UNDERSTANDING THE COMPANY

What is the purpose of the company and its role in society? From their origin in medieval times to their modern incarnation as powerful transnational bodies, companies remain an important part of business and society at large. Drawing from a variety of perspectives, this book adopts a normative approach in understanding the modern company and provides insights into how companies should be conceptualized. It considers key topics such as the development of corporate theory, the rights and obligations of the company, and the means and ends of corporate governance. Written by leading experts of different jurisdictions, this book provides important international viewpoints on some of the most pressing corporate governance questions.

BARNALI CHOUDHURY is a senior lecturer at University College London. She is the author of *Public Services and International Trade Liberalization: Human Rights and Gender Implications* (Cambridge University Press, 2012) as well as of over 20 articles and book chapters. She has delivered lectures internationally and her research has been cited by the UK House of Lords EU Select Committee, arbitral tribunals, and nongovernmental organizations. Prior to joining academia, she practiced corporate and international investment law.

MARTIN PETRIN is a senior lecturer at University College London and the deputy director of its Centre for Commercial Law. He holds an S.J.D. specializing in corporate law from the University of California, Los Angeles, a Ph.D. from the University of St. Gallen, Switzerland, and an LL.M. from Columbia University. Martin has practiced law with a leading international business law firm and has been admitted to the Bar in New York and Switzerland. He has been a visiting scholar at the University of Cambridge, Faculty of Law and the Max Planck Institute for Comparative and Private Law in Hamburg. Martin has published and presented widely on corporate governance topics.

UNDERSTANDING THE COMPANY

Corporate Governance and Theory

Edited by

BARNALI CHOUDHURY

University College London

MARTIN PETRIN

University College London

CAMBRIDGE
UNIVERSITY PRESS

CAMBRIDGE
UNIVERSITY PRESS

University Printing House, Cambridge CB2 8BS, United Kingdom

One Liberty Plaza, 20th Floor, New York, NY 10006, USA

477 Williamstown Road, Port Melbourne, VIC 3207, Australia

4843/24, 2nd Floor, Ansari Road, Daryaganj, Delhi–110002, India

79 Anson Road, #06-04/06, Singapore 079906

Cambridge University Press is part of the University of Cambridge.

It furthers the University's mission by disseminating knowledge in the pursuit of education, learning, and research at the highest international levels of excellence.

www.cambridge.org
Information on this title: www.cambridge.org/9781107146075
DOI: 10.1017/9781316536384

First published 2017

A catalogue record for this publication is available from the British Library.

Library of Congress Cataloging-in-Publication Data

Names: Choudhury, Barnali, 1974- editor. | Petrin, Martin, 1978- editor.
Title: Understanding the company : corporate governance and theory / edited by Barnali Choudhury, University College London, and Martin Petrin, University College London.
Description: Cambridge, United Kingdom ; New York, NY : Cambridge University Press, 2017. | Includes papers presented at a conference held in London in May 2015, funded by Queen Mary University of London and University College London.—ECIP Acknowledgement. | Includes bibliographical references and index.
Identifiers: LCCN 2016049296 | ISBN 9781107146075 (hardback)
Subjects: LCSH: Corporate governance—Law and legislation—Congresses.
Classification: LCC K1327.A6 U53 2017 | DDC 346/.066—dc23 LC record available at https://lccn.loc.gov/2016049296

ISBN 978-1-107-14607-5 Hardback

For Kaya

CONTENTS

FIGURES

TABLES

CONTRIBUTORS

REUVEN S. AVI-YONAH is the Irwin I. Cohn Professor of Law and director of the International Tax LL.M. Program at the University of Michigan Law School. He has served as a consultant to the US Department of the Treasury and the Organisation for Economic Co-operation and Development (OECD) on tax competition, and is a member of the steering group for OECD's International Network for Tax Research. He is also a trustee of the American Tax Policy Institute, a member of the American Law Institute, a fellow of the American Bar Foundation and the American College of Tax Counsel, and an international research fellow at Oxford University's Centre for Business Taxation. In addition to prior teaching appointments at Harvard University (law) and Boston College (history), he practiced law with Milbank, Tweed, Hadley & McCloy in New York; with Wachtell, Lipton, Rosen & Katz in New York; and with Ropes & Gray in Boston. After receiving his B.A., *summa cum laude*, from Hebrew University, he earned three additional degrees from Harvard University: an A.M. in history, a Ph.D. in history, and a J.D., *magna cum laude*. He has published more than 150 books and articles, including *Advanced Introduction to International Tax* (2015), *Global Perspectives on Income Taxation Law* (2011), and *International Tax as International Law* (Cambridge University Press, 2007).

WILLIAM W. BRATTON is the Nicholas F. Gallicchio Professor of Law at the University of Pennsylvania Law School and the codirector of the Institute for Law and Economics. Bill is recognized internationally as a leading writer on business law. He brings an interdisciplinary perspective to a wide range of subject matters that encompass corporate governance, corporate finance, accounting, corporate legal history, and comparative corporate law. His work has appeared in the Cornell, Michigan, Northwestern, Pennsylvania, Stanford, and Virginia law reviews, and the Duke and Georgetown law journals, along with the *American Journal of Comparative Law* and the *Common Market Law Review*. His book, *Corporate Finance: Cases and Materials* (7th edn., 2012), is the leading law school text on the subject. Bill is a research associate of the European Corporate Governance Institute. In 2009, he was installed as the Anton Philips Professor at the Faculty of Law of Tilburg University in The Netherlands, the fifth American academic to hold the chair.

CHRISTOPHER M. BRUNER is the William Donald Bain Family Professor of Corporate Law at Washington and Lee University, where he also serves as Director of the Frances Lewis Law Center. Christopher's articles have appeared in a variety of law and policy journals, and he has twice received the Law School's Ethan Allen Faculty Fellowship for scholarly excellence. His comparative study of US and UK corporate governance, "Power and Purpose in the 'Anglo-American' Corporation," won the 2010 Association of American Law Schools Scholarly Papers competition. His book, *Corporate Governance in the Common-Law World: The Political Foundations of Shareholder Power* (Cambridge University Press, 2013), develops a new comparative theory of corporate governance in common-law countries. Christopher currently serves as a member of the Executive Committee for the Association of American Law Schools' Section on Business Associations, and a member of the Scholarship Advisory Group to the Younger Comparativists Committee of the American Society of Comparative Law.

KARIN BUHMANN is an associate professor at Copenhagen Business School and Associate Professor of Business Studies at Roskilde University, Denmark. Karin holds a Dr.scient.adm (doctor scientiarum administrationis) from Roskilde University, a Ph.D. in law from Aarhus University, a Master of International Law from the Raoul Wallenberg Institute of Human Rights Law and Humanitarian Law at Lund University and a degree in East Asian Studies from Copenhagen University. Karin is a member of the Danish National Contact Point (NCP) under the OECD's Guidelines for Multinational Enterprises and chairs the CSR Legal Research Network (CSRLRN) and the interdisciplinary network "The BHRight Initiative for research and teaching on Business & Human Rights." She has published extensively and her latest book, *Normative Discourses and Public–Private Regulatory Strategies for Construction of CSR Normativity: Towards a Method for Above-National Public–Private Regulation of Business Social Responsibilities*, was published by Multivers Academic in 2014.

BARNALI CHOUDHURY is a senior lecturer at University College London. She is the author of *Public Services and International Trade*

Liberalization: Human Rights and Gender Implications (Cambridge University Press, 2012) as well as over 20 articles and book chapters. Her work has been cited by the House of Lords EU Select Committee and by arbitral tribunals and she has given talks in China, Canada, France, Germany, Lebanon, Spain, Switzerland, the United States, and the United Kingdom. Prior to joining academia, she practiced as a corporate and investment arbitral lawyer.

BRANDON L. GARRETT is the Justice Thurgood Marshall Distinguished Professor of Law at the University of Virginia Law School. He is the author of *Too Big to Jail: How Prosecutors Compromise with Corporations* (2014), among numerous other publications. Brandon's work has been widely cited by courts, including the US Supreme Court, lower federal courts, state supreme courts, and courts in other countries, such as the Supreme Courts of Canada and Israel. Brandon is a frequent speaker about criminal justice matters before legislative and policy-making bodies, groups of practicing lawyers, law enforcement, and in local and national media.

MARTIN GELTER is a professor at Fordham Law School. Previously, he was an assistant professor in the Department of Civil Law and Business Law at the WU Vienna University of Economics. Martin has been a Terence M. Considine Fellow in Law and Economics and a John M. Olin Fellow in Law and Economics at Harvard Law School, a visiting fellow at the University of Bologna, and is a research associate with the European Corporate Governance Institute. His scholarship has been published widely in distinguished journals including the *Harvard International Law Journal, the NYU Journal of Law and Business*, and *Fordham International Law Journal.*

DIONYSIA KATELOUZOU is a lecturer in law at King's College London, specializing in the areas of comparative and transnational corporate governance and corporate law, with a particular interest in shareholder activism and empirical legal studies. She holds a Ph.D. and an LL.M. from the University of Cambridge and an LL.B. from the University of Athens. Dionysia's articles have appeared in the *Journal of Corporate Law Studies, University of Pennsylvania Journal of Business Law, Virginia Law and Business Review*, and *Journal of Comparative Law*, among others. She is currently a research associate at the London Centre for Corporate Governance and Ethics at the University of Birkbeck and has also been a visiting researcher at the University of Pennsylvania.

ANDREW KEAY is Professor of Corporate and Commercial Law at the University of Leeds. He is the author of numerous books, including *The Enlightened Shareholder Value Principle and Corporate Governance* (2012) and *The Corporate Objective* (2011). He has published widely throughout the United Kingdom and internationally and his work has appeared in the *Modern Law Review*, *European Business Organization Law Review*, and the *Cambridge Law Journal*, among other journals. His work has been cited by courts in several countries including the Privy Council, the Supreme Court of New Zealand, the High Court of Australia, the Supreme Court of Appeal in South Africa, the Singapore Court of Appeal, and the High Court of England and Wales. Andrew is a barrister practicing in the Chancery field and was previously a partner in an Australian business law firm and a Deputy Registrar of the Australian Federal Court.

IAN B. LEE is an associate professor at the University of Toronto. Ian clerked with Justice Claire L'Heureux-Dubé of the Supreme Court of Canada and Justice Mark MacGuigan of the Federal Court of Appeal, and later served as a legal researcher with the Privy Council Office. He practiced with Sullivan & Cromwell LLP in Paris, France, and New York before joining the Faculty of Law in 2003. His teaching and research interests are in the areas of constitutional law, corporate law, and European Union law. Ian also teaches in the Law and Business Program at the University of Sydney Law School and is admitted to the bars of Ontario and New York.

MARC T. MOORE is Reader in Corporate Law at the University of Cambridge. He previously taught at University College London and the University of Bristol and was a visiting professor in the Adolf A. Berle, Jr. Center on Corporations, Law & Society at Seattle University School of Law. In 2012 Marc was awarded a prestigious Philip Leverhulme Prize, for outstanding scholars who have made a substantial and acknowledged contribution to their field of study. His 2013 book, *Corporate Governance in the Shadow of the State*, was shortlisted for the SLS Peter Birks Prize for Outstanding Legal Scholarship. Marc is currently Director of the Centre for Corporate and Commercial Law (3CL) at the University of Cambridge.

MARTIN PETRIN is a senior lecturer at University College London. He holds an S.J.D. specializing in corporate law from the University of California, Los Angeles, a Ph.D. in law from the University of St. Gallen, Switzerland, and an LL.M. from Columbia University. Martin's articles have appeared in the *Modern Law Review*, *American University Law*

Review, *Virginia Law and Business Review*, among others. Martin previously practiced corporate law with a leading international business law firm and is admitted to the bar in New York and Switzerland. He has also been a visiting researcher at the Max Planck Institute for Comparative and Private Law in Hamburg, Germany and at the University of Cambridge Law Faculty.

BEATE SJÅFJELL is Professor Dr. Juris at the University of Oslo, Faculty of Law. Beate is head of the faculty's research group Companies, Markets, Society and the Environment, and also of the international Sustainable Companies Project (2010–14), and the international network Sustainable Market Actors (jus.uio.no/companies under Projects and Networks). Beate's publications include *Towards a Sustainable European Company Law* (2009), the edited volumes *The Greening of European Business under EU Law: Taking Article 11 TFEU Seriously* (2015; coeditor: Anja Wiesbrock) and *Company Law and Sustainability: Legal Barriers and Opportunities* (Cambridge University Press, 2015; coeditor: Benjamin Richardson).

LYNN STOUT is the Distinguished Professor of Corporate & Business Law at Cornell Law School. Lynn is an internationally recognized expert in the fields of corporate governance, securities regulation, financial derivatives, law and economics, and moral behavior. She is the author of numerous articles and books on these topics and lectures widely. Her most recent book is *The Shareholder Value Myth: How Putting Shareholders First Harms Investors, Corporations and the Public* (2012), which was named 2012 Governance Book of the Year. Lynn serves on the Board of Governors of the CFA Institute, on the Financial Research Advisory Committee to the US Treasury, as a member of the Board of Advisors for the Aspen Institute's Business & Society Program, as executive advisor to the Brookings Institution Project on Corporate Purpose, and as a research fellow for the Gruter Institute for Law and Behavioral Research.

PREFACE

In May 2015, a group of scholars gathered in London to discuss the modern company. Their purpose was to shed light on this familiar, yet often misunderstood entity. Alongside a group of esteemed commentators, the scholars set out to provide depth and breadth to the question of what the corporation is and what its role in society should be.

The day began early and was, for London, unusually warm. Alongside a packed (and often highly engaged) audience, the scholars and commentators converged into a non-air-conditioned and stuffy lecture hall to discuss, debate, and offer their thoughts on key questions ranging from what corporate governance mechanisms are most effective to what constitutional rights a company should have and whether a company is public or private in nature and beyond. Despite the lack of ideal conditions, unique ideas were presented, pivotal topics were discussed and, most importantly, questions in need of answers were given just that.

The outcomes and discussions that began in that lecture hall can now be found as the substance of this book. We are aware that the discussions surrounding the nature of the company and its purpose are still continuing and our hope is that this book helps to engage with those discussions.

ACKNOWLEDGMENTS

Most feats today rely on the assistance and goodwill of others and putting together this book was no exception. Thanks are due first to Queen Mary University of London and University College London for generously funding the conference whose output ultimately became this book. In particular, we would like to thank Kevin Warne, Anett Loosz, Tatjana Wingender, and Lisa Penfold for ably assisting in the administrative aspects of the conference.

A hearty thanks is also due to all of the speakers at the conference, most of whom are listed as contributors to this book. Thanks are also due to Paddy Ireland, who so eloquently (and humorously) spoke on the history of the company, but was unable to contribute to this book due to his appointment shortly after the conference as Dean of Bristol Law School. We would further like to thank our commentators Janet Dine, Robin Brooks, and Luca Enriques for their insights and thoughts on the speakers' papers as well as the audience at the conference for their engagement and interest.

Riccardo Savona Siemens took on the herculean task of correcting the footnotes for each of the chapters. We thank him for his tremendous efforts.

Finally, we thank the team at Cambridge University Press for their assistance with the publication process. Thanks are due in particular to Kim Hughes, for early support of this project, as well as to Rebecca Roberts and Chloe Harries.

Introduction

BARNALI CHOUDHURY AND MARTIN PETRIN

In 2011, Starbucks CEO Howard Schultz declared that it was "no longer enough" for companies to serve shareholders, but that companies have a responsibility, even a duty, "to serve the communities where we do business by helping to improve" aspects of citizens' daily lives.[1] Shortly thereafter, in 2012, it was revealed that Starbucks had paid only £8.6m in taxes in the United Kingdom on £3bn of sales since 1998, a practice that its UK CEO said "didn't bother [him] at all."[2]

The dichotomy of the Starbucks example serves to highlight the lack of understanding surrounding what a company is and what its purpose should be. Is a company, as Schultz opines, duty bound to improve aspects of citizens' lives or is it, as his UK colleague suggests, an entity that can – and perhaps should – minimize or even circumvent tax obligations, as a means of improving its bottom line, with a clear conscience?

Indeed, the struggle to define the company is not new. Since its origin in medieval times as vehicles by which governments could grant institutional status to universities to their modern incarnation as transnational bodies that traverse nations, the company remains an important, yet highly misunderstood entity. Understanding the company (or, as it is commonly referred to in US parlance, *corporation*),[3] what its rights and duties are, and to whom it should be accountable – as the Starbucks example serves to remind – remains a persistent and enduring debate.

[1] Howard Schultz, "Invest in Communities to Advance Capitalism," *Harvard Business Review* (October 17, 2011), available at https://hbr.org/2011/10/ceos-should-invest-in-communit.

[2] "We won't pay normal UK tax until 2017 – Starbucks CEO," *Financial Director*, (December 4, 2014), available at www.financialdirector.co.uk/financial-director/news/2384484/-we-won-t-pay-normal-uk-tax-until-2017-starbucks-ceo.

[3] In this book, the terms "company" and "corporation" will normally be used interchangeably and we did not edit the chapters to achieve uniformity in this regard. References to the "company" or "corporation" thus do not necessarily mean that an author refers to a specific jurisdiction.

However, with society operating increasingly under the dominance of businesses and businesses being exposed to increasingly dense regulation, it has become more imperative than ever to understand the modern company and its function and place in society. In recent years, the hazards of defining companies and their purpose too narrowly have become apparent. Thus, the view of the company as primarily an economic vehicle is thought to have contributed to short-termism and excessive risk-taking, which contributed to the rise of the last financial crisis. At the same time, an understanding of the company as a public body has, in some instances, stifled the entrepreneurial spirit and competition necessary for economic growth. Even an attempt to reach a compromised view on defining the company, such as in section 172 of the UK's 2006 Companies Act, has raised more questions than it answered.[4]

A failure to understand what the company is has further impacted contemporary rules on corporate liability.[5] This is because courts have been unable to disentangle themselves from the lingering effects of ancient theoretical notions that a company is an aggregate, a real person, a fiction or something else entirely. Longstanding discussions and struggles in this area have also complicated fundamental questions of corporate and corporate governance law, which remain unsettled and in flux.

Understanding the company, therefore, continues to be a modern mystery and a question in need of an answer. This book tackles important aspects of this question by engaging in three main research questions. First, it aims to discover what a company is by employing a historical review of the development of corporate theories as well as by exploring modern corporate theories. Corporate theories can help elucidate the nature of the company as they define the company's roles and functions. This can then provide a basis by which to consider related issues, such as those considered in the further research questions.

Second, it examines what types of rights and duties companies have and should have. Having better understood the nature, role and function of a company, it becomes easier to ascertain whether this nature or role gives rise to certain rights for the company as well as any obligations.

Finally, it explores the means and ends of corporate governance. Thus, it examines the structure of corporate decision-making and seeks to clarify the corporation's beneficiaries.

[4] See, e.g., A. Keay, "Ascertaining the Corporate Objective: An Entity Maximisation and Sustainability Model" (2008) 71:5 *Modern Law Review* 663.

[5] See, e.g., *Citizens United* v. *FEC*, 558 U.S. 310 (2010); *Burwell* v. *Hobby Lobby Stores, Inc.*, 134 S. Ct. 2751 (2014).

What Is the Nature of the Company?

Despite the persistent debate over the nature of a company, attempts to define the "firm" are longstanding. Since Roman and medieval times, scholars have attempted to capture the nature or characteristics of what today are companies and other legal or business entities. In the nineteenth century the discussion gained intensity and, with some periods of relative "calm" in this regard, flared up again in recent years. In some jurisdictions, including the United Kingdom and Continental European civil law countries, scholars and courts have largely given up on trying to define the "nature of the firm." Still, the law in this regard remains often shaped by historical oddities but – apart from occasional complications, including the difficulties in holding companies criminally liable – there is now a stable and pragmatic arrangement with the status quo.

Conversely, in the United States, the Supreme Court's 2010 decision in *Citizens United*[6] and its 2014 decision in *Hobby Lobby*[7] have sparked a new wave of controversy and academic explorations in this regard. Although the Supreme Court had no intention of – and indeed tried to avoid – shaping the theory of the firm, these decisions, nevertheless, re-ignited the debate through their support of corporate rights and the court's varying perceptions of the corporation. In some ways, it is curious that corporate theory came to the forefront in the above-mentioned cases, which were mainly concerned with constitutional law and related statutory rights. But what is even more striking is that the US Supreme Court decided the cases based on antiquated corporate theories, suggesting the need for clarification and progress in this area.[8]

Two Schools of Thought

Today, discussions on the nature of the firm tend to begin based on one of two schools of thought: the nexus of contracts model or the stakeholder model. Both these theoretical perspectives, and those that derive from them, provide a lens through which the company can be viewed and therefore may provide answers on related issues such as corporate purpose and the role of a company.

[6] *Citizens United*, above n 5.

[7] *Hobby Lobby*, above n 5.

[8] See Martin Petrin's contribution in this book, "A Balancing Approach to Corporate Rights and Duties." See also E. Pollman, "Corporate Law and Theory in Hobby Lobby" in M. Schwartzman, C. Flanders, and Z. Robinson *The Rise of Corporate Religious Liberty* (Oxford University Press, 2016) p. 149.

The first of these competing theories, the nexus of contracts model, describes the corporation as a bundle of formal and informal "contractual" relationships between various constituencies, which act together to produce goods and services and thus form a "firm."[9] Far from being a "new" invention,[10] the nexus of contracts theory has, in many academic circles, become a dominant approach by which to conceptualize today's corporations.[11]

Intertwined with law and economics approaches to corporate law, the nexus of contracts view of the firm emphasizes the private nature of corporations and corporate regulation. It sees corporate law primarily as a tool by which to provide "contracting" parties with a set of off-the-rack terms, thereby saving or reducing the cost of negotiating and contracting individually. On a normative level, the model suggests that the parties involved should also be able to change the default provisions as they see fit. Of course, this means that mandatory legal rules that govern corporations or the relationships within the "nexus" are difficult to reconcile with the model, despite the fact that such rules have grown heavily in the past years and decades. In addition, the nexus of contracts theory is traditionally associated with shareholder primacy and shareholder value maximization – the notion that shareholder interests take precedence over other stakeholders' interests – as well as the view that corporations do not bear any social or moral duties. At the same time, however, the contractarian view accepts that the role of shareholders in the modern corporation is a relatively passive one, which is seen as justified from a cost–benefit perspective.

Conversely, stakeholder theory focuses on the idea that companies owe duties, not only to shareholders but also to a variety of other corporate constituents as additional stakeholders. The reasons for this conclusion are varied, and unlike the nexus of contracts theory model do not draw from a unified theory.

Some possibilities for the justification of companies having to take into account the interests of stakeholder are by viewing it as a social or

[9] The director primacy theory elegantly extends this idea stating that the guiding idea is not that the firm *is* a nexus of contracts, but that it *has* a central nexus, the board of directors. S.M. Bainbridge, "Director Primacy: The Means and Ends of Corporate Governance" (2003) 97 *Northwestern University Law Review* 547 at 554–60.

[10] The theory, which can be traced to Ronald Coase and other economists, emerged around the 1970s.

[11] An outline of the theory can be found, for example, in F.H. Easterbrook and D.R. Fischel, *The Economic Structure of Corporate Law* (Harvard University Press, 1991) p. 12.

public institution,[12] for reasons of morality,[13] due to the need to maximize social welfare,[14] because otherwise shareholders could inflict harms on stakeholders,[15] or because the "legal, economic, political and moral challenges" to the current nexus of contracts view of the firm require it.[16]

Despite the lack of a unified underlying theory, stakeholder theorists generally arrive at three conclusions. First, that there is a need for a company to consider the interests of stakeholders; second, that wealth maximization should not be an overriding concern guiding corporate decision-making;[17] and third, that corporate decision-making should balance the interests of all stakeholders, including shareholders, against each other.[18]

Of course, not all corporate theories neatly fit into either of these two categories. For instance, the enlightened shareholder value paradigm, which underlies contemporary UK company law, derives from stakeholder theory, but introduces the prioritization of shareholder interests over stakeholder interests, a practice not found in stakeholder theory.[19] Similarly, the well-known "Team Production" theory is a modification of the "nexus of contracts" view of companies but one that deviates from a contractarian view by introducing the notion that corporate managers should consider the interests of all stakeholders who have made firm-specific investments.[20]

[12] A.A. Berle, Jr. and G.C. Means, *The Modern Corporation and Private Property* (New York: Harcourt, Brace & World, Inc., 2nd ed. 1968) p. 46; T.L. Hazen, "The Corporate Persona, Contract (and Market) Failure, and Moral Value" (1991) 69 *North Carolina Law Review* 273 at 309; D.K. Millon, "New Directions in Corporate Law: Communitarians, Contractarians, and the Crisis in Corporate Law" (1993) 50 *Washington and Lee Law Review* 1373 at 1379.

[13] W. Bradford, "Beyond Good and Evil: The Commensurability of Corporate Profits and Human Rights" (2012) 26 *Notre Dame Journal of Law, Ethics and Public Policy* 141, 148.

[14] K. Greenfield, "Defending Stakeholder Governance" (2008) 58 *Case Western Reserve Law Review* 1043 at 1055.

[15] R.M. Green, "Shareholders as Stakeholders, Changing Metaphors of Corporate Governance" (1993) 50 *Washington and Lee Law Review* 1409, 1417.

[16] R.E. Freeman, "A Stakeholder Theory of the Modern Corporation" in T.L. Beauchamp and N.E. Bowie (eds.), *Ethical Theory & Business* (Upper Saddle River: Prentice Hall College Division, 6th ed., 2000) p. 39.

[17] J. Kaler, "Differentiating Stakeholder Theories" (2003) 46 *Journal of Business Ethics* 71.

[18] M.M. Blair and L.A. Stout, "A Team Production Theory of Corporate Law" (1999) 85 *Virginia Law Review* 247 at 281; Freeman, above n 16 at 44; Bradford, above n 13 at 149.

[19] P. Davies, K.J. Hopt, R.G.J. Nowak, and G. van Solinge, "Boards in Law and Practice: A Cross-Country Analysis in Europe" in P. Davies, *et al.* (eds.), *Corporate Boards in European Law: A Comparative Analysis* (Oxford University Press, 2013) p. 93; P. Davies, "Corporate Boards in the United Kingdom" in P. Davies (ed.), *Corporate Boards in European Law: A Comparative Analysis* (Oxford University Press, 2013) p. 753.

[20] Blair and Stout reformulate the nexus of contracts theory to argue that a corporation is a "nexus of firm-specific investments." See Blair and Stout, above n 18 at 275, 285, 286.

The Influence of Corporate Theories

As the US Supreme Court's reliance on old corporate theories to decide contemporary constitutional rights for companies has highlighted, the impact of these theories – old and new – remains considerable. Corporate theories influence the way we define the role and function of companies; the extent to which they should be subject to governmental intervention and control; corporate rights and duties; the question of how to balance and allocate corporate power and decision-making; and others. If we revisit the Starbucks case study described at the outset of this chapter, we see that the nexus of contracts theory suggests that the UK CEO of Starbucks is correct in his views insofar as Starbucks' tax strategies benefit its shareholders, while the stakeholder theory supports the assertions of Howard Schultz. Corporate theory, therefore, has the potential to help define the role of twenty-first century-companies and guide those that are in control of them. Still, there is growing skepticism regarding the validity and usefulness of existing corporate theories and orthodox descriptions of the corporation and its governing framework. Of course, if we reject corporate theory, as it stands today or perhaps even altogether, the next question to arise is what should fill the resulting void. This book reflects on and contributes to aspects of this discussion.

Corporate Rights and Duties

A second focus of this book is on the rights and duties of companies, an area that flows naturally from the earlier discussion on the nature and theory of the company. One field of study within this area is the development, reasoning, and potential reform in the allocation of constitutional and (sometimes related) statutory rights for the benefit of corporate entities. The US Supreme Court's jurisprudence in this regard is particularly rich and multi-faceted. Although future developments of this jurisprudence, which continues to evolve, are uncertain, we can make some predictions – and recommendations – based on an analysis of historical patterns. Although, as discussed in the preceding section, the US Supreme Court now tends to brush aside the importance of corporate theory in adjudicating corporate constitutional rights, in reality corporate law and corporate law scholars play an important role in helping develop appropriate frameworks that can provide guidance.

Furthermore, the questions of how, to what extent, and based on what justification corporate entities can or should be held liable in tort and criminal law continue to preoccupy courts, legislatures, and scholars alike. Again, this is an area that remains – depending on the jurisdiction and type of liability involved – influenced by corporate theories. Traditionally, but with effects lasting today, the fiction theory stood in the way of holding legal entities such as corporations criminally responsible since purely fictitious beings could not have the necessary state of mind required to commit a crime. The real entity theory partially changed this position and, at least in some jurisdictions, became prevalent in instances of corporate tortious and criminal liability that imposed responsibility on companies via its "directing minds" or "managing agents" – the metaphoric "hands and mouth" of the company.[21]

Conversely, the contemporary nexus of contracts theory has little to say about corporate rights and duties in relation to third parties. However, it has been interpreted to suggest that companies as fictional connection points for various contracts are incapable of owing obligations that are social or moral in nature. For proponents of corporate social responsibility and related obligations, the idea of the nexus of contracts is therefore particularly problematic. Moreover, if we were to apply the nexus of contracts theory to constitutional, tort, and criminal law, the result would necessarily be that neither corporate rights nor liabilities could be convincingly explained.

While this is understandable (the nexus of contracts theory is not geared towards answering such questions), it shows the need for different or complementary theories. Indeed, stakeholder theory may be better suited to defining corporate rights and duties and, in this regard, is particularly relied upon by those who favor the notion of corporations bearing social obligations. Yet, stakeholder theory also suffers from limitations, including the problem that it fails to define which of the many stakeholder interests companies and their boards should be obliged to protect, particularly when there are conflicts between these interests.[22]

The prevailing views on how to conceptualize companies by relying on corporate theories can thus be usefully contrasted with alternative approaches. For example, examining corporate rights and duties through the lens of externalities and cost internalization, non-legal social and

21 This is how one of the major proponents of the Germanic real entity or "organic" theory explained its attribution mechanism. See O. von Gierke, *Die Genossenschaftstheorie und die Deutsche Rechtsprechung* (Berlin: Weidmann, 1887) p. 603–10.

22 For an overview of these limitations, see B. Choudhury, "Aligning Corporate and Community Interests: From Abominable to Symbiotic" (2014) 2013:3 *Brigham Young University Law Review* 101.

moral signals, or the notion of balancing the negative effects of businesses on society with enlarged societal obligations, can offer useful impulses for future changes in policies and law. Modern corporate theories focus mostly on governance questions that arise between directors, managers, and shareholders, but are not typically concerned with rights and duties based on constitutional and other non-corporate laws. This leaves a lacuna to be filled by future scholarship.

Means and Ends

Finally, this book focuses on the notion of what can be called the "means and ends" of corporate governance.[23] This refers to two central questions: First, who should have the ultimate decision-making power in the corporate structure? Second, for whose benefit should corporations primarily operate?

The first question – which often represents the struggle between board/managerial powers and shareholder empowerment – can be usefully rephrased as "how should different stakeholder powers be balanced?" or, relatedly, "how can different stakeholders act as a system of checks and balances within the corporation, with different constituents sharing or allocating amongst them at least some powers?" The second question can be extended by adding the inquiry as to whom the company (or its board of directors) should be accountable. The company's beneficiaries may well be identical to those to whom the company is accountable, such as in a traditional shareholder primacy model. However, this is not necessarily the case as can be seen in models where, for example, the company is said to be running for the benefit of "itself" and accountability is owed to a separate body within the company,[24] or in stakeholder-oriented models where the beneficiaries are a wider group of individuals than simply shareholders.[25]

Defining corporate powers, objectives and accountability has far-reaching consequences. For instance, an overly narrow focus on shareholders (and shareholder powers) and shorter-term profitability may contribute to scenarios such as what was encountered during the last financial crisis, while defining the corporate role too widely can impair its ability to contribute to wealth creation and economic growth. Recognizing this gravity, shareholder powers

[23] See Bainbridge, above n 9.

[24] This is proposed by Andrew Keay in his contribution to this book, "Board Accountability and the Entity Maximization and Sustainability Approach."

[25] See, e.g., the discussion of labor-oriented models in Martin Gelter's chapter of this book, "Comparative Corporate Governance: Old and New."

and the corporate objective have long been the subject of intense academic discussion as well as regulatory activities. In terms of the latter, recent years have seen an international trend towards enhanced "shareholder democracy," with shareholders' "say on pay" as a prominent example, and – in the United Kingdom – the introduction of new statutory language on corporate goals.[26]

While strongly shareholder-oriented approaches remain dominant, it should be noted that commentators from across the ideological spectrum have begun to express doubt as to whether the prevalent preference for shareholder primacy and shareholder wealth maximization,[27] as promulgated by the nexus of contracts model, is in fact beneficial for shareholders. As one prominent scholar has observed, a number of strong shareholder value advocates have backed away from a commitment to shareholder value maximization as the exclusive goal of corporate governance.[28] Following the financial crisis, the EU Commission – normally a proponent of shareholder empowerment – has also stated that the "confidence in the model of the shareholder-owner who contributes to the company's long-term viability has been severely shaken."[29] In sum, it appears as though the means and ends of corporate governance are in need of a re-calibration.

The Contributions

Against this background, this book seeks to elucidate depth and breadth to the question of what the company is and what its role in society should be, specifically by drawing from the three research questions outlined above. The contributions to this book are organized into four parts.

Part I

Part I begins with an exploration of the company from comparative and historical perspectives. In "The Four Transformations of the Corporate Form," Reuven Avi-Yonah describes the evolution of the corporate entity,

[26] See Companies Act 2006, s. 172.

[27] Note that these two terms are not synonymous.

[28] See M.M. Blair, "Corporate Law and the Team Production Problem" in C.A. Hill and B.H. McDonnell (eds.), *Research Handbook on the Economics of Corporate Law* (Cheltenham: Edward Elgar, 2012) p. 33.

[29] *Commission Green Paper on Corporate Governance and Remuneration Policies for Financial Institutions*, COM (2010) 284 (June 2, 2010). Although in the case of the EU Commission the conclusion was that more – not fewer – shareholders powers would provide the adequate cure to the malaise.

tracing the history from its Roman law origins until today. He shows how this evolution progressed through four major transformations during which the corporation was first recognized as a separate legal entity and given some of its other typical "corporate" attributes and then shifted from a non-profit to a for-profit entity. This shift was followed by the corporate form's development from closely held to widely held, publicly traded entities before finally emerging – and continuing to evolve – as multinational enterprises. As Avi-Yonah demonstrates, three major corporate theories provided the backdrop to these transformations: the aggregate theory, the artificial entity theory, and the real entity theory. Nevertheless, for reasons that the chapter explores in detail, the real entity theory prevailed each time.

Martin Gelter's chapter, "Comparative Corporate Governance: Old and New," moves Part I from the development of the company from a strictly historical perspective to a comparative perspective, focusing on the differences in the development of companies between the United States and Continental Europe, especially Germany. His focus is on the interaction between corporate ownership structures – concentrated versus dispersed – and employees or labor as potential corporate constituencies. Gelter describes an emerging "new" or at least "modified" corporate governance in which shareholders – led by institutional investors – are gaining powers, which results in a shifting equilibrium between the traditional power balance of managers, shareholders, and labor. He concludes that although the basic structures of corporate governance systems in the United States and Continental Europe persist even in the age of "new" governance, they have become more complex through the ongoing changes caused by increasing influence of strong outside investors.

Part I concludes with another comparative perspective on the development of company law, this time with a focus on US–UK law. In "The Corporation's Intrinsic Attributes," Christopher Bruner takes a closer look at the attributes commonly regarded as being "intrinsic" to the corporation or essential for its economic utility. Using historical and comparative perspectives, however, he questions the static nature of these attributes, particularly as they are thought to give rise to the optimal division of power between boards and shareholders, the degree of regard for shareholder interests, and/or degree of liability exposure for boards and shareholders. Instead, he argues that issues of power, purpose, and risk-taking may not be best resolved by reference to purported "typical" or core corporate characteristics and paradigms. Using three examples – shareholder bylaw authority, board discretion to consider non-shareholder interests, and regulation of financial risk-taking – as illustrations of his argument, Bruner concludes that the key to resolving regulatory and governance issues in corporate law lies in political discourse.

Part II

Part II adds to the earlier historical and comparative discussions on the nature of the firm by focusing on the issues surrounding the company's private or public nature. Marc Moore's chapter, "Understanding the Modern Company through the Lens of Quasi-Public Power," begins this part by arguing – contrary to the nexus of contracts theory and its reliance on private relationships as the firm's core – the case for viewing the company as a public entity. Companies, he argues, entail power, legitimacy, and accountability, which give these entities a public dimension. This view leads to the normative claim that the main purpose of company law should be to ensure that managers give account to shareholders, which in turn leads to legitimacy and sustainability.

Dionysia Katelouzou re-examines the nature of the company against the backdrop of modern shareholder activism and stewardship. Although the contractarian "private" paradigm of the corporation suggests that increased shareholder monitoring of managers is not necessary, in "Reflections on the Nature of the Public Corporation in an Era of Shareholder Activism and Stewardship," Katelouzou finds that the rise of activist institutional shareholders has challenged this notion. As these shareholders have the incentives and necessary resources to monitor management, she finds a shift away from the contractarian and agency paradigm towards an "investor paradigm" for company law. Within this new paradigm, however, public and private elements co-exist in the company.

Beate Sjåfjell's chapter, "Regulating for Corporate Sustainability: Why the Public-Private Divide Misses the Point" – which concludes this part of the book – takes a different view entirely. Sjåfjell argues that the public-private divide misses the point and is inconsequential. Instead, the essential question should be how to regulate for corporate sustainability. As Sjåfjell explains, a holistic approach is necessary to achieve this goal. She introduces the notion of a "planetary boundaries" framework, which determines the safe operating space for humanity, as a reference point for company law and guidelines in balancing economic, social, and environmental interests. Sjåfjell concludes that company law should be reformed by redefining both the purpose of the company and the role and the duties of the board in order to achieve greater sustainability.

Part III

Having provided context on the nature of the company, Part III of this book is dedicated to issues surrounding the company's rights and duties. In "The Constitutional Rights of Corporations in the United States," Brandon Garrett explores, in an in-depth manner, corporate constitutional rights in the United States. Drawing from case law from the early nineteenth century to the recent Supreme Court decisions in *Hobby Lobby* and *Citizens United*, Garrett discusses a wide range of constitutional rights that have been granted or, as the case may be, denied to corporations. In doing so, he analyzes commonalities in the reasoning behind the various rulings, highlights the potential conflicts between individual and corporate constitutional rights, and ultimately paves the way to a better understanding of the future direction of corporate constitutional litigation.

Moving from rights to duties, in "Understanding Corporate Criminal Liability," Ian Lee focuses on corporate criminal liability and explores the rationale behind imposing such duties on corporations. Taking an intermediate position between neoclassical and agency approaches, Lee suggests that criminal liability of corporations is useful where it can be established that individuals within the corporation have violated certain norms but their identity remains unknown. Lee argues against the utility of having to construe whether corporate acts are intentional or whether it is efficient to impose criminal liability on legal entities. Instead, he finds that through the shame and guilt of criminal penalties, corporate criminal liability can function as a tool to influence non-legal social and moral norms observed by the individuals who act for a corporation.

Continuing with the idea of defining a company's duties, in "Human Rights and Business: Expectations, Requirements, and Procedures for the Responsible Modern Company," Karin Buhmann explores the modern company's human rights obligations. Buhmann describes how changing social expectations and policy debates have led to various binding and non-binding regulatory and other instruments that make up today's human rights for business regime. She also explores the United Nations Guiding Principles on Business and Human Rights as well as the due diligence process for human rights as one of the central recommendations that flow from these principles. Looking ahead, she predicts that businesses can expect even more human rights obligations in years to come.

Part III concludes with an examination of both a company's rights and duties. In "A Balancing Approach to Corporate Rights and Duties," Martin Petrin revisits the perennial debate as to which rights and duties a legal entity can or should have. He begins by observing that the debate remains in flux, as most recently demonstrated in the area of constitutional law in the United States. However, the analysis does not end with constitutional law and Petrin explores how corporate rights and duties also pertain to tortious and criminal liability, statutory rights and obligations, and corporate social responsibility. He describes how these areas remain influenced by corporate theories and why this leads to various problems. The chapter suggests that a new model is needed in order to appropriately assign corporate rights and duties and argues in favor of a balancing approach.

Part IV

The final part of this book focuses on the issue of corporate governance in a narrower sense. Part IV explores who should be in charge of corporate decision-making and for whose benefit the company should be governed. This part considers three very different approaches to answering these questions.

In "Corporate Law Reform in the Era of Shareholder Empowerment," William Bratton first examines corporate law reform proposals in light of the shareholder empowerment movement. He finds that corporate paradigms are not important in deciding the fundamental corporate governance questions of our times, such as anti-takeover regulation or shareholder influence over the corporate agenda. Bratton finds that these paradigms are not supported by firm empirical evidence. Ultimately, he concludes that the status quo is currently the best option and that the balance between shareholder and board powers should not be changed as there is not a convincing case for law reform.

In "Board Accountability and the Entity Maximization and Sustainability Approach," Andrew Keay takes a decidedly different approach than Bratton. Keay argues that the accountability of boards of directors is "essential to corporate governance." Accordingly, his focus is on exploring the board's accountability using an entity maximization and sustainability approach. Keay offers two options for holding the board accountable. First, drawing from the notion of supervisory boards common in Germany, he introduces the idea of an accountability council to which the board would be accountable. Second, he builds on the idea of an accountability council to argue that this body would be accountable to the general meeting acting for the company as a whole. In order to ensure that shareholders will act accordingly, Keay explores the idea of imposing a fiduciary duty on shareholders to act in the best interests of the company.

Finally, in "The Corporation and the Question of Time," Lynn Stout conceptualizes the company's nature and purpose using the metaphor of a time machine. Indeed, she provides a direct answer to the question of what a company is by arguing that it represents a vehicle for serving intergenerational equity and efficiency. Stout's view of companies as sempiternal legal persons necessitates a much longer lens for viewing corporate governance roles than a shareholder-centric view of the firm. As a result, not only does she argue that future generations should be considered as additional corporate stakeholders but also that corporate performance should be assessed by viewing the company as a system. This latter notion allows for evaluation of companies by "optimizing within constraints" instead of focusing on the maximization of one performance metric – such as shareholder value – alone.

Conclusion

The debate over what a company or its purpose is remains persistent. From US Supreme Court justices to legislators to even former presidential hopeful Mitt Romney – who once declared that "Corporations are people"[30] – the omnipresent uncertainties over the nature of this legal entity endure in our daily lives. The "age of darkness" for this entity, however, need not remain. The contributors in this book have been brought together to encourage discussions and to promote new ideas and lenses through which the modern company can be better understood. The hope is that their contributions will unravel some of the layers of mystery surrounding the nature of the firm and inform and inspire future discussions.

[30] P. Rucker, "Mitt Romney says 'corporations are people,'" *Washington Post* (August 11, 2011).

PART I

Comparative and Historical Perspectives

1

The Four Transformations of the Corporate Form

REUVEN S. AVI-YONAH

1.1 Introduction

This chapter will describe the historical evolution of the corporation form. Historically, the corporation evolved from its origins in Roman law in a series of four major transformations. First, the concept of the corporation as a separate legal person from its owners or members had to be developed, and this development was only completed with the work of the civil law commentators in the fourteenth century. By the end of the Middle Ages, the membership corporation, i.e., a corporation with several members who chose others to succeed them, had legal personality (the capacity to own property, sue and be sued, and even bear criminal responsibility) and unlimited life, was well established in both civil and common law jurisdictions. The next important step was the shift from non-profit membership corporations to for-profit business corporations, which took place in England and the United States in the end of the eighteenth and beginning of the nineteenth century. The third transformation was the shift from closely held corporations to corporations whose shares are widely held and publicly traded, and with it the rise of limited liability and freedom to incorporate, which took place by the end of the nineteenth and the beginning of the twentieth century. Finally, the last major transformation was from corporations doing business in one country to multinational enterprises whose operations span the globe, which began after World War II and is still going on today.

Each of these four transformations was accompanied by changes in the legal conception of the corporation. What is remarkable, however, is that throughout all these changes spanning two millennia, the same three theories of the corporation can be discerned. Those theories are the aggregate theory, which views the corporation as an aggregate of its members or shareholders; the artificial entity theory, which views the corporation as a creature of the State; and the real entity theory, which views the corporation as neither the sum of its owners nor an extension of the state, but as a separate entity controlled by its managers.[1] Every time there was a shift in the role of the corporation, all three theories were brought forward in cyclical fashion. However, each time the real entity theory prevailed, for reasons we will discuss below, and it was the dominant theory during periods of stability in the relationship between the corporation, the shareholders, and the state.

1.2 First Transformation: The Establishment of the Corporation as a Legal Person

Scholars have been debating for a long time whether classical Roman law had in fact developed a concept of the corporation as a legal person with legal attributes (owning property, the capacity to sue and be sued) separate not just from its members as individuals but also from its members as a group.[2] The classical texts are in fact ambiguous and reflect different views.[3] But one can already discern in them the three views of the corporation outlined in the introduction above: the aggregate theory, the artificial entity theory, and the real entity theory.

The artificial entity view, for example, is reflected in the following excerpt from the classical jurist Gaius:

> Partnerships, *collegia*, and bodies of this sort may not be formed by everybody at will; for this right is restricted by statutes, *senatus consulta*, and imperial *constitutiones*.[4]

The emphasis here is on the authority granted to the various types of corporation by the state: without imperial permission, they could not

[1] These three theories are the standard ones in the literature. See, e.g., David Millon, "Theories of the Corporation" (1990) 201 *Duke Law Journal* 201 at 261–2.

[2] P.W. Duff, *Personality in Roman Private Law* (Cambridge University Press, 1938) argues in the affirmative; F. Schulz, *Classical Roman Law* (Oxford: Clarendon Press, 1951), pp. 88–102 and O. von Gierke, *Associations and Law: The Classical and Early Christian Stages* (University of Toronto Press, 1977), pp. 95–142, in the negative.

[3] These texts are taken from the Corpus Juris Civilis, the major compilation of Roman law performed under the Emperor Justinian in 528–534 AD. The Corpus Juris Civilis consists of three parts: The Institutes (Inst.), an introduction to the law in general; the Digest (D.), a collection of pronouncements of individual jurists, mostly from the classical period (the first two centuries AD); and the Code (C.), a collection of imperial statutes. The views of the classical jurists thus come to us in fragmentary fashion, and with the possibility of later editing or interpolation, so it is hard to be sure what any classical jurist actually said. For the Digest, I used the text edited by Mommsen and Krueger, in Alan Watson (ed. and transl.), *The Digest of Justinian* (Philadelphia: University of Pennsylvania Press, 1985).

[4] Gaius, D. 3.4.1 pr.-1 (transl. Alan Watson).

have legal personality, own property, or have an agent who can act in their name. In fact, we know from other sources that the Roman emperors were suspicious of private corporations, especially in the provinces, as potentially seditious, and refused permission to set up such corporations even for seemingly innocuous purposes.

The aggregate view of the corporation as equivalent to its members acting collectively is reflected in the following excerpt from the classical jurist Paul:

> Citizens of a municipality can possess nothing of themselves, because the consent of all is not possible. Hence, they do not possess the marketplace, public buildings, and the like, but they use them in common.[5]

This refers to the Roman concept of possession (*possessio*), which requires animus and corpus, the intention to possess and the capacity to hold[6]; Paul is saying that since the members of a corporation cannot have a single animus, they cannot actually own anything. The same view is also reflected in the classical prohibition against instituting corporate bodies as heirs because they are "uncertain," i.e., their membership is changing.

The real view, finally, is mostly reflected in the excerpts of the classical jurist Ulpian. For example:

> If members of a municipality or any corporate body appoint an attorney for legal business, it should not be said that he is in the position of a man appointed by several people; for he comes in on behalf of a public authority or corporate body, not on behalf of individuals.[7]

Ulpian here uses *universitas* (corporate body) as equal to the *municipes* (members), and speaks of the representative as acting for the corporate body rather than on behalf of the "individuals," which can be consistent with the aggregate view; but he also states that the representative does not act for the "several people," which favors the real entity view that he acts for the corporation itself.

Similarly, consider the following:

> As regards decurions or other corporate bodies, it does not matter whether all the members remain the same or only some or whether all have changed. But if a corporate body is reduced to one member, it is usually conceded

[5] Paul, D. 41.2.1.22 (transl. Alan Watson).

[6] D. 41.2.3.1; cf. W.W. Buckland, *A Text-Book of Roman Law: From Augustus to Justinian* (Cambridge University Press, 1963), pp. 199–202.

[7] Ulpian, D. 3.4.2.

> that he can sue and be sued, since the rights of all have fallen to one and the corporate body continues to exist in name only.[8]

In this text Ulpian envisages the corporate body as remaining unchanged as the membership changes, and he even considers the possibility of a "corporation sole." This is the clearest evidence of the real entity view in the Roman texts; but note that not even Ulpian could imagine a corporation continuing to exist without any members.

The same debate continued through the Middle Ages. Consider the following examples, which come from the Ordinary Gloss by Franciscus Accursius (1182–1258), which was written around 1250 and summarized the previous century's work by the jurists in Bologna of commenting on the Corpus Juris Civilis.

First, the artificial entity view:

> Of others: . . . And because certain societies are permitted, as the text says, it is clear that normally they are prohibited . . . But can a society, such as that of scholars living in one inn, appoint an agent [to sue]? It seems they can, if the case is the society's, as it is a permitted society.[9]

Here Accursius emphasizes the need for a society to obtain permission from the state to have legal personality, just as Gaius did in the text he was commenting upon. The identity of the state has changed (the Bolognese jurists professed allegiance to the German emperors), as did the identity of the corporations, but the concept is similar.

The aggregate view can be seen in Accursius' definition of the agent as "Syndicus: Who acts for any corporate body, but only for the many . . . for he is called syndicus because he argues (*dicens*) cases for the single ones (*singulorum*)."[10] Here the agent is seen as speaking for the members as a collective, as opposed to the members as individuals. Similarly, Accursius rejected the concept of limited liability, requiring the members to be liable for debts of the corporation, which again reflects the aggregate view. And he allows departing members to take their share, although not of inheritances or other property that belonged to the corporation itself.

In yet other locations, the real entity view predominates, even when it requires challenging the Roman authorities. For example:

> It is as if [Paul] said not easily, because they cannot will together easily . . . but they can with difficulty, so as when a bell is tolled, because

[8] Ulpian, D. 3.4.7.2.

[9] Franciscus Accursius, Glossa Ordinaria (1658) (henceforward GO) on D. 3.4.1.1, v. aliorum. The translation of this and other medieval texts is mine.

[10] GO on D.3.4.1.1, v. syndicum.

> all are considered to have done what the council or a majority did . . . and they can commit intimidation . . . and obtain possession . . . and elect a tribune or leader . . . for this question notes the rarity, not the impossibility [of doing so].[11]

Here Accursius rejects Paul's view that corporate bodies cannot own anything because they cannot will together, referring to the notion that the majority of the members can act for the corporate body. Likewise,

> What if a member of a corporate body injures you, can the corporate body be said to have done it and be sued by you? It seems that not, because he did it out of his own will, not as a corporate body, i.e., after deliberation and sounding a bell or having been otherwise gathered together. On the contrary, yes, because a corporate body is nothing more than the people who are there.[12]

The last sentence clearly reflects the aggregate view. However, when Accursius considers the question what happens when the membership changes, he seems to reject the aggregate view in favor of the real entity view:

> Some say that goods that belong to a college belong to the people, or to many single individuals . . . but they do not concede that if those [individuals] die the people is dead, because others are considered (*finguntur*) to take their place. Thus the emitted cry perishes, but not your voice.[13]

This text conceives of the membership corporation as unchanging even though the individual members change. This could still be consistent with the aggregate view (the membership remains as a collective), but the rejection of the view that the goods belong to "many single individuals" and the citation to Ulpian suggest the real entity view.

Finally, consider the following:

> Even though a single person cannot be a corporate body, he still retains the rights of the corporate body, even though a single person cannot constitute a corporate body initially, but only three persons . . . But can he appoint a syndicus, who argues cases for the many, or [at least] for two? It seems so . . . But what if nobody at all remains? . . . The college is then dissolved, and the goods belong to nobody, like inherited goods. But if thereafter by authority of the Pope or whoever is in charge of that college, someone is appointed to that college, by the artifice of the law the goods are considered (*fingitur*) to belong to him . . . Even though some Bishop Moses said that the walls themselves possess even during the existence of the college,

[11] GO on D. 4.3.15.1, v. facere possunt.
[12] GO on D.3.4.7.1, v. non debetur.
[13] GO on D.47.22.1.1, v. competit.

> which seems very difficult to say and contrary to the law. To the contrary, in no way do the goods belong to anyone, but once the college has been dissolved, by the law they belong to the fisc or the Pope. . . . But it can be said for Moses, that the church is frequently called the place itself which is surrounded by walls and consecrated; and it is also said that the church can have rights and possess and sue . . . thus the location itself, or the walls, possess even while the college exists, through the priest, like a private person through an agent.[14]

In this gloss on Ulpian, Accursius goes beyond his Roman source to ask what happens if all members of a corporation die. He then resorts to the artificial entity theory to argue that the state should appoint a replacement; alternatively, he states that the college ceases to exist, consistent with the aggregate view. But he also mentions the possibility that the "location" of the corporation continues to exist, which is closer to the real entity view. There is no resolution: all three views co-exist in this text.

A hundred years later, however, the real entity view comes to predominate. This can be seen in the following examples from the work of Bartolus of Sassoferato (1314–57), the most important of the Commentators, the generation that followed the Glossators in further developing the interpretation of the Roman text. The work of Bartolus was influential well into the nineteenth century, i.e., until the codification movement, which replaced the Corpus Juris Civilis as the main source of civil law.

Bartolus clearly adhered to the real entity view of the corporation. First, he rejected the artificial entity view that permission by the state is needed to set up a corporation: "If some people want to settle in some place, and create a city, castle, or village, they can do so, as it is permitted by the law of nations."[15] This is understandable because by Bartolus' time the Holy Roman Empire had ceased to exist as a force in Italian political life and the Italian city-states were independent municipal corporations.

Second, Bartolus clearly envisaged the corporation remaining even if all of its members perish: "What if this university [Perugia] were to perish by pestilence, and nobody remained? . . . The privileges would remain in the place where it was."[16] This commentary was probably written after the Black Death of 1347–8 swept through Europe, so it reflects the reality of Bartolus' time. But it also goes beyond Accursius and Ulpian to reject the aggregate view.

[14] GO on D. 3.4.7.2, v. nomen universitatis.

[15] Bartolus of Sassoferato, Commentary on D.3.4.1.1 (1653).

[16] Bartolus, Comm. on D. 47.22.4.

Instead, Bartolus developed the concept of the corporation as *persona representata*, i.e., a legal personality that is separate from both the state and its members, but that had to act through agents. For example:

> A corporate body is a legal name, and it does not have a soul or an intellect. Therefore it cannot commit crimes . . . Others say, that corporate bodies can commit crimes . . . We must consider first, whether a corporate body differs from its members? Some say no, like the philosophers and canonists, who hold that the whole does not really differ from its parts. The truth is, that if we speak about reality proper, those say the truth. For a university of scholars is nothing other than the scholars. But according to legal fiction they err. For a university represents a person, which is different than the scholars, or its members . . . Thus, if some scholars leave and others return, nevertheless the university stays the same. Similarly if all members of a people die and others take their place, the people is the same . . . and thus a corporate body is different from its members, by legal fiction . . ..[17]

This text shows that Bartolus had a clear vision of the corporation as separate both from the state and from its members. It was a "legal fiction" that could have the basic attributes of legal personality, i.e., the capacity to own property, sue and be sued, and even commit crimes, although in all these respects it had to act through its agents, and it was not subject to certain kinds of punishment.

What enabled Bartolus to go beyond his Roman and medieval sources to reach this conclusion? In part, it was a natural evolution of moving away from and beyond the ancient text through the process of commentary and debate. But Bartolus was also influenced by external factors, the most important of which were the decline of the Holy Roman Empire, which led to the abandonment of artificial entity theory that corporations needed imperial permission to exist, and the rise of independent corporations in Italy such as the city-state and the Italian universities. For these corporations to maintain their independence, they needed to be seen as separate both from the state and from their members, since even the collective membership could perish. Bartolus and his colleagues did not want the privileges and property of the university to revert to the Popes or the Emperors should the membership all change at once. Hence, the natural theory for Bartolus to embrace as representative of the university was real entity theory, which enabled the university to maintain its independence both from the state and from its members.

We thus see that in the period between the classical Roman jurists in the second century AD and the Commentators in the fourteenth century

[17] Comm. on D. 48.19.16.10.

the concept of the corporation as a legal person gradually evolved, and that as this evolution proceeded all three theories of the corporation (aggregate, artificial entity, and real entity) were brought forward by various legal commentators. We also see that in the end, aided by external factors such as the decline of the state, real entity theory, which most closely reflects the views and interests of corporate management, emerges as the dominant theory. As we shall see, this pattern of debate among the three theories followed by the triumph of real entity theory is typical of subsequent transformations in the role of the corporation as well.

1.3 Second Transformation: From Non-Profit to For-Profit Corporations

The period between Bartolus (mid-fourteenth century) and the late eighteenth century was one of relative stability in the development of the corporate form. The corporation was established as a membership corporation, i.e., a corporation made up of members who selected their own successors, like the President and Fellows of Harvard College still do today. As such, a corporation had legal personality, i.e., the rights to own property, sue and be sued, act under a common seal, and other such "chestnuts."[18] Private corporations were used primarily for non-profit purposes (e.g., hospitals and universities), but by the eighteenth century there were also some commercial ones (e.g., the East India Company).[19]

From our perspective, there were two significant developments in this period. The first was the reassertion of royal control over corporations; in England and other European countries corporations could only be established by royal charter. Blackstone notes that although in Roman law corporations could be established without "the prince's consent," "with us in England, the king's consent is absolutely necessary."[20] Second, some degree of outside control over management was established through the institution of the committee of visitors, which represented the interests of the founder and of the wider community.[21]

[18] R.C. Clark, *Corporate Law* (Rotterdam: A.A Balkema, 1989). As we have seen these "chestnuts" were not at all self-evident.

[19] See the classification and description of various corporations in W. Blackstone, *Commentaries on the Laws of England* (Oxford: Clarendon Press, 1765), ch. XVIII.

[20] *Ibid.* at 460; *Tipling* v. *Pexall*, 3 Bulstrode 233 (1614) ("the King creates them").

[21] Blackstone, above n 19 at 467–9.

But other than in extraordinary cases, the real entity view of the corporation prevailed throughout this period and management (the members) were firmly in control. "A corporation aggregate of many is invisible, immortal, and rests only in intendment and consideration of the law."[22] As such, it was a self-perpetuating body subject to relatively little outside regulation. Corporations, Blackstone notes, are "artificial persons, who may maintain a perpetual succession, and enjoy a kind of legal immortality."[23] When the members "are consolidated and united into a corporation, they and their successors are then considered as one person in law: as one person, they have one will, which is collected from the sense of the majority of the individuals . . . for all the individual members that have existed from the foundation to the present time, or that shall ever hereafter exist, are but one person in law, a person that never dies."[24] This one person then acquires all the rights of corporations, including perpetual succession, the right to sue and be sued, the right to own property, to have a common seal, to make bylaws, and to be subject to certain criminal liabilities.[25] The king constituted corporations, and the king or other visitors exercised some degree of supervision over them, but once established the corporation (i.e., its members) remained subject to relatively little outside regulation.

This situation meant that corporate status was very desirable, especially since the members also enjoyed limited liability for corporate debts. But the English Kings were very cautious with granting corporate charters, especially in the case of for-profit enterprises; only corporations that were clearly vested with a public purpose and benefited the public fisc, like the East India and Hudson Bay Companies, received royal approval and accumulated vast power. As more capital was required for commercial enterprises this resulted in promoters organizing corporations with transferable shares and claiming that under authority of a lost or obsolete charter the shareholders enjoyed limited liability. After the South Sea Bubble burst in 1720, this problem (and the desire of the East India Company to retain its monopoly) led to the Bubble Act under which it became a crime to organize such corporations without explicit royal consent.[26] Although prosecutions under the Bubble Act were rare, it meant that the entire Industrial

[22] *Sutton's Hospital Case*, 10 Co Rep 1, 973 (1612).

[23] Blackstone, above n 19 at 455.

[24] *Ibid.* at 456.

[25] *Ibid.* at 463.

[26] The Bubble Act, 6 Geo. I c. 18 (1720). See R. Harris, *Industrializing English Law: Entrepreneurship and Business Organization 1720–1844* (Cambridge University Press, 2000).

Revolution in England (1760–1820) took place outside the corporate form and without limited liability. The Bubble Act was ultimately repealed in 1825, after the Industrial Revolution was over, but with the provision of unlimited liability for shareholders, which continued to be the rule in England until 1855.[27]

This situation, which can be seen as a way of maintaining state control over corporations through restrictions on charters, meant that the next great shift in the use of the corporate form took place in the fledgling United States. There, once the revolution was over, every state could issue corporate charters. The result was an explosion of charters for commercial enterprises. One of the first treatises written on corporate law was Joseph Angell and Samuel Ames' Treatise on the Law of Private Corporations Aggregate, published in Boston in 1832. Angell and Ames begin their book by stating that:

> The reader does not require to be told, that we have in our country an infinite number of corporations aggregate, which have no concern whatever with affairs of a municipal nature. These associations we not only find scattered throughout every cultivated part of the United States, but so engaged are they in all the varieties of useful pursuit, that we see them directing the concentration of mind and capital to . . . the encouragement and extension of the great interests of commerce, agriculture, and manufacturing. There is a great difference in this respect between our own country, and the country from which we have derived a great portion of our laws. What is done in England by combination, unless it be the management of municipal concerns, is most generally done by a combination of individuals, established by mere articles of agreement. On the other hand, what is done here by the co-operation of several persons is, in the greater number of instances, the result of a consolidation effected by an express act or charter of incorporation.[28]

The main reason for this proliferation of corporations in the United States was the second great transformation in the role of the corporation in society: from primarily a not-for-profit to primarily a for-profit enterprise. As Judge Kent stated, "the multiplication of corporations in the United States, and the avidity with which they are sought, have arisen in consequence of the power which a large and consolidated capital gives them over business of every kind; and the facility which the incorporation

[27] Bubble Act Repeal, 6 Geo. IV c. 91 (1825); Limited Liability Act, 18 & 19 Vict. C. 133 (1855).

[28] J.K. Angell and S. Ames, *Treatise of the Law of Private Corporations Aggregate* (Boston: Little, Brown & Co., 1861), v.

gives to the management of capital, and the security which it affords to the persons of its members, and to their property not vested in the corporate stock."[29]

This was a profound shift, and not surprisingly it led to a revival of the centuries-old debate about the nature of the corporate form and its relationship to the shareholders and to the state. This debate can be seen if we examine the opinions on the subject issued by the first great American jurist, John Marshall. Three of Marshall's opinions, written decades apart, are particularly relevant here: *Bank of the United States* v. *Deveaux* (1809), *Dartmouth College* v. *Woodward* (1819), and *Bank of the United States* v. *Dandridge* (1827).[30] These opinions represent the evolution of his thinking on corporations, which moved from the aggregate view (*Deveaux*) to the artificial entity view (*Dartmouth College*) to the real entity view (*Dandridge*).

Deveaux involved an attempt by the state of Georgia to tax the Savannah branch of the Bank of the United States, a corporation established by Congress in 1791, as part of the early struggles around federalism. The Bank was a membership corporation ("The President, Directors and Company of the Bank of the United States") and all the members were citizens of Pennsylvania. The Bank refused to pay the tax and the State sent its collectors to enforce payment, whereupon the Bank sued the collectors in federal court, claiming diversity jurisdiction. The issue facing the court was whether a corporation made up of members from one state could sue citizens of another state in federal court on diversity grounds. This in turn required deciding between the view that "the individual character of the members is so wholly lost in that of the corporation, that the court cannot take notice of it," and the contrary view that "a corporation is composed of natural persons," i.e., between the entity (artificial or real) and aggregate views.[31]

Marshall decided in favor of the aggregate view. He stated that the corporation itself, "that mere legal entity," cannot be a citizen or sue in federal court, unless it can be regarded as "a company of individuals."[32] However, since the reasons that led Congress to enact diversity jurisdiction applied

29 *Ibid.* at 36, citing 2 Kent's Com. 219. The last sentence refers to limited liability, which will be discussed below.

30 *Bank of the United States* v. *Deveaux*, 9 US (5 Cranch) 61 (1809); *Trustees of Dartmouth College* v. *Woodward*, 17 US (4 Wheat.) 518 (1819); *Bank of the United States* v. *Dandridge*, 25 US (12 Wheat.) 64 (1827).

31 *Deveaux*, above n 30 at 63–4.

32 *Ibid.* at 86–7.

to corporations as well, Marshall was inclined to see the controversy as being between the members "suing in their corporate character" and their opponents.[33] "The controversy is substantially between aliens, suing by a corporate name, and a citizen . . . in this case the corporate name represents persons who are members of the corporation."[34] The Court therefore held that federal jurisdiction existed.

Ten years later Marshall was faced with another difficult issue involving corporations. In the famous *Dartmouth College* case, the state of New Hampshire attempted to alter the charter of Dartmouth College (incorporated as a membership corporation by George III in 1769, under the name of The Trustees of Dartmouth College), by transferring the appointment of trustees to the state, thereby effectively taking it over. The trustees objected, arguing that the charter constituted a contract and altering it violated the contracts clause of the Constitution.[35]

Marshall held that as the College was a private corporation, its charter was a contract and was protected by the contracts clause. He began by noting that the funds for the College came from private sources and its educational character did not make it public either. He then got to the heart of the question – whether the act of incorporation by the state makes it possible for the state to take it over. In frequently quoted language, Marshall held that:

> A corporation is an artificial being, invisible, intangible, and existing only in contemplation of law. Being the mere creature of law, it possesses only those properties which the charter of its creation confers upon it, either expressly, or as incidental to its very existence.[36]

This language reflects the artificial entity view of the corporation. But Marshall then went on to note that, having created the corporation, the state may not treat it as a mere extension of itself: "[T]his being does not share in the civil government of the country, unless that be the purpose for which it was created."[37] Even though its object is to promote governmentally approved aims, this does not make corporations into mere instruments of government. Instead, the corporation exists to represent the interest of the founder and his descendants in the aims for which it was founded. This interest is in the United States protected by the contracts

[33] *Ibid.* at 87–8.
[34] *Ibid.* at 91.
[35] *Trustees of Dartmouth College*, above n 30.
[36] *Ibid.* at 636.
[37] *Ibid.*

clause, although in England, Marshall recognized, Parliament had the power to annul the charter.[38] In this country "the body corporate, as possessing the whole legal and equitable interest, and completely representing the donors, for the purpose of executing the trust, has rights which are protected by the constitution."[39]

It should be noted that while Marshall held that the state may not take over a private corporation, even one founded for public ends, the emphasis on the artificial nature of the corporation left ample room for state regulation via the original charter. Since states were busy granting charters by the hundreds, the *Dartmouth* opinion thus enabled the states to regulate corporations, should they wish to do so.

Finally, six years later, Marshall was once more called to opine on the nature of corporations in another case involving the Bank of the United States.[40] The case involved a suit by the Bank on a bond executed by Dandridge, one of its cashiers, in which the defendant argued that the bond had never been approved by the Board of Directors, as required by the charter of incorporation. The key issue was whether the level of evidence required of corporations was higher than that required of individuals, since corporations are incapable of acting not in writing. Justice Story for the Court held that no distinction should be made: "The same presumptions are . . . applicable to corporations."[41] Marshall, however, dissented. He argued that:

> The corporation being one entire impersonal entity, distinct from the individuals who compose it, must be endowed with a mode of action peculiar to itself, which will always distinguish its transactions from those of its members. This faculty must be exercised according to its own nature . . . This can be done only in writing.[42]

The Court's view was the more pragmatic one, but Marshall's view was more consistent with the real entity view of the corporation as distinct from its members, individually or collectively. It certainly forms an interesting contrast with the views he expressed in the *Deveaux* case sixteen years earlier.

How can one explain the shift in Marshall's view of the corporation from aggregate (*Deveaux*) to artificial (*Dartmouth College*) to real (*Dandridge*)?

38 *Ibid.* at 642–3.
39 *Ibid.* at 654.
40 *Dandridge*, above n 30.
41 *Ibid.* at 70.
42 *Ibid.* at 91–2.

In part, this stems from the circumstances of these particular cases. In *Deveaux*, Marshall wanted to confer diversity jurisdiction to protect a federal institution (he was after all a Federalist), and the only way to do so was to look through the corporation to its members. In *Dartmouth College*, the issue involved the relationship of private corporations (albeit "imbued with a public purpose"; the full-fledged private/public distinction had not yet evolved) to the state, and thus Marshall emphasized the role of the state in creating the corporation, while placing clear limits on its ability to regulate corporations thereafter. These limits were required as the result of the proliferation of corporations, especially for-profit business corporations, since otherwise the state would be able to take over purely private businesses. The result in *Dartmouth College* favored in practice the real entity view, since once a private corporation was created, it could no longer be taken over or perhaps even be overly regulated by the state. Thus, it may not be surprising that by the time he came to write his *Dandridge* dissent Marshall took the real entity view, even though it contradicted his opinion in *Deveaux* (which is not mentioned).

1.4 Third Transformation: From Closely Held to Widely Held Corporations

The situation between the 1820s and the end of the Civil War was thus the proliferation of for-profit corporations, incorporated under general incorporation laws with minimal interference by the state, and whose shareholders enjoyed limited liability. Those shareholders were, however, relatively limited in number; despite the Angell and Ames' quotation above, few corporations before 1865 required massive amounts of capital, and most were small, closely held enterprises. This enabled the Civil War income tax on corporate income to be imposed directly on the shareholders of corporations.

This state of affairs began to change with the advent of the railroads, followed by the steel and oil companies. With the rise of large corporate enterprises, massive amounts of capital were required, and between 1865 and the 1890s the widely held, publicly traded, non-owner managed enterprise gradually became the norm for US business activities. This was followed from 1890 to 1906 by a wave of consolidation that left several important business areas dominated by monopolies run by the "robber barons."

The shift from small, closely held enterprises to massive, publicly held ones once again necessitated a re-examination of the corporate form, and again all three theories of the corporation appear. A classic example of the aggregate view is the *Santa Clara* case, ultimately decided by the Supreme Court in 1886. This case is famous for Chief Justice Waite's statement that "[t]he court does not wish to hear argument on the question whether the [equal protection clause] applies to these corporations. We are all of the opinion that it does."[43] Some scholars identified this as an application of the real entity view to corporations, but Professor Horwitz has shown by examining Justice Field's opinion in the court below that it actually represented an application of the aggregate view.[44] Specifically, Field held that the equal protection clause must apply to corporations for the following reasons:

> Private corporations consist of an association of individuals united for some lawful purpose, and permitted to use a common name in their business and have succession of membership without dissolution . . . But these members do not, because of such association, lose their right to protection, and equality of protection . . . Whatever affects the property of the corporation – that is, of all the members united by the common name – necessarily affects their interests . . . So, therefore, whenever a provision of the constitution or of a law guarantees to persons protection in their property . . . the benefits of the provision are extended to corporations; not to the name under which different persons are united, but to the individuals composing the union. The courts will always look through the name to see and protect those whom the name represents [citing *Deveaux*].[45]

A clearer statement of the aggregate view can hardly be imagined; most remarkable is Field's reliance on *Deveaux* despite the fact that the Supreme Court overturned its results forty years earlier. Similarly, in *Pembina Consolidated Silver Mining Co.* v. *Pennsylvania*, decided two years later, Justice Field for the Court stated that "[u]nder the designation of person there is no doubt that a private corporation is included. Such corporations are merely associations of individuals united for a special purpose."[46]

However, the artificial entity view was also raised in these cases. In *Santa Clara*, the railroad corporations made the argument that because they were operating under special congressional legislation they should be regarded as an extension of the federal government and

[43] *Santa Clara County* v. *Southern Pacific Railroad Company*, 118 US 394 at 396 (1886).

[44] M.J. Horwitz, "Santa Clara Revisited: The Development of Corporate Theory" (1985) 88 *West Virginia Law Review* 173.

[45] *Santa Clara County* v. *Southern Pacific Railroad Company*, 18 F 385 (C.D.D. Cal. 1883) at 409–10.

[46] *Pembina Consolidated Silver Mining Co.* v. *Pennsylvania*, 125 US 181 at 189 (1888).

therefore California could not tax them.[47] Field rejected this view (citing *Dartmouth College*), but noted that "when the instrumentality is the creation of the state – a corporation formed under its laws – and is employed or adopted by the general government for its convenience . . . it remains subject to the taxing power of the state."[48] And notably, in *Pembina* Field followed Taney in rejecting the argument that the privileges and immunities clause applied to corporations because they were not "citizens," even though the aggregate view he adopted in *Santa Clara* might have led to the contrary position. Instead, Field emphasized the relationship between the corporation and the incorporating state under the artificial entity view:

> The term citizens, as used in this clause, applies only to natural persons, members of the body politic owing allegiance to the State, not to artificial persons created by the legislature, and possessing only such attributes as the legislature has prescribed . . . a grant of corporate existence was a grant of special privileges to the corporators, enabling them to act for certain specified purposes as a single individual, and exempting them, unless otherwise provided, from individual liability.[49]

Moreover, all three views of the corporation appear in *Hale* v. *Henkel*, decided by the Supreme Court in 1906. The issues were whether an agent of a corporation could invoke the Fifth Amendment privilege against self-incrimination or the Fourth Amendment protection against unreasonable search and seizure in the name of the corporation. On the Fifth Amendment issue, the Court held that the right against self-incrimination does not apply to corporations:

> The right of a person under the Fifth Amendment to refuse to incriminate himself is purely a personal privilege of the witness . . . The question whether a corporation is a "person" within the meaning of this Amendment really does not arise . . . since it can only be heard by oral evidence in the person of some one of its agents or employees.[50]

This is closest to the real entity view, since it rejects (like Marshall in *Dandridge*) the aggregate position of looking through a corporation to its shareholders, and takes into account the special characteristics of the corporation itself.

[47] *Santa Clara County*, above n 45 at 387.
[48] *Ibid.* at 389.
[49] *Pembina Consolidated*, above n 46 at 187–8.
[50] *Hale* v. *Henkel*, 201 US 43 at 69–70 (1906).

On the other hand, on the Fourth Amendment issue, the Court at first emphasized the artificial entity view, using it to justify regulation by the state:

> Conceding that the witness was an officer of the corporation under investigation, and that he was entitled to assert the rights of the corporation with respect to the production of its books and papers, we are of the opinion that there is a clear distinction in this particular between an individual and a corporation, and that the latter has no right to refuse to submit its books and papers for an examination at the suit of the State. The individual may stand upon his constitutional rights as a citizen . . . Upon the other hand, the corporation is a creature of the State. It is presumed to be incorporated for the benefit of the public. It receives certain special privileges and franchises, and holds them subject to the laws of the State and the limitations of its charter . . . It would be a strange anomaly to hold that a State, having chartered a corporation to make use of certain franchises, could not in the exercise of its sovereignty inquire how these franchises had been employed, and whether they had been abused, and demand the production of the corporate books and papers for that purpose.[51]

However, having clearly stated its reasons for limiting the application of the constitutional right, the Court suddenly reverts to the aggregate view when facing the question whether corporations have any Fourth Amendment rights at all:

> [W]e do not wish to be understood as holding that a corporation is not entitled to immunity, under the Fourth Amendment, against unreasonable searches and seizures. A corporation is, after all, but an association of individuals under an assumed name and with a distinct legal entity. In organizing itself as a collective body it waives no constitutional immunities appropriate to such body. Its property cannot be taken without compensation. It can only be proceeded against by due process of law, and is protected, under the Fourteenth Amendment, against unlawful discrimination. Corporations are a necessary feature of modern business activity, and their aggregated capital has become the source of nearly all great enterprises.[52]

What can explain this remarkable oscillation between the three views? The key is the last sentence quoted. As noted above, the period between 1890 and 1906 marked the height of the debate on the rise of the great corporations. The Court is trying to strike a balance between the rights of the corporations, which can best be protected under either the aggregate

[51] *Ibid.* at 74–5.

[52] *Ibid.* at 76 (citations omitted).

or the real entity views, and the regulatory power of the state, which is best reflected in the artificial entity view. On the one hand, as the Court states, "[c]orporations are a necessary feature of modern business activity" and must be protected. On the other hand, the right of the state to regulate must also be preserved, especially since the context of *Hale* v. *Henkel* was an antitrust investigation into two major corporations, the American Tobacco Company and MacAndrews & Forbes Inc.

Ultimately, however, the real entity view prevailed. This involved first the rejection of the aggregate view. For example, in *Western Turf Association* v. *Greenberg*, decided just one year after *Hale* v. *Henkel*, Justice Harlan emphasized that a corporation is a separate entity from its shareholders, and therefore is not a "citizen" for purposes of the privileges and immunities clause or entitled to the protection of the due process clause: "the liberty guaranteed by the Fourteenth Amendment against deprivation without due process of law is the liberty of natural, not artificial, persons."[53] But by itself this position would have led to too much state regulation for the Lochner court. Thus, in *Southern Railway Co.* v. *Greene*, decided in 1909, the Court came out clearly for the position that the corporation *as such* was entitled to constitutional protection under the equal protection clause, without any reference to its shareholders: "the corporation . . . is within the meaning of the Fourteenth Amendment, a person within the jurisdiction of the state of Alabama, and entitled to be protected against any statute of the State which deprives it of the equal protection of the laws."[54]

Once again, the triumph of the real entity view can be explained by several factors. The aggregate view was raised by Field and others to protect the rights of corporations, but it was even more incongruous in the context of the mega-corporations of the 1890s, with thousands of shareholders, than in the pre-civil days. It also gave the corporation too many rights vis-à-vis the state, as seen in *Hale* v. *Henkel* and in *Greenberg*. The artificial entity view gave the state too much power to regulate corporations, as the *Hale* v. *Henkel* court came to realize when it laid out its implications. The real entity view was the most congruent with business realities as well as the one most suited to some balance between corporations and the state. By 1909, it was well established as the dominant view of the corporation, as reflected in contemporary debates surrounding the enactment of the corporate tax.

[53] *Western Turf Association* v. *Greenberg*, 204 US 359 at 363 (1907).

[54] *Southern Railway Co.* v. *Greene*, 216 US 400 at 417 (1910).

1.5 Fourth Transformation: From National Corporations to Multinational Enterprises

The last transformation in the nature of the corporation began in the 1950s and is still going on, so that its ultimate outcome is hard to judge. This is the transformation from corporations based mostly in one country to multinational enterprises based in many countries.

Multinationals, in the sense of corporations owning assets overseas, have existed since the seventeenth century. However, as recently as the 1950s, the shareholders and other sources of capital, the management, most of the production facilities, and most of the markets of even large multinationals tended to be in one country, so that "what was good for G.M. was good for America." By the 1990s, however, this has changed profoundly. As more countries opened up to foreign direct investment, communications improved, and many products became lighter and easier to ship, more and more corporations became "globalized." In a globalized multinational world, the sources of capital are in many countries: The shares of large multinationals trade on as many as twenty exchanges, and borrowing facilities are similarly diversified. Research and development and production facilities are likewise spread throughout the globe, as are markets. The only thing that usually ties a modern multinational to its home country is the location of management.

In this context, the debate over the nature of the corporation has reopened. There is abundant academic writing on the relationship between multinationals and the state, and most writers from both left and right concede that this relationship has changed profoundly so that the home state (the state of incorporation) has become powerless to control "its" multinationals; it is hard even to identify to which country multinationals "belong." On a practical level this situation has led to attempts by home states to control the behavior of multinationals abroad in areas as diverse as trading with the enemy, antitrust, corruption and others with varying success. The most recent development in this regard has been "inversion" transactions, in which the management changes the country of incorporation of a multinational's parent corporation. These transactions are undertaken primarily for tax reasons, but they have corporate governance implications as well. Specifically, the artificial entity theory becomes hard to maintain when management can pick weak countries like Bermuda as the country of incorporation for the parent of a multinational.

The relationship with shareholders has also undergone changes as shareholders now tend to come from many countries. One implication of this has been that the securities laws of the weakest country tend to dominate because of cross-country price arbitrage. Another is academic proposals to let management choose the country of securities law as well as the country of incorporation. On a practical level, globalization has led the SEC to relax requirements for some foreign issuers. This trend has tended to weaken the applicability of the aggregate view as well. It is hard to predict where these trends will lead, but at the moment they appear once more to favor the real entity view.

To summarize: Throughout all the transformations we have studied, the same pattern recurs. As the relationship of the corporation to the state, to society and to its members or shareholders changes, all three views of the corporation emerge, submerge and then re-emerge in a slightly different but fundamentally similar form. In the end, however, the real entity view prevails.

Why does the real entity view prevail? In part, this is no doubt due to the fact that it represents the most congenial view to corporate management, because it shields them from undue interference from both shareholders and the state. Corporate management wields political power and it influences the outcome of the debate; judges again and again refer to the importance of corporations, by which they mean corporate management. But the very fact that corporate management wields this power shows that there is another reason why the real entity view prevails: It fits reality much more than the other two. In some periods (e.g., the Roman Empire or the eighteenth-century Europe) the power of the state is overwhelming and the artificial entity view seems plausible, and in other periods (the medieval membership corporation, the nineteenth-century close corporation) the aggregate view seems plausible, but in most periods equating the corporation either with the state or with shareholders must have seemed to most non-academics highly implausible. The real entity view prevailed because it was more *real* than the others. And that reality has implications for modern debates about the corporate form, such as issues relating to corporate governance and corporate social responsibility, which are addressed in other chapters.

2

Comparative Corporate Governance: Old and New

MARTIN GELTER

2.1 Introduction

Whose interests should a corporation serve? Should it have a higher social purpose beyond the financial gain of shareholders? These questions have befuddled theorists of corporate law since the Berle–Dodd debate in the early 1930s in the United States,[1] and the discussion in Germany in the 1920s and 1930s about the *Unternehmen an sich* – a term aptly coined by opponents of the writings of Walther Rathenau, who seemed to endorse a public purpose for the corporation.[2] Since then, the discussion has flared up with predicable recurrence both in common law and civil law jurisdictions over the past century, and without clear winning arguments, even if one model or the other has dominated at times.[3]

[1] A.A. Berle, Jr., "Corporate Powers as Powers in Trust" (1931) 44 *Harvard Law Review* 1049; E. Merrick Dodd, Jr., "For Whom Are Managers Trustees?" (1931) 45 *Harvard Law Review* 1145; A.A. Berle, Jr., "For Whom Corporate Managers Are Trustees: A Note" (1931) 45 *Harvard Law Review* 1365.

[2] W. Rathenau, *Vom Aktienwesen: Eine geschäftliche Betrachtung* (Berlin: Fischer Verlag, 1917). Rathenau's leading critic was Hausmann. See F. Haussmann, *Vom Aktienwesen und vom Aktienrecht* (Mannheim: Besheimer, 1928), p. 20; F. Haussmann, "Gesellschaftsinteresse und Interessenpolitik in der Aktiengesellschaft" (1930) 30 *Bank-Archiv* 57 at 64–5. For an overview of the debate in English, see, e.g., M. Gelter, "Taming or Protecting the Modern Corporation? Shareholder–Stakeholder Debates in a Comparative Light" (2011) 7 *New York University Journal of Law & Business* 641 at 686–6.

[3] Gelter, above n 2 at 667–78 (discussing the United States), 678–704 (Germany), and 704–18 (France). For some recent contributions, see, e.g., L.M. Fairfax, "The Rhetoric of Corporate Law: The Impact of Stakeholder Rhetoric on Corporate Norms" (2006) 31 *Journal of Corporation Law* 675; W.W. Bratton and M.L. Wachter, "Shareholder Primacy's Corporatist Origins: Adolf Berle and the Modern Corporation" (2009) 34 *Journal of Corporation Law* 99 at 101; R. Reich-Graefe, "Deconstructing Corporate Governance: Absolute Director Primacy" (2011) 5 *Brooklyn Journal of Corporate, Financial & Commercial Law* 341; L. Stout, *The Shareholder Value Myth: How Putting Shareholders First Harms Investors, Corporations, and the Public* (San Francisco: Berrett-Koehler Publishers, 2012); W.W. Bratton and M.L. Wachter, "Shareholders and Social Welfare" (2013) 36 *Seattle University Law Review* 489;

Meanwhile, comparative corporate governance debates have focused on two important issues. The first issue concerns ownership structure: are large corporations in a particular corporate governance system owned by a multitude of disempowered shareholders, thus effectively giving management free rein? Or are corporations typically governed by a controlling shareholder or a coalition of controlling shareholders that keep management on a tight leash, but have their own devices for the corporation?[4]

The second issue is the role of other "constituencies" of the corporation besides shareholders, of which labor is most central to the debate, as the question of corporate purpose comes into play more directly. Some jurisdictions explicitly give labor an influential voice in corporate affairs,[5] whereas in others its influence is developed through factual power or through either unintended or subtly intended consequences of legislation.[6]

This chapter explores the interactions between ownership of firms and labor, focusing on the United States on the one hand and Continental Europe, particularly Germany, on the other. I distinguish between "old" and "new" comparative corporate governance, the former referring to the dichotomy studied by scholars of comparative corporate law up to the 1990s and 2000s. Recent changes, heralded by intermediated, but widespread share ownership, are leading us to a brave new world of corporate governance whose contours have only begun to emerge. The central tenet, in any event, is that labor matters for corporate governance and is thus

K. Greenfield, "Sticking the Landing: Making the Most of the 'Stakeholder Moment'" (2015) 26 *European Business Law Review* 147.

[4] For example R.K. Morck, "Introduction," in R.K. Morck (ed.), *Concentrated Ownership Structure* (University of Chicago Press, 2000), p. 1; R.J. Gilson, "Controlling Shareholders and Corporate Governance: Complicating the Corporate Taxonomy" (2006) 119 *Harvard Law Review* 1641 at 1645–50 (both summarizing cross-country evidence).

[5] Several jurisdictions require employee representation on the supervisory board or board of directors. This includes Germany, Austria, the Netherlands, Slovenia, Slovakia, Hungary, Luxembourg, Denmark, Sweden, and Norway. See, e.g., T. Raiser, "Unternehmensmitbestimmung vor dem Hintergrund europarechtlicher Entwicklungen" (2006) Gutachten B für den 66. *Deutschen Juristentag* at B 42; M. Gelter and G. Helleringer, "Lift not the Painted Veil! To Whom Are Directors' Duties Really Owed?" (2015) *University Of Illinois Law Review* 1069 at 1077–9.

[6] See generally M. Gelter, "The Dark Side of Shareholder Influence: Managerial Autonomy and Stakeholder Orientation in Comparative Corporate Governance" (2009) 50 *Harvard International Law Journal* 129 at 168–73; L.E. Strine, Jr., "The Soviet Constitution Problem in Comparative Corporate Law: Testing The Proposition That European Corporate Law is More Stockholder-Focused Than U.S. Corporate Law," *Research Paper No. 15-39* (University of Pennsylvania Institute for Law and Economics, 2015), available at http://ssrn.com/abstract=2688018, at 17.

important for a proper comparison. Section 2.2 begins by describing the traditional juxtaposition of the United States and Continental (mainly German) corporate governance in the comparative literature and Section 2.3 discusses the changes of the past twenty years, and the new world in which we seem to be moving. Section 2.4 concludes.

2.2 Old Comparative Corporate Governance

2.2.1 The United States: Berle–Means or "Strong Managers–Weak Owners"

Old corporate governance in the United States was characterized – in Berle and Means's words – by the "separation of ownership and control,"[7] or – maybe more precisely in Mark Roe's words – by "strong managers and weak owners."[8] Regardless of the terminological question whether it is legally and economically accurate to characterize shareholders as owners,[9] what is clear is that shareholders had very little influence over the corporation. With its relatively high proportion of retail investors[10] and a securities law that made coordination between institutional investors difficult[11] – backed by a managerially oriented state corporate law – management remained nearly all-powerful while shareholders suffered from a classic collective action problem that quashed any nascent influence that may have existed.[12]

The situation gave rise to the development of agency theory.[13] With management distant from the masses of shareholders, but affecting

[7] A.A. Berle, Jr. and G. Means, *The Modern Corporation and Private Property* (New York: Macmillan, 1932), p. 90.

[8] M.J. Roe, *Strong Managers, Weak Owners – The Political Roots of American Corporate Finance* (Princeton University Press, 1994).

[9] M.M. Blair, "Corporate 'Ownership'" (1995) 13 *Brookings Review* 16.

[10] See, e.g., R.J. Gilson and J.N. Gordon, "The Agency Costs of Agency Capitalism: Activist Investors and the Revaluation of Governance Rights" (2013) 113 *Columbia Law Review* 863 at 874 (noting that in 1950 "[e]quities were still held predominately by households").

[11] M.J. Roe, "A Political Theory of American Corporate Finance" (1991) 91 *Columbia Law Review* 10 at 26 9.

[12] See, e.g., H. Wells, "Shareholder Power in America, 1800–2000: A Short History," in J.G. Hill and R.S. Thomas (eds.), *Research Handbook on Shareholder Power* (Northampton, MA: Edward Elgar Publishing, 2015), pp. 13, 21. ("In the Berle–Means corporation, shareholder powerlessness was a given.")

[13] M.C. Jensen and W.H. Meckling, "Theory of the Firm: Managerial Behavior, Agency Costs and Ownership Structure" (1976) 3 *Journal of Financial Economics* 305. On the rise of agency theory see, e.g., R. Khurana, *From Higher Aims to Hired Hands: The Social*

shareholders' financial well-being with its decisions, the corporation became the paradigmatic case for the application of agency theory. In the mainstream view, employees became mainly a distraction from efficiency.[14] At best, unaccountable managers did not make sufficient efforts to keep labor in line, thus squandering more shareholder wealth. At worst, they were, in the purely shareholder-focused agency perspective, actively collaborating with employees against shareholders; takeovers – which historically were opposed both by managers and shareholders – serve as a good example.[15] Overall, corporate governance institutions such as boards of directors were not well-tailored to monitoring management.[16]

While the manager–labor coalition may have carried the day during that period, the role of labor needs to be seen in a more nuanced light. Corporate defined benefits (DB) pension plans from the 1950s through 1970s typically had features tying employees to the firm by penalizing job changes. Admittedly, the so-called Taft–Hartley pension plans were often jointly administrated by firms and unions and seen as a way of securing labor peace.[17] However, since workers had pension wealth that was often tied to the firm,[18] and because they may sometimes have had specialized human capital as well, it is unlikely that the situation was one where workers were too strongly exposed to opportunism by or on behalf of shareholders, given that they otherwise would not have allowed themselves

Transformation of American Business Schools and the Unfulfilled Promise of Management as a Profession (Princeton University Press, 2007), p. 316; Roe, above n 11 at 23.

[14] See L.A. Stout, "Takeovers in the Ivory Tower: How Academics Are Learning Martin Lipton May be Right" (2005) 60 *Business Lawyer* 1435 at 1445 (criticizing that principal-agent thinking has pushed the interests of labor to the margins of corporate law debates); e.g., F.H. Easterbrook and D.R. Fischel, *The Economic Structure of Corporate Law* (Cambridge: Harvard University Press, 1991), p. 11 (discussing how employees are sufficiently protected by contract).

[15] See, e.g., E.W. Orts, "Beyond Shareholders: Interpreting Corporate Constituency Statutes" (1992) 61 *George Washington Law Review* 14 at 24–5 (discussing labor support for antitakeover legislation).

[16] See, e.g., J.N. Gordon, "The Rise of Independent Directors in the United States 1950–2005: Of Shareholder Value and Stock Market Prices" (2007) 59 *Stanford Law Review* 1465 at 1514–26 (tracing the development from a managerial board to a monitoring board).

[17] See, e.g., S. Sass, "The Development of Employer Retirement Income Plans: From the Nineteenth Century to 1980," in G.L. Clark and A.H. Munnell (eds.), *Oxford Handbook on Pensions and Retirement Income* (Oxford University Press, 2007), pp. 76, 86.

[18] See generally R.A. Ippolito, *Pension Plans and Employee Performance: Evidence, Analysis, and Policy* (Chicago University Press, 1997), pp. 10–29 (discussing how DB plans were used to create an implicit contract between employers and employees that resulted in low turnover); M. Gelter, "The Pension System and the Rise of Shareholder Primacy" (2013) 43 *Seton Hall Law Review* 909 at 922–3.

to be exposed to such a situation. The prevailing corporate governance arrangements thus must have helped to protect worker interests. Overall, a "balancing" board of directors, as proposed by Blair and Stout's team production theory,[19] thus provides a good fit for the "old" system of corporate governance in the United States.[20] Both capital and labor contributed, and the board was neither strongly accountable to either group, nor did it have incentives to favor shareholders over other interests in the corporation, which began to emerge during the 1980s.[21]

2.2.2 *Continental Europe: Conflict and Legal Arrangement*

From a global perspective, the Berle–Means corporation remained an exception.[22] Even in the United Kingdom, which developed dispersed ownership during the second half of the twentieth century, institutional investors held a larger proportion of shares than in the United States[23] and were able to coordinate and influence the trajectory of corporate law and governance more strongly when ownership dispersion established itself.[24] In Continental Europe, dispersed ownership was not fully developed yet; as late as the 2000s, in major countries such as Germany, France, and Italy, large firms remained dominated by large owners, including financial institutions, government entities, families, and other businesses, with a different controlling coalition in each country.[25]

[19] See generally M.M. Blair and L.A. Stout, "A Team Production Theory of Corporate Law" (1999) 5 *Virginia Law Review* 247.

[20] Similarly, Gordon, above n 16 at 1514, footnote 187.

[21] See, e.g., Wells, above n 12 at 24 (describing increasing shareholder power and changing corporate governance in the 1980s).

[22] See, e.g., B.R. Cheffins, *Corporate Ownership and Control: British Business Transformed* (Oxford University Press, 2008), pp. 5–6.

[23] See, e.g., B.S. Black and J.C. Coffee, Jr., "Hail Britannia? Institutional Investor Behavior Under Limited Regulation" (1994) 92 *Michigan Law Review* 1997 at 2002; J. Armour, B.R. Cheffins, and D.A. Skeel, Jr., "Corporate Ownership Structure and the Evolution of Bankruptcy Law: Lessons from the United Kingdom" (2002) 55 *Vanderbilt Law Review* 1699 at 1750 (both noting that as of the 1990s, 70% of UK stock were held by institutional investors, while the figure was only 50% in the United States); *ibid.* at 344–6 (discussing the rise of institutional share ownership in the United Kingdom during the mid-twentieth century).

[24] See, e.g., J. Armour and D.A. Skeel, Jr., "Who Writes the Rules for Hostile Takeovers, and Why? – The Peculiar Divergence of U.S. and U.K. Takeover Regulation" (2007) 95 *Georgetown Law Journal* 1727 at 1767–76 (discussing how UK institutional investors established their influence in the 1950s and 1960s – much earlier than their US counterparts – and used it to shape takeover regulation).

[25] See, e.g., M. Becht and A. Roëll, "Blockholdings in Europe: An International Comparison" (1999) 43 *European Economic Review* 1049; R. La Porta, F. Lopez-de-Silanes, and A. Shleifer,

Corporate black-letter law in Continental Europe did not follow the lead of US corporate law and avoided a managerialist turn over the course of the twentieth century. Shareholders retained stronger powers relating to agenda setting, regarding the appointment and removal of directors, and financial decision-making such as share issues, preemptive rights, and dividends. In some jurisdictions, including France and the United Kingdom, shareholders formally retained the power to give binding instructions to management, a power they never had in the United States.[26]

The origin of this important distinction – which, strangely, was hardly touched upon in the comparative corporate law literature until the 2000s – is not entirely clear. One possibility is that in the United States, management came into a position where it could exploit the regulatory competition process to erode shareholder powers, a mechanism that was not available in Europe.[27] In any event, with the exception of the United Kingdom, in Europe managers would not have been in the position to capture such a process.[28] Continental Europe had, of course, controlling shareholders to take advantage of a shareholder-centric core corporate law. Even if corporate laws had taken a managerial turn, the law likely would have done little to curb shareholder power. Even in the United States, we see that controlling shareholders typically do not find it difficult to impose their will on

"Corporate Ownership Around the World" (1999) 54 *Journal of Finance* 471; M. Faccio and L.H.P. Lang, "The Ultimate Ownership of Western European Corporations" (2002) 65 *Journal of Financial Economics* 365 at 379–80; P.A. Gourevitch and J. Shinn, *Political Power and Corporate Control: The New Global Politics of Corporate Governance* (Princeton University Press, 2005), p. 18; P.D. Culpepper, *Quiet Politics and Business Power* (Cambridge University Press, 2011), pp. 31–2; W.-G. Ringe, "Changing Law and Ownership Patterns in Germany: Corporate Governance and the Erosion of Deutschland AG" (2015) 68 *American Journal of Comparative Law* 493 at 496–8 (discussing different types of blockholders in Germany).

[26] See, e.g., S. Cools, "The Real Difference in Corporate Law between the United States and Continental Europe: Distribution of Powers" (2005) 30 *Delaware Journal of Corporate Law* 697 at 737–50.

[27] One example is the directors' power to issue stock without seeking shareholder approval and without preemptive rights that would hinder managerial flexibility. As Marco Venturozzo notes, "[it] might be argued that in listed or publicly held corporations, where the separation between ownership and control is more profound in the U.S., directors and managers influenced the development of corporate law toward the abolition of mandatory preemptive rights." M. Ventoruzzo, "Issuing New Shares and Preemptive Rights: A Comparative Analysis" (2013) 12 *Richmond Journal of Global Law and Business* 517 at 542.

[28] Regulatory arbitrage opportunities in Europe are more likely to be exploited by controlling shareholders. See, e.g., M. Gelter, "The Structure of Regulatory Competition in European Corporate Law" (2005) 52 *Journal of Corporate Law Studies* 247 at 269–75.

managers[29] – given their ability to elect directors – and the hurdles setup in securities law against shareholder influence really only affect the coordination between institutional investors.[30] Consequently, both the European and US experience seem to suggest that corporate law reflects a particular ownership structure, and helps to entrench it, rather than to precipitate it.

On another level, however, Continental European corporate laws do not appear shareholder-friendly at all, namely when we look at the role of labor.[31] The major Continental European countries are known for stronger pro-labor employment laws that, for example, make firing workers or changing workplace conditions more costly and thus give more bargaining powers to unions.[32] While corporate governance analysts have often overlooked the very important role of these labor and employment law mechanisms, they were strongly aware of German codetermination, which allows employees and unions to appoint half of the directors of the largest firms.[33] Similar mechanisms – although these, with the exception of the Netherlands[34], were not quite as extensive – were implemented in several

[29] This is illustrated by the imposition of a fiduciary duty of loyalty on controlling shareholders in the United States. See, e.g., W.T. Allen, R. Kraakman, and G. Subramanian, *Commentaries and Cases on the Law of Business Organization* (New York: Aspen Publishers, 2012), pp. 295–309.

[30] See in particular Roe, above n 11 at 26; Gelter, above n 6 at 148–9 (discussing coordination problems between institutional investors exacerbated by Rules under §§ 13 and 14 of the Securities Exchange Act.

[31] See, e.g., Strine, above n 6 at 17–18.

[32] See, e.g., Gelter, above n 6 at 171–3.

[33] See, e.g., L. Enriques, H. Hansmann, and R. Kraakman, "The Basic Governance Structure: Minority Shareholders and Non-Shareholder Constituencies," in R. Kraakman, J. Armour, P. Davies, *et al.* (eds.), *The Anatomy of Corporate Law* (New York: Oxford University Press, 2009), pp. 90, 100–2; M.J. Roe, "German Codetermination and German Securities Markets" (1998) *Columbia Business Law Review* 167.

[34] Under the "structure regime," one-third of the members of the supervisory board of the largest firms is nominated by the works council (although elected by shareholders). See A. de Jong and A. Roëll, "Financing and Control in the Netherlands: A Historical Perspective," in R.K. Morck (ed.), *A History of Corporate Governance around the World* (University of Chicago Press, 2005), pp. 467, 473; P.J. Phoelich, "Report from the Netherlands" (2009) 6 *European Company Law* 92 at 92–4. Until the 2004 reform, board members were appointed following a system of co-optation that only gave veto powers to both shareholders and the works council. P.W. Moerland, "Complete Separation of Ownership and Control: The Structure Regime and Other Defensive Mechanisms in the Netherlands," in J.A. McCahery, P. Moerland, T. Raaijmakers, and L. Renneboog (eds.), *Corporate Governance Regimes* (New York: Oxford University Press, 2003), pp. 286, 287–8; E. Groenewald, "Corporate Governance in the Netherlands: From the Verdam Report of 1964 to the Tabaksblat Code of 2003" (2005) 6 *European Business Organization Law Review* 291 at 297.

other Central, Eastern, and Northern European countries.[35] Even in countries that did not have employee participation on boards, such as (until recently) France[36] and Italy, labor unions were influential. Mechanisms such as mandatory works councils in much of Continental Europe[37] and, more generally, restrictive employment laws that made dismissals difficult and costly enhanced the bargaining position of unions. While this likely was not the only relevant factor, it clearly detracted from corporations' ability to focus on producing returns for shareholders even without labor's formal involvement in corporate decision-making.

2.2.3 *Explaining the Difference*

Why did the United States and Continental Europe integrate both capital and labor into corporate governance in such distinct ways? One possibility is that the corporate law systems of Continental European countries are inefficient.[38] The law and finance literature provided significant fodder for this point of view. Studies have found a correlation between corporate

[35] This includes Austria, Denmark, Finland, Hungary, Luxembourg, Norway, Slovakia, Slovenia, Sweden, and formerly the Czech Republic. See, e.g., G. Jackson, "Employee Representation on the Board Compared: A Fuzzy Sets Analysis of Corporate Governance, Unionism and Political Institutions" (2005) 12 *Industrielle Beziehungen* 1 at 4–6; T. Raiser, above n 5 at B 43–B 44; J. Lau Hansen, "The Danish Green Paper on Company Law Reform – Modernising Company Law in the 21st Century" (2009) 10 *European Business Organization Law Review* 73 at 89–90; see C. Rose, "The Challenges of Employee-Appointed Board Members for Corporate Governance: The Danish Evidence" (2008) 9 *European Business Organization Law Review* 215 at 224–6; Enriques *et al.*, above n 33 at 100 and footnote 47; M. Gelter, "Tilting the Balance between Capital and Labor? The Effects of Regulatory Arbitrage in European Corporate Law on Employees" (2010) 33 *Fordham International Law Journal* 792 at 803–4.

[36] France has recently introduced employee representatives on the board. See Code de Commerce art. L225-27-1, introduced by Loi n° 2013-504 14 June 2013 relative à la sécurisation de l'emploi. See S. de Vendeuil and O. Rault-Dubois, "Représentation des salariés au conseil d'administration ou de surveillance de grandes entreprises" (2013) *JCP E Etude* 1379.

[37] See, e.g., L.A. Cunningham, "Commonalities and Prescriptions in the Vertical Dimension of Global Corporate Governance" (1999) 84 *Cornell Law Review* 1133 at 1141–2; Gelter, above n 6 at 171–2. For a discussion of the interaction between board representation and the works council in Germany, see P. Davies, "Efficiency Arguments for the Collective Representation of Workers," *Law Working Paper No. 279/2015* (European Corporate Governance Institute, 2015), available at http://ssrn.com/abstract=2498221, at 19.

[38] See, e.g., H. Hansmann and R. Kraakman, "The End of History for Corporate Law" (2001) 89 *Georgetown Law Journal* 439 at 443–51 (characterizing corporate governance models deviating from shareholder primacy as inefficient, and mustering market forces as driving forces for convergence).

law protecting investors on the one hand and developed capital markets and ownership dispersion on the other, with "good corporate law" leading to greater dispersion and larger capital markets, and "bad corporate law" resulting in concentrated ownership.[39]

This empirical observation can be explained in various ways. A potential functional explanation is that powerful blockholders are needed to curb excessive managerial power and to keep agency costs in check,[40] particularly when pro-labor mechanisms such as codetermination render pro-shareholder institutions such as the board of directors dysfunctional.[41] However, it is equally plausible that the absence of an effective corporate law makes the persistence of controlling shareholders more likely because a controlling shareholder retains the ability to extract private benefits of control, thus creating an incentive to remain in a controlling position.[42]

Mark Roe has explained the persistence of concentrated ownership with political factors. In an influential body of scholarship, he treats labor codetermination and other pro-employee laws as an exogenous influence on corporate governance, resulting from the political necessity of the tumultuous times of the mid-twentieth century. By making pro-shareholder mechanisms (such as the board in the case of codetermination) ineffectual, it necessitated and allowed the persistence of blockholders, and thus inhibited the development of capital markets.[43]

[39] R. La Porta, F. Lopez-de-Silanes, A. Shleifer, and R.W. Vishny, "Legal Determinants of External Finance" (1997) 52 *Journal of Finance* 1131; R. La Porta, F. Lopez-de-Silanes, A. Shleifer, and R.W. Vishny, "Law and Finance" (1998) 106 *Journal of Political Economics* 1113 at 1145–51; S. Djankov, R. La Porta, F. Lopez-de-Silanes, A. Shleifer, R.W. Vishny, "The Law and Economics of Self-Dealing" (2008) 88 *Journal of Financial Economics* 430.

[40] See, e.g., J.C. Coffee, Jr., "The Future as History: The Prospects for Global Convergence in Corporate Governance and Its Implications" (1999) 93 *Northwestern University Law Review* 641 at 647–8; B.S. Black, "The Legal and Institutional Preconditions for Strong Securities Markets" (2001) 48 *UCLA Law Review* 781 at 834–5; B.R. Cheffins, "Does Law Matter? The Separation of Ownership and Control in the United Kingdom" (2001) 30 *Journal of Legal Studies* 459 at 461–5.

[41] M.J. Roe, *Political Determinants of Corporate Governance Political Context, Corporate Impact* (New York: Oxford University Press, 2003), pp. 29–37.

[42] L.A. Bebchuk, "A Rent-Protection Theory of Corporate Ownership and Control," *NBER Working Paper No. 7203* (National Bureau Economic of Research, 1999); W.W. Bratton and J.A. McCahery, "Incomplete Contracts Theories of the Firm and Comparative Corporate Governance" (2001) 2 *Theoretical Inquiries in Law* 1 at 34–6; Gilson, above n 4 at 1644 at 1654.

[43] M.J. Roe, "Political Preconditions to Separating Ownership from Corporate Control" (2000) 53 *Stanford Law Review* 539 at 542; Roe, above n 41.

Yet, it does not seem plausible that a simple inefficiency explanation can account for international differences that have persisted over long periods of time. How can it be that economically successful nations such as Germany retain governance structures so different from the ones typically perceived to be economically efficient in the predominant paradigm?

A way forward may be to integrate the interests, incentives, and investments of workers not just within a political analysis, but also within the economic paradigm by studying how corporate governance may help to secure labor supply. Such a perspective can be grounded in human capital theory. An employee's human capital – that is knowledge and skills that are used on the job – can in principle be firm-specific,[44] meaning that it cannot be transferred to another job either because the skill or combination of skills can only be used to its full productive potential at the current job[45] or because alternative positions are, for example, geographically distant, thus hindering transfers of human capital with transaction costs.[46]

For a contract to fully protect an employee's specific investment, the contract would have to be complete contingent; that is, all future possible states of the world are foreseen and verifiable with payoffs being specified for each possible future states of the world.[47] In the context of long-term employment relationships, this is a very unrealistic condition, thus rendering a key element of prevalent shareholder primacy theory

[44] See generally G.S. Becker, *Human Capital: A Theoretical and Empirical Analysis, with Special Reference to Education* (Chicago University Press, 1964), pp. 11–36; see also H. Hansmann, *The Ownership of Enterprise* (Cambridge: Harvard University Press, 1996), p. 26; J.M. Malcomson, "Individual Employment Contracts," in O. Aschenfelter and D. Card (eds.), *Handbook of Labor Economics* (Amsterdam: Elsevier, 1999) vol. 3, pp. 2291, 2311–37 (reviewing the literature on contractual protection of specific investment); D. Neumark, "Productivity, Compensation, and Retirement" in Clark and Munnell, above n 17 at 721, 722.

[45] E.P. Lazear, *Inside the Firm* (Oxford University Press, 2011), p. 342 (giving the example of work in a tax software company requiring knowledge of computer programming, economics, and tax law).

[46] See A.L. Saxenian, *Regional Advantage: Culture and Competition in Silicon Valley and Route 128* (Cambridge: Harvard University Press, 1994), p. 35 (quoting an engineer comparing the difficulty of getting another job in the same industry in Texas and in Silicon Valley). Social capital may also reduce worker mobility by making relocation more costly for employees due to the need to reorient social relationships. See M. Bräuninger and A. Tolciu, "Should I Stay or Should I Go? Regional Mobility and Social Capital" (2011) 167 *Journal of Institutional and Theoretical Economics* 434 at 434–6.

[47] For a definition of incomplete contracts, see, e.g., A. Schwartz, "Incomplete Contracts," in P. Newman (ed.), *The New Palgrave Dictionary of Economics and the Law* (London: Palgrave Macmillan, 1998), vol. 2, p. 277.

highly problematic.[48] Consequently, with shareholders enjoying at least some control rights and management working on behalf of shareholders, employees are subject to the risk of "hold-up," meaning that quasi-rents that employees may have been expecting based on their investment in the employer–employee relationship will be expropriated for the benefit of shareholders.[49]

Another important factor has traditionally related to company pensions. In the United States, in the heyday of the Berle–Means corporation, firms typically provided employees with DB pensions that made it financially costly to switch to another firm because pensions could not be fully transferred.[50] Consequently, human capital that was by its nature not firm-specific sometimes became firm-specific, thus tying workers to the corporation.[51]

If we widen the analysis to include employees, the dichotomy between the United States, on the one hand, and the Continental European jurisdictions, on the other, gains a new dimension. In the United States, "strong managers" and a powerful board were relatively well-positioned to balance the interests of various stakeholder groups. The function of the board must thus have been to "slow down" the exercise of shareholder power to avoid short-termism and to prevent it from overwhelming other constituencies.[52] However, as we have explored earlier, the disempowerment

48 See, e.g., K. Greenfield, *The Failure of Corporate Law: Fundamental Flaws and Progressive Possibilities* (Chicago University Press, 2006), pp. 55–9 (arguing that workers are residual claimants like shareholders because of pension benefits and their inability to diversify).

49 See, e.g., T. Eger, "Opportunistic Termination of Employment Contracts and Legal Protection against Dismissal in Germany and the USA" (2004) 23 *International Review of Law and Economics* 381 at 384–5 (discussing opportunistic wage renegotiations); J.C. Coffee, Jr., "Shareholders Versus Managers: The Strain in the Corporate Web" (1986) 85 *Michigan Law Review* 1 at 70, footnote 194 (discussing termination of pension plans).

50 Pension benefits were often calculated on the basis of the highest yearly salaries or a fixed dollar amount for each year of service. See, e.g., E.A. Zelinsky, *The Origins of the Ownership Society: How the Defined Contribution Paradigm Changed America* (Oxford University Press, 2007), p. 1; A.H. Munnell, "Employer-Sponsored Plans: The Shift from Defined Benefit to Defined Contribution," in Clark and Munnell, above n 17 at 359, 365; E.A. Zelinsky, "The Cash Balance Controversy" (2000) 19 *Virginia Tax Review* 683 at 687.

51 See generally Ippolito, above n 18 at 10–29 (discussing how DB plans were used to create an implicit contract between employers and employees that resulted in low turnover); A.H. Munnell and A. Sundén, *Coming Up Short: The Challenge of 401(k) Plans* (Washington, DC: Brookings Institution Press, 2004), p. 2; Munnell, above n 50 at 365; Sass, above n 17 at 87 (explaining that typically pension claims only vested after ten years with the same employer).

52 R.B. Thompson, "The Power of Shareholders in the United States," in Hill and Thomas, above n 12 at 441, 446.

of shareholders in the United States – combined with the equally idiosyncratic ownership structure – is also unusual among capitalist economies.[53] The longstanding influence of institutional shareholders in the United Kingdom, and even more so given the power of controlling shareholders in Continental Europe, clearly pose a problem to those theories extolling the virtues of managerial power.

How can the board provide any form of corporate commitment to any constituency if it serves essentially at the discretion of a controlling shareholder or coalition of large blockholders? Hierarchical theories of the corporation, such as the team production[54] and director primacy[55] models, and the commitment model[56] of the corporation, therefore face considerable hurdles as positive theories of the nature of the corporation outside the Anglo-Saxon world.[57] For a comparative analysis, however, such an explanation is less than satisfactory. For instance, in the German (or generally Continental European) system, corporations are characterized by strong owners and weak managers, but also by strong labor.[58] A strong power of management vis-à-vis shareholders can only manifest itself if the CEO himself is a significant blockholder in the firm, or in individual cases, where a particularly strong personality in top management is able to assert the board's strength vis-à-vis a controlling shareholder.

The various institutions strengthening the power of labor (board representations and labor laws strengthening union power) can thus be seen as protecting employees vis-à-vis hold-up risks emanating from the presence of influential large shareholders who potentially have both the incentive to expropriate labor – at least at certain points in time – and the power to do it if it were not for the presence of pro-labor laws and regulations.[59] The weighing and balancing of interests between capital and labor, which in the mediating hierarch model of US corporate governance is left to a

[53] See above n 26–30 and accompanying text.

[54] Blair and Stout, above n 19.

[55] S.M. Bainbridge, "Director Primacy: The Means and Ends of Corporate Governance" (2003) 97 *Northwestern University Law Review* 547.

[56] C. Mayer, *Firm Commitment: Why the Corporation is Failing Us and How to Restore Trust in It* (Oxford University Press, 2013); C. Mayer, "Conceiving Corporate Commitment: Creation and Confirmation" in Hill and Thomas, above n 12 at 211.

[57] See L.A. Bebchuk, "The Case for Increasing Shareholder Power" (2005) 118 *Harvard Law Review* 833 at 908–9 (defending shareholder empowerment on the grounds that those supporting limitations on the power of dispersed shareholders would equally have to "support limiting the intervention power of controlling shareholders").

[58] See above n 31–7 and accompanying text.

[59] Gelter, above n 6 at 168–73.

A	weak shareholders weak labor	B	strong shareholders weak labor
C	weak shareholders strong labor	D	strong shareholders strong labor

Figure 2.1 Local optima of shareholder influence and labor power

board serving as a large independent third party, is, in the European context, thus put on the level of influences of shareholders – created by strong share ownership – and legally buttressed by the influence of labor. Thus, the weighing of interests between these groups happens at the level of the law rather than at the level of a board.

To put it differently, economic and legal arrangements can be seen as commitment mechanisms protecting the firm – and those with specific investments in it – from the excessive influence of one group, which includes particularly large or well-coordinated shareholders. In the United States, capital has traditionally resigned itself to a residual influence and provided commitment through the Berle–Means structure and backed up by managerialist corporate law. In concentrated ownership systems, it was able to do so only through a legal arrangement that strengthened the powers of the most important non-capital group, namely labor. Ultimately, the US and Continental equilibria may thus achieve relatively similar results, but they do it by incorporating two different elements, namely weak labor and weak owners on one side of the Atlantic, and strong owners and strong labor on the other, thus yielding two different balances of power.

As shown in Figure 2.1, one might speculate that strong shareholders must be balanced by strong labor to foster human capital development, while in situations with weak shareholders, strong labor power would be problematic because it would exacerbate agency problems.[60]

In this light, one is tempted to conclude that a political theory deriving concentrated ownership from labor power may have it backward. Chronologically, it is clear that concentrated ownership came first, and labor-strengthening laws came later, often fully falling into place after

[60] For a more detailed explanation, see *ibid.* at 176–81.

World War II.[61] In contrast, concentrated ownership is inevitably the primeval state of the world for a corporate governance system, since firms are normally set up by a founder, and the separation of ownership and control can only be set at a subsequent stage when firms are already big enough to make use of the capital market as their primary means of finance.

As Ugo Pagano suggests, control of capital in the early twentieth century may have reflected the larger picture of political and social organization in a particular country, namely either democratic or aristocratic and family-oriented, with the respective pattern perpetuating itself in economic governance.[62] The reasons why particular systems originally came into place may have been exogenous and mainly political at that point in time,[63] and they may have perpetuated long-standing social structures. It appears that to some extent two elements – namely strong labor and strong shareholders on one hand and weak labor and weak shareholders on the other – reinforced each other as a set of institutional complementarities.[64] Changing one without changing the other would have been costly and would have either exacerbated hold-up risk, increased agency costs, or caused costly regulation without much benefit. Consequently, each system exhibited inertia and path-dependent resistance to change.

2.3 New Comparative Corporate Governance

2.3.1 The United States

In the United States, the transition to the new corporate governance model began in the 1970s. Corporations became more mindful of their shareholders and dissatisfaction with the performance of the board of directors led to the corporate governance movement and the American Law Institute's ALI Principles.[65] Concurrently, the SEC became more strongly

[61] Roe, above n 41 at 78; Gelter, above n 6 at 181–4.

[62] U. Pagano, "The Evolution of the American Corporation and Global Organizational Biodiversity" (2012) 35 *Seattle University Law Review* 1271 at 1279–90.

[63] See also M.J. Roe, "Legal Origins, Politics, and Modern Stock Markets" (2006) 120 *Harvard Law Review* 461 at 295–500 (suggesting that political disruption inflicted by the Depression and World War II may be responsible for the persistence of concentrated ownership in Continental Europe).

[64] M.J. Roe and M. Vatiero, "Corporate Governance and Its Political Economy," *Discussion Paper No. 5/2015* (Harvard Olin Center, 2015), available at http://ssrn.com/abstract=2588760, at 14.

[65] The ALI project was initiated in 1978, a first draft was produced in 1982, and the final "Principles of Corporate Governance" were promulgated in 1992. See R.B. Perkins,

involved with corporate governance issues, for example, by providing rules requiring boards to have independent directors that were intended to monitor on behalf of shareholders.[66]

The 1980s saw the takeover wave, which allowed shareholders in some cases to extract rents at the expense of labor,[67] but often also to make firms more efficient.[68] This was followed by the introduction of performance-oriented executive compensation, which helped make managers more focused on stock prices. While this may seem the normal state of affairs to us today, this was not typically the case in prior periods. However, the market for corporate control remained incomplete as a mechanism for focusing managerial actions on shareholder interests given the scarcity of takeovers and the reticence of Delaware law, which essentially entrenched managerialism by permitting firms to defend against takeovers with the *Moran*[69] and *Unocal*[70] doctrines.[71] Similarly, executive compensation turned out to be, to a significant extent, a rent-seeking device for

---

"The Genesis and Goals of the ALI Corporate Governance Project" (1987) 8 *Cardozo Law Review* 661 at 666–8 (discussing the Corporate Governance project as a way of addressing corporate problems and preempting federal regulation); S.M. Bainbridge, "Independent Directors and the ALI Corporate Governance Project" (1993) 61 *George Washington Law Review* 1034 at 1044–52 (discussing crisis as the initial impetus for launching the project); Gordon, above n 16 at 1481 ("Throughout the 1980s and 1990s, various panels and "blue ribbon" committees developed somewhat influential "best practice" guidelines for relationship tests.").

66 See, e.g., R.S. Karmel, "Is the Independent Director Model Broken?" (2014) 37 *Seattle University Law Review* 775 at 780–1 (describing SEC involvement relating to independent directors). Note, however, that the empirical evidence on the effects of independent board members on shareholder wealth is, at best, mixed. See M.M. Blair, "Boards of Directors and Corporate Performance under a Team Production Model" in Hill and Thomas, above n 12 at 249, 250–5.

67 The theory of LBOs in particular as redistributing from employees to shareholders was established in, for example, A. Shleifer and L. Summers, "Breach of Trust in Hostile Takeovers," in A.J. Auerbach (ed.), *Corporate Takeovers: Causes and Consequences* (University of Chicago Press, 1988), pp. 33, 37. It is most plausible in the context of pension plan "terminations for reversion." See M.A. Petersen, "Pension Reversions and Worker–Stockholder Wealth Transfers" (1992) 107 *Quarterly Journal of Economics* 1033; M.M. Blair, "The Great Pension Grab: Comments on Richard Ippolito, Bankruptcy and Workers: Risks, Compensation and Pension Contracts" (2004) 82 *Washington University Law Quarterly* 1305; Gelter, above n 18 at 933–6.

68 For an overview of the empirical literature, see S. Bhagat and R. Romano, "Empirical Studies of Corporate Law," in A.M. Polinsky and S. Shavell (eds.), *Handbook of Law and Economics* (Amsterdam: Elsevier, 2007), vol. 2, pp. 945, 987–92.

69 *Moran* v. *Household International, Inc.*, 500 A 2d 1346 (Del. 1985).

70 *Unocal Corp.* v. *Mesa Petroleum Co.*, 493 A 2d 946 (Del. 1985).

71 The *Unitrin* test arguably made it easier for boards to defend against hostile bids under the *Unocal* test. *Unitrin, Inc.* v. *American General Corp.*, 651 A 2d 1361 (Del. 1995).

corporate management[72] and has arguably often been a driver of corporate short-termism.[73]

Consequently, corporate governance analysts put high hopes into institutional investors, whose shareholder activism became more noticeable from the 1990s onward.[74] With state pension funds leading the way, this movement bore full fruition only in the second half of the first decade of the 2000s when various elements of the voting system were changed. This led commentators to declare that US corporations had now entered a "shareholder-centric reality";[75] that is, a situation resembling that of the United Kingdom. At the same time, commentators observed a "re-concentration of share ownership,"[76] namely a higher proportion of shares being held by institutional investors with retail investors progressively leaving the market. With share ownership being slightly more concentrated within firms and strongly more concentrated across the market, the political situation for more shareholder power seems ripe. Even Delaware judges are becoming more skeptical about their treasured managerialism, given that shareholders are now more sophisticated and probably less in need of self-protection.[77]

The labor side of corporate governance has concurrently become weaker. Not only has labor become more mobile and its share in the income of the American economy decreased in the past decades, but also in an environment with higher labor mobility, workers are less strongly dependent on specific jobs. Pension plans have gradually moved from the DB to the DC system – for regulatory reasons largely outside of the purview of corporate governance[78] – thus likely reducing the degree to which human capital is

[72] See, e.g., L.A. Bebchuk and J.M. Fried, "Executive Compensation as an Agency Problem" (2003) 17 *Journal of Economic Perspectives* 71.

[73] P. Bolton, J. Scheinkman and W. Xiong, "Pay for Short-Term Performance: Executive Compensation in Speculative Markets" (2005) 30 *Journal of Corporate Law* 721.

[74] See, e.g., E.B. Rock, "The Logic and (Uncertain) Significance of Institutional Shareholder Activism" (1991) 79 *Georgetown Law Journal* 445.

[75] E.B. Rock, "Adapting to the New Shareholder-Centric Reality" (2013) 161 *University of Pennsylvania Law Review* 1907.

[76] Gilson and Gordon, above n 10 at 886–8.

[77] See, e.g., *Air Products and Chemicals* v. *Airgas*, 16 A 3d 48 at 57 (Del. Ch. 2011) (suggesting that the poison pill has served its purpose in this case, but that precedent case law dictates that the courts respect the board's decision in identifying a "cognizable threat" under *Unocal*).

[78] US Department of Labor, Employee Benefits Security Administration, "Private Pension Plan Bulletin Historical Tables and Graphs" (2009), available at www.dol.gov/ebsa/pdf/1975-2006historicaltables.pdf (tracing historical trends in occupational pensions); See Zelinsky, above n 50 at 38–55; G.A. (Sandy) MacKenzie, *The Decline of the Traditional*

artificially rendered firm-specific.[79] The transition has also ensured that employees are no longer creditors of their employer with a fixed DB pension claim, but rather shareholder investors and typically much more diversified in the market. Americans have become more dependent on the capital market with their retirement wealth since employers' guarantees do not exist in a DC plan.

Paradoxically, the most active institutional investors are normally DB plans – often those connected with government employees – and not mutual funds with whom 401(k) money is typically invested.[80] While mutual funds are not typically shareholder activists,[81] they often "vote with their feet" by selling shares if they are discontent with management.[82] In an environment where corporate managers are often dependent on their firms' stock price because of executive pay practices, an alignment of managerial performance with shareholder interests does not require shareholder activism since market prices similarly create the appropriate incentives. In any event, on the political level, pro-shareholder policies

---

Pension (Cambridge University Press, 2010); Gelter, above n 18 at 929–36 (all discussing reasons for the shift).

[79] Gelter, above n 18 at 947–8; see also Munnell, above n 50 at 367 (discussing the fit between DB plans and industries with a stable workforce on the one hand, and the fit between DC plans higher labor mobility on the other); S.M. Jacoby, "Labor and Finance in the United States," in C.A. Williams and P. Zumbansen (eds.), *The Embedded Firm: Corporate Governance, Labor, and Finance Capitalism* (Cambridge University Press, 2011), pp. 277, 286 (suggesting that firms no longer invest in long-term projects such as employee training due to the short-term horizon of institutional investors).

[80] See, e.g., S.M. Jacoby, "Convergence by Design: The Case of CalPERS in Japan" (2007) 55 *American Journal of Comparative Law* 239 at 243–54 (describing the history of shareholder activism by CalPERS); S.J. Choi and J.E. Fish, "On Beyond CalPERS: Survey Evidence on the Developing Role of Public Pension Funds in Corporate Governance" (2008) 61 *Vanderbilt Law Review* 315 at 315; A. Lucchetti and J.S. Lublin, "Corporate Governance: Calpers Targets Directors Who Neglect Holders," *Wall Street Journal*, 16 April 2016, at p. C1 (describing CalPERS's renewed efforts at shareholder activism); see also *Westland Police & Fire Retirement Systems* v. *Axcelis Technologies Inc.*, 1 A 3d 281 (Del. 2010) (public sector pension plan seeking to put a majority voting bylaw amendment on the target company's proxy statement).

[81] L.E. Strine, Jr., "The Delaware Way: How We Do Corporate Law and Some of the New Challenges We (and Europe) Face" (2005) 30 *Delaware Journal of Corporate Law* 673 at 687; see also S.M. Jacoby, "Finance and Labor: Perspectives on Risk, Inequality, and Democracy" (2008) 30 *Comparative Labor Law & Policy Journal* 17 at 55; A. Tucker, "The Citizen Shareholder: Modernizing the Agency Paradigm to Reflect How and Why a Majority of Americans Invest in the Market" (2012) 35 *Seattle University Law Review* 1299 at 1302–7 (highlighting agency problems between investors and mutual funds managers).

[82] See, e.g., D. Gross, "Some Mutual Funds Are Joining the Activist Bandwagon," *New York Times*, January 15, 2006, available at www.nytimes.com/2006/01/15/business/mutfund/15active.html (quoting an investment analyst).

have gained ground relative to pro-labor policies, given that the retirement wealth of politically relevant American voters means that Middle America has a large stake in corporate America. It is therefore not surprising that the center-left has sometimes taken up the cause of pro-shareholder reforms, which some political scientists have described as a "transparency coalition" between shareholders and workers.[83]

Theories of US corporate governance emphasizing managerial power, including those emphasizing an equilibrium between stakeholder groups or commitment to them as central for corporate law, face serious problems in light of the developments of the past decades. If interpreted as descriptive theories, they are certainly less persuasive in today's environment where the balance is increasingly tipping toward shareholders. While managerial powers and the central role of the board have only been eroded on the margins, the incentive of the relevant actors are now much more strongly tied to shareholder interests than they were thirty years ago. If we interpret managerial theories as normative prescriptions, however, then US corporate governance clearly has been pushed out of a balance that served the country well.

Alternatively, one might argue that an increased attention to shareholder interests may well be efficient *ceteris paribus*, given that Americans have become so strongly dependent on the capital market with their retirement wealth.[84] If the classical agency problem of separation of ownership and control has thus been largely resolved,[85] the issue of intermediated agency capitalism comes to the fore: Do fund managers actually pursue the best interest of their investors when filling the shareholder role? Future corporate governance analysis will thus have to shed light on the agency problem between shareholders and fund managers, both in the domestic and comparative dimensions.

2.3.2 *Continental Europe*

On the other side of the Atlantic, corporate governance in the various Continental European systems underwent considerable change during the period most strongly identified with the movement toward convergence,

[83] The term goes back to Gourevitch and Shinn, above n 25 at 210–11. See also J.W. Cioffi, *Public Law and Private Power* (New York: Cornell University Press, 2010), pp. 108–36; C.M. Bruner, "Corporate Governance Reform in a Time of Crisis" (2011) 36 *Journal of Corporation Law* 309 at 338; Gelter, above n 18 at 949–50.

[84] Gelter, above n 18 at 946–48.

[85] Rock, above n 75 at 1926 (suggesting that the "shareholder–manager agency cost problem has been brought under control").

namely the late 1990s and early 2000s. Abandoning or eroding state-centric and labor-centric corporate governance models, countries across the continent began to implement reforms ostensibly strengthening shareholders, in particular, outside investors not belonging to the traditional elite coalition. This trend went hand in hand with a growing international dispersion of ownership, which was made possible by more open capital markets that allowed an influx of institutional investment. CalPERS, ever at the vanguard of corporate governance trends, began to promote a set of "Global Corporate Governance Principles" with an international audience in the 1990s.[86]

During this period a European "corporate governance movement" arose, which was characterized by the adoption of corporate governance codes following the British "comply or explain" model.[87] Most countries introduced pro-shareholder reforms, such as the German Control and Transparency Act of 1998,[88] the French "Nouvelles régulations économiques" of 2001[89], and the Italian reforms of 2004.[90] Subsequently, the EU Commission's "High Level Report of Company Law Experts" of 2002[91] promoted the shareholder

[86] T.J. André, "Cultural Hegemony: The Exportation of Anglo-Saxon Corporate Governance Ideology to Germany" (1998) 73 *Tulane Law Review* 69 at 76–83 (describing CalPERS' portfolio and its code of principles).

[87] R.V. Aguilera and A. Cuervo-Cazurra, "Codes of Good Governance" (2009) 17 *Corporate Governance* 376 at 377–9 (describing the spread of codes from their English origins). The European Corporate Governance Institute provides a list at www.ecgi.org/codes/all_codes.php

[88] Gesetz zur Kontrolle und Transparenz im Unternehmensbereich (KonTraG), 3 March 1998, BGBl I Nr. 24 S. 786, 30 April 1998. See, e.g., M. Pargendler, "State Ownership and Corporate Governance" (2011), available at http://ssrn.com/abstract=1854452 (discussing the role of the KonTraG and privatization for the development of shareholder value thinking in Germany); P.-Y. Gomez and H. Korine, *Entrepreneurs and Democracy: A Political Theory of Corporate Governance* (Cambridge University Press, 2008), p. 192; However, the ostensible motivation of this comprehensive legal reform was actually a number of corporate failures in the late 1990s. For an overview of the act, see U. Seibert, "Control and Transparency in Business (KonTraG): Corporate Governance Reform in Germany" (1999) *European Business Law Review* 70 at 70 (describing the collapse of Metallgesellschaft as a main trigger for the debate).

[89] B. Clift, "French Corporate Governance in the New Global Economy: Mechanisms of Change and Hybridisation within Models of Capitalism" (2007) 55 *Political Studies* 546 at 553–7.

[90] See also L. Enriques and P.F. Volpin, "Corporate Governance Reforms in Continental Europe" (2007) 21 *Journal of Economic Perspective* 117 at 127–37 (surveying Continental European reforms).

[91] High Level Group of Company Law Experts, "Report on a Modern Framework for Company Law in Europe," November 4, 2002.

agenda, and the 2007 Shareholder Rights Directive[92] required a number of reforms compliant to the tastes of English and American institutional investors. Since a 2006 amendment, the EU Accounting Directive has required that publicly traded firms must disclose whether the company applies a corporate governance code and explain if it does not apply some of its provisions.[93] Nevertheless, the significance of these codes in Continental Europe is questionable, given that there is little – if any – empirical evidence showing positive effects. In retrospect, corporate governance codes seem to have been mainly a marketing instrument.[94] They provided a superficial benefit to "international investors" in order to tap international capital markets and keep institutions interested, while at the same time, did little that would actually harm the dominant corporate governance coalition.

Even if these adjustments remained minor, they need to be understood against the backdrop of societal and cultural changes that brought the European "coordinated capitalism" more in line with American (and English) "liberal" capitalism.[95] One major cultural, if not yet economic, change emanated from the retirement system. Spurred by the OECD, Continental Europeans were told for at least a quarter of a century that their pensions – which tend to be governed-run, DB-style systems – are

[92] Directive 2007/36/EC of the European Parliament and of the Council of 11 July 2007 on the exercise of certain rights of shareholders in listed companies, OJ 2007 No. L184/17 (implementing, e.g., a record date system and facilitating voting for international investors).

[93] Since 2013, the provision is in art. 20 of the recast Accounting Directive. Directive 2013/34/EU of the European Parliament and of the Council of June 26, 2013 on the annual financial statements, consolidated financial statements, and related reports of certain types of undertakings, amending Directive 2006/43/EC of the European Parliament and of the Council and repealing Council Directives 78/660/EEC and 83/349/EEC, OJ No. L182/19.

[94] For alternative interpretations, see S. Thomsen, "The Hidden Meaning of Codes: Corporate Governance and Investor Rent Seeking" (2006) 7 *European Business Organization Law Review* 845 (interpreting codes as a rent-seeking mechanism for institutional investors); L.-C. Wolff, "Law as Marketing Gimmick – The Case of the German Corporate Governance Code" (2004) 3 *Washington University Global Studies Law Review* 115 at 132–33 (plausibly describing the German code as a marketing instrument aimed at foreign investors); A. Zattoni and F. Cuomo, "Why Adopt Codes of Good Governance? A Comparison of Institutional and Efficiency Perspectives" (2008) 16 *Corporate Governance* 1 at 13 (suggesting that the content and adoption process of codes supports a "legitimation theory" for the adoption of codes in civil law countries); M.M. Siems, *Convergence in Shareholder Law* (Cambridge University Press, 2008), pp. 56–9.

[95] See generally P.A. Hall and D. Soskice, "An Introduction to Varieties of Capitalism," in P.A. Hall and D. Soskice (eds.), *Varieties Of Capitalism: The Institutional Foundations of Comparative Advantage* (Oxford University Press, 2001), p. 1.

unsustainable for demographic reasons.[96] Encouraged to reform their PAYGO retirement systems by the OECD and the World Bank, Continental European countries thus attempted to move to a more balanced mix of the "three pillars" in retirement, thereby strengthening the role of individual responsibility in the form of private pension accounts.[97] Private stock ownership and private investment were also heavily promoted and, at least for a while, obtained a significance in the public perception that they probably did not have at any time since the Great Depression.[98] All of this may have resulted in a greater political acceptance of shareholder interests in corporate governance.[99]

It remains yet to be seen what impact the financial crisis will have on the new, emerging balance. Many private (but tax-subsidized) pension plans have run into considerable problems in the late 2000s.[100] Continental capital markets have not, in many cases, regained the vigor of the convergence

[96] See, e.g., L. Schruff, "Pensions and Post-Retirement Benefits by Employers in Germany" (1998) 64 *Brooklyn Law Review* 795 at 797–8 (describing demographic trends in Germany); D. Blanchet and F. Legros, "France. The Difficult Path to Consensual Reforms," in M. Feldstein and H. Siebert (eds.), *Social Security Pension Reform in Europe* (Chicago University Press, 2002), pp. 109, 113–6 (describing the 1990 reform debate in France); D. Franco, "Italy. A Never-Ending Pension Reform" (describing demographic problems in Italy) and B. Rürup, "The German Pension System. Status Quo and Reform Options" at 160 (describing the German PAYGO system as "threatened by demographic changes within German society") (both in the same volume edited by M. Feldstein and H. Siebert); Mackenzie, above n 78 at 145 (table showing the growth of life expectancy in 10 OECD countries).

[97] The "three pillars" represent a commonly used definitional framework proposed by the World Bank. See World Bank, *Averting the Old Age Crisis* (Oxford University Press, 1994), p. 15; J. Marshall and S. Butterworth, "Pensions Reform in the EU: The Unexplored Time Bomb in the Single Market" (2000) 37 *Common Market Law Review* 739 at 741–4.

[98] See, e.g., J.A. Fanto, "Persuasion and Resistance: The Use of Psychology by Anglo-American Corporate Governance Advocates in France" (2002) 35 *Vanderbilt Journal of Transactional Law* 1041 at 1086–7 (suggesting that Anglo-American "corporate governance advocates – consciously or not – used psychological factors to manipulate or persuade [French] policymakers . . . to support a particular form of corporate finance and governance").

[99] See Gourevitch and Shinn, above n 25 at 220–1 (suggesting a shift in the political preferences of workers toward minority shareholder protection); Gelter, above n 18 at 967–8; see also A. Dignam and M. Galanis, *The Globalization of Corporate Governance* (Farnham: Ashgate Publishing, 2009), pp. 66–70 (discussing retirement savings of workers as reason for the political importance of shareholders); G.F. Davis, "The Twilight of the Berle and Means Corporation" (2011) 34 *Seattle University Law Review* 1121 at 1129.

[100] See, e.g., B. Ebbinghaus, "The Privatization and Marketization of Pensions in Europe: A Double Transformation Facing the Crisis" (2015) 1 *European Policy Analysis* 56 at 56–7 ("The financial market crash in 2007/2008, however, has challenged the merits of private funded pensions as their assets experienced a substantial decline within a short time . . . As a result, trust in the expected long-term returns of funded pensions has been shattered at a time when saving for retirement has become more important.").

period. Union membership is still eroding across the continent and employment protection has been under attack in the name of more flexibility and lower unemployment for at least two decades. The "convergence in corporate governance" period led to a discussion about codetermination in Germany, but not to a fundamental reassessment or change.[101] Ultimately, the political power of labor and its entrenched institutions were yet too resilient and not sufficiently eroded to give way during this now infamous phase. However, the Netherlands – often an outlier on the Continent in many parts of the political economy – weakened its co-optive "structure model" of employee participation to a more moderate one in 2004.[102]

With the financial crisis having led to a prolonged recession, no clear trend in labor and corporate governance seems to be emerging. Whereas one country – the Czech Republic – abandoned employee representation on the board recently,[103] the recent espousal of employee representation by France seems a much greater victory for the idea. Employee representation in France was introduced in the wake of the election of President Hollande within the context of pro-employment reforms that seemed to be bringing back some traditional left-wing policies.[104]

We can probably say that the "convergence in corporate governance" period has been the result of political and possibly demographic developments exogenous to the financial system. In contrast to the United States, it seems that no stable equilibrium state of the politics of corporate governance has emerged yet. Political scientists have pointed out that German corporate governance systems have been shifting toward a "transparency coalition," which pitches the interests of investors and workers against those of managers and other corporate insiders.[105] That coalition, however, did not prove itself stable with the failure of the largely pro-shareholder Schroeder government – which was cannibalized from the left – being a prominent example.[106] Subsequently, the financial crisis dealt a significant blow to the emerging liberal consensus of the previous decade.

[101] See, e.g., E. McGaughey, "The Codetermination Bargains: The History of German Corporate and Labour Law," *LSE Law, Society and Economy Working Papers No. 10/2015* (London School of Economics and Political Science Law Department, 2015), available at http://ssrn.com/abstract=2579932, at 40–2 (surveying recent debates and noting that codetermination has not been seriously questioned since 1979).

[102] Groenewald, above n 34 at 297–300.

[103] L. Fulton, "Board Representation" (Czech Republic), available at www.worker-participation.eu/National-Industrial-Relations/Countries/Czech-Republic/Board-level-Representation

[104] Code de Commerce art. L225-27-1, above n 36.

[105] Gourevitch and Shinn, above n 25 at 160–7.

[106] Cioffi, above n 83 at 9 (pointing out that pro-shareholder reforms were spearheaded by the center-left Schröder government). This episode may illustrate Marco Pagano and

Nevertheless, it seems that the time of the government as an important shareholder, the all-powerful role of banks and other financial institutions and the eminent role of unions of decades past are not destined to return. Institutional investors, rather international than local ones, continue to gain ground on the Continent. In Germany, in particular, it appears that large shareholders are losing ground with the ownership structure of the largest corporations no longer resembling the "powerful blockholder" dynamic of old, but a new equilibrium transitional between dispersed and concentrated ownership.[107] The end result will likely be a modified version of the respective traditional corporate governance system of each country, with the powers of large shareholders and other insiders only diminished slightly, but coupled with larger and more restless outside investors. While power structures will likely be more balanced than they were in the past, this is not the sea change the convergence literature expected.

2.4 Conclusion

Over the past decades, outside investors have gained in power both in the United States and in Continental Europe. However, neither in the United States nor in Continental Europe has the traditional corporate governance system been completely superseded by a new one. The United States is still to a large extent manager-centric, although managerial incentives are more aligned with shareholder interests. The role of labor has changed fundamentally, and employees have effectively become shareholders as a result of defined contribution pension plans. Continental Europe still has coordinated corporate governance systems, with powerful large shareholders, and often powerful other groups. Labor as an independent force has remained more important than in the United States, but outside institutional investors – sometimes from the United States – have become a player to be reckoned with. One could say that investor influence has added an additional layer of complexity to the respective corporate governance system. The underlying substrate or deep structure of each system persists.

Paolo Volpin's theory, according to which proportional voting systems are more likely than majoritarian ones to produce stronger employment and weaker investor protection. M. Pagano and P.F. Volpin, "The Political Economy of Corporate Governance" (2005) 95 *American Economic Review* 1005.

[107] Ringe, above n 25 at 508–17.

3

The Corporation's Intrinsic Attributes

CHRISTOPHER M. BRUNER

Numerous treatises, casebooks, and other resources commonly present concise lists of attributes said to be intrinsic to the modern corporation and/or essential to its economic utility. Such descriptions of the corporate form often constitute introductory matter, conditioning how students, professionals, and public officials alike approach corporate law by presenting a straightforward framework to distinguish the corporate form from other types of business entities. There are two significant problems with such frameworks, however, from a pedagogic perspective. First, these frameworks describe the corporation by reference to purportedly fixed intrinsic attributes, conflicting sharply with the flux and dynamism that have in fact characterized the history of corporate law. Second, these frameworks differ markedly from each other in how they characterize the corporation's attributes, each embodying a contestable perspective on the nature of the corporate form.

The diversity of perspectives that such inquiry reveals calls into question the degree to which we can validly deduce a single correct or optimal (1) division of power between boards and shareholders, (2) degree of regard for shareholder interests, and/or (3) degree of liability exposure for boards and shareholders, based exclusively on premises purportedly intrinsic to corporate law itself – that is, without express appeal to external policy considerations and related regulatory fields. These matters map onto three core issues of corporate law and governance – power, purpose, and risk-taking, respectively – and the inability to resolve them by reference to the corporation's purportedly intrinsic features suggests that re-conceptualizing the corporate form might facilitate more effective assessment of its capabilities.

This chapter undertakes that project. Section 3.1 begins with an historical discussion of the corporation's emergence and early deployment for business in the United Kingdom and the United States. Section 3.2 turns to various contemporary descriptions of the corporation's intrinsic attributes presented in modern reference materials, exploring their commonalities, differences, and theoretical implications. Section 3.3 explores the impossibility of resolving core issues of power, purpose, and risk-taking by reference to such conceptions of the corporate form, providing three US examples that map onto these respective issues – the scope of shareholders' bylaw authority, the degree of board discretion to consider non-shareholder interests in hostile takeovers,[1] and the regulation of financial risk-taking following the recent crisis. Each illustrates the necessity of resort to political discourse – a reality underscored through comparison with the United Kingdom, which reveals substantial divergence on such issues notwithstanding broad similarities between the US and UK corporate governance regimes.

The chapter concludes, in Sections 3.4 and 3.5, by proposing that we refrain from describing the corporate form by reference to purportedly fixed intrinsic attributes. I argue that it would pay to re-conceptualize the modern corporation by reference to the tools it offers, and how those tools can be deployed – a series of governance "levers," I suggest, that can be adjusted and calibrated in various ways to pursue a broad range of governance-related goals.

3.1 Corporate Constituents and Corporate Assets

Early English descriptions suggest that, in its origin, the corporation arose as a stable vehicle to facilitate ongoing deployment of assets toward collective institutional goals outlasting the involvement of particular individuals. Sir Edward Coke, writing in the early seventeenth century, described the "corporation aggregate of many" as "invisible" and "immortal."[2] Sir William Blackstone, writing in the eighteenth century, employed a river analogy, characterizing the corporation's changing constituency as "but one person in law, a person that never dies: in like manner as the river Thames is still the same river, though the parts which compose it are changing every instant."[3] Sir Matthew Bacon, also writing in the eighteenth

[1] On these two issues, see also William Bratton's chapter in this book, "Corporate Law Reform in the Era of Shareholder Empowerment."

[2] E. Coke, *The Reports of Sir Edward Coke, Knt. in Thirteen Parts* (Clark, NJ: The Lawbook Exchange Ltd., 2002), vol. V, p. 32b (reporting on *The Case of Sutton's Hospital*).

[3] W. Blackstone, *Commentaries on the Laws of England*, W. Morrison (ed.), (London: Cavendish Publishing, 2001), vol. I, p. 468.

century, similarly turned to metaphor, describing the corporation as a "Body Politick," the "Ligaments of which . . . are the Franchises and Liberties thereof, which bind and unite all its members together; and the whole Frame and Essence of the Corporation consist therein."[4] Though less reliant on metaphor, contemporary accounts of the corporation's utility similarly reflect this fundamental insight, one prominent treatise on English company law explaining that an association "with a large and fluctuating membership" calls for a form of organization that "ideally should confer corporate personality on the association, that is, should recognize that it constitutes a distinct legal person, subject to legal duties and entitled to legal rights separate from those of its members."[5]

This notion of substituting for actual people a structure capable of holding and deploying collective assets indefinitely has been identified as "the sine qua non of the legal entity." Henry Hansmann, Reinier Kraakman, and Richard Squire emphasize the capacity of "entity shielding" – that is, "rules that protect a firm's assets from the personal creditors of its owners" – to facilitate commercial transactions by creating a stable pool of assets to which counterparties can look to assess a business' creditworthiness.[6] Intriguingly, they argue that unlike limited liability – a form of "ownership shielding" – entity shielding lies at the very heart of any business entity because, while the former can be achieved through contract, the latter "can be achieved only through the special property rules of entity law." The strength of such rules varies from one form of business entity to another, ranging from general partnerships with relatively "weak" entity shielding, to corporations with "strong" entity shielding, to non-profits and charitable trusts with "complete" entity shielding.[7] This capacity to establish a stable pool of assets associated with a business undertaking contributes directly to certain characteristics commonly ascribed to the

[4] M. Bacon, *A New Abridgment of the Law* (London: Printed by his Majesty's Law-Printers, 1768), vol. I, pp. 499–500. For further discussion see C.M. Bruner, "The Enduring Ambivalence of Corporate Law" (2008) 59 *Alabama Law Review* 1385 at 1387–9; C.M. Bruner, "Agency and the Ontology of the Corporation" (2012) 69 *Washington and Lee Law Review* 355 at 355–6.

[5] P.L. Davies, *Gower and Davies' Principles of Modern Company Law* (London: Sweet & Maxwell, 2008), pp. 4–6.

[6] See H. Hansmann, R. Kraakman, and R. Squire, "Law and the Rise of the Firm" (2006) 119 *Harvard Law Review* 1335 at 1336–8.

[7] See *ibid.* at 1337–8, 1340–3. See also D.A. Moss, *When All Else Fails: Government as the Ultimate Risk Manager* (Cambridge: Harvard University Press, 2004), pp. 80–3 (acknowledging that limited liability could be achieved through contract but suggesting that such negotiations would likely prove awkward and costly).

modern corporation and corporate finance – notably by reducing creditors' monitoring costs, constraining borrowing, and simplifying bankruptcy proceedings (through clear rules associating particular assets with particular contracts), while at the same time stabilizing going-concern value, facilitating investment diversification, and promoting share transferability (by limiting asset withdrawals, thereby reducing the significance of fellow investors' financial circumstances).[8]

Despite having established commercial dominance in Europe by the late seventeenth century, "institutional conservatism prevented English law from developing in lockstep with commerce."[9] By the mid-nineteenth century, however, "the country had produced useful, general-purpose commercial entities" providing effective entity shielding – notably the "joint stock company."[10] Starting in the seventeenth century, several undertakings organized through trading guilds were granted Parliamentary or Crown charters providing monopoly privileges in specific regions. While initially structured as one-off ventures that contemplated dividing their cargoes among investors, joint stock companies were soon placed on a permanent footing by eliminating investors' right to withdraw assets while allowing them "to sell their shares without the consent of other owners, a compromise that reconciled a company's need for fixed capital with a shareholder's need for liquidity."[11] While certain joint stock company charters provided for limited liability, not all did so – which Hansmann, Kraakman, and Squire cite as evidence that "limited liability is not a prerequisite of tradable shares."[12]

As English commerce continued to expand, chartering failed to keep pace with demand, prompting development of an "unincorporated" form of joint stock company. A direct predecessor to the modern English company, the unincorporated joint stock company represented "a union of the trust form and the partnership," essentially involving "a partnership-like form whose assets were held in trust for the partners by trustees whom the partners had themselves selected."[13] This provided strong entity shielding, in turn permitting shares to be traded without regard to the buyer's financial wherewithal – and without limited liability, which parties sometimes

[8] See Hansmann, Kraakman, and Squire, above n 6 at 1343–50.

[9] *Ibid.* at 1375.

[10] *Ibid.* at 1375–6.

[11] *Ibid.* at 1376–7.

[12] See *ibid.* at 1378. See also Davies, above n 5 at 21.

[13] Hansmann, Kraakman, and Squire, above n 6 at 1383.

endeavored to create through contract, but which was not clearly endorsed by courts until the mid-nineteenth century. By the turn of the nineteenth century there were almost one thousand unincorporated joint stock companies in England, and when general incorporation was adopted in 1844, such companies "with transferable shares or more than twenty-five members" were required to "register as public corporations and follow uniform disclosure rules."[14] Limited liability would be added to the statute over a decade later, in 1855, "and even then it was optional."[15] In fact, limited liability was initially available only to companies with at least twenty-five members.[16] While these thresholds would be phased out over time, imposing no meaningful constraint by the turn of the twentieth century, it remains noteworthy that the statutory requirement of multiple members to receive limited liability was not formally removed from the statute until after the turn of the millennium.[17]

In the United States, state legislatures "were less stingy than Parliament in granting charters, and they were also quicker to enact general incorporation statutes," beginning with New York in 1811.[18] As in England, however, the basic trade-off involved the sacrifice of withdrawal rights in exchange for share tradeability,[19] with limited liability often coming later – in some cases, much later. While "the world's first limited liability statutes were enacted in the United States in the early nineteenth century," with New York again leading the way (through a provision included in its 1811

[14] *Ibid.* at 1386.

[15] *Ibid.* at 1387. See also Davies, above n 5 at 495–6; H. Hansmann and R. Kraakman, "Toward Unlimited Shareholder Liability for Corporate Torts" (1991) 100 *Yale Law Journal* 1879 at 1923–4. Davies observes that the directors often "were themselves the trustees," explaining why British directors' duties of loyalty derive from trust law. While directors of incorporated companies are not literal trustees, "it was not unnatural that the courts should extend [such duties] to them by analogy" in order to conform directors' duties in the two settings. Davies, above n 5 at 495–6.

[16] See Davies, above n 5 at 5.

[17] Davies explains that "the requirement was effectively undermined by the decision in *Salomon's* case," [1897] AC 22, permitting it to be "met through the use of bare nominees rather than shareholders who held the shares beneficially as well as legally." See Davies, above n 5 at 5, 211–12.

[18] Hansmann, Kraakman, and Squire, above n 6 at 1394.

[19] See *ibid.* at 1394–6. See also Moss, above n 7 at 54. By the 1880s, "general acts of incorporation had become the norm" in the United States. W.T. Allen, R. Kraakman, and G. Subramanian, *Commentaries and Cases on the Law of Business Organization* (New York: Aspen Publishers, 2007), p. 88.

general incorporation statute),[20] and while "most American states had adopted limited liability for corporations in general by the 1850's,"[21] not all had done so. Indeed, "California imposed unlimited pro rata liability by statute on the shareholders of both domestic and foreign corporations from statehood in 1849 until 1931, evidently without crippling industrial and commercial development."[22] These developments mapped closely onto the emergence of large-scale American industry, and corporate law gradually liberalized beginning in the 1890s – permitting corporations, for example, to "amend their certificates of incorporation, own and vote stock of other corporations, own land without limit, and merge with other corporations." Additionally, "the evolution of a new class of managers and the rise of liquid markets for stock" reflected and facilitated the larger-scale corporate structures built to pursue American industrialization.[23]

The foregoing accounts of the emergence of the modern corporation in the United Kingdom and the United States, though cursory, are sufficient to suggest that the intrinsic attributes of the corporate form are less static and rigid than contemporary accounts often suggest. The capacity to hold and deploy collective assets indefinitely would indeed appear central to any business entity, but beyond that one can speak only of generalized tendencies. To be sure, trends toward limited liability for shareholders, free transferability of stock, and centralized management are readily discernible since the early nineteenth century in each country, and their general association with industrialization would appear straightforward. As we will see, however, such generalizations in fact provide little insight regarding fundamental questions of corporate governance that continue to vex us today – including the optimal division of power between boards and shareholders, degree of regard for shareholder interests, and degree of liability exposure for boards and shareholders.

20 See Moss, above n 7 at 54–7. See also C.M. Bruner, *Corporate Governance in the Common-Law World: The Political Foundations of Shareholder Power* (New York: Cambridge University Press, 2013), pp. 216–17.

21 Hansmann and Kraakman, above n 15 at 1924.

22 *Ibid.* David Moss recounts that "New Hampshire, Connecticut, and Vermont had begun granting limited liability on a regular basis to their incorporated manufacturers in the late 1810s; and Maine, just recently separated from Massachusetts in 1820, enacted a broad rule of limited liability for its manufacturing corporations in 1823." Massachusetts would follow in 1830, while California maintained its distinctive regime of unlimited pro rata liability until 1931. Moss, above n 7 at 61, 68–9, 72–3. See also Allen, Kraakman, and Subramanian, above n 19 at 94.

23 See Allen, Kraakman, and Subramanian, above n 19 at 88–90. See also Moss, above n 7 at 70.

3.2 Intrinsic Corporate Attributes

As described above, the attributes commonly associated with the modern corporation did not spring into the world fully formed – they emerged and evolved in various jurisdictions at different times, and in different ways. Today, lists of the corporation's intrinsic attributes appearing in treatises, casebooks, and other resources reflect discernible trends of the sorts noted above, yet present them in a static form that implies a higher degree of inevitability and rigidity than either history or contemporary practice bear out – a topic taken up in subsequent sections of the chapter.

In fact, while broadly resembling one another, these lists do differ in ways that gesture toward enduring theoretical disagreements – even within a single jurisdiction. For purposes of discussion I have selected four representative lists, summarized for the reader's convenience in Table 3.1, from highly regarded US scholars of corporate law. In this section of the chapter, I discuss the distinguishing features of these lists and briefly consider some theoretical divergences reflected in them.

Though broadly similar, these lists of intrinsic corporate attributes do differ in discernible ways, reflecting points of contention among these commentators regarding fundamental issues of corporate law. Robert Clark, in his 1986 treatise, provides the sparsest list, identifying four characteristics that help account for "the continued preference for the corporate form of organization."[24] These include (1) "limited liability for investors"; (2) "free transferability of investor interests"; (3) "legal personality (entity-attributable powers, life span, and purpose)"; and (4) "centralized management."[25] Essentially Clark's list recognizes the fundamental requirement of a legal entity possessing distinct powers, and then summarizes the general historical trends described above toward limited liability for shareholders, free transferability of stock, and centralized management that emerged over the nineteenth and twentieth centuries.

William Allen, Reinier Kraakman, and Guhan Subramanian, then, provide a similar list but include five "basic characteristics of the corporate form" that they present as neutralizing "the contracting problems engendered by the UPA-style general partnership."[26] These include (1) "legal personality with indefinite life"; (2) "limited liability for investors"; (3) "free transferability of share interests"; and (4) "centralized management"

[24] R.C. Clark, *Corporate Law* (New York: Aspen Law & Business, 1986), p. 2.

[25] *Ibid.*

[26] Allen, Kraakman, and Subramanian, above n 19 at 83.

Table 3.1 *Lists of Intrinsic Corporate Attributes*

	Clark	Allen, Kraakman, and Subramanian	Bainbridge	Klein, Coffee, and Partnoy
Entity	• "Legal personality (entity-attributable powers, life span, and purpose)"	• "Legal personality with indefinite life"	• "Legal personality" • "Indefinite duration"	• "Separate entity" • "Indefinite duration"
Shareholder liability	• "Limited liability for investors"	• "Limited liability for investors"	• "Limited liability"	• "Limited liability"
Investment transfers	• "Free transferability of investor interests"	• "Free transferability of share interests"	• "Freely alienable ownership interests"	• "Transferable and tradable shares and debt obligations"
Control	• "Centralized management"	• "Centralized management" • "Appointed by equity investors"	• "Separation of ownership and control"	• "Centralized control and separation of ownership and control"
Creation			• "Formal creation as prescribed by state law"	
Ownership				• "Divisible ownership"
Assets				• "Assets separated from shareholders"

who are (5) "appointed by equity investors." The close resemblance to Clark's list is apparent (and acknowledged in a footnote),[27] though Allen, Kraakman, and Subramanian add an additional element to the list,[28] presumably to emphasize what they regard as the fundamental significance of the shareholder franchise – a point to which I return below.

Like Allen, Kraakman, and Subramanian, who characterize the attributes they identify as responding to "contracting problems" associated with partnerships, Stephen Bainbridge lists those attributes thought to "give the corporate form considerable advantages for large businesses as compared to the other forms of business organizations available under U.S. law." Bainbridge, however, identifies "six attributes," including (1) "formal creation as prescribed by state law"; (2) "legal personality"; (3) "separation of ownership and control"; (4) "freely alienable ownership interests"; (5) "indefinite duration"; and (6) "limited liability."[29] In its general contours, Bainbridge's list resembles the foregoing lists, each of which lumps life span together with "legal personality." His list does differ marginally in emphasizing the affirmative effort required to create a corporation, though this too is broadly consistent with Allen, Kraakman, and Subramanian's list in spirit, as a requirement of "formal creation" clearly distinguishes corporate law from the residual nature of partnership law.[30] A more significant and illuminating distinction, however, emerges in the description of centralized management. Whereas Allen, Kraakman, and Subramanian emphasize the significance of the shareholder's ability to elect directors, suggesting that accountability to shareholders is fundamental to the form, Bainbridge refers to a "separation of ownership and control," a phrase historically employed to suggest precisely the opposite – a de facto insulation of management power from meaningful accountability to dispersed and rationally apathetic minority shareholders in large public companies.[31]

The list offered by William Klein, John Coffee, and Frank Partnoy broadly resembles Bainbridge's list in suggesting relative freedom from substantial accountability to shareholders, while perhaps going further in emphasizing finance-relevant dimensions of the corporation particularly

[27] *Ibid.* at footnote 1.

[28] This element is management's appointment by equity investors.

[29] S.M. Bainbridge, *Corporate Law* (New York: Foundation Press, 2009), p. 1.

[30] See Uniform Partnership Act 1997 § 202(a)–(b) (last amended 2013).

[31] See A.A. Berle, Jr. and G.C. Means, *The Modern Corporation and Private Property* (New York: Harcourt, Brace & World, Inc., 2nd ed. 1968), p. 5 (coining this term). See also Bruner, "Enduring Ambivalence," above n 4 at 1391, footnote 25 (discussing the term's ubiquity).

pertinent to creditors. Their list includes seven "characteristics that, collectively, account for [the public corporation's] success in organizing economic activity on a large scale," including (1) "separate entity"; (2) "divisible ownership"; (3) "assets separated from shareholders"; (4) "limited liability"; (5) "indefinite duration"; (6) "transferable and tradable shares and debt obligations"; and (7) "centralized control and separation of ownership and control."[32] Here, specifying the divisibility of equity interests amounts to a marginal distinction (presumably being taken for granted in the others' specification of share transferability). More noteworthy aspects, however, include placing emphasis on a "separation of ownership and control," connoting de facto insulation from meaningful accountability to shareholders, as in Bainbridge's list, and their unique attention to creditors, which tends further to decentralize shareholders. Unlike the others, Klein, Coffee, and Partnoy cite the significance of transferability of "debt obligations," and underscore that corporate assets are "separated from shareholders."[33] Though perhaps implicit in the other lists' specification of "legal personality," emphasizing the shareholders' inability to access or withdraw corporate assets gestures toward the "entity shielding" concept described above, which tends to identify creditor protection as the very heart of the business entity's utility.[34]

These differing views on the intrinsic or essential attributes of the modern corporation – from highly regarded scholars within a single jurisdiction – point toward markedly divergent normative positions regarding the role of shareholders and their interests, and distinct concerns regarding how corporations function. For example, it is unsurprising that the list offered by Allen, Kraakman, and Subramanian would underscore that the board is "appointed by equity investors," given that the first named author, as Delaware Chancellor, had penned the famous *Blasius* opinion in which the "shareholder franchise" was described as "the ideological underpinning upon which the legitimacy of directorial power rests."[35] Conversely, it is unsurprising that the list offered by Bainbridge would alternatively emphasize a "separation of ownership and control,"

[32] W.A. Klein, J.C. Coffee, Jr. and F. Partnoy, *Business Organization and Finance: Legal and Economic Principles* (New York: Foundation Press, 2010), pp. 108–110 (emphasis and capitalization removed).

[33] *Ibid.* at 109.

[34] Cf. *ibid.* at 108–109 and footnote 4 (citing Hansmann and Kraakman's work on asset partitioning).

[35] *Blasius Industries, Inc.* v. *Atlas Corp.*, 564 A 2d 651 at 659 (Del. Ch. 1988) (per Allen, Chancellor).

given his "director primacy" theory of corporate law and governance in which the board is described as "a sort of Platonic guardian – a *sui generis* body serving as the nexus for the various contracts making up the corporation and whose powers flow not from shareholders alone, but from the complete set of contracts constituting the firm."[36]

At the same time, creditor-oriented elements of the list offered by Klein, Coffee, and Partnoy reflect a distinct set of concerns relating to risk, time horizon, and financial stability of the enterprise. In explaining the centrality of separating corporate assets from the shareholders they suggest that a shareholder's inability to withdraw assets "protects the stability of the corporation and the interest of the other shareholders in that stability," but that a "more important" function of this limitation on shareholder power may be that "it protects the creditors of the corporation," who (as described above) can accordingly extend credit more confidently, knowing that they possess downside priority over shareholders' personal creditors.[37]

In light of this diversity of concerns and views – from respected scholars within a single jurisdiction – it is unsurprising that such formulations offer little meaningful guidance when it comes to resolving fundamental corporate governance problems of power, purpose, and risk-taking. The remainder of the chapter examines such problems more closely, arguing that the challenge they pose requires a more nuanced way of thinking about the modern corporation's intrinsic attributes.

3.3 Three Core Issues: Power, Purpose, and Risk-Taking

This section briefly examines three prominent examples of corporate governance problems arising in the United States that implicate power, purpose, and risk-taking, respectively, and then contrasts US law on such matters with approaches taken in the United Kingdom. Ultimately, I argue that the inability to resolve such problems without resort to political discourse suggests a need to re-conceptualize the core attributes and functions of corporations.

3.3.1 The Shareholders' Bylaw Authority

US corporate law has long remained ambivalent regarding who ought to hold the upper hand in corporate governance. Is it the board of directors,

[36] S.M. Bainbridge, "Director Primacy: The Means and Ends of Corporate Governance" (2003) 97 *Northwestern University Law Review* 547 at 554–60.

[37] See Klein, Coffee, and Partnoy, above n 32 at 108.

whose sweeping statutory authority to manage the "business and affairs" of the corporation[38] has been interpreted by the Delaware Supreme Court to include "the selection of a time frame for achievement of corporate goals,"[39] and whose judgments are substantially reinforced by various common-law and statutory structures insulating them from second-guessing?[40] Or is it the shareholders, who possess statutory authority to elect directors and (at least in theory) to remove them?[41]

An important reflection of this ambiguity arises from the shareholders' bylaw authority – a singular form of unilateral action open to Delaware shareholders that, if interpreted expansively, could permit them to carve back substantially at the board's governance power.[42] The problem arises from the lack of any clear statutory resolution to the collision between the board's power under § 141 of the Delaware General Corporation Law to manage the corporation's business and affairs "except as may be otherwise provided in this chapter," which might be read to include the shareholders' bylaw authority, and the shareholders' power under § 109 to "adopt, amend or repeal bylaws" relating to the corporation's business and affairs that are "not inconsistent with law," which might be read to include the board's management authority.[43] Aptly termed a "recursive loop,"[44] this statutory conundrum could be broken only by Delaware's judiciary, who were forced to acknowledge that the statute itself provided no meaningful guidance as to the core division of power between boards and shareholders in this area.[45]

Ultimately put to the Delaware Supreme Court through certification from the US Securities and Exchange Commission (who asked whether a shareholder proposal for a bylaw requiring reimbursement of shareholder proxy expenses could be excluded from a company's proxy statement due

[38] See Delaware General Corporation Law § 141(a).

[39] *Paramount Communications, Inc.* v. *Time Inc.*, 571 A 2d 1140 at 1154 (Del. 1990). I focus on Delaware due to its significance as the jurisdiction of incorporation for most US public companies. See Delaware Department of State, Division of Corporations, "About Agency," available at http://corp.delaware.gov/aboutagency.shtml.

[40] For additional background see Bruner, above n 20 at 37–42; Bruner, "Enduring Ambivalence," above n 4 at 1422–4.

[41] See Delaware General Corporation Law §§ 141(k), 211(b).

[42] See generally C.M. Bruner, "Managing Corporate Federalism: The Least-Bad Approach to the Shareholder Bylaw Debate" (2011) 36 *Delaware Journal of Corporate Law* 1. See also Bruner, above n 20 at 48–53.

[43] See Delaware General Corporation Law §§ 109(a)–(b), 141(a).

[44] J.N. Gordon, "'Just Say Never?' Poison Pills, Deadhand Pills, and Shareholder-Adopted Bylaws: An Essay for Warren Buffett" (1997) 19 *Cardozo Law Review* 511 at 546–7.

[45] See *CA, Inc.* v. *AFSCME Employees Pension Plan*, 953 A 2d 227 at 232 (Del. 2008).

to inconsistency with state law),[46] the matter placed the Delaware judiciary in an untenable position because a non-arbitrary answer effectively required judicial policymaking. Those favoring greater shareholder power would naturally favor elevating § 109 over § 141, while those favoring greater board power would naturally favor the opposite.

As a consequence, the court's 2008 *CA, Inc.* opinion was less than compelling, finding that § 141 trumps because board authority is "a cardinal precept of the DGCL" – a rationale coupled with no explanation of how one knows a "cardinal precept" when one sees it, and why the shareholders' § 109 bylaw authority did not qualify for this status.[47] Concluding that board authority trumps because it is "a cardinal precept" effectively amounts to burying the conclusion in the premise – though it bears emphasizing that the court could offer little more due to the lack of guidance from the political branch on this fundamentally political issue.

The court did, to be sure, conclude that the proposed bylaw was a proper subject for shareholder action under Delaware law, because it implicated procedure as opposed to substance – the former type of limit on board authority being permissible while the latter is not.[48] The court nevertheless nixed the bylaw, however, by concluding that adopting it would require the board to violate its fiduciary duties by reimbursing proxy expenses where the board itself considered this contrary to the company's interests. No theoretical rationale is provided for this formulation of fiduciary duty, rendering the move another example of burying the conclusion in the premise. As I have argued elsewhere, the (entirely comprehensible) aim was apparently to dodge the fundamental issue of governance power implicated, allowing the court "to avoid endorsing a shareholder-centric conception of the corporation without expressly rejecting it"[49] – an approach responding to the inevitable tension involved in a case forcing the judiciary to make a fundamentally political decision.

3.3.2 Discretion to Consider Non-shareholders in Hostile Takeovers

In much the same manner that the shareholder bylaw debate has forced Delaware's courts to make policy regarding the core division of power,

[46] See *ibid.* at 229–30.

[47] See *ibid.* at 232 and footnote 7.

[48] See *ibid.* at 234–6. This distinction may prove useful, though its application remains murky at the margin. See Bruner, above n 20 at 52.

[49] See Bruner, above n 20 at 51–2.

in the takeover context the judiciary has been forced to determine who controls the outcome, and whose interests count, in responding to a hostile bid. Delaware judges have (in a law review article) noted the "legislative vacuum" arising from the General Assembly's reluctance to tackle takeovers in the statute, rendering it "unavoidable that the [adjudication] process for developing those legal rules will involve policy choices"[50] – a candid admission that the case law in this area rests upon normative judgments, effectively constituting political decision-making. Indeed, just as in the bylaw context,[51] the court's fundamental move in the takeover context has been to obscure the political dimensions of its case law by reframing the core issue as a matter of fiduciary duties – effectively burying the conclusion in the premise once again.

In its 1990 *Time, Inc.* decision, the Delaware Supreme Court determined that a board could deploy potent defenses to prevent shareholders from accepting an all-cash, all-shares, premium bid, reasoning that "Time shareholders might elect to tender into Paramount's cash offer in ignorance or a mistaken belief of the strategic benefit which a business combination with Warner [the board's preferred strategic partner] might produce."[52] In essence, shareholder autonomy was constrained by reference to the shareholders' own interests – a move permitted by subsuming the conclusion of board authority in the premise of a duty to protect shareholders from themselves. At the same time, however, the court indicated that in responding to a bid the board could pay some regard to "the impact on 'constituencies' other than shareholders,"[53] a nod to prior case law permitting a board facing a hostile bid to consider "its effect on the corporate enterprise" as a whole, as well as particular impacts on "creditors, customers, employees, and perhaps even the community generally."[54] In this manner, the court again avoids expressly confronting the policy choices inevitably involved in a form of transaction requiring prioritization of various constituencies' competing interests – a political reality reflected

[50] W.T. Allen, J.B. Jacobs, and L.E. Strine, Jr., "The Great Takeover Debate: A Meditation on Bridging the Conceptual Divide" (2002) 69 *University of Chicago Law Review* 1067 at 1068–70.

[51] The bylaw debate essentially arose from the takeover debate, in so far as aggressive use of shareholder bylaws aimed at constraining takeover defenses responded directly to dissatisfaction with the takeover regime described here. See Bruner, above n 20 at 51.

[52] *Paramount Communications*, above n 39 at 1152–3.

[53] *Ibid.* at 1153.

[54] *Unocal Corp.* v. *Mesa Petroleum Co.*, 493 A 2d 946 at 955 (Del. 1985).

in the statutory treatment of takeovers in most US states,[55] yet obscured in Delaware by toggling between fundamentally divergent shareholder- and constituency-oriented rationales.[56]

3.3.3 *Post-Crisis Risk Regulation*

The recent financial crisis – and the widespread belief that excessive risk-taking in financial firms contributed substantially to its magnitude and duration – led to searching reappraisals of how corporate governance can function to amplify or dampen risk-taking incentives.[57] Accordingly, regulatory responses to the crisis in the United Kingdom and the United States alike included corporate governance-related reforms (of which more below).[58]

The turn to corporate governance in this context reflects the straightforward reality that core features of corporate law function to calibrate risk-taking incentives. While the "business judgment rule" emerged for multiple reasons (including institutional modesty on the part of courts), one of those reasons is undoubtedly that insulating directors from personal monetary liability for simple negligence tends to promote entrepreneurial risk-taking. As then-Chancellor Allen explained in his 1996 *Gagliardi* opinion,

> [if] corporate directors were to be found liable for a corporate loss from a risky project on the ground that the investment was too risky... their liability would be joint and several for the whole loss... Given the scale of operation of modern public corporations, this stupefying disjunction between risk and reward for corporate directors threatens undesirable effects . . . Obviously, it is in the shareholders' economic interest to offer sufficient protection to directors from liability for negligence, etc., to allow directors to conclude that, as a practical matter, there is no risk that, if they act in good faith and meet minimal proceduralist standards of attention, they can face liability as a result of a business loss.[59]

This rationale clearly presumes that the shareholders themselves favor greater risk-taking, and from this perspective the business judgment rule

55 For a brief discussion see Bruner, above n 20 at 44.

56 See *ibid.* at 41–4, 51–2.

57 See generally S.M. Bainbridge, *Corporate Governance after the Financial Crisis* (Oxford University Press, 2012); C.M. Bruner, "Corporate Governance Reform in a Time of Crisis" (2011) 36 *Journal of Corporation Law* 309.

58 See Bruner, above n 57 at 317–22.

59 *Gagliardi* v. *Trifoods International, Inc.*, 683 A 2d 1049 at 1052–3 (Del. Ch. 1996).

and limited liability go hand-in-hand – the latter peaking the shareholders' appetite for risk while the former frees up management to direct the company accordingly.[60]

While it is widely understood that limited liability and the business judgment rule both tend to encourage entrepreneurial risk-taking, fewer have explored the converse – that greater liability exposure for shareholders and/or managers might reduce socially undesirable risk-taking. A noteworthy exception is the work of Henry Hansmann and Reinier Kraakman, who closely examine the costs of limited liability in the tort context and argue that partially relaxing shareholders' limited liability protection would reduce detrimental risk-taking.[61] Observing that, particularly in areas such as harms to the environment and product liability, where there is a real prospect of tort damages exceeding the corporation's net worth, limited liability may result in insufficient precautionary measures and excessive investment in "hazardous industries" (problems exacerbated by debt financing, shareholder authority to liquidate, and personal bankruptcy protection).[62] And unlike "voluntary" creditors who have an opportunity ahead of time to assess the corporation's creditworthiness and negotiate protections, "involuntary" creditors such as tort victims get no such opportunity by hypothesis.[63] Accordingly, Hansmann and Kraakman argue for a rule of unlimited pro rata shareholder liability in tort.[64] They of course understand that this would dampen risk-taking incentives – this being their explicit aim – but contend that this would likely impact solely those "firms that, under the prevailing norms of tort law, impose net costs on society."[65]

As to managers, on the other hand, Hansmann and Kraakman take the position that expanding liability exposure in such a manner would not work because if "prospective tort losses were very large relative to the personal assets of the liability targets," then "imposing personal liability for the firm's entire tort losses on its managers would create a powerful incentive

60 See Bruner, above n 20 at 216–17; Moss, above n 7 at 72–8.

61 See generally Hansmann and Kraakman, above n 15.

62 See *ibid.* at 1880–5.

63 See Bruner, above n 20 at 216–17; Moss, above n 7 at 71–2.

64 See Hansmann and Kraakman, above n 15 at 1892–4, and also 1896–7, 1921 (advocating a "claims-made" timing rule and a tort-based approach to choice of law).

65 *Ibid.* at 1933. For an historical discussion of why limited liability prevailed over unlimited pro rata liability throughout the United States, see Moss, above n 7 at 78–80 (observing, among other things, the difficulty of reducing one's unlimited pro rata liability through diversification in the nineteenth century, and the resulting uncertainty regarding overall liability exposure).

to overinvest in safety measures or, what is more likely, to resign."[66] While there is certainly room for reasonable minds to differ regarding their proposed expansion of shareholder liability exposure and/or their reluctance to pursue the same with respect to managers,[67] for present purposes the point is simply that Hansmann and Kraakman's argument reflects an underlying awareness of the potential to calibrate risk-taking incentives by expanding or contracting shareholder and/or manager liability exposure.

More generally, it has been argued that there are whole categories of firms where fully limited liability promotes excessive risk-taking. Hansmann and Kraakman gesture in this direction in suggesting that the unlimited pro rata shareholder liability regime advocated would be particularly attractive in specific "hazardous industries" where harms are more likely to exceed a corporation's net worth, and likewise in their further observation that the federal regime enacted in the United States through the Comprehensive Environmental Response Compensation and Liability Act (CERCLA) already imposes "a diluted form of de facto unlimited liability" upon those who "own" or "operate" a hazardous waste facility.[68] Historically, however, corporate law provides a more striking and illustrative example of the use of shareholder and manager liability exposure as tools to reduce risk-taking – financial firms.

Notwithstanding the general aim of incentivizing entrepreneurial risk-taking, US corporate law long sought to constrain risk-taking in banks by imposing greater liability exposure on directors and shareholders alike. Bank directors faced a more demanding duty of care (in some cases accomplished through diminished business judgment rule protection), and shareholders faced "double liability" rules, which sought to protect creditors by providing that shareholders of a failed bank could be assessed up to the sale price of their stock (rendering them doubly liable, in that they already lost what they initially invested). In some states, then, these structures were reinforced by treating depositors as beneficiaries of directors' fiduciary duties. In each case, such policies aimed to reduce risk-taking in banks to stabilize the banking system,[69] and it is noteworthy

[66] Hansmann and Kraakman, above n 15 at 1929.

[67] For example, Hansmann and Kraakman do not consider caps or other mechanisms to avoid excessive management liability exposure.

[68] See Hansmann and Kraakman, above n 15 at 1880–3, 1928.

[69] See Bruner, above n 20 at 264–5; C.M. Bruner, "Conceptions of Corporate Purpose in Post-Crisis Financial Firms" (2013) 36 *Seattle University Law Review* 527 at 529–41 (observing that double liability applied in national banks from the 1860s until the 1930s, after which use at the state level declined as well). On the duty of care applicable to bank

that Australia, Canada, and the United Kingdom historically employed multiple liability regimes as well.[70]

In light of this history, some have argued that we ought to consider reinvigorating director and shareholder liability in financial firms to mitigate the impulse toward excessive risk-taking thought to leave us vulnerable to crisis[71] – an approach that has not found favor to date. Indeed, both US and UK post-crisis reform agendas aimed to empower shareholders further in the apparent belief that risk-preferring shareholders would (for some unspecified reason) exert themselves to constrain reckless managers – a response reflecting a decidedly cramped conception of the corporation's core governance dynamics and the range of potential responses to excessive risk-taking (a problem explored further below).[72] The essential point highlighted by these examples, however, is simply that a single correct or optimal level of liability exposure for shareholders and/or boards cannot be deduced from the corporate form itself; the history of corporate law illustrates employment of starkly different calibrations of liability exposure and risk-taking incentives in different times and industries.

3.3.4 *Corporate Law in Comparative and Historical Context*

Stepping back from corporate law as a field, this indeterminacy of the corporate form should hardly surprise us. Indeed, as complex social constructs, corporations are neither more nor less than what we make of them.[73]

directors, see generally P.A. McCoy, "A Political Economy of the Business Judgment Rule in Banking: Implications for Corporate Law" (1996) 47 *Case Western Reserve Law Review* 1. On double liability rules in the United States, see generally J.R. Macey and G.P. Miller, "Double Liability of Bank Shareholders: History and Implications" (1992) 27 *Wake Forest Law Review* 31.

70 See generally L.T. Evans and N.C. Quigley, "Shareholder Liability Regimes, Principal-Agent Relationships, and Banking Industry Performance" (1995) 38 *Journal of Law and Economics* 497; J.D. Turner, "'The Last Acre and Sixpence': Views on Bank Liability Regimes in Nineteenth-Century Britain" (2009) 16 *Financial History Review* 111.

71 See, e.g., Bruner, above n 69 at 560–1; P. Conti-Brown, "Elective Shareholder Liability" (2012) 64 *Stanford Law Review* 409; C. Hill and R. Painter, "Berle's Vision beyond Shareholder Interests: Why Investment Bankers Should Have (Some) Personal Liability" (2010) 33 *Seattle University Law Review* 1173; J.R. Macey and M. O'Hara, "Solving the Corporate Governance Problems of Banks: A Proposal" (2003) 120 *Banking Law Journal* 326. Cf. Hansmann and Kraakman, above n 15 at 1925 (observing that the move away from more expansive shareholder liability exposure since the nineteenth century "should not be taken to indicate that it would be inefficient today").

72 See generally Bruner, above n 57; Bruner, above n 69.

73 See Bruner, "Enduring Ambivalence," above n 4 at 1388–9.

As Max Weber observed over a century ago, when it comes to appraisal of social institutions, there is little room for deduction. For Weber the distinctiveness of "problems of economic and social policy" lay in the fact that they "cannot be resolved merely on the basis of purely technical considerations which assume already settled ends."[74] Accordingly, he rejects outright the notion that "the goal of the cultural sciences" can be "to construct a closed system of concepts, in which reality is synthesized in some sort of *permanently* and *universally* valid classification and from which it can again be deduced."[75] Weber's insight applies straightforwardly to corporations, in so far as they represent social constructs and objects of "economic and social policy" that exist solely because we have created them, and solely to pursue ends that we collectively define. When novel questions regarding fundamental issues of corporate architecture and the scope of potential corporate functions arise, we are called upon to make political decisions – which can only be framed by reference to values external to corporate law as such.

Writing from the jurisprudential perspective, H.L.A. Hart arrived at a very similar conclusion through examination of legal definition, including the term "corporation." Observing that such terms lack "counterparts in the world of fact which most ordinary words have," Hart suggests that "out of these innocent requests for definitions of fundamental legal notions . . . have arisen vast and irreconcilable theories, so that not merely whole books but whole schools of juristic thought may be characterized by the type of answer they give to questions like 'What is a right?', or 'What is a corporate body?'"[76] Critically, Hart recognizes that embedded within such a question "is often an amalgam of issues that should be distinguished." For example, claims to the effect that corporations are, or are not, "real persons" are not truly questions of definition in the conventional sense, but rather "ways of asserting or denying the claims of organized groups to recognition by the State," rendering the purported definitional project "a criss-cross between logical and political criteria."[77] Ultimately, such terms can be sensibly defined only by reference to rules that we ourselves create, and by our own choices regarding the contexts in which to use such terms. To purport to "deduce" what corporations can (or ought to) do from

[74] M. Weber, "'Objectivity' in Social Science and Social Policy," in E.A. Shils and H.A. Finch (trans., eds.), *Max Weber on the Methodology of the Social Sciences* (Glencoe, IL: The Free Press, 1949), p. 56.

[75] *Ibid.* at 84.

[76] H.L.A. Hart, "Definition and Theory in Jurisprudence," in H.L.A. Hart, *Essays in Jurisprudence and Philosophy* (Oxford University Press, 1983), p. 23.

[77] *Ibid.* at 25.

conclusory statements regarding their intrinsic characteristics simply obscures the fact that such issues really pose enduring questions about ourselves – our values, the social aims we pursue, and how we endeavor to solve associated problems.[78]

As discussed above, the answers to such questions have not remained fixed over time or across industries. For the same reasons, they have not taken the same form across jurisdictions – even among legal systems and market cultures as similar as those in the United States and the United Kingdom.[79] As I have explored elsewhere, the UK corporate governance system has, in general, favored shareholders much more substantially than the US approach has; relative to their US counterparts, UK shareholders possess far greater legal authority and practical capacity to call special meetings, remove directors without cause, control the content of core governance documents, limit the use of takeover defenses, and compel board action.[80] Similarly, UK shareholders' interests are expressly established as the sole legitimate aim of director decision-making in the Companies Act (2006) – a provision with no counterpart in the Delaware General Corporation Law.[81] Such stark divergences between the US and UK corporate governance systems clearly cannot be deduced from any singular,

[78] See *ibid.* at 35, 40–5. See also E.W. Orts, "The Complexity and Legitimacy of Corporate Law" (1993) 50 *Washington and Lee Law Review* 1565 at 1570–4.

[79] See J. Armour and D.A. Skeel, Jr., "Who Writes the Rules for Hostile Takeovers, and Why? – The Peculiar Divergence of U.S. and U.K. Takeover Regulation" (2007) 95 *Georgetown Law Journal* 1727 at 1751.

[80] See Bruner, above n 20 at 28–65. See also C.M. Bruner, "Power and Purpose in the 'Anglo-American' Corporation" (2010) 50 *Virginia Journal of International Law* 579.

[81] Companies Act 2006, § 172(1) ("A director of a company must act in the way he considers, in good faith, would be most likely to promote the success of the company for the benefit of its members as a whole . . .."). See also Bruner, above n 20 at 34–5, 44–5. Delaware Chief Justice Leo Strine has suggested in a recent working paper that Delaware directors are duty-bound "to make stockholder welfare the sole end of corporate governance within the limits of their legal discretion." See L.E. Strine, Jr., "The Dangers of Denial: The Need for a Clear-Eyed Understanding of the Power and Accountability Structure Established by the Delaware General Corporation Law," *Research Paper No. 15-08* (University of Pennsylvania Institute for Law and Economics, 2015), available at http://ssrn.com/abstract=2576389, at 3. Strine can point to no statute expressing clear legislative intent to make shareholder welfare the corporation's "sole" legitimate aim, however. Relying on the "signal" purportedly conveyed by the fact that shareholders are uniquely favored in various ways (*ibid.* at 7). Strine ignores the extraordinary limits upon the power of Delaware shareholders that comparative analysis of this sort reveals. As discussed below, relative to its counterparts in other common-law jurisdictions, Delaware law remains aptly characterized as "ambivalent" regarding the desirability of shareholder governance power and single-minded focus on their interests.

fixed conception of the corporate form and its intrinsic characteristics. Rather, these divergences reflect their differing political economies – of which the corporate governance system of each jurisdiction constitutes just one part – and the differing normative and political judgments arising from those political economies.

For example, why does the UK takeover regime favor shareholders in a manner, and to a degree, vastly exceeding the US approach? The short answer is that the Labour Government of the 1960s – that is, the UK's political *left* – concluded that takeovers could facilitate larger and more globally competitive British companies, while remaining confident that downside costs facing their own key constituency could be managed through the relatively robust UK welfare state.[82] As economic historian Leslie Hannah observed, by the 1960s "earlier fears of Labour leaders that mergers and rationalization created unemployment had . . . given way to a feeling that larger (and, it was hoped, more productive) units would in the long run be better for employment," and that "social costs faced by unemployed workers were also more broadly shared as a result of the redundancy payments scheme initiated by Labour."[83] In the US political economy of the 1980s, however, neither prong of this rationale held sway. Accordingly, during the ascendance of the modern US political *right*, state legislatures (and, in the case of Delaware, state courts) ensured that management possessed adequate discretion to subordinate shareholder interests to long-term stability – an approach reflecting widespread concerns that leveraged hostile takeovers would bring little economic benefit while leaving workers thrown out of their jobs to the vagaries of a weak US welfare state.[84] In neither case was the balance of power in hostile takeovers, or the degree of conceptual emphasis to be placed on the shareholders' interests, resolved by reference to any purportedly intrinsic features of the corporate form. These were purely political decisions reflecting context-specific normative judgments regarding which policy would best serve broader social aims in the particular historical circumstances facing a particular jurisdiction.

[82] See Bruner, above n 20 at 147–60.

[83] L. Hannah, *The Rise of the Corporate Economy: The British Experience* (Baltimore: Johns Hopkins University Press, 1976), p. 172 and footnote 26.

[84] See Bruner, above n 20 at 166–73. Intriguingly, Australia's takeover regime resembled the stakeholder-oriented US approach during the 1980s, when Australia's social welfare system remained unstable, yet resembled the shareholder-oriented UK approach at the turn of the millennium, by which time Australian social welfare protections had more fully coalesced. See *ibid.* at 176–93.

In light of the foregoing, it is to be expected that no compelling universal descriptive theory of corporate law – or the role of shareholders within it – has emerged, or could. Shareholder-centric theories of corporate law may appear to hold considerable descriptive power as applied to the United Kingdom, but to the extent this is the case, it has more to tell us about British politics than it does about economics as a social science. In the United States, corporate law has long reflected deep "ambivalence" regarding the governance role of shareholders and compatibility of their interests with broader social aims.[85] These realities suggest that we require a more nuanced way of conceptualizing what corporations are, and what they can do, than relying on conclusory statements reflecting purportedly fixed intrinsic characteristics.

3.4 Fine-Tuning the Corporate Machinery

The foregoing discussion of corporate law's inevitable contingency with respect to fundamental issues of power, purpose, and risk-taking suggests that re-conceptualizing the corporation's intrinsic attributes would offer tangible benefits. This final section of the chapter argues that what is truly of the essence is not some set of static attributes, accounts of which tend to overstate the level of fixity and specificity of the corporate form. Rather the corporation is better conceptualized as a set of tools – a series of governance "levers," I suggest – that can be adjusted and calibrated in various ways to pursue a broad range of governance-related goals.

To be sure, it is widely understood that corporate statutes provide substantial flexibility, on a firm-by-firm basis, to address the sorts of issues discussed here through corporate organizational documents. For example, the Delaware General Corporation Law contemplates charter provisions "for the management of the business and for the conduct of the affairs of the corporation," including provisions "creating, defining, limiting and regulating the powers of the corporation, the directors, and the stockholders"; provisions requiring higher shareholder and/or director voting thresholds than those expressly required in the statute; a provision "limiting the duration of the corporation's existence"; a provision "imposing

[85] *Ibid.* See also Bruner, "Enduring Ambivalence," above n 4; L. Johnson, "The Delaware Judiciary and the Meaning of Corporate Life and Corporate Law" (1990) 68 *Texas Law Review* 865; Orts, above n 78 at 1612–3 (arguing that "corporate law does not follow any unified conception of the corporation," and that corporate law "requires a legal and political 'metatheory' to contain and justify it").

personal liability for the debts of the corporation on its stockholders"; a provision "eliminating or limiting the personal liability of a director to the corporation or its stockholders for monetary damages" for duty of care breaches[86]; and a provision creating a "restriction on the transfer . . . of securities of a corporation, or on the amount of a corporation's securities that may be owned by any person or group of persons."[87] It further remains open to the corporation to include in the charter a more expansive statement of the "nature of the business or purposes to be conducted or promoted," beyond the boilerplate suggested by the statute.[88]

As the foregoing discussion suggests, however, what is at issue is not simply the capacity of individual firms to make idiosyncratic deviations from established default rules, but rather how we think about the regulatory content and structure of corporate law – which ought to be informed by recognition that core issues of corporate governance have been resolved in varying ways in differing historical, cultural, and social contexts, often resulting in context-specific approaches that deviate markedly from the prevailing conceptions discussed in Section 3.2 of this chapter. To be clear, the scholars presenting those various conceptions of the corporation's intrinsic attributes understand this, as the careful and nuanced analyses presented throughout the cited texts reflect. The point here is not to suggest that they themselves fail to grasp the contingency of issues related to corporate power, purpose, and risk-taking,[89] but rather that a different mode of representation of the corporation's intrinsic attributes provides an opportunity to highlight from the outset – in casebooks and treatises widely consulted and relied upon by students, practitioners, and public officials alike – the innate and considerable flexibility of the corporate form, and the range of governance-related problems it is capable of addressing.

The analysis provided above suggests that the corporate form is better conceptualized as a complex governance machinery with a variety of "levers" that can be set and fine-tuned in different ways to address various types of problems thought amenable to resolution (or at least mitigation)

[86] Delaware General Corporation Law § 102(b)(1), (4)–(7).

[87] *Ibid.* § 202(b). See also § 203 (Delaware's business combination statute).

[88] *Ibid.* § 102(a)(3) ("It shall be sufficient to state . . . that the purpose of the corporation is to engage in any lawful act or activity for which corporations may be organized under the General Corporation Law of Delaware . . ..").

[89] Note, for example, that Kraakman's presentation of the corporation's intrinsic attributes (in his co-authored casebook) is implicitly contrasted here with his own historical work on the utility of distinct business entities, general incorporation, and limited liability.

through corporate governance. While a more granular account might include others, these levers minimally would include:

- *governance centralization*, reflecting the balance of power between boards and shareholders;
- *board liability exposure*, reflecting the degree of insulation (for example, business judgment rule protection) and the resulting strength of risk-taking incentives;
- *shareholder liability exposure*, reflecting the degree of insulation (that is, limited liability protection) and the resulting strength of risk-taking and monitoring incentives;
- *shareholder orientation*, reflecting the balance of emphasis between shareholders' and other stakeholders' interests; and
- *share transferability*, reflecting the degree of capital mobility into and out of the business.

For the reader's convenience Figure 3.1 provides a visual depiction of this corporate governance machinery.

It will be apparent that this schema starts with certain attributes included in the lists presented in Table 3.1, but re-conceptualizes each as a spectrum, inviting critical thought regarding where each lever ought to be set, and how the relevant balance ought to be struck. One important addition worth emphasizing, however, relates to board liability exposure – a curious omission from the lists of intrinsic attributes discussed above, given the widely acknowledged centrality in US corporate law of the business judgment rule and associated mechanisms aimed at regulating the personal liability of directors.[90]

Again, one could imagine a more granular account including any of a number of other levers. The aim is simply to illustrate the potential for a rendering capturing something of the corporate form's dynamism and flexibility – which these five levers suffice to convey. Depicted in these terms, one might readily imagine the typical public company looking something like Figure 3.2.

In this depiction the various levers are set to reflect the attributes typically associated with public companies the stock of which is widely

[90] See above notes 59–60 and the accompanying text. On the profound governance impacts of the business judgment rule see, e.g., M.M. Blair and L.A. Stout, "A Team Production Theory of Corporate Law" (1999) 85 *Virginia Law Review* 247 at 299–309; E. Elhauge, "Sacrificing Corporate Profits in the Public Interest" (2005) 80 *New York University Law Review* 733 at 770–6.

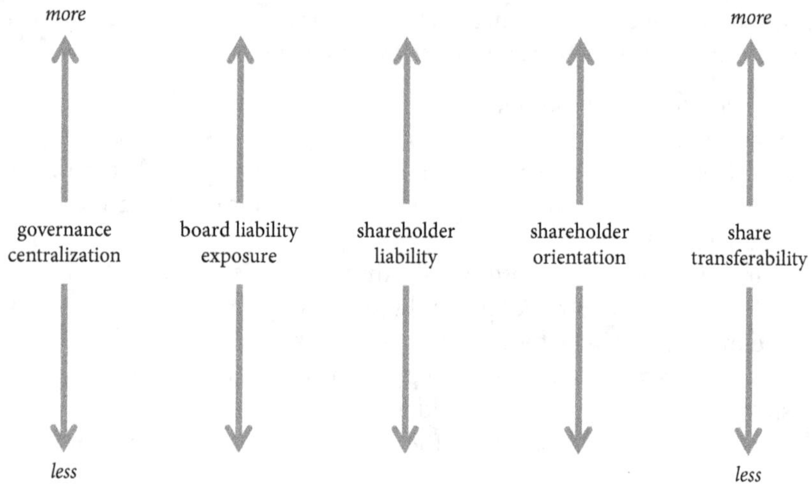

Figure 3.1 Corporate governance machinery: five levers

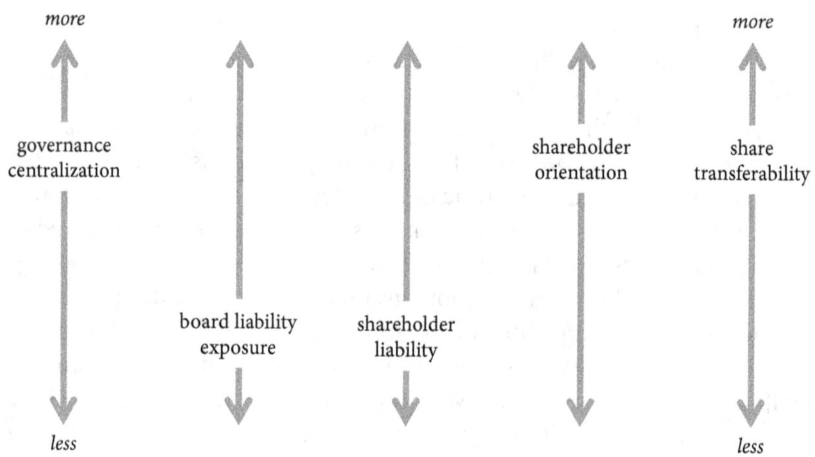

Figure 3.2 Corporate governance machinery: typical public company

dispersed – relatively more board power, relatively less liability exposure for boards and shareholders, relatively more emphasis on generating returns for shareholders, and relatively more investment liquidity. For the reasons discussed above, however, some refinements would be required in order to provide accurate comparative depictions of corporate governance

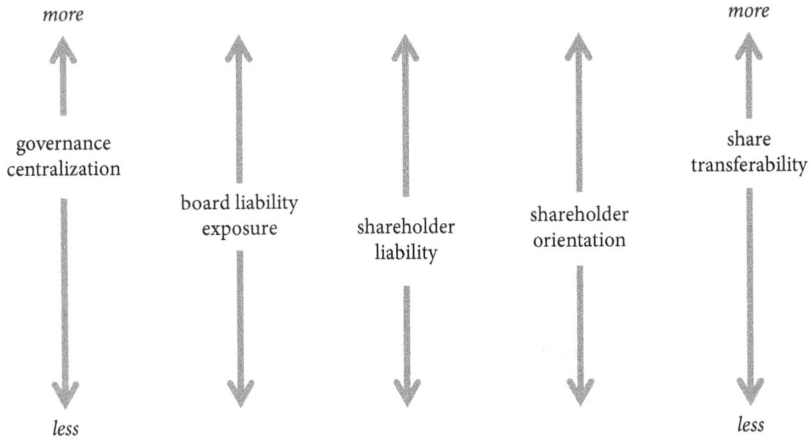

Figure 3.3 Corporate governance machinery: financial firms (historical)

in the United States and the United Kingdom. If Figure 3.2 were said to represent the typical US public company, for example, then a relative depiction of its UK counterpart would require adjusting "governance centralization" somewhat lower (reflecting the greater governance powers of UK shareholders), "shareholder orientation" somewhat higher (reflecting express statutory prioritization of their interests), and "share transferability" somewhat higher (reflecting UK shareholders' ability to limit takeover defenses).[91]

Looking further afield, then, starkly different configurations are entirely comprehensible, as we have seen – depicting, say, how bank governance functioned in the past (and how some have argued it might be improved in the future), as reflected in Figure 3.3.

Relative to the configuration now associated with the typical public company, this depiction reflects higher board and shareholder liability exposure (due to the more demanding duty of care and double liability rules historically applied), and lower shareholder orientation (due to designation of depositors as beneficiaries of director fiduciary duties).[92]

[91] See above notes 79–85 and the accompanying text.

[92] See above notes 69–71 and the accompanying text. Note that other adjustments might be required, based on these adjustments. For example, if shareholder liability exposure inspired heightened monitoring, perhaps "board centralization" would have to be adjusted downward as well.

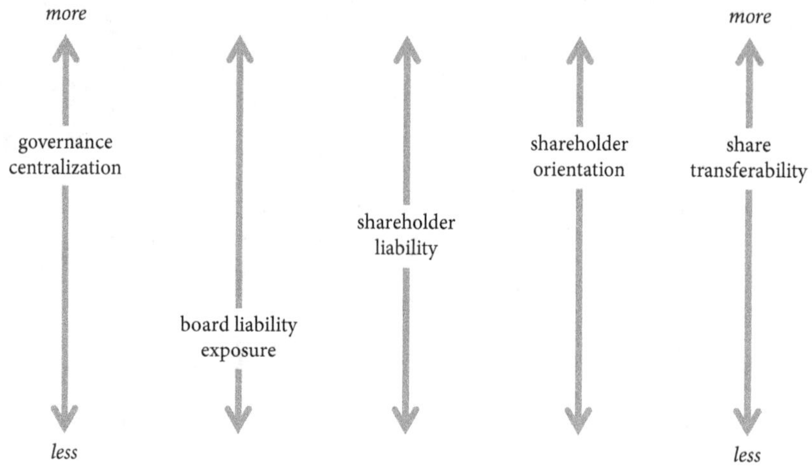

Figure 3.4 Corporate governance machinery: hazardous industries (Hansmann and Kraakman)

Critically, this mode of depicting the corporation's intrinsic capacities invites development of a creative impulse – broadly lacking among contemporary legislators, regulators, and judges[93] – regarding adjustments that might be made in a number of areas, toward a number of goals. For example, if we determined that more entrepreneurial risk-taking would be broadly favorable, then we might start with the depiction of a typical public company in Table 3.1 and set "board liability exposure" and "shareholder liability exposure" even lower. Conversely, if we determined that less risk-taking would be favorable, either broadly or in a particular industry such as finance, then precisely the opposite adjustments would be called for (as reflected in Figure 3.3). If we determined that particularly hazardous industries were imposing intolerable net costs on society, then – per Hansmann and Kraakman's proposal for an unlimited pro rata shareholder liability regime in tort – we might set "shareholder liability exposure" higher in those particular industries (while leaving "board liability exposure" alone), as reflected in Figure 3.4.[94]

If we determined that competitiveness concerns militated in favor of more corporate consolidations, then we might set "governance centralization" lower (giving shareholders more power), "shareholder orientation"

[93] See Bruner, above n 69 at 560–1. See also above notes 71–2 and accompanying text.

[94] See above notes 61–7 and the accompanying text.

higher (demanding greater focus on their interests), and "share transferability" higher (giving shareholders greater latitude to accept a hostile bid), as the UK takeover regime has effectively done. Conversely, if we determined that social concerns militated in favor of fewer corporate consolidations, then precisely the opposite adjustments would be called for, as the US takeover regime has effectively done.

3.5 Conclusion

There is no pretense here of answering the normative and political questions embedded in the foregoing in any particular industry context or any particular society, let alone in the abstract. Such value judgments require open and vigorous public debate.[95] The aim is to present the corporate form and corporate law in a manner that invites challenging questions that ought to be carefully considered and answered by policymakers too often inclined to accept the status quo as fixed and eternal.

Purporting to deduce answers to pressing economic and social policy questions implicating corporate governance by reference to a static conception of the corporate form comes at the matter from the wrong direction. Rather, we ought to be revisiting the corporate form itself to assess comprehensively the governance-related tools available, and how they might be deployed. To be sure, in some instances we might reasonably decide that extra-corporate legal and regulatory structures offer better means of attacking a particular problem.[96] Minimally, however, the sort of re-conceptualization of the corporate form offered here might help us ensure that we are asking the right questions, and thinking through the relevant trade-offs. In so doing, we may find that corporate governance offers a broader range of solutions than fixed conceptions of the corporate form now lead many to believe.

[95] See above notes 73–8 and the accompanying text.

[96] Cf. Bruner, above n 20 at 194–6 (discussing "the interrelated nature of corporate law, labor law, social welfare policy, and other forms of regulation in addressing risks faced by employees in large corporate enterprises").

PART II

The Company: Public or Private?

4

Understanding the Modern Company through the Lens of Quasi-Public Power

MARC T. MOORE

4.1 Introduction

The Anglo-American public company is one of the most heavily studied institutions within modern western society. However, over recent decades there has been an increasingly pervasive tendency amongst social-scientists – and particularly law and economics scholars – to seek to depict and understand companies in purely instrumental or anatomical terms, by reference to the prudential private incentives of their individual participants. Most notable in this regard is the influential "nexus of contracts" theory of the firm, which presents the company as a merely fictional negotiating hub around which its various economic "input-providers" notionally bargain with one another, to determine their respective shares of the economic "output" resulting from the firm's productive operations.[1]

Such reductionist and individualistic depictions of the company have an undoubted analytical value, insofar as they provide a simplified and intellectually digestible portrayal of an otherwise complex and multi-faceted subject matter. But this key analytical strength of the nexus of contracts paradigm is also – curiously – the theory's main conceptual weakness, insofar as its narrow fixation on private, consent-based interactions encumbers it

[1] See, e.g., A.A. Alchian and H. Demsetz, "Production, Information Costs and Economic Organization" (1972) 62 *American Economic Review* 777; M.C. Jensen and W. Meckling, "Theory of the Firm: Managerial Behavior, Agency Costs and Ownership Structure" (1976) 3 *Journal of Financial Economics* 305; E.F. Fama, "Agency Problems and the Theory of the Firm" (1980) 88 *Journal of Political Economy* 288; E.F. Fama and M.C. Jensen, "Separation of Ownership and Control" (1983) 26 *Journal of Law and Economics* 301; F.H. Easterbrook and D.R. Fischel, "The Corporate Contract" (1989) 89 *Columbia Law Review* 1416; F.H. Easterbrook and D.R. Fischel, *The Economic Structure of Corporate Law* (Cambridge: Harvard University Press, 1991), ch. 1; B.R. Cheffins, *Company Law: Theory, Structure and Operation* (Oxford University Press, 1997).

with a descriptive "blind spot" when it comes to the more "public" aspects of the company's structural architecture. In particular, by relying on the notion of implicit mutual consent – and, in turn, presumptive efficiency – as its ideological bedrock for explaining and legitimizing prevailing legal-institutional features of the company, the nexus of contracts model necessarily excludes from its ambit of vision the significant role of extra-contractual *power* in conditioning the company's inherent governance dynamics.[2]

Moreover, the concept of power – as it is typically manifested within the internal relational architecture of the modern company – cannot properly be understood by reference to the orthodox "private" reference point of the discrete reciprocal transaction. This is because, as will be explained below, the aspect of the corporation that is typically regarded as its most inherently private feature – namely the central equity relation between its shareholders and management – is, in itself, fundamentally *unrepresentative* of a discrete reciprocal transaction in the classically understood sense. In contrast, as will be shown, the corporate equity relation is in fact characterized by an inherent structural imbalance, as a result of which management is customarily vested with a significant ambit of power in allocating shareholders' invested funds. Such power, moreover, is *not fundamentally dissimilar from* the type of power exercised by the state in allocating public revenue streams committed by citizens. This is a phenomenon that will be referred to in the discussion that follows as management's "discretionary administrative power" (or DAP) vis-à-vis shareholders.

Essentially, DAP denotes the legally constituted capacity of an incorporated business entity to collect and administer externally contributed resources from investors on a centralized basis, and on unilaterally established terms that the contributing investors may *or may not* share. In this regard, DAP can be regarded as tantamount to a quasi-public power of ex ante taxation on corporate earnings via management's unilateral capacity for discretionary earnings retention, which is typically coupled with a corresponding ambit of unilateral executive discretion with respect to the specific ways in which such retained resources are allocated internally by management.

Accordingly, just as the public power of the state must be "checked" by effective accountability mechanisms to secure its legitimacy in the eyes of citizen subjects, so too – correspondingly – must the quasi-public power of the company (and, in particular, its management) be effectively "checked" so as to secure the continuing acquiescence of shareholders in their subjection to

[2] On this, see M.T. Moore, *Corporate Governance in the Shadow of the State* (Oxford: Hart Publishing, 2013), pp. 87–8.

management's discretionary prerogative. It will be suggested that this helps to explain the framework of mandatory corporate governance laws – especially those with respect to the annual shareholders' meeting (or, in UK companies, Annual General Meeting) and associated proxy process – which have the effect of compelling periodic account-giving by management to shareholders.

The present chapter thus proceeds as follows. First, it provides a working problematization of corporate power for the purpose of the examination at hand, focused on the so-called "internal" or proprietary-relational element of the corporate power dynamic, and – in particular – the unilateral power dynamic arising from the core corporate equity relation between management and shareholders. Here corporate power will be understood – for present purposes – in terms of the quasi-public phenomenon referred to above as DAP. This chapter subsequently examines the legal foundations of DAP in the above sense, noting in particular how the dual allocative and appropriative dimensions of DAP are underpinned by fundamental and longstanding corporate law doctrines. It then highlights the structural necessity of legitimizing DAP, as a necessary prelude to securing the continuing acquiescence of the subjects of such power in the ensuing relational imbalance. It will further be explained here how, in the context of the corporate equity relation, power-legitimacy is customarily reflected on a practical level in a criterion widely referred to as "cost of capital." Finally, this chapter explains the role of formal accountability mechanisms – both in corporate and non-corporate settings – in fulfilling the above power-legitimation function. It then illustrates this claim by reference to some of the core managerial accountability mechanisms that are mandated by US and UK corporate governance law. This chapter concludes by advancing an important normative claim based on the preceding analysis.

4.2 Problematizing Corporate Power

4.2.1 The Multifarious Nature of Power as a Social Phenomenon

Power is a ubiquitous phenomenon: it has been said that "next to sex and love, [it] is perhaps the oldest social phenomenon in human history."[3] However, power is also an opaque and contested phenomenon,[4] and

[3] A.A. Berle, Jr., *Power without Property: A New Development in American Political Economy* (New York: Harcourt, Brace & World, 1959), p. 77.

[4] J.E. Parkinson, *Corporate Power and Responsibility: Issues in the Theory of Company Law* (Oxford University Press, 1993), p. 8.

"[f]ew words are used so frequently with so little seeming need to reflect on their meaning."[5]

Constructing an objectively defensible definition of power is a highly difficult – some might say intractable – intellectual challenge.[6] To a Marxist, the notion of power denotes that prevailing economic, political, and legal institutions are inextricably linked to bourgeoisie class domination over industrial society. Feminist or critical theorists, meanwhile, frequently rely on the concept to refer to overt or tacit forms of societal domination stemming from other underlying factors such as gender, race, or technology.

Even within the specific *corporate* domain, the origins, nature, and significance of power remain largely ambiguous issues. While law and economics scholars typically conceptualize power in the narrow and relationship-specific guise of "agency costs,"[7] progressive theorists have advanced a broader understanding of corporate power in terms of "social decision-making power"[8]: that is to say, the discretion that socially significant corporations enjoy to "make private decisions which have public results."[9] Indeed, corporate power has been described as "one of the great enigmas of political science . . . [a] complex phenomenon possessing economic, legal, political, and social significance."[10]

Within social-scientific literature, corporate power has been categorized as taking two distinct but overlapping forms, namely "internal" and "external" power. According to Bowman, the internal dimension of corporate power denotes power arising from the contractual or quasi-contractual control relationships intrinsic to the functioning of the firm as a productive entity. This is in distinction from the external dimension, which encapsulates the power wielded by corporations within the broader framework of society including their political lobbying power and consequent influence over the governmental policy-making process.[11]

[5] J.K. Galbraith, *The Anatomy of Power* (Boston: Houghton Mifflin, 1983), p. 1.

[6] Interpreted in its most general sense, power can be defined as "the ability of A to cause B to behave in a manner intended by A that B would not have done without A's intervention"; insofar as "A has some form of control over B, or at least a strong bargaining position that enables A to score a 'victory' over B." See Parkinson, above n 4 at 8.

[7] See, e.g., Jensen and Meckling, above n 1.

[8] See Parkinson, above n 4 at 10.

[9] *Ibid.*

[10] S.R. Bowman, *The Modern Corporation and American Political Thought: Law, Power and Ideology* (University Park, PA: Penn State University Press, 1996), p. 1.

[11] See *ibid.* especially chs. 2–4.

Given the complexity and substantive indeterminacy of corporate power, any rigorous academic account of the concept must inevitably adopt a degree of selectivity in defining its subject matter. The present chapter will therefore focus exclusively on *internal* corporate power. This type of power is of particular interest from the perspective of corporate lawyers, in that it pertains directly to the corporate equity relation between shareholders and management, which is generally acknowledged to lie at the heart of corporate governance as it is conventionally understood in both the United States and the United Kingdom.[12]

4.2.2 Internal Corporate Power as Discretionary Administrative Power

The most comprehensive and renowned academic exponent of the power phenomenon (at least within the English-speaking world) as it exists in the economic-organizational context is the economist John Kenneth Galbraith. For this reason, Galbraith's definition of power represents the most appropriate theoretical starting point in any enquiry into the nature of corporate power viewed from a legal perspective.

Fundamentally, Galbraith understood power in Weberian terms as enabling the imposition by some person or group of "its will and purpose or purposes on others, including on those who are reluctant or adverse."[13] Galbraith observed that *all* organizations – economic or otherwise – are by their very nature sources of power in this sense, insofar as the essence of an organization is "a number of persons or groups . . . united for some purpose or work."[14] This presupposes that the relevant individuals "in one degree or another, have *submitted to* the purposes of the organization in pursuit of some common purpose."[15]

However, the business corporation – in comparison to other non-corporate organizational forms – is possessed with an extraordinary capacity to impose its will and purposes on others in the Galbrathian sense. This is on account of a phenomenon that will be termed *discretionary administrative power* (or DAP), which is largely (albeit not wholly) distinct to the corporate form of economic organization. In essence, DAP denotes

[12] This is not to deny, though, that the scope of external power wielded by a corporation vis-à-vis wider society is affected *indirectly* by its internal legal constitution of power.

[13] Galbraith, above n 5 at 2.

[14] *Ibid.*

[15] *Ibid.* at 55 (emphasis added).

the capacity that public companies enjoy to collect and administer the resources or funds of others in the pursuit of autonomously determined objectives that the contributors may *or may not* commonly share.

DAP arises where an organization collects and administers externally contributed economic resources from investors on a centralized and substantially autonomous basis, and in an endeavor in which the external resource providers retain a common material interest. Thus DAP necessarily entails the sacrifice by an individual investor of her autonomy or freedom of action with respect to a given asset or resource, in the expectation that this will ultimately bring about a net gain in her material welfare. The situation can be rationalized in accordance with social contract logic, insofar as a group of individuals submit part of their individual freedom of action over economic affairs to centralized organizational control, in return for the benefits that they each stand to derive as passive beneficiaries of some greater collective scheme.[16]

The concept of DAP in the above sense is manifested most extensively in the governmental context, where social services and/or productive functions are administered within the bureaucratic state apparatus using public economic resources. In a communist command economy, the primary economic resource advanced by citizens in this regard is their labor or human capital. In the archetypical case, such capital is allocated and coordinated by government unilaterally in the service of centrally determined social objectives; the most common of which being the generation of a sufficient quantity of essential goods and services to satisfy projected public need. In a liberal market economy, on the other hand, the main economic resource collected by government is public taxation revenues. These revenues are then used to purchase human and physical capital on free and decentralized labor and goods markets in the pursuit of objectives that are, in the last place, determined democratically.

In both instances, however, the basic point stands that a collectivized process of resource accumulation – and subsequent administration – is taking place. The only differences are the identity of the principal resource that is being accumulated by government (whether human or financial capital), and the extent of the public accumulation process as a proportion of overall national economic activity; such proportion typically being much higher in command economies than in market economies.

[16] For the classical philosophical exposition of this concept, see T. Hobbes, *The Leviathan* (Harmondsworth: Penguin, 1968).

When one moves from the public to the private sector of a market economy, a fundamentally similar tendency can be observed within the corporate form of economic organization. In the same way that the dual institutions of taxation and executive government permit the centralized administration of public resources, the significant powers vested by law in *corporate* controllers enable the collectivization of privately invested capital *outside of* the democratic state apparatus. The existence of DAP in the corporate setting accordingly provides the basis for a form of non-statist quasi-taxation, whereby formally private officeholders wield substantial discretion in appropriating and allocating economic resources outside of the reach of direct proprietary or democratic control.[17]

There are two distinct but interlocking components of DAP that together constitute the basis of the corporation's characteristic autonomy in this regard. The first of these is *allocative* power, which relates to the range of uses or "ends" to which an invested (financial or non-financial) resource can be devoted *without* the specific agreement of the resource provider. The second constituent component of DAP is *appropriative* power, which denotes the legal capacity of corporate controllers to determine the rate of return on an externally provided resource *without* seeking the direct consent of the resource provider thereto. In this way – as will be explained below – appropriative power gives a corporation considerable latitude to establish its current rate of capital accumulation, and also the extent to which such accumulation will be financed at the collective expense of its external resource providers.

4.2.3 *Power Imbalance in the Corporate Equity Relation*

It is widely accepted by law and finance scholars that equity or "risk" capital represents a unique form of investment, especially in the context of business enterprise. While debt is a largely "fixed" or contractually determinate method of financing in terms of durability, price, and terms of advancement, equity on the other hand is inherently "open-ended": that is to say, it is contractually *indeterminate* with regard to its longevity, compensatory rate of return, and also the substantive conditions under which its productive use in enterprise is sanctioned.[18]

[17] On the common fundamental features of the centralized resource accumulation process within communistic and capitalistic-corporate organizations, see Berle, above n 3 at 151.

[18] See O.E. Williamson, *The Mechanisms of Governance* (Oxford University Press, 1996), ch. 7; O.D. Hart, "Incomplete Contracts and the Theory of the Firm" (1988) 4 *Journal of Law, Economics and Organization* 119.

From this premise, it is commonly argued that the technical incapacity of equity investors to exercise effective control over their capital by orthodox contractual means necessitates that they be protected instead via extra-contractual hierarchical rights over the productive venture in which that capital is used.[19] It follows that equity investors should be granted ultimate power of direction over the *entire enterprise* in which their capital is invested,[20] together with the corresponding entitlement to appropriate surplus cash flows in excess of the firm's fixed contractual liabilities to other (non-equity) investors.[21] This reasoning purportedly explains why equity (as opposed to debt or human) capital in the ordinary case "owns" the business firm, in the sense of enjoying residual control and distributional rights in it, as ex ante compensation for standing last in line in the event of any periodic or terminal distribution of its funds or assets.[22]

In the case of *unincorporated* business entities the above logic could certainly be said to hold true. In such instances, the equity investor's peculiar contractual vulnerability can be regarded as a quid quo pro trade-off for the exclusive management and agency rights that he or she enjoys in respect of the running of the firm's business, whether individually (as a sole proprietor) or collectively (as a partner). It can accordingly be said that the equity investor here gives up full ex ante control over her capital in return for pervasive proprietary powers of direction, appropriation, and disposal over the firm as a whole including its unsecured assets and cash flows.[23]

In the corporate[24] setting, however, such structural reciprocity is not present in the equity relation. Indeed, the essence of *corporate* governance

[19] See G. Kelly and J. Parkinson, "The Conceptual Foundations of the Company: A Pluralist Approach," in A. Gamble, G. Kelly and J. Parkinson (eds.), *The Political Economy of the Company* (Oxford: Hart Publishing, 2000), ch. 6, p. 120.

[20] See Williamson, above n 18 at 567, 579.

[21] Within the latter group are included not only professional and unprofessional (i.e. trade) debt investors, but also human capital investors (i.e. employees).

[22] In this context, the term "ownership" is deployed in a purely technical sense to denote the purported status of equity investors as exclusive collective bearers of the residual risk of firm's underperformance or failure. It is thus not intended to denote any of the moral-proprietary considerations traditionally associated with ownership in the orthodox (i.e. non-corporate) sense of the term. For a critical perspective on the notion of corporate ownership, see P. Ireland, "Company Law and the Myth of Shareholder Ownership" (1999) 62 *Modern Law Review* 32.

[23] See S.J. Grossman and O.D. Hart, "The Costs and Benefits of Ownership: A Theory of Vertical and Lateral Integration" (1986) 94 *Journal of Political Economy* 691 at 692.

[24] The word "corporate" in this context is used to refer specifically to *public* or widely held corporations. In private or closely held incorporated firms, the common dual capacity of equity investors as shareholder-directors, or at least close associates or overseers of management, frequently gives them the effective status of "quasi-partners" (and thus quasi-owners) irrespective of their formal legal control rights over the firm.

as an organizational activity is that it necessarily entails submission by equity investors of executive authority to a substantially autonomous central body (namely the board of directors, and – indirectly – the board's senior-managerial delegates), which is charged with coordinating the various inputs of external resource providers in pursuit of internally formulated objectives and strategies.[25] More fundamentally, since independent corporate personhood acts as a formal ownership partition between the respective assets of the corporate entity and its shareholders, the act of *corporate* equity investment consequently demands outright submission by investors of any proprietary entitlement to their capital whether in money or physical asset form.[26] Instead, equity investors acquire the relatively limited and artificially prescribed bundle of rights consequent to their shareholding in the company,[27] with the curious effect that *no one* – except for the corporate entity itself – can be said to own the company in either a juridical or beneficial sense.[28]

It logically follows that no external resource – *even equity* – is legally entitled to usurp the board's constitutional prerogative to control the company's business affairs and transact on its behalf (whether directly or, in the more common case, indirectly by delegated managerial authority), except in the specific ways (if any) that are provided for in advance by the corporate constitution.[29] Indeed, a fundamental trade-off at the heart of any large-scale organization, including business corporations, is that the freedom of action of the organization itself is – in large part – contingent on the denial of formal executive influence to individual organizational participants. In other words, corporate autonomy is – by its very nature – paradoxically predicated on the collective *loss of* individual autonomy by corporate resource providers in determining the direction

[25] On this generally, see S.M. Bainbridge, "Director Primacy: The Means and Ends of Corporate Governance" (2003) 97 *Northwestern University Law Review* 547.

[26] On the dual corporate legal attributes of "defensive" and "affirmative" asset partitioning, see H. Hansmann and R. Kraakman, "The Essential Role of Organizational Law" (2000) 110 *Yale Law Journal* 387.

[27] For an influential judicial exposition of the Hohfeldian concept of the corporate share as a "bundle of rights," see *Borland's Trustee* v. *Steel Bros. & Co.* [1901] 1 Ch. 279 at 288.

[28] For judicial dictum to this effect, see *Short* v. *Treasury Commissioners* [1948] 1 KB 116 (CA) at 122; *Gramophone and Typewriter Co.* v. *Stanley* [1908] 2 KB 89; *Macaura* v. *Northern Assurance Co.* [1925] AC 619 (HL). See also Ireland, above n 22 at 47.

[29] See *Automatic Self-Cleansing Filter Syndicate Co.* v. *Cunninghame* [1906] 2 Ch. 34 (CA); *John Shaw & Sons* v. *Shaw* [1935] 2 KB 113. For an influential academic rationalization of this position (in a US context), see M. Blair and L.A. Stout, "A Team Production Theory of Corporate Law" (1999) 85 *Virginia Law Review* 248.

of the enterprise in which their capital is invested.[30] This inherent tension between individual and corporate autonomy stems from the fact that, where bureaucratic scale and complexity render egalitarian methods of rule impractical or inefficient, effective organizational control necessitates prioritizing hierarchy over accountability as the principal criterion of governance effectiveness.[31]

Therefore, in contrast to the situation with unincorporated entities, the sacrifice by corporate equity investors of determinative control over their capital is *not* matched by the corresponding acquisition of control over the productive enterprise in which their invested capital is mobilized. The consequent incapacity of equity investors to constrain the exercise of the board's managerial prerogative whether contractually or hierarchically means that – in contrast to other corporate resource providers – equity investors are *entirely subjected* to the DAP of the corporation and its controlling officers. The effect is to render the corporate equity relation uniquely indeterminate and vulnerable from the investor's perspective insofar as both the rate of return on equity, and also the uses to which such capital is put, are inherently uncertain and susceptible to ongoing variation by management on a unilateral (that is non-negotiated) basis.

4.3 The Legal Foundations of Internal Corporate Power Imbalance

Both the allocative and appropriative dimensions of the DAP possessed by a corporation vis-à-vis its equity investors are attributable to the corporation's unique structural characteristic of centralized board decision-making. This feature is in turn principally dependent on two fundamental and interlocking corporate law principles.

The first of these is the principle of board primacy,[32] which entitles the board of directors (or, more commonly, its senior-managerial delegates) to make executive policy decisions with respect to the internal allocation of corporate cash flows unimpeded by interference from shareholders or

[30] On this, see Berle, above n 3 at 81.

[31] On this, see Bainbridge, above n 25; K.J. Arrow, *The Limits of Organization* (New York: Norton, 1974), pp. 68–70.

[32] I have deliberately used the term "board primacy" in distinction from Professor Stephen Bainbridge's term "director primacy." However, both terms should be regarded as essentially equivalent in meaning. I deviate from Professor Bainbridge with respect to terminology in the personal belief that the former term better depicts the collective (as opposed to individual) nature of the executive decision-making authority that is vested in corporate directors. On Bainbridge's concept of director primacy, see Bainbridge, above n 25.

other "outside" parties. The second such principle is that of board control over corporate dividends, whereby the board of directors is vested with exclusive constitutional power to set the uppermost limit on the extent to which the corporation's periodic profits will be distributed to shareholders, as opposed to being appropriated by management internally in the form of retained earnings.

Under the law of the US State of Delaware, where the majority of larger listed US corporations are registered, the executive primacy of the board is established by section 141 of the State's General Corporation Law, which affirms that "[t]he business and affairs of every corporation . . . shall be managed by or under the direction of a board of directors."[33] The same basic position is established within UK company law by Article 3 of the governmentally prescribed Model Articles, which provides that "[s]ubject to the articles, the directors are responsible for the management of the company's business, for which purpose they may exercise all the powers of the company."[34] Under the law of both jurisdictions, moreover, the board's supreme managerial function is constituted not just as a responsibility but, more significantly, as a constitutional *right* (or, more accurately, a set of constitutionally guaranteed powers) that is consequently defensible by the board against any outside party or group – including equity – which seeks to challenge or displace the board's executive prerogative in any regard.[35]

Within the traditional US legal model of corporate governance, the principle of board primacy is carried to its logical extreme insofar as the board's powers are, at common law, deemed to be "original and undelegated . . . in the sense of being received from the State in the act of incorporation."[36] According to this logic, "the individual directors making up the board are not mere employees, but [rather are] a part of an elected body of officers constituting the executive agents of the corporation."[37] Furthermore, a company's constitutional charter is purportedly vested with the force of law by virtue of the act of incorporation alone, meaning

33 Delaware General Corporation Law § 141(a).

34 The Companies (Model Articles) Regulations 2008 (SI 2008 No. 3229), Schedule 3 ("Model Articles for Public Companies"), art. 3.

35 On this, see *Automatic Self-Cleansing Filter Syndicate*, above n 29; *John Shaw & Sons*, above n 29. For an influential academic rationalization of this position (in a US context), see Blair and Stout, above n 29.

36 *Hoyt* v. *Thompson's Executor*, 19 NY 207 at 216 (Court of Appeals of New York) (1859) (per Comstock J.).

37 *People ex rel. Manice* v. *Powell*, 201 NY 194 at 201 (Court of Appeals of New York) (1911) (per Chase J.).

that the corporate governance arrangements established in the charter – as supplemented by generally applicable corporate laws – are perceived to emanate directly from the State as the formal grantor of corporate status. It follows that, insofar as the corporate charter and general law (at individual State level) vest executive authority for the running of the business in the hands of a company's board (as opposed to its shareholders), then the board's constitutional discretion over executive affairs can be regarded as sovereign and absolute.[38]

Thus shareholders of Delaware corporations, inter alia, have no right to give any legally binding directions – whether specific or general – to the board regarding the running of the business,[39] or to acquire any broader constitutional authority over managerial affairs absent the assent thereto of the board itself.[40] More fundamentally, section 141 arguably establishes the board's executive prerogative as an inalienable phenomenon, meaning that shareholders are necessarily precluded from revoking the board's decision-making supremacy within the corporate-organizational hierarchy.

Therefore, whereas in unincorporated firms, equity has hierarchical superiority over (delegated) management; in Delaware corporations, this lexical order is reversed so that equity is hierarchically subordinated to the board (and, indirectly, management), with the latter constituting the supreme executive and rulemaking organ within the corporate-constitutional framework, and the former representing little more than an economic functionary with no "sovereign" governance status.[41] Moreover, as a result of Delaware law's underlying presumption in favor

[38] See *Hoyt*, above n 36; *Olcott* v. *Tioga Railroad Co.*, 27 NY 546 (1863); *Continental Securities Co.* v. *Belmont*, 206 NY 7 (1912).

[39] On the contrasting position of UK corporate law in this regard, see the Model Articles for Public Companies, above n 34, art. 4.

[40] See L.A. Bebchuk, "The Case for Increasing Shareholder Power" (2005) 118 *Harvard Law Review* 833 at 844–5. While shareholders admittedly have joint authority (alongside the board) under Delaware law to initiate changes to the corporation's bylaws, the necessary invalidity of any bylaw provisions that contradict the superseding charter of incorporation (which only the board may initiate amendments to) renders this power of limited practical effectiveness. See Delaware General Corporation Law § 109(b).

[41] In addition to their structural exclusion from managerial affairs in the above ways, shareholders have no legally guaranteed power under Delaware law to remove directors without cause before expiration of office. Rather, the "default" statutory right that shareholders enjoy in this regard can be disapplied (or "opted out of") by a corporation on the voluntary classification of its board. The effect is to render the directors of many Delaware corporations formally irremovable throughout the period of their official tenure. See Delaware General Corporation Law § 141(d).

of management control, the board – and, indirectly, its senior-managerial delegates – are in effect vested "by default" with any corporate functions or powers not specifically reserved for shareholders.[42]

It is thus arguable that residual legal "ownership" of US corporations – if it can be said to rest with any particular constituency – resides squarely in *the board* (and, indirectly, senior management) rather than the shareholders. This position is, of course, contrary to the orthodox portrayal of equity's formal status within the firm as expounded within law and finance literature. And, significantly for present purposes, it serves to highlight the extensive degree of DAP with which US boards – and, in turn, managers – are formally vested in allocating equity as a corporate resource.

The British legal model of corporate governance is commonly portrayed as being much more shareholder-centric than its US counterpart, and in some specific regulatory respects this is undoubtedly true. However, the most fundamental conceptual difference between the two systems is the fact that, under UK company law, the corporate constitution – including any corporate governance arrangements established therein – is vested with the formal status of a private (and thus alterable) contractual agreement binding together a company's "members" or shareholders.[43]

Prima facie, the exclusive quasi-membership entitlement of shareholders to act as signatories to the notional corporate-constitutional "contract" might be thought to confer a corresponding degree of hierarchical supremacy over a company's controlling officers. However, the foundational English case law on the division of corporate decision-making power makes clear that the legal relationship between a company's shareholders and board of directors is a reciprocal one between contracting equals, as opposed to a hierarchical relation founded on any sense of either group – whether shareholders or the board – enjoying constitutional supremacy over the other.

This position was put most emphatically by Greer LJ in *John Shaw & Sons v. Shaw*, who explained the doctrinal nature of the board primacy principle at common law in the following (resolutely *non*-hierarchical) terms:

> If powers of management are vested in the directors, they and they alone can exercise those powers. The only way in which the general body of shareholders can control the exercise of the powers vested by the articles in the directors is by altering the articles, or, if the opportunity arises under the

[42] On the development of US (and particularly Delaware) corporate law's general presumption in favor of managerial (over shareholder) control, see Bowman, above n 10, ch. 3.

[43] See Companies Act 2006, s. 33.

> articles, by refusing to re-elect the directors of whose actions they disapprove. *They cannot themselves usurp the powers which by the articles are vested in the directors any more than the directors can usurp the powers vested by the articles in the general body of shareholders.*[44]

It follows that shareholders have no subjective power over the corporation or its management under UK company law, in the sense of any general capacity to demand deference to their expressed interests.[45] On the contrary, UK company law – like its Delaware counterpart – ultimately affirms the DAP of the board (and, indirectly, management) by establishing that shareholders are, in the ordinary course of things,[46] formally *subject to* the executive prerogative of the board with respect to the allocation of corporate cash flows – including externally invested equity – in the service of centrally determined organizational objectives.[47]

Accordingly, whereas in the United States – as explained above – management's allocative power vis-à-vis equity derives at root from the board's exclusive and statutorily entrenched prerogative over internal corporate affairs, in the United Kingdom, by comparison, such power is understood to derive from the notional mutual agreement of shareholders and directors regarding the proper allocation of decision-making powers within the corporate-constitutional framework. Structurally, however, the basic doctrinal result – namely *board primacy* – is the same in both environments.[48]

The board primacy doctrine is supplemented and reinforced by the second major legal principle underpinning DAP in the corporate equity relation, which is the principle of board control over corporate dividends. This latter principle is the doctrinal source of the board's traditional and continuing authority to divert corporate cash flows to capital

[44] *John Shaw & Sons*, above n 29 at 134 (emphasis added).

[45] It may be argued that managerial deference to shareholders' interests is compelled by the director's general statutory duty of loyalty under Companies Act 2006, s. 172, which requires directors to promote the success of their employer company for the benefit of its shareholders as a whole. However, the duty of loyalty – like all directors' general duties – operates exclusively on an ex post facto basis as a response to conduct already committed or proposed by directors, and in any event defers wide subjective discretion on the board (and, indirectly, management) in conducting the company's business affairs.

[46] That is, at least pending usurpation of the board's managerial powers by collective amendment of the articles under Companies Act 2006, s. 21, which in a public company is both highly impractical and also counter to the basic logic of the corporation as a business entity characterized by centralized control and oversight.

[47] See M.T. Moore and A. Rebérioux, "Revitalizing the Institutional Roots of Anglo-American Corporate Governance" (2011) 40 *Economy and Society* 84 at 97–9.

[48] *Ibid.* at 99.

accumulation, most notably via unilateral retention of dividends. As such, it represents – in conjunction with the more general board primacy doctrine – the formal foundation of the significant *appropriative* power that exists in the corporate equity relation.

Under Delaware law, the board is vested with ultimate constitutional control over the declaration and payment of dividends as a default statutory rule, with the effect that shareholders have no formal power to displace directors' collective determination in these regards.[49] While UK law by contrast vests the default power to declare dividends in the shareholders by way of ordinary resolution, any resolution to declare a dividend is necessarily contingent on the board first recommending the amount of dividend that is to be declared.[50] Crucially, shareholders are in the ordinary course of things prohibited from declaring a dividend higher than the amount that is recommended by the directors.[51] The effect of the above provision is that, in virtually all US and UK public companies, shareholders are formally excluded from the important periodic decision as to whether a company's free cash flow should be retained and reinvested within the business internally, or else distributed to shareholders for subsequent reinvestment or consumption on a macro (i.e. economy-wide) level. This is the essence of the appropriative power phenomenon as it operates within the wider social context.

The concept of appropriative power has historically been the most conspicuous and, consequently, controversial dimension of DAP within the corporate decision-making framework. One of the most noted critics of this aspect of corporate power was Adolf Berle, who observed that its effect is to vest a public company's management with unchecked discretion over "whether and to what extent its profits shall be distributed, and to what extent these profits shall be dedicated to capital formation."[52] The most worrying implication of appropriative power, according to Berle, is its tendency to permit "perpetual accumulation" by corporations with "no top limit" thereon.[53] Berle described the practice of discretionary corporate earnings retention as a form of "forced savings" imposed by managers on both shareholders and consumers (to whom the benefits of corporate

49 Delaware General Corporation Law § 170(a).

50 Model Articles for Public Companies, above n 34, art. 70(2).

51 *Ibid.*

52 Berle, above n 3 at 52.

53 *Ibid.* Indeed, in this regard, it is worth noting that the total amount of global corporate cash reserves (as of 2014) has recently been estimated at $7 trillion (or £4.5 trillion). See B. Marlow and A. Armstrong, "Global Firms Sitting on $7 Trillion Dollar War Chest," *The Telegraph*, 17 August 2014.

profitability are consequently not passed on), which is tantamount to "a sales tax whose proceeds were ticketed for capital expansion of the corporation" without prior public consultation.[54]

4.4 The Structural Imperative of Legitimizing Internal Corporate Power

4.4.1 The Centrality of Power-Legitimacy in Sustaining Internal Power Imbalance

In any organization where the power of senior officeholders rests on the consent of the direct subjects of that power, the formal accountability of officeholders to subjects is of key importance in securing the *legitimacy* of the former group's possession and exercise of executive power. "Legitimacy" is understood here to denote a general and inherent quality of public "rightness."

In the context of social organizations and power structures (including business corporations), such rightness derives from a popular understanding "that the holders of power are considered by the community to be justified in their tenure of it," so that "the system conforms to the general consensus on a moral base."[55] Basic social contract logic dictates that the holder of power should not be free to exercise it in her own interest, but rather in the interests of those affected by it. Hence the distinctive feature of a non-totalitarian governance system is that the centralization of power, which is necessary for administrative efficiency, is counterbalanced by "checks" placed on that power.[56]

[54] Berle, above n 3 at 148. Berle noted the fundamental parallels between this process and the system of arbitrary conscription of productive capital by the state in the command economy of the Soviet Union at the time of his writing. However, he believed that in the American system, the process of "capital gathering . . . is better since the taking is painless, is acquiesced in, and provides comfortably for future development, while the Soviet system is obviously marred by compulsion" (*ibid.* at 151). Moreover, it may be said that in instances where retained earnings are dedicated not to capital formation but rather to other more socially objectionable forms of corporate expenditure (e.g. managerial enrichment or "empire building"), the politically problematic character of the practice is exacerbated. This is because, in such cases, the community is effectively being "taxed" for the support of activities or projects that – unlike industrial capital formation – cannot be said to have acquiesced in even in the broadest possible sense, thereby establishing a material democratic deficit at the level of society as a whole.

[55] A.A. Berle, Jr., *The American Economic Republic* (New York: Harcourt, Brace & World, 1963), p. 42.

[56] Moore and Rebérioux, above n 47 at 94.

Where the use of power is subjected, by appropriate institutional checks, to the collective will of the subjects of that power, the resulting governance framework can be referred to – in the words of the liberal political philosopher Alan Gewirth – as a "hierarchy of authority."[57] That is to say, the possession and exercise of DAP is legitimately authorized – or at least widely acquiesced in – by those who are principally affected by it.[58] It follows that the individual contractual autonomy or freedom[59] of those subject to the relevant power is not undermined, or – at least – where it is, any such loss of autonomy can be regarded as a generally acceptable trade-off for the material benefits that follow from submission to the authority structure in question. Consequently in such cases, organizational and individual autonomy can legitimately (and thus sustainably) co-exist even though the pursuit of collective corporate objectives will inevitably entail curtailment of the pursuit of individual goals by the subjects of authority.

On the other hand, where these conditions are in large part absent from an organization's governance framework, the organization in question is more appropriately termed a "hierarchy of power."[60] In such instances, the absence of subordinate authorization for the possession and exercise of power by senior officeholders means that the latter's position and privileges are incapable of deriving legitimacy from representational criteria.[61] Accordingly, the dual phenomena of organizational and individual

[57] See A. Gewirth, *The Community of Rights* (University of Chicago Press, 1996), p. 271.

[58] *Ibid.* This institutional characteristic is most clearly manifested in liberal-democratic political systems, where the dual phenomena of free contested elections and the rule of law ensure that incumbent officeholders lack determinative control over their successors to government, and also over the constitutionally established scope of their executive powers – both of which are, in the last place, determined at the collective behest of citizens.

[59] My understanding of the often-nebulous term "freedom" in this context is premised on Gewirth's understanding of freedom as individual autonomy. In Gewirthian political philosophy, freedom is explained as a logically necessary precondition of action and successful action in general as a prospective purposive agent. Accordingly "all persons have a generic right to freedom, which consists in controlling one's behavior by one's unforced choice while having knowledge of relevant circumstances." See *ibid.* at 18–19, 266. Admittedly, this very short summary can in no way do justice to the intellectual richness and complexity of Gewirth's theory of rights and his Principle of Generic Consistency (PGC).

[60] *Ibid.*

[61] This is on the commonly held understanding within liberal-democratic political economies that "[p]ower (aside from its crude or brute form) cannot exist apart from some idea or principle justifying it and, therefore, entitling holders of it to expect allegiance and cooperation." See Berle, above n 3 at 100. However, this is notwithstanding the fact that, within *non*-representational governance frameworks, popular elections may comprise at least a nominal part of the formal leadership selection process and a formal source of the system's public legitimacy. A notable example of this is the political system of the People's Republic

autonomy will be incapable of co-existing in a legitimate manner, insofar as sacrifice of individual freedom of action will be widely regarded as an unjustifiable concession on the part of those subject to the unauthorized power in question.

Crucially, the fact that a particular organizational power structure may, as a matter of fact, be overall efficient or utility-maximizing from an economic point of view does not eliminate the possibility that its conditions may still fail to secure the acquiescence of those directly subject to the relevant power. On the assumption that organizational participants operate under conditions of bounded rationality (and consequent informational incompleteness), there will inevitably be an informational disparity between "inside" (managerial) officeholders and (non-managerial) "outsiders" insofar as the former group – by virtue of its innate positional advantage – will have greater access than the latter group to organization-relevant knowledge and expertise. This renders it impossible for outsider participants to determine reliably whether their submission to internal organizational goals represents an acceptable price to pay in return for the material benefits that are expected to flow from organizational membership. It follows that some degree of formal accountability (or checks) on the exercise of executive power is an essential structural precondition to securing widespread membership "buy-in" to the ensuing power imbalance, in the absence of complete or equal informational access between organizational participants.[62]

4.4.2 Cost of Capital as the Principal Criterion of Internal Corporate Power-Legitimacy

In the democratic governmental context, the legitimacy of senior executive officeholders' continuing possession and exercise of DAP (what may be referred to in shorthand as "executive power-legitimacy") is, in general,

of China, whereby the principle of universal franchise is constitutionally guaranteed in form, albeit substantially meaningless in practice given the ruling Communist Party's pervasive control over the electoral process.

[62] In this regard, Bowman has observed (writing in the context of US society) that "[t]he conception of *balance* as a remedy for concentrated power permeates the fabric of American institutions and informs the distinctive development of American liberalism." The logic of Madisonian Republicanism dictates that, so long as organizational power is politically "checked" by a "systemic balance of forces" to prevent it from straying out of its proper functional bounds, such power can be exercised both legitimately *and* largely autonomously within those bounds – thus functioning in effect as a form of "limited oligarchy." On this, see Bowman, above n 10 at 217 (emphasis added).

manifested in their popular mandate to hold office as reflected in periodic election outcomes and ongoing opinion polls. Vice versa, revocation of the mandate to govern is manifested in the withdrawal of public support for incumbent officeholders, which renders their continuing possession and exercise of executive power normatively unsustainable.

However, given the general informational disparity between governmental and non-governmental actors, and the resultant incapacity of "outsider" citizens or representatives to exert effective control over the executive allocation of public revenue streams via executive appointment alone, it follows that other supplementary accountability (or "checking") mechanisms are called for in order to secure the continuing acquiescence of citizens in the centralized possession and exercise of DAP within the state-organizational framework. Hence the preponderance of transparency requirements, committee structures, and other formalized review mechanisms, which have the collective effect of ensuring that, in any developed democratic state, public-governmental powers are possessed and exercised in a manner that – broadly speaking – is acquiesced in by the subject citizenry as a whole.

In the corporate context, meanwhile, executive power-legitimacy is, in general, manifested in a criterion that can crudely be termed "cost of capital." For the purpose of the argument at hand, cost of capital should be understood as denoting the general willingness of outside investors to purchase a firm's securities (especially equity) on primary and secondary markets. Such willingness is contingent not just on the perceived risk-adjusted return that an investor expects to make by purchasing the firm's securities, but also on the opportunity cost of that investment: that is, the return that an investor expects to receive from an alternative investment at the same price and with the same risk exposure. It follows that the firm (or, specifically, its management), by reducing the perceived risk exposure of its securities (all other factors being equal) will effect a reduction in its cost of capital insofar as an alternative lower-risk investment will have lower projected net returns than an alternative higher-risk investment (after accounting for risk), thereby increasing the relative attractiveness of the firm's securities and – in turn – the market valuation of its equity.[63]

To the extent that the continuing survival of a firm is ordinarily contingent to some extent on access to outside investment, maintaining a low cost of capital can be regarded as a central managerial goal in its own right. However, cost of capital is for the most part a means to an end from

[63] On this concept generally, see F. Modigliani and M. Miller, "The Cost of Capital, Corporation Finance and the Theory of Investment" (1958) 48 *American Economic Review* 261.

managers' perspective, in that an exceptionally low demand for a particular firm's securities – and the consequent devaluation in equity that this entails – can prompt the displacement of the incumbent management team via revocation of its continuing investor license to hold office (as manifested most typically, at least in the United States, in the case of a proxy contest aimed at ousting the incumbent board of directors).[64]

Given the inherent informational disparity between managerial and non-managerial actors, outside investors are generally incapable of exerting effective control over the executive allocation of private revenue streams via securities selection (coupled with occasional managerial displacement) alone. It follows that other supplementary accountability (or checking) mechanisms are called for in order to ensure the continuing acquiescence of investors (and, in particular, equity) in the centralized possession and exercise of DAP within the corporate-organizational framework. Hence the availability of a range of formal legal governance mechanisms,[65] which have the collective effect of ensuring that, in any capitalistic corporate enterprise, private-governmental powers are possessed and exercised by managers in a manner that – broadly speaking – is acquiesced in by the subject shareholders as a whole.

As the following discussion will show, in order to secure the legitimacy – and corresponding acquiescence of equity investors – in the continuing possession and exercise of DAP by management, the key quality that a corporate governance system must engender is *accountability*. That is to say, management must be continuously and formally called upon to give an account of themselves to those who are directly subject to their executive power (namely shareholders), as a precondition to obtaining the latter's acquiescence in the underlying power imbalance inter se.

Of course, greater managerial accountability – absent other factors – will not in itself engender enhanced corporate performance (however defined), or eliminate scope for managerial diminution of shareholder wealth in other ways. The key point, however, is that where bounded rationality[66] inhibits the capacity of outside investors to evaluate the

[64] On this, see H.G. Manne, "Mergers and the Market for Corporate Control" (1965) 73 *Journal of Political Economy* 110.

[65] For a brief analysis of some of the most noteworthy mechanisms available within US and UK public companies, see below nn 79–84 and accompanying text.

[66] On the dual concepts of bounded rationality and inherent uncertainty as developed within behavioral economics literature generally, see H.A. Simon, "Theories of Decision-Making in Economics and Behavioral Science" (1959) 49 *American Economic Review* 253; A.A. Alchian, "Uncertainty, Evolution, and Economic Theory" (1950) 58 *Journal of Political Economy* 211; Williamson, above n 18 at 55–7.

diversity of variables determining the overall riskiness of a firm's securities, the *accountability* of its senior executive office-holders is prone to be perceived as an important – albeit imperfect – bulwark against misappropriation or wastage of shareholder wealth. At the very least, formal managerial accountability serves to legitimize the basic structure of the equity relation within any corporation, which – as explained above – is essential to the firm's ongoing capacity to raise and allocate capital on terms that – prima facie at least – are fundamentally inconsistent with the continuing contractual autonomy of external equity providers.

4.5 Accountability as the Key Factor in Legitimizing Internal Corporate Power Imbalance

4.5.1 Accountability as a General Social Phenomenon

Accountability has been described as "one of the most powerful symbols in modern politics and administration,"[67] and – more fundamentally – as something intrinsic to the moral character of a human being.[68] Understood in its simplest and most general sense, accountability entails "the giving and demanding of reasons for conduct,"[69] and as such is "a chronic feature of daily conduct"[70] derived from the innate nature of human beings as "reason seeking/giving animals."[71] A relationship of accountability by definition involves at least two actors (namely the account-giver and account-recipient(s)), and the key relational quality of accountability

[67] M.J. Dubnick and H.G. Frederickson, *Public Accountability: Performance Measurement, the Extended State, and the Search for Trust* (Dayton, OH: The Kettering Foundation, 2011), p. 3.

[68] In his *Theory of Moral Sentiments* (1759, III, 1), Adam Smith famously proclaimed that "[a] moral being is an accountable being" (cited in Dubnick and Frederickson, above n 67 at 52).

[69] J. Roberts and R. Scapens, "Accounting Systems and Systems of Accountability – Understanding Accounting Practices in their Organizational Contexts" (1985) 10 *Accounting, Organizations and Society* 443 at 447. On this, see also A. Sinclair, "The Chameleon of Accountability: Forms and Discourses" (1995) 20 *Accounting, Organizations and Society* 219.

[70] A. Giddens, *Central Problems in Social Theory: Action, Structure, and Contradiction in Social Analysis* (Berkeley, CA: University of California Press, 1991), p. 57; cited in Roberts and Scapens, above n 69 at 448.

[71] Quote from well-known American sociologist Professor Charles Tilly, cited in M.J. Dubnick, "Sarbanes-Oxley and the Search for Accountable Corporate Governance," in J. O'Brien (ed.), *Private Equity, Corporate Governance and the Dynamics of Capital Market Regulation* (London: Imperial College Press, 2007), ch. 9, p. 246.

practices are their intended effect in enabling the "settling up or getting right" of a matter between the account-giver and account recipient(s).[72]

It has been observed that "modern governance – public as well as private – is at its core based on some form of accountability [in the above sense]."[73] Drawing on historical evidence of the governance of embryonic nation-states in the late medieval period, Dubnick has observed that – from a governance perspective – the principal value of accountability processes resides in their capacity to enable rulers "to maintain and sustain authority over autonomous subjects who were becoming increasingly aware of [the rulers'] capacity for discretionary action."[74] In other words, formal accountability processes evolved historically as a natural counterbalance to DAP, and as an essential means of legitimizing and sustaining such power in the face of potential resistance by those who were subject to it.[75]

The act of account-giving is highly significant on a normative or political level, especially when it occurs within relationships or organizations that are characterized by relative power disparity between participants. In the public-governmental environment, it has been said that "[n]othing is more fundamental to representative democratic government than is political accountability to citizens," to the extent that "we commonly equate democracy with accountable governance – and vice versa."[76] However, within any organizational context – governmental or otherwise – the extent to which senior decision-makers are rendered accountable to those principally subject to or affected by their decisions or actions is normatively crucial on both an individual and collective level.

First, effective accountability mechanisms are central to protecting the individual autonomy of those parties subject to DAP, in that where individual preferences are formed by deliberative processes and not simply by "external circumstances" (such as relative distributions of power and influence), they can be regarded as emanating first and foremost from the power of reason as opposed to being imposed or manipulated by dominant organizational interests (such as senior executive officeholders).[77]

[72] Dubnick and Frederickson, above n 67 at 3.

[73] *Ibid.* at 228.

[74] *Ibid.*

[75] On the general concept of institutional counterbalance via "countervailing power," see J.K. Galbraith, *American Capitalism: The Concept of Countervailing Power* (Boston: Houghton Mifflin, 1952).

[76] Dubnick and Frederickson, above n 67 at 18.

[77] J. Cohen, "Deliberation and Democratic Legitimacy," in A. Hamlin and P. Pettit (eds.), *The Good Polity: Normative Analysis of the State* (New York: Blackwell, 1989).

Second, effective accountability mechanisms are essential in establishing the legitimacy of the relevant organization as a whole, by demonstrating the *non*-inconsistency of its internal power imbalance(s) with the basic democratic principle of fair collective representation.

This is because the procedural requirement of account-giving, based on the elicitation of reasons that are generally acceptable to an organization's participants, in effect "neutralizes" any underlying power imbalance(s) by ensuring that (objective) reasons "trump" (inter-subjective) relative influence or resources as the principal determinant of fundamental, important, or controversial organizational decisions.[78] As a result, the basic representational inclination of organizational controllers is – in outward appearance at least – not impaired by the fact that the vast majority of their decisions are made on a centralized and autonomous basis. This preserves the aforementioned link between collective (organizational) and individual (participant) autonomy that is a precondition of executive decision-makers' continuing ability to possess and exercise power on *legitimate* – that is to say, generally acquiesced in – terms.

4.5.2 Accountability (and Consequent Power-Legitimacy) as the Principal Rationale for Formal Corporate Governance Mechanisms

Rationalizing the modern public company – and, in particular, the equity relation at the heart of orthodox Anglo-American corporate law – through the lens of the quasi-public phenomenon of DAP, has significant implications for how one understands the function of formal *corporate governance* mechanisms. Indeed, by an extension of the above logic, it can reasonably be surmised that the principal and definitive purpose of corporate governance law should be understood as that of *engendering an effective and ongoing process of managerial account-giving to shareholders*. In this way, the law has the effect of legitimizing – and thus sustaining – the necessary reciprocal power imbalance between management and shareholders at the heart of the public company, notwithstanding the fact that the basic structural characteristics of this relation are fundamentally averse to investors' continuing contractual autonomy as economic actors.

[78] In the so-called "ideal" speech scenario envisaged by the social theorist Jürgen Habermas, "no force except that of the better argument is exercised." See J. Habermas, *Legitimation Crisis* (Boston: Beacon Press, 1975), p. 108.

Accordingly, it is submitted that the central dual function of mandatory managerial accountability mechanisms in Anglo-American corporate governance law is: first, to provide an appropriate formal forum for the bilateral deliberation of fundamental, important, or controversial issues pertaining to the corporate equity relation; and, second, to effect an equalization – or, at least, moderation (in shareholders' favor) of the relative power and resources that managers and shareholders, respectively, bring to the proverbial corporate discussion table. In these ways, corporate governance law seeks to engender more effective deliberative conditions than would be possible by recourse to management-shareholder private ordering alone. The ultimate effect of such extensive regulatory intervention is to secure the legitimacy – and, in turn, sustainability – of the corporate equity relation, by demonstrably ensuring its *non*-inconsistency with the basic liberal-democratic principle of individual (investor) autonomy.

The most obvious and fundamental respect in which Anglo-American corporate governance law provides for the effective giving and receipt of accounts by management in the above sense is by mandating the annual shareholders' meeting (or, in the UK, Annual General Meeting) as the formal fulcrum for periodic management-shareholder deliberations within public companies.[79] In the Delaware case of *Hoschett* v. *TSI International Software*,[80] the Court of Chancery articulated a powerful normative justification for regarding the annual shareholders' meeting – and associated corporate election procedure – as compulsory and irreducible elements of corporate governance. Chancellor Allen explained that, "while the model of democratic forms should not too strictly be applied to the economic institution of a business corporation . . ., it is nevertheless a not unimportant feature of corporate governance that at a noticed annual meeting *a form of discourse . . . among investors and between shareholders and managers is possible*."[81] Accordingly, he emphasized that "[t]he theory of the meeting *includes the idea that a deliberative component of the meeting may occur*" and, whilst in reality "meetings are very far from deliberative convocations . . . a keen realization of the reality of the degree of deliberation that is possible, should make the preservation of residual mechanisms of corporate democracy more, not less, important."[82]

[79] See Delaware General Corporation Law § 211(b); UK Companies Act 2006, s. 336(1).

[80] *Hoschett* v. *TSI International Software*, 683 A 2d 43 (Del. Ch. 2006).

[81] *Ibid.* at 45–6 (emphasis added).

[82] *Ibid.* at 46 (emphasis added).

Clearly, this deliberative logic is applicable to the basic procedure of the meeting itself including the laying of accounts and reports, and the raising of questions by investors in anticipation of reasoned answers by the board thereto. It could furthermore be said to extend to the procedure for voting on the election of directors and other issues proposed for resolution, including the rules regarding the preparation and solicitation of proxies by both management and shareholders. Of course, the capacity of the annual shareholders' meeting and surrounding proxy solicitation process to serve as an effective deliberative forum is contingent on the extent to which investors are able to vote, speak, and act on an informed basis. Otherwise, managerial account-giving is rendered impossible. Accordingly, it may be said that the key purpose of mandatory disclosure requirements – especially those pertaining to the publication of ongoing firm performance and extraordinary business transactions and events – is to mitigate the innate informational disparity between management and shareholders by providing an objective and credible informational floor to their common deliberations. This brings the corporate communications process closer to the hypothetical ideal speech scenario by enabling shareholders to evaluate managerial proposals (including directorial nominees) in the light of information additional to that provided voluntarily by management itself.

Mandatory disclosure requirements also enhance the rigor of managerial account-giving by providing investors with the informational capacity – in appropriate cases – to initiate proxy proposals independently of those advanced by management, ranging from ad hoc strategic recommendations to calls for outright managerial displacement.[83] While such "insurgent" proposals are usually highly unlikely to command majority shareholder support, their very (actual or potential) advancement is in itself prone to prompt the giving of reasons by management in defense of its current policies or position.[84] And, as explained above, such deliberative reason-giving is essential to maintaining the legitimacy of management's possession and exercise of DAP vis-à-vis shareholders and the corresponding acquiescence of investors therein.

[83] On the shareholder proxy process generally, see SEC Regulation 14A, especially Rule 14A-8 (on precatory shareholder proposals).

[84] On the frequent effectiveness of shareholder proxy proposals in prompting change in established managerial attitudes and corporate governance norms in US public companies, see M. Kahan and E. Rock, "Embattled CEOs" (2010) 88 *Texas Law Review* 987; R. Thomas and J. Cotter, "Shareholder Proposals in the New Millenium: Shareholder Support, Board Response, and Market Reaction" (2007) 13 *Journal of Corporate Finance* 368.

4.6 Conclusion

The essential argument of this chapter is that corporate power – in the quasi-public sense described above – is *structurally unsustainable* in the absence of an underpinning framework of effective managerial accountability mechanisms. Such mechanisms, as explained above, *must* – and, for the most part, *are* – designed to legitimize management's continuing possession and exercise of power, by securing the acquiescence of those principally subject to such power (namely shareholders) in the ensuing relational imbalance.

Hence this chapter's normative claim is ultimately a (small "c") conservative one. In short, it is that existing key managerial accountability mechanisms within Anglo-American corporate governance law – on the face of things at least – would appear to be doing a reasonably commendable job of fulfilling what this chapter perceives to be their core motivating purpose: that is to say, securing the legitimacy – and, in turn, sustainability – of management's DAP, by ensuring that such power is possessed and exercised against the background of a robust network of countervailing formal checks.

The concern thus is not that existing laws in this regard are unfit for purpose, but rather that the effectiveness of those laws has tended to be evaluated by reference to an overly narrow (orthodox private-economic) conceptual paradigm, thereby detracting from their fundamental structural value. The corresponding hope is that once the broader and inherently *public* dimensions of power, legitimacy, and accountability as social phenomena come to be universally appreciated within Anglo-American corporate law scholarship, students of the modern public company will have a more sophisticated array of conceptual vantage points from which to observe the full institutional complexity of their subject matter.

5

Reflections on the Nature of the Public Corporation in an Era of Shareholder Activism and Stewardship

DIONYSIA KATELOUZOU

5.1 Introduction

The nature and origins of the Anglo-American public company – or, in the American usage, public corporation[1] – are subject to a century-old discourse swirled around the debates of shareholder primacy versus stakeholderism, the legitimacy of management power, and the balance of authority between the management team[2] and shareholders. Disputes over whether the public corporation is "private" or "public" in nature have featured prominently on the radar of this scholarly discourse since the early twentieth century, especially in the United States, echoing the intellectual dualism of a neoliberal market-oriented view of the corporation versus a state-centric tradition of corporate governance and the broader discussion of the relationship between economy and society.[3]

One strand of the debate, known as the "contractarian" or "nexus of contracts" paradigm of corporate governance, analogized the public corporation to a "nexus" of contractual relationships to demonstrate its *private* nature. The contractual corporation (or firm)[4] is understood as a private body arising from the contracts of free and rational economic actors (such

[1] In this chapter the term "public corporation" is used to specifically refer to the large, publicly listed and dispersed-owned company.

[2] For the purposes of this chapter it is assumed that directors and managers act together as a management team, regardless of who actually is in charge. The differences between managers and directors are beyond the scope of this chapter, which focuses on the relationship between shareholders on the one hand and the management team as a whole on the other.

[3] See, e.g., K. Polanyi, *The Great Transformation: The Political and Economic Origins of Our Time* (Boston: Beacon Press, 2001).

[4] In this chapter, I use the terms "corporation" and "firm" interchangeably. But see C.R.T. O'Kelley, "Coase, Knight, and the Nexus-of-Contracts Theory of the Firm: A Reflection on Reification, Reality, and the Corporation as Entrepreneur Surrogate" (2012) 35 *Seattle University Law Review* 1247 (explaining the differences in the use of these two terms).

as shareholders, directors, officers, employees, creditors, customers, suppliers, and other factors of production) with the aim to improve the utility or welfare of the contracting parties. This picture, in effect, implies a facilitative, cost-reductive role for corporate law whereby legal rules are essentially reflective of individual preferences or firm-specific circumstances.[5] The classic statement of this limited facilitative role for corporate law, and public policy more generally, is mainly attributed to Frank Easterbrook and Daniel Fischel who, in their 1991 book, advocated that "corporate law should contain the terms people would have negotiated, were the costs of negotiating at arm's length for every contingency sufficiently low," and that corporate law "almost always conforms to this model."[6] This is a strong deregulatory position that accords institutional primacy to the market.[7] On the other side of the debate, a competing group of scholars view the corporation as a *public* phenomenon seeking to advance the public interest,[8] and assert that management should be subject to additional legal and socially determinative controls.[9] The result of this debate has been a voluminous body of theoretical work, especially within the United States but which has also spread to English scholarship.[10]

Whereas there has been much discussion about the normative implications of both sides of this debate for the nature of corporate law (enabling versus paternalistic), the effects of this public–private divide on the role of shareholders in the public corporation remained on the sidelines for decades. For the supporters of the private nature of the corporation, shareholders have in general been viewed as the main beneficiaries of

[5] See generally, J.R. Macey, "Corporate Law and Corporate Governance: A Contractual Perspective" (1993) 18 *Journal of Corporation Law* 185.

[6] F.H. Easterbrook and D.R. Fischel, *The Economic Structure of Corporate Law* (Cambridge: Harvard University Press, 1991), p. 15.

[7] Contractarians, however, ascribe a gap-filling function to corporate law. See *ibid.* at 34–5.

[8] See, e.g., J.E. Parkinson, *Corporate Power and Responsibility: Issues in the Theory of Company Law* (Oxford: Clarendon Press, 1993), p. 23 (viewing corporations as "social enterprises" on the basis of a political theory about the legitimacy of private power).

[9] On the distinction between socially determinative and non-socially determinative conceptions of the purpose of corporate law, see D. Millon, "Communitarians, Contractarians, and the Crisis in Corporate Law" (1993) 50 *Washington and Lee Law Review* 1373.

[10] In the United Kingdom, the most prominent application of the contractual perspective to UK company law can be found in B.R. Cheffins, *Company Law: Theory, Structure and Operation* (Oxford: Clarendon Press, 1997). More recently, Marc Moore favors an expanded contractarian paradigm that accounts for the significant public dimensions of the Anglo-American corporate governance regulation. See M.T. Moore, *Corporate Governance in the Shadow of the State* (Oxford: Hart, 2013), pp. 228–79.

the corporate activity,[11] whereas the adherents of the public model have embraced a stronger stakeholder-oriented corporate governance system.[12] However, none of these positions coherently account for who shareholders are today and their changed nature from "passive holders" to "activist owners" in recent years. Rather they both rely on an outdated theoretical conceptualization of the firm and a series of assumptions about the efficacy of either private ordering or state regulation.

In addition, trapped in the old economic-oriented theories, both sides of this public–private debate suffer from a monolithic view of the functions of the firm as they do not consider the relevance of history, culture, or politics in explaining the development of the modern corporation and the related company laws. This deficiency has been increasingly filled in recent years by prominent political theories of comparative corporate governance, including the social democracy theory,[13] the varieties of capitalism approach,[14] and the social welfare theory.[15] What is striking, however, is that like the economic-oriented approaches, the political theories take an excessively national view of corporate governance systems and the laws relating to them, disregarding real-word developments and the substantial privatization of norm-making in corporate law in recent years.[16] It is in this context that this chapter deconstructs the contractarian portrayal of the role of shareholders within the internal functioning of the corporation,[17]

[11] Easterbrook and Fischel, above n 6 at 38 (asserting that "maximizing profits for equity investors assists the other 'constituencies' automatically"). However, the variants of the neoclassical view of the public corporation, including the team production theory, the director primacy theory, and the shareholder primacy theory deviate sharply in relation to the corporation's purpose. See M.M. Blair and L.A. Stout, "A Team Production Theory of Corporate Law" (1999) 5 *Virginia Law Review* 247; S.M. Bainbridge, "The Case for Limited Shareholder Voting Rights" (2006) 53 *UCLA Law Review* 601; L.A. Bebchuk, "The Myth of Shareholder Franchise" (2007) 93 *Vanderbilt Law Review* 675, respectively.

[12] See, e.g., M. Gelter, "The Dark Side of Shareholder Influence: Managerial Autonomy and Stakeholder Orientation in Comparative Corporate Governance" (2009) 50 *Harvard International Law Journal* 129.

[13] M.J. Roe, *Political Determinants of Corporate Governance: Political Context, Corporate Impact* (New York: Oxford University Press, 2003).

[14] P.A. Hall and D. Soskice, *Varieties of Capitalism: The Institutional Foundations of Comparative Advantage* (Oxford: Oxford University Press, 2001).

[15] C.M. Bruner, *Corporate Governance in the Common-Law World: The Political Foundations of Shareholder Power* (New York: Cambridge University Press, 2013).

[16] See, e.g., P. Zumbansen, "Rethinking the Nature of the Firm: The Corporation as a Governance Object" (2012) 35 *Seattle University Law Review* 1469.

[17] This chapter will not explore the implications of the public version of this debate. Instead, the focus of this chapter is on the challenges raised by the contractarian model due to the changing role of shareholders within the internal functioning of the modern corporation.

taking input from the institutionalization of shareholder ownership in recent decades and the emergence of shareholder activism, especially the one associated with activist hedge funds.

Critiques of the nexus of contracts theory are not new. Earlier commentators exposed various weaknesses of the economic analysis of the corporation and, by the mid-to-late-twentieth century, it was largely recognized that the corporation cannot be regarded as an essentially private and quasi-contractual institution.[18] Much of the mainstream debate, however, still weds the neoliberal contractarian view of the corporation with the agency theory, reaffirming the norm of shareholder primacy.[19] Within this framework it is asserted that management accountability to shareholders is the best means to achieve aggregate social welfare for all stakeholders.[20] Contractarianism goes further, dispelling the notion of shareholder "ownership," and thereby relying on the efficacy of individual contracting and the constraining forces of various markets to control managerial discretion and reduce monitoring costs. Within the contractarian framework, there is no a priori reason why shareholders should exercise control over managerial decision-making and any legally imposed reform to empower the monitoring role of shareholders is viewed as unnecessary and counterproductive.

It will be shown that these contractarian assertions do not hold anymore in the face of the parallel rise in the holdings and influence of institutional investors in recent years.[21] At the same time, the increasing "financialization"[22] of the modern corporation and the role of activist shareholders in corporate law practices need to be taken into account. Most shares today are owned by institutional investors. Among them, activist hedge funds are well-positioned to monitor management because of their strong incentives to raise the stock price. Hedge fund activism

[18] See, e.g., V. Brudney, "Corporate Governance, Agency Costs, and the Rhetoric of Contract" (1985) 85 *Columbia Law Review* 1403.

[19] R. Kraakman, J. Armour, P. Davies, *et al.* (eds.) *The Anatomy of Corporate Law* (New York: Oxford University Press).

[20] H. Hansmann and R. Kraakman, "The End of History for Corporate Law" (2001) 89 *Georgetown Law Journal* 439.

[21] The implications of having multiple intermediaries in the holding chain for the contractarian model will not be addressed as this extends beyond the scope of this chapter.

[22] See G.A. Epstein, *Financialization and the World Economy* (Cheltenham, UK: Edward Elgar Publishing, 2005), p. 3 (attributing the increasing financialization of the modern corporation to "the increasing role of financial motives, financial markets, financial actors and financial institutions"); P. Ireland, "The Financialization of Corporate Governance" (2009) 60 *Northern Ireland Legal Quarterly* 1.

also mitigates the traditional passivity of mainstream institutional investors as the latter not only are the main source of investment capital for activist hedge funds but they also directly or indirectly support their activist campaigns.

To understand the changed nature of shareholders, as this is embraced by activist hedge funds, one needs to move away from contractarian accounts of the shareholder franchise on the basis of residual claims or principal-agent relationships. An alternative theoretical foundation for promoting the shareholder franchise can be found in Paul Edelman, Randall Thomas, and Robert Thompson's proposed theory of shareholder voting, which is based on the sensitivity of shareholders to the share price.[23] Building on this positive theory it will be shown that activist hedge funds are tied closely to the stock price of the corporation and thus it is in their interests that the firm's value be maximized. Activist hedge funds, therefore, have interests coincident with the rest of shareholders, while maximizing shareholder values can also have ancillary social benefits.

The idea that shareholder power is a positive corporate governance attribute underpins recent policy efforts to instill greater shareholder democracy into the modern corporation on both sides of the Atlantic. These efforts include the Dodd-Frank reforms in the United States,[24] the introduction of binding "say on pay" regulations in the United Kingdom,[25] and the proposed amendments to the Shareholder Rights Directive in the EU,[26] which aims to increase shareholder influence on both executive remuneration and related party transactions.[27] Nevertheless, with power comes responsibility. While compliance with shareholder value maximization as a proxy for aggregate social welfare is increasingly promulgated by

[23] P.H. Edelman, R.S. Thomas, and R.B. Thompson, "Shareholder Voting in an Age of Intermediary Capitalism" (2014) 87 *Southern California Law Review* 1354.

[24] Dodd-Frank Wall Street Reform and Consumer Protection Act of 2010, Pub. L. No. 111-203, 124 Stat. 1376 (2010).

[25] UK Companies Act 2006, ss. 226B, 226C, 439, and 439A.

[26] Proposal for a Directive of the European Parliament and of the Council amending Directive 2007/36/EC as regards the encouragement of long-term shareholder engagement and Directive 2013/34/EU as regards certain elements of the corporate governance statement, published 9 April 2014, Parliament amended version of 8 July 2015, Arts. 9a and 9b, available at www.europarl.europa.eu/sides/getDoc.do?pubRef=-//EP//TEXT+TA+P8-TA-2015-0257+0+DOC+XML+V0//EN ("Amendments to Shareholder Rights Directive").

[27] On how recent regulatory developments in Anglo-American corporate law "de-privatize" the subject matter, see M.T. Moore, "The De-Privatisation of Anglo-American Corporate Law?," *Research Paper No. 57/2015* (University of Cambridge Faculty of Law, 2015), available at http://ssrn.com/abstract=2698288.

regulatory developments and enforced through shareholder activism, the notion of shareholder "stewardship," introduced by the UK Stewardship Code and recently espoused by the proposed Shareholder Rights Directive, harnesses shareholder power to protect the long-term interests of other shareholders and the economy as a whole. While the United States has yet to track the recent developments in shareholder stewardship, concerns over the likely dysfunctionality of shareholders' accountability are shared by American scholars.[28]

These recent empirical and regulatory developments undermine the contractarian view of shareholders and arguably mark a paradigm shift for Anglo-American[29] corporate law from contractarianism and agency theory to what can be described as an "investor paradigm" for corporate law. Within this paradigm, institutional investors are expected to act in a twofold way: (1) as a monitoring mechanism promoting shareholder value maximization and (2) as an accountability mechanism protecting the interests of other shareholders and the economy as a whole through the promotion of shareholder stewardship.

The rest of this chapter is organized as follows. It first addresses what has become something of an orthodoxy, especially within economists' circles: the view of the public corporation as a "nexus of contracts," and the role of shareholders within it. Next, the chapter examines the emergence of shareholder activism, especially hedge fund activism, and its implications for the nature of the public corporation. It will be shown that the recent wave of hedge fund activism, and the shareholder-centric policy reforms accompanying it have prompted a re-examination of the conclusions drawn by the nexus of contracts model of the corporation that put faith on the institutional primacy of the market over shareholders' intervention.[30] Although shareholders still play a subordinate role in the governance of the modern corporation,[31] their monitoring role is crucial.

[28] See, e.g., I. Anabtawi and L.A. Stout, "Fiduciary Duties for Activist Shareholders" (2008) 60 *Stanford Law Review* 1255.

[29] This chapter does not discuss the implications of the proposed Shareholder Rights Directive in terms of the various ways in which the public corporation is perceived by the EU Member States (shareholder-oriented versus stakeholder-oriented approaches).

[30] Recent shareholder-centric reforms empowering shareholders also sit uneasily with the proponents of the public nature of the corporation who reject shareholder maximization as the only legitimate corporate purpose embracing public interests and see no reason why only the shareholders (and not other stakeholders, such as employees) should have an input into the company's decision-making.

[31] See M.T. Moore's chapter in this book, arguing that shareholders under both UK and US company law are subordinate to the board – and indirectly to management – in respect of the allocation of decision-making power.

The positive attributes of shareholder engagement have been recognized by recent shareholder empowerment regulatory efforts. It will be asserted, however, that the notion of "power entailing responsibility" underpins the recent regulatory developments establishing shareholder stewardship and marks a shift towards an "investor paradigm" in corporate law. The last part advances the case for an approximation of the different theories of the firm and real-world developments to present a more thickly textured picture of the position of shareholders as active monitors and stewards within the modern corporation.

5.2 The Contractarian View of Shareholders

For the greater part of the twentieth century the role of shareholders within the public corporation was conceptualized within the contractarian framework influenced by the neoliberal emphasis on market efficiency.[32] The contractarian or "nexus of contracts" theory of the corporation (or firm) is routinely traced to Ronald Coase's famous 1937 article, *The Nature of the Firm*,[33] which, despite being initially neglected among scholars, was rediscovered by Alchian and Demsetz, and Jensen and Meckling in the 1970s.[34] Since then, it has largely dominated both American and English (economic and legal) discourses on the nature of the public corporation.[35] The contractarian theorists famously asserted that a corporation is a "legal fiction" that serves as a network of explicit and implicit bargains among individual factors of production, or, in other words, a nexus of contracting relationships joining inputs (such

[32] G.J. Ronald and R. Kraakman, "The Mechanisms of Market Efficiency" (1984) 70 *Virginia Law Review* 549.

[33] R.H. Coase, "The Nature of the Firm" (1937) 4 *Economica* 386 at 390–5 (explaining "firms" and "markets" as alternative forms of "organization," with the "costs of organizing" (transaction costs) determining the choice between the two methods of allocating resources). See, however, O'Kelley, above n 4 at 1248–50, 1259–67 (asserting that Coase's theory of the firm supports a very different contractarian account of the corporation than the one presented by the nexus of contracts theory).

[34] A.A. Alchian and H. Demsetz, "Production, Information Costs, and Economic Organization" (1972) 62 *American Economic Review* 777; M.C. Jensen and W.H. Meckling, "Theory of the Firm: Managerial Behavior, Agency Costs and Ownership Structure" (1976) 3 *Journal of Financial Economics* 305.

[35] Although there is no single view of the contractarian theory, there is a fairly consistent view among the contractarian theorists and this is presented in this part of the chapter. For different versions of the contractarian theory, see W.W. Bratton, Jr., "The 'Nexus of Contracts' Corporation: A Critical Appraisal" (1989) 74 *Cornell Law Review* 407 at 419.

as equity or debt) to outputs (such as dividends or interest).[36] Within this framework, there is no generic distinction between "insiders," such as shareholders and employees, and "outsiders," such as suppliers or customers.[37] All the firm's constituencies are defined by their contractual rights and the firm itself is merely a facility for exchanges of inputs and outputs, much like a stock market.[38]

The firm, taken as a neoclassical nexus of contracts, is not viewed in hierarchical terms,[39] but rather as a series of bilateral contracts between rational economic actors,[40] which take place under effective competition.[41] As has been famously argued, the nexus of contracts firm has "no power of fiat, no authority, no disciplinary action,"[42] and therefore, management is understood as one of the firm's many production factors,[43] and does not hold a strategic position in the firm. Financial and business economists in the 1970s and 1980s, therefore, displaced the management-centered concept of the firm (managerialism),[44] which prevailed in US scholarship in the first half of the twentieth century,[45] and married the neoliberal

36 Alchian and Demsetz, above n 34 at 778, 794–5; Jensen and Meckling, above n 34 at 310–11. See also E.F. Fama and M.C. Jensen, "Separation of Ownership and Control" (1983) 26 *Journal of Law and Economics* 301 at 302; M.C. Jensen, "Organization Theory and Methodology" (1983) 58 *Accounting Review* 319 at 326.

37 Jensen and Meckling, above n 34 at 311. See, however, E.B. Rock and M.L. Wachter, "Islands of Conscious Power: Law, Norms, and the Self-Governing Corporation" (2011) 149 *University of Pennsylvania Law Review* 1619 at 1628–9 (characterizing this "emptiness" of the firm as the main weakness of the nexus of contracts theory).

38 Alchian and Demsetz, above n 34 at 777.

39 It is noteworthy, however, that not all contractarian theorists see the firm merely as a non-hierarchical unit of contractual arrangements among maximizing individuals. The so-called institutionalist variant of the contractarian theory, influenced by Ronald Coase, and mainly taken by Oliver Williamson, sees the firm as a "governance structure," with authority distinguishable in a meaningful way from market contracting. On the development of these two variants of the contractarian theory, see Bratton, above n 35 at 420–3.

40 E.F. Fama, "Agency Problems and the Theory of the Firm" (1980) 88 *Journal of Political Economy* 288 at 289.

41 Jensen, above n 36 at 322, 327.

42 Alchian and Demsetz, above n 34 at 777.

43 See, e.g., *ibid.* at 794; Fama, above n 40 at 290 (describing management as "a continuous process of negotiation of successive contracts" and "type of labor but with a special role-coordinating the activities of inputs and carrying out the contracts agreed [upon] among [the] inputs," respectively).

44 On how the nexus of contracts theory (or what he terms "the new economic theory of the firm") displaces managerialism, see W.W. Bratton, "The New Economic Theory of the Firm: Critical Perspectives from History" (1989) 41 *Stanford Law Review* 1471 at 1475–7, 1493–1501.

45 For the history of managerial capitalism in the United States, see B. Cheffins, "Corporate Governance since the Managerial Capitalism Era" (2015) 89 *Business History Review* 717.

contractarian view of the corporation with the "agency theory." According to agency theory, the shareholders ("principals") acting through the board of directors delegate decisional authority to the firm's managers ("agents"), but they are not always able to monitor them, thereby giving rise to "agency problems."[46] While managers have the incentive to "shirk" and act in their own self-interests (rather than in the shareholders' interest), contractarians claim that the costs of managerial shirking (agency costs) – to the extent it is cost efficient to do so – are decreased by the terms of the contractual relationships and structures within the corporation.[47]

Within the nexus of the firm, shareholders are merely one of the parties who enter into contracts through the medium of the firm and therefore occupy the same contractual space as the other corporate constituencies, such as managers, directors, employees, customers, creditors, and suppliers.[48] In the words of Eugene Fama, while the shareholders own the equity capital that they supply to the firm,

> [o]wnership of capital should not be confused with ownership of the firm. Each factor [of production] in a firm is owned by somebody. The firm is just the set of contracts covering the ways inputs are joined to create outputs and the way receipts from outputs are shared among inputs.[49]

Viewed in this way, the corporation cannot be *owned* by the shareholders or anyone else and the ownership of the corporation becomes "an irrelevant concept."[50] The contractarian view of the shareholders, therefore, dismantles the notion of shareholders' ownership of private property famously advanced by Professor Adolf Berle.[51]

Despite this downgrade in the shareholders' standing within the corporation, contractarians tend to reaffirm the norm of shareholder primacy.[52]

[46] See Jensen and Meckling, above n 34 at 308.

[47] *Ibid.* at 308–10.

[48] See, for instance, J.R. Macey, "Fiduciary Duties as Residual Claimants: Obligations to Nonshareholder Constituencies from a Theory of the Firm Perspective" (1999) 84 *Cornell Law Review* 1266 at 1267–8.

[49] Fama, above n 40 at 290.

[50] *Ibid.* at 288, 290.

[51] According to Berle shareholders own passive (and not active) property, which entails "a set of economic expectations evidenced by a stock certificate . . . representing an infinitesimal claim on massed industrial wealth and funnelled income-stream" and leave their property rights in the hands of the board of directors who take on a role similar to a trustee. See, further, A.A. Berle, Jr., "For Whom Corporate Directors Are Trustees: A Note" (1932) 45 *Harvard Law Review* 1365 at 1369–70.

[52] J. Velasco, "The Fundamental Rights of the Shareholder" (2006) 40 *University of California Davis Law Review* 407 at 445–8. See, however, M.A. Eisenberg, "The Conception that the Corporation

Shareholders retain a significant position in the neoclassical model, because they are the "residual claimants" or "residual risk bearers" to the firm's income stream.[53] Shareholders have a right to the surplus that remains after all the contractual claims of employees, creditors, and the other factors of production have been met and, hence, voluntarily accept a more uncertain future return.[54] Conversely, other corporate constituencies, such as employees and creditors, have fixed claims and can (in theory at least) protect themselves through contractual arrangements.[55] Despite not being the owners of the corporation, shareholders are vested with significant property rights, under corporate law, such as the right to elect directors, the right to receive dividends, and the right to vote on important matters relating to the corporate affairs, such as mergers, significant transactions and amendments to the constitutional documents of the corporation.[56]

The right to the residual earnings of the firm ("what is left over") provides shareholders with an incentive to maximize the performance of the firm and to decrease management shirking.[57] Shareholders, it is argued,

is a Nexus of Contracts, and the Dual Nature of the Firm" (1999) 24 *Journal of Corporation Law* 819 at 833: "[T]he nexus-of-contracts conception is connected in a fundamental way, not to shareholder primacy, but to a communitatian conception of the corporation in which all groups with an interest in the corporation are put on an equal footing."

53 Easterbrook and Fischel, above n 6 at 67.

54 An alternative approach, the "transaction cost approach," associated principally with Oliver Williamson, points to the asset-specific character of the shareholders' investment in the firm, which can be obtained by the firm only on terms that the firm will maximize profits for shareholder. For a concise summary and critical analysis of both the "incentive-residual rights" theory and the transaction cost approach, see L.L. Dallas, "Two Models of Corporate Governance: Beyond Berle and Means" (1989) 22 *University of Michigan Journal of Law Reform* 19 at 53–63, 69–80.

55 See, however, M.M. Blair, "Firm-Specific Human Capital and Theories of the Firm," in M.M. Blair and M.J. Roe (eds.), *Employees and Corporate Governance* (Washington, DC: Brookings Institution Press, 1999), p. 58 (exposing the weakness of the contractarian theory of the firm to account for firm-specific employee investment).

56 For an examination of the shareholder rights under the contractarian theory, see Velasco, above n 52 at 448–51.

57 Fama and Jensen, above n 36 at 302–3 (arguing that "[t]he residual risk – the risk of the difference between stochastic inflows of resources and promised payments to agents – is borne by those who contract for the rights to net cash flows . . . Having most uncertainty borne by one group of agents, residual claimants, has survival value because it reduces the costs incurred to monitor contracts with other groups of agents and to adjust contracts for the changing risks borne by other agents"). See, however, S. Deakin and G. Slinger, "Hostile Takeovers, Corporate Law, and the Theory of the Firm" (1997) 24 *Journal of Law and Society* 124 at 129 (challenging the view that shareholders bear the residual risk on the basis of evolutionary theories of the firm that see the firm in terms of organizational processes that are distinct from those of the market).

will perform this monitoring function by selling their shares, thereby causing the company's stock price to fall.[58] For the supporters of the nexus of contracts theory, shareholder powerlessness was not a cause of concern in view of the economic rationality of shareholders' actions. After all, shareholders can ensure that their contracts contain the terms necessary to safeguard their interests against managerial incompetence and shirking and, if they are dissatisfied with the way the corporation is managed, they will exit the firm rather than incurring the costs of exercising their "voice"[59] and attempting to effect changes in the firm's policy or managerial personnel.

In addition, it was claimed that the disciplinary forces of various markets (capital, product, management, and labor) will further cause the survival of the most efficient and cost-saving governance arrangements.[60] Putting faith in the neoliberal axiom that the market allocates resources more efficiently than organizations and advocating the ineffectiveness of internal corporate control mechanisms,[61] contractarianism sees hostile takeovers in the "market for corporate control" as the key device for disciplining low-performing managers and increasing managerial efficiency.[62] Within this framework it becomes clear that "no reason exists why investors, who provide the firm with capital in anticipation of receiving a certain rate of return generated by the firm's assets, should have any input into the firm's decision-making processes."[63] Nor, it is argued, do the shareholders wish to be involved, or gain any benefits, from an active engagement with the company's incumbents, mainly because of a series of legal and extra-legal obstacles to shareholders' active involvement, such as diversification concerns, conflicts of interests, free-rider, and collective action problems.[64]

58 See Alchian and Demsetz, above n 34 at 788 (noting that "[r]ather than try to control the decisions of the management . . . unrestricted salability provides a more acceptable escape to each stockholder from continued policies with which he disagrees").

59 For a theory of the choice between exiting the firm, exercising voice and exhibiting loyalty to the incumbent management, see A.O. Hirschman, *Exit, Voice and Loyalty: Responses to Decline in Firms, Organizations and States* (Cambridge, MA: Harvard University Press, 1970).

60 See Easterbrook and Fischel, above n 6 at 8–15.

61 M.C. Jensen, "The Modern Industrial Revolution, Exit, and the Failure of Internal Control Systems" (1993) 48 *Journal of Finance* 831.

62 H. Manne, "Mergers and the Market for Corporate Control" (1965) 73 *Journal of Political Economy* 110.

63 D.R. Fischel, "The Corporate Governance Movement" (1982) 35 *Vanderbilt Law Review* 1259 at 1276.

64 Further on the factors behind shareholder passivity, see A.F. Conrad, "Beyond Managerialism: Investor Capitalism?" (1988) 22 *Journal of Law Reform* 117 at 152–63; *ibid.* at 1277; B.S. Black, "Shareholder Passivity Re-examined" (1990) 89 *Michigan Law Review* 520.

Albeit to a different extent, both US and UK corporate law have traditionally promoted centralized managerial authority via the board of directors, coinciding with the contractarian logic of shareholders' deprivation of any direct interference with the firm's internal management. Through most of the twentieth century, this contractarian orthodoxy of the rather passive role of shareholders also coincided with practice. At most of the largest corporations in the United Kingdom and the United States, share ownership remained dispersed among thousands of individual shareholders until the early 1980s.[65] The dispersion of shareholding and consequent inability of individual shareholders to oversee management left professional executives firmly in control of the corporation.[66] During this era "managers led, and directors and shareholders followed," particularly in the United States.[67] The tendency of shareholders to eschew active engagement was not a cause for concern, however, given the proliferation of hostile takeovers in the 1980s.[68] During this period, sometimes referred to as "the Deal Decade,"[69] the hostile takeover activity acted as an "external" corporate governance mechanism motivating managers to focus on shareholders returns.[70] The rationale was that managers would reward shareholder investors more diligently if they recognized a risk of being replaced by hostile takeovers. Accordingly, management and shareholder interests were adequately aligned by the operation of the market for corporate control and therefore the separation of ownership and control in the large public and widely dispersed corporation was not a cause for concern,

[65] On ownership patterns in the United States and the United Kingdom, see, e.g., M.J. Roe, *Strong Managers Weak Owners: The Political Roots of American Corporate Finance* (Princeton University Press, 1993), p. 5; M. Goergen and L. Renneboog, "Strong Managers and Passive Institutional Investors in the United Kingdom," in F. Barca and M. Becht (eds.), *The Control of Corporate Europe* (Oxford University Press, 2001), pp. 259–84; B.R. Cheffins, *Corporate Ownership and Control: British Business Transformed* (Oxford University Press, 2008), pp. 14–15.

[66] A.D. Chandler, Jr., *The Visible Hand: The Managerial Revolution in American Business* (Cambridge: Harvard University Press, 1977).

[67] J. Pound, "The Promise of the Governed Corporation" (1995) 78 *Harvard Business Review* 89.

[68] B. Cheffins, "The History of Corporate Governance," in M. Wright, D.S. Siegel, K. Keasey, and I. Filatotchev (eds.), *The Oxford Handbook of Corporate Governance* (Oxford University Press, 2013), pp. 46–64, 52.

[69] M.M. Blair, *The Deal Decade: What Takeovers and Leveraged Buyouts Mean for Corporate Governance* (Washington, DC: Brookings Institution Press, 1993).

[70] J.P. Welsh and J.K. Seward, "On the Efficiency of Internal and External Corporate Control Mechanisms" (1990) 15 *Academy of Management Review* 421.

as Berle and Means famously suggested,[71] but the product of a search for greater contractual efficiency.[72]

With the subsequent decline of hostile takeovers in the 1990s,[73] however, the contractarians' belief in the adequacy of market forces to align shareholders' and managers' interests and the contractual efficiency of shareholder passivity has been deeply challenged. A key parallel development, as will be shown in the next part, was a change in the dominant ideologies associated with the role of shareholders in the public corporation, assisted by the continuing institutionalization of share ownership and the accompanying shareholder-centric policy reforms.

5.3 The Eroding Contractarian Paradigm: Shareholders' Role Transformed

5.3.1 The Rise of Institutional Ownership and Shareholder Activism

As early as the 1960s, when managerialism was still at its peak, Anthony Crosland, in his book *The Future of Socialism*, raised the prospect of a "shareowning democracy" via institutional investors' equity ownership as an alternative form of capitalism in the United Kingdom.[74] A few years later, Peter Drucker, in his book *The Unseen Revolution*, warned that "pension fund socialism" would soon displace American managerialism.[75] Despite the rise of institutional investors – pension funds, bank trusts, insurance firms, endowment funds, and money managers – as major "intermediary"[76] holders of global corporate equity in the years that followed, little in the way of a "shareowning democracy" or "pension fund socialism" came to pass. Although pension funds' stockholdings grew

71 A.A. Berle, Jr. and G. Means, *The Modern Corporation and Private Property* (New York: Macmillan, 1932).

72 Fama and Jensen, above n 36 at 302, 305, 321–3.

73 M.C. Jensen, "The Eclipse of the Public Corporation" (1989) 5 *Harvard Business Review* 61.

74 A. Crosland, *The Future of Socialism* (London: Jonathan Cape, 1956). See also B. Jones, *Corporate Power and Responsible Capitalism? Towards Social Accountability* (Cheltenham, UK: Edward Elgar Publishing, 2015), pp. 61–73 (analyzing the political infrastructure of the transformed nature of the modern corporation in the United Kingdom).

75 P.F. Drucker, *The Unseen Revolution: How Pension Fund Socialism Came to America* (New York: Harper and Row, 1976).

76 For the several layers of conflicts of interest caused by financial intermediation, see R.C. Clark, "The Four Stages of Capitalism: Reflection on Investment Treatises" (1981) 94 *Harvard Law Review* 561.

rapidly as anticipated, especially since the 1980s,[77] most beneficiaries continue to lack control over the funds' assets and have little say over the fund itself.[78] With the rise in the equity holdings of institutional investors and the parallel lull in takeovers, however, an economic, political, and ideological base for what has been called "investor capitalism"[79] or, more recently, "agency capitalism"[80] has emerged.

Since the 1990s, legal academics and policy makers, alike, turned their attention to the ability of institutional investors to engage in active monitoring of portfolio company performance and advocated engaged share ownership.[81] For many, the growth of institutional investors' assets in equities was thought to enhance the skills and incentives of the re-concentrated institutional shareholders, especially pension funds, to reduce the agency problems arising from the familiar Berle-Means separation of ownership and control.[82] Indeed with increasing equity holdings, some institutional investors transformed from passive holders to engaged owners. A leading example of this transformation in the US equities market is the California Public Employees Retirement Scheme (CalPERS), which turned to direct challenges of what it considered to be shareholder-unfriendly practices, demanding lower takeover barriers, greater board independence, greater

[77] In the United States, institutional investors hold about 70% in equities. See M. Tonello and S. Rabimov, "The 2010 Institutional Investment Report: Trends in Asset Allocation and Portfolio Composition," *Research Report No. R-1468-10-RR* (The Conference Board Inc., 2010), available at http://ssrn.com/abstract=1707512; R.B. Thompson, "The Power of Shareholders in the United States," in J.G. Hill and R.S. Thomas (eds.), *Research Handbook on Shareholder Power* (Northampton, MA: Edward Elgar Publishing, 2015), pp. 441–58, 447. In the United Kingdom, financial institutions now hold the vast majority of equities with foreign (non-UK) investors holding about 50% of listed UK equities. See P. Davies, "Shareholders in the United Kingdom," in J.G. Hill and R.S. Thomas (eds.), *Research Handbook on Shareholder Power* (Northampton, MA: Edward Elgar Publishing, 2015), pp. 355–82, 356.

[78] R.B. Davis, *Democratizing Pension Funds: Corporate Governance and Accountability* (Vancouver: UBC Press, 2008); J.E. Fisch, "Securities Intermediaries and the Separation of Ownership from Control" (2010) 33 *Seattle University Law Review* 877.

[79] M. Useem, *Investor Capitalism: How Money Managers Are Changing the Face of Corporate America* (New York: Basic Books, 1996).

[80] R.J. Gilson and J.N. Gordon, "The Agency Costs of Agency Capitalism: Activist Investors and the Revaluation of Governance Rights" (2013) 113 *Columbia Law Review* 863.

[81] See, e.g., B. Black, "Agents Watching Agents: The Promise of Institutional Investor Voice" (1992) 39 *UCLA Law Review* 811; J.C. Coffee, Jr., "Liquidity Versus Control: The Institutional Investor as Corporate Monitor" (1991) 91 *Columbia Law Review* 1277; R.J. Gilson and R. Kraakman, "Reinventing the Outside Director: An Agenda for Institutional Investors" (1991) 43 *Stanford Law Review* 863.

[82] Berle and Means, above n 71 at 112–116.

disclosure, fewer barriers to shareholder proposals and tighter links between executive compensation and firm performance.[83]

This form of shareholder activism, mainly developed in the United States, has been described as "defensive."[84] Defensive shareholder activism occurs when a shareholder – institutional or otherwise – with a pre-existing stake in a company, reacts to managerial deficiencies by promoting changes that are largely related to the corporate governance practices of the company and could improve long-term performance. However, for a long time, defensive activism remained the exception rather than the rule. Throughout the twentieth century there were a handful of US institutional shareholders, mainly pension funds and mutual funds, that took an active role in corporate decision-making, but they were outliers. On the other side of the Atlantic, institutional shareholders were slower to take up an activist role but informal engagement was observed in the United Kingdom on an ad hoc basis.[85] Overall, the vast majority of institutional shareholders remained "rationally apathetic" over the last century, choosing to diversify risk by spreading their equity holdings rather than engaging in time-consuming and costly monitoring of managerial practices.[86]

The situation changed rapidly after the turn of the century. Alternative investment funds, such as hedge funds and private equity firms, became significant global corporate equity owners during the past decade and a half, while pension funds' assets in equities diminished.[87] A handful of hedge fund managers turned to corporate governance as an investment

[83] M.P. Smith, "Shareholder Activism by Institutional Investors: Evidence from CalPERS" (1996) 51 *Journal of Finance* 227; S.M. Jacoby, "Convergence by Design: The Case of CalPERS in Japan" (2007) 55 *American Journal of Comparative Law* 239 at 243–54.

[84] I.H-Y. Chiu, *The Foundations and Anatomy of Shareholder Activism* (Oxford: Hart Publishing, 2010), chs. 1 and 2; B.R. Cheffins and J. Armour, "The Past, Present and Future of Shareholder Activism by Hedge Funds" (2011) 37 *Journal of Corporation Law* 51.

[85] B.S. Black and J.C. Coffee, "Hail Britannia: Institutional Investor Behavior under Limited Regulation" (1994) 92 *Michigan Law Review* 1997.

[86] For the United States, see R. Romano, "Public Pension Fund Activism in Corporate Governance Reconsidered" (1993) 93 *Columbia Law Review* 795; B.S. Black, "Shareholder Activism and Corporate Governance in the United States," in P. Newman (ed.), *The New Palgrave Dictionary of Economics and the Law* (London: Palgrave Macmillan, 1998), p. 459; S.J. Choi and J.E. Fisch, "On Beyond CalPERS: Survey Evidence on the Developing Role of Public Pension Funds in Corporate Governance" (2008) 61 *Vanderbilt Law Review* 315. For the United Kingdom, see Cheffins, above n 65 (illustrating the "hands-off" approach of UK institutional investors especially up to 1990).

[87] For statistics, see, among others, G.L. Clark and D. Wojcik, *The Geography of Finance: Corporate Governance in a Global Marketplace* (Oxford: Oxford University Press, 2007).

strategy.[88] As a result, a new form of shareholder activism, called "offensive"[89] shareholder activism, emerged in the United States in the early 2000s. Activist hedge funds have been the main publicized participants of this style of shareholder activism, which involves taking substantial equity positions in underperforming companies and agitating for changes that will realize improved returns. Unlike mainstream institutional shareholders, who have pre-existing stakes and engage in defensive shareholder activism only in egregious times when they become dissatisfied with management, activist hedge funds accumulate their equity stakes *proactively*. That is, despite not having a pre-existing stake in the target company or having only a small stake, they quickly increase their investment when they decide to adopt a hands-on strategy.[90]

Activist hedge funds target companies for the purposes of maximizing shareholder value. They campaign for certain capital- or operational-related measures to be taken such as share buy-backs, distributions of dividends, sales of assets, and redirections of investments.[91] Such funds may also make demands for governance improvements including more board independence, concerns over executive compensation or anti-takeover mechanisms.[92] This corporate-governance-related hedge fund activism shares many similarities with earlier efforts by mainstream activist shareholders to improve corporate governance practices, but it is doubtful whether this type of activism is linked to the activist hedge funds' value-creation agenda.[93]

[88] Activist hedge funds comprise only a relatively small portion of the hedge fund sector. See M. Tonello, "Hedge Fund Activism: Findings and Recommendations for Corporations and Investors," *Research Report No. R-1343-08-RR* (The Conference Board Inc., 2008), available at http://ssrn.com/abstract=1107027.

[89] Cheffins and Armour, above n 84 at 56.

[90] See, further, D. Katelouzou, "Worldwide Hedge Fund Activism: Dimensions and Legal Determinants" (2015) 17 *University of Pennsylvania Business Law Review* 789.

[91] D. Katelouzou, "Myths and Realities of Hedge Fund Activism: Some Empirical Evidence" (2013) 7 *Virginia Business and Law Review* 459 at 491–5; W.W. Bratton, "Hedge Funds and Governance Targets" (2007) 95 *Georgetown Law Journal* 1375; A. Brav, W. Jiang, F. Partnoy, and R. Thomas, "Hedge Fund Activism, Corporate Governance, and Firm Performance" (2008) 63 *Journal of Finance* 1729 at 1735–6.

[92] Katelouzou, above n 91 at 492.

[93] See M. Schor and R. Greenwood, "Investor Activism and Takeovers" (2009) 32 *Journal of Financial Economics* 362 (presenting evidence that any value creation generated by hedge fund activism is mainly due to the ability of activist hedge funds to force target companies into a takeover).

Less often, activist hedge funds intersect with the market for corporate control in engaging in transfers of control by "vote" or "sale."[94] Activist hedge funds may also attempt to direct the affairs of the target company by replacing the majority of the board members to facilitate control transactions such as mergers and sales of the company to third parties, or more rarely, to make an offer to buy the target company themselves.[95] Although this kind of shareholder activism implies a considerable overlap with the market for corporate control, activist hedge funds are not generally interested in taking control of the target companies themselves[96] and they therefore engage in the so-called "market for corporate influence."[97]

Although hedge fund activism emerged in the United States, it quickly spread to other countries in Europe and Asia, but not necessarily as duplicates of the American practice.[98] Within Europe, the United Kingdom has the greatest concentration of activist hedge funds and activist campaigns.[99] Hedge fund activism in the United Kingdom is handled in various forms, from private discussions with the target board and other shareholders to public clashes with target companies.[100] Among the highlighted activist instances in the UK market is the hedge fund-driven reverse in strategy of Cadbury Schweppes,[101] which separated its drinks and confectionery operations in March 2007 following the offensive accumulation of a 3% ownership stake by Trian Funds, an investment vehicle controlled by the veteran American shareholder activist Nelson Peltz.[102]

[94] R.J. Gilson and A. Schwartz, "Sales and Elections as Methods of Transferring Corporate Control" (2011) *Theoretical Inquiries in Law* 783 at 790.

[95] Katelouzou, above n 91 at 493.

[96] Empirical evidence on the ownership stakes amassed by activist hedge funds lends support to this claim as activist hedge funds acquire around 5% to 10% stakes. See Katelouzou, above n 90 at 840–1.

[97] Cheffins and Armour, above n 84 at 51.

[98] On hedge fund activism outside the United States, see M. Becht, J.R. Franks and J. Grant, "Hedge Fund Activism in Europe," *Finance Working Paper No. 283/2010* (European Corporate Governance Institute, 2010), available at http://ssrn.com/abstract=1616340; J. Buchanan, D.H. Chai, and S. Deakin, *Hedge Fund Activism in Japan: The Limits of Shareholder Primacy* (Cambridge: Cambridge University Press, 2014); Katelouzou, above n 90 at 832–5.

[99] Katelouzou, above n 90 at 833.

[100] Katelouzou, above n 91 at 484–90.

[101] Cadbury Schweppes was renamed Cadbury plc in May 2008 and acquired by Kraft in February 2010.

[102] J. Wiggins, "Cadbury's Bitter-Sweet Dilemma," *Financial Times*, 14 March 2007, p. 20.

To the surprise of their academic detractors,[103] activist hedge funds have been extremely successful in forcing their demands and generating above-market rates of returns for the funds and their investors.[104] There is also some recent empirical evidence suggesting that hedge fund activism, at least as of 2007, is able to achieve not only its investment objective of profiting from shareholder activism, but also a form of discipline, especially relating to the agency problems associated with free cash flows and to the improvement of long-term performance.[105] Concerns over the "dark-side" of hedge fund activism have been empirically refuted,[106] and the existing empirical literature is consistent with arguments that activist hedge funds can act "like real owners,"[107] or as a "corrective mechanism"[108] in corporate governance, and effectively monitor managerial discretion.

The high success rate of hedge fund activism is attributable to several factors. First, activist hedge funds face fewer conflicts of interest than mainstream institutional shareholders since they are usually independent investment vehicles unaffiliated with other institutions[109] and they have better incentives to monitor due to their compensation structures.[110] Second, the unique organizational features of hedge funds, including their ability to lock-up investor capital, make them more suited to activism.[111] Third, hedge funds use unique financial instruments, such as short-selling techniques and the purchase of securities in margin, to facilitate their

[103] See, e.g., Anabtawi and Stout, above n 28 at 1255; M. Lipton, "Bite the Apple; Poison the Apple; Paralyze the Company; Wreck the Economy," (Wachtell, Lipton, Rosen & Katz memorandum, 2013), available at http://corpgov.law.harvard.edu/2013/02/26/bite-the-apple-poison-the-apple-paralyze-the-company-wreck-the-economy.

[104] For a review of the empirical literature, see A. Brav, W. Jiang, and H. Kim, "Hedge Fund Activism: A Review" (2009) 4 *Foundations and Trends in Finance* 185; J.C. Coffee, Jr., and D. Palia, "The Impact of Hedge Fund Activism: Evidence and Implications," *Law Working Paper No. 266/2014* (European Corporate Governance Institute, 2014).

[105] See L.A. Bebchuk, A. Brav, and W. Jiang, "The Long-Term Effects of Hedge Fund Activism" (2015) 114 *Columbia Law Review* 1085 (finding improved operating performance of companies following activist interventions).

[106] Katelouzou, above n 91.

[107] M. Kahan and E.B. Rock, "Hedge Funds in Corporate Governance and Corporate Control" (2007) 155 *University of Pennsylvania Law Review* 1021 at 1047.

[108] P. Rose and B. Sharfman, "Shareholder Activism as a Corrective Mechanism in Corporate Governance" (2015) 2014 *Brigham Young University Law Review* 1015.

[109] Kahan and Rock, above n 107 at 1066–8.

[110] *Ibid.* 1064–6.

[111] K.-W. Chueh, "Is Hedge Fund Activism New Hope for the Market?" (2008) 2008 *Columbia Business Law Review* 724.

activism.[112] An activist hedge fund could focus on a handful of underperforming companies and hedge by "shorting" other companies that offset the firm or industry-specific risk. Fourth, in the United States, where the bulk of hedge fund activity takes place, activist hedge funds also face fewer regulatory impediments and they are not subject to diversification or investment strategies restraints.[113] Finally, despite first appearing to be unsympathetic to the interests of shareholders as a class, hedge fund activism is increasingly gaining in reputation with large institutional investors, some of which now vocally support activist hedge fund campaigns.[114] Mainstream institutional shareholders, therefore, have been transformed from "rationally apathetic" investors to "rationally reticent" in that they are increasingly willing to support activist hedge funds' proposals, but are unlikely themselves to initiate them.[115]

5.3.2 Toward an "Investor Paradigm": Policy Attempts to Promote Shareholder Engagement and Stewardship

In the complex processes that explain the transformation of the role of shareholders in recent years, a key parallel development to the rise and influence of institutional investors, including activist hedge funds, is the attempted strengthening of the legal status of shareholders.[116] Governments, particularly, in the Anglo-Saxon world, have actively long promoted an "equity culture" and espoused the notion of "shareholder democracy"[117] premised on the idea that shareholder power is a positive regulatory mechanism.

[112] F.S. Partnoy and R.S. Thomas, "Gap Filling, Hedge Funds, and Financial Innovations," in Y. Fuchita and R.E. Litan (eds.), *New Financial Instruments and Institutions: Opportunities and Policy Challenges* (Nomura Institute of Capital Markets Research, 2007), p. 119.

[113] *Ibid.* at 117–18. Investment Company Act of 1940, Pub. L. 112-90, approved 3 January 2012, r. 2a-7.

[114] Katelouzou, above n 90 at 792.

[115] Gilson and Gordon, above n 80 at 867.

[116] However, despite several legislative measures strengthening shareholders' status within the corporation, the level of "formal" shareholder protection world-wide did not dramatically change in the years following the financial crisis. For relevant statistics, see D. Katelouzou and M. Siems, "Disappearing Paradigms in Shareholder Protection: Leximetric Evidence for 30 Countries, 1990–2013" (2015) 15 *Journal of Corporate Law Studies* 127.

[117] R. Dore, "Financialization of the Global Economy" (2008) 17 *Industrial and Corporate Change* 1097.

In the United States, shareholder-centric policy reforms have a long and diverse history revolving around the debates of shareholder primacy versus director primacy. For shareholder empowerment proponents, the lack of shareholder engagement has contributed to excessive risk-taking by managers and corporate failures.[118] For the opponents of shareholder empowerment, however, the locus of authority in a public corporation is the board of directors, which is in the best position to make the most important decisions on behalf of the company. Accordingly, any strengthening of shareholder powers will undermine the benefits of centralized decision-making authority and therefore cannot guarantee that shareholders will use the powers made available to them to prevent a future crisis.[119] Although this debate is still lively,[120] recent years have seen several developments aiming to increase the accountability of listed company boards to shareholders and to enhance shareholders' direct involvement in the firm's internal management. Likely, the most significant development is the expanded ability of shareholders to use shareholder proposals under Rule 14a-8 to effect changes in corporate election procedures, calibrated by section 971 of the Dodd-Frank Act.[121]

Shareholder empowerment developments have been also promoted in recent years in the area of executive pay. Since 2002, the United Kingdom has been the forerunner in mandating that public companies allow shareholders an advisory vote on the annual remuneration report,[122] while in 2013 it introduced a binding shareholder vote on remuneration policy in addition to an advisory vote on implementation.[123] Many countries around the world including Australia, Belgium, Denmark, France,

[118] L.A. Bebchuk, "The Case for Increasing Shareholder Power" (2005) 118 *Harvard Law Review* 833; Commission on Capital Markets Regulation, Interim Report 93 (2006), available at http://capmktsreg.org/press/interim-report.

[119] See, among others, S.M. Bainbridge, "Director Primacy: The Means and Ends of Corporate Governance" (2003) 97 *Northwestern University Law Review* 547; W.W. Bratton and M.L. Wachter, "The Case against Shareholder Empowerment" (2010) 158 *University of Pennsylvania Law Review* 653 at 653–4, 657–9.

[120] See, e.g., J.G. Hill, "Images of the Shareholder – Shareholder Power and Shareholder Powerlessness," in J.G. Hill and R.S. Thomas (eds.), *Research Handbook on Shareholder Power* (Northampton, MA: Edward Elgar Publishing, 2015), pp. 53–74 (discussing how this debate is underpinned by a range of competing images of the shareholder).

[121] Dodd-Frank Act, above n 24 s. 971. Another post-crisis legislative measure that increased shareholder protection was the introduction of majority (rather than plurality) voting in the election of directors. See, further, S.M. Bainbridge, *Corporate Governance after the Financial Crisis* (New York: Oxford University Press, 2011), pp. 206–20.

[122] The Directors' Remuneration Report Regulations 2002, SI 2002 No. 1986.

[123] UK Companies Act 2006, ss. 226B, 226C, 439, and 439A.

Germany, Italy, the Netherlands, Norway, Spain, Sweden, Switzerland, and the United States, have followed the UK's model and introduced "say on pay" in various forms.[124] These reforms seeking to promote "say on pay" reflect the view that shareholder participation rights can act as a useful check and balance on high executive remuneration.[125] The latest addition to this impressive record of bolstering shareholder involvement in the setting of executive pay worldwide is the proposed amendments to the Shareholder Rights Directive (2007/36/EC) seeking to improve the level and quality of shareholder engagement and proposing, among others, a "say on pay" vote at least every three years.[126]

Whilst the purported aim of these regulatory developments has been to promote managerial accountability by according shareholders with more powers, public trust cannot be restored in the post-crisis market unless the dysfunctionality of shareholders' accountability is also addressed. Many commentators on both sides of the Atlantic have voiced concerns in recent years about the potential vulnerability of public corporations to short-term pressures in view of the increasing powers of activist shareholders.[127] These concerns have been addressed by the idea of "shareholder stewardship," first introduced in the United Kingdom.

In the post-crisis UK market, the lack of shareholder engagement is believed to have contributed to the excessive risk-taking by the management of some banking institutions, while at the same time excessive short-termism has been blamed for recent corporate failures and a lack

[124] "Say on pay" involves allowing shareholders to vote on corporations' compensation packages and policies. For a comparative study on say on pay, encompassing eight jurisdictions, see R.S. Thomas and C. Van der Elst, "The International Scope of Say on Pay," *Law Working Paper No. 227/2013* (European Corporate Governance Institute, 2013), available at http://ssrn.com/abstract=2307510, at 5–64. A shorter overview for 11 European countries can be found in R. Barontini, S. Bozzi, G. Ferrarini, and M.C. Ungureanu, "Directors' Remuneration before and after the Crisis: Measuring the Impact of Reforms in Europe," in M. Belcredi and G. Ferrarini (eds.), *Boards and Shareholders in European Listed Companies* (Cambridge: Cambridge University Press, 2013), p. 251, table 1.

[125] However, in practice shareholders approve almost all executive pay packages except in the most egregious cases of high pay. See J.F. Cooter, "The First Year of Say-on-Pay under Dodd-Frank: An Empirical Analysis and Look Forward" (2013) 81 *George Washington Law Review* 967 at 978.

[126] Amendments to Shareholder Rights Directive, above n 26.

[127] See, e.g., A. Dignam "The Future of Shareholder Democracy in the Shadow of the Financial Crisis" (2013) 36 *Seattle University Law Review* 639; L.E. Strine, Jr., "Can We Do Better by Ordinary Investors? A Pragmatic Reaction to the Dueling Ideologists of Corporate Law" (2014) 114 *Columbia Law Review* 449.

of investment in research and development.[128] At the urging of such calls, the Financial Reporting Council, as part of the regulatory response to the challenges of managerial failures and short-termism practices, enacted, in July 2010, the Stewardship Code as a set of best practices for institutional shareholders.[129] The UK Stewardship Code, revised in 2012, is a "soft law" code of best practices for institutions and asset managers in conducting their relationships with their investee companies. Although the Code is not mandatory, voluntary signatories to the Code are required to comply with the principles or explain their lack of compliance.[130] The Code has attracted 302 voluntary signatories to date,[131] including all major UK and international institutions, asset managers and proxy advisory agencies.

The UK Stewardship Code envisages engagement as a "purposeful dialogue"[132] with investee companies, which can be escalated where necessary. Such escalation activities include holding meetings with the incumbents (management, chairman, or directors), making public statements or actively exercising shareholder rights such as submitting shareholder resolutions at general meetings or requisitioning general meetings.[133] In this way, both defensive and offensive forms of shareholder activism have to conform to the standards in the Code.

The concept of stewardship encourages institutional investors and asset managers to engage with corporate management and boards in a constructive way across a range of issues "such as strategy, performance, risk, capital structure, and corporate governance, including culture and remuneration,"[134] with a sense of "duty"[135] to the long-term interests of their investee companies and their own end-investors. Stewardship assumes that more effective shareholder engagement in corporate affairs should

[128] D. Walker, "A Review of Corporate Governance in UK Banks and other Financial industry Entities: Final Recommendations" (2009), available at http://webarchive.nationalarchives.gov.uk/+/, www.hm-treasury.gov.uk/d/walker_review_261109.pdf; J. Kay, *The Kay Review of UK Equity Markets and Long-Term Decision Making* (Final Report, 2012).

[129] See Financial Reporting Council, *The UK Stewardship Code* (2012), available at www.frc.org.uk/getattachment/e2db042e-120b-4e4e-bdc7-d540923533a6/UK-Stewardship-Code-September-2012.aspx.

[130] On the comply or explain approach, see further J.G. Parkinson and G. Kelly, "The Combined Code of Corporate Governance" (1999) 70 *Political Quarterly* 101.

[131] These include: 203 asset manager signatories, 86 asset owners, and 13 proxy advisory agencies.

[132] UK Stewardship Code, above n 129 at 5.

[133] *Ibid.* at 8.

[134] *Ibid.* at 1.

[135] *Ibid.* The Principles of the UK Stewardship Code can evolve into concrete institutional shareholder duties – a duty to engage, a duty to avoid conflicts of interests, and a duty to vote.

not only improve the governance and performance of investee companies, but should also assist the efficient operation of the markets and strengthen the credibility of the market economy as a whole.[136] Terms, such as "long-term success," "responsibility," "purposeful dialogue," and "transparency," figure emblematically in the concept of shareholder stewardship.[137]

Adapted versions of the UK Stewardship Code have since been introduced in various jurisdictions, by quasi-regulatory bodies such as the Malaysian Stock Exchange[138] and the Institute of Directors in South Africa[139] as well as shareholder constituencies such as the Japanese National Pension Fund[140] and the Swiss Institutional Investors Association – the Economiesuisse.[141] More recently, the proposed Shareholder Rights Directive requires institutional investors and asset managers to develop an engagement policy and imposes disclosure obligations of institutions' investment policies and strategies, their arrangements with asset managers, and the accountability of asset managers to institutions.[142] While the policy directions towards stewardship have, to date, been voluntary in nature and encouraged by regulators without direct state intervention as part of the emerging de-centered regulatory landscape,[143] the proposed Directive is arguably not far from imposing a "duty" to demonstrate engagement on the part of institutions.[144] This somewhat "hardening" of shareholder

[136] *Ibid.* at 2.

[137] *Ibid.* at 1, 6, 10.

[138] *Malaysian Code for Institutional Investors* (2014), available at www.sc.com.my/wp-content/uploads/eng/html/cg/mcii_140627.pdf

[139] Committee on Responsible Investing by Institutional Investors in South Africa, *The Code for Responsible Investing in South Africa* (2011), available at http://c.ymcdn.com/sites/www.iodsa.co.za/resource/resmgr/crisa/crisa_19_july_2011.pdf

[140] Council of Experts Concerning the Japanese Version of the Stewardship Code, *Principles for Responsible Institutional Investors: Japan's Stewardship Code* (2014), available at www.fsa.go.jp/news/25/singi/20140227-2/05.pdf

[141] *Guidelines for Institutional Investors Governing the Exercising of Participation Rights in Public Limited Companies* (2013), available at www.ethosfund.ch/upload/publication/p432e_130121_Guidelines_for_institutional_investors.pdf

[142] Proposed Shareholder Rights Directive above n 26, arts. 3f–3h.

[143] C. Scott, "Analysing Regulatory Space: Fragmented Resources and Institutional Design" (2001) *Public Law* 329; C. Scott, "Reflexive Governance, Meta-regulation and CSR," in N. Boeger, R. Murray and C. Villiers (eds.), *Perspectives on Corporate Social Responsibility* (Cheltenham: Edward Elgar Publishing, 2008), ch. 9.

[144] For a detailed discussion of the notion of shareholder stewardship promulgated by the Proposed Shareholder Rights Directive, see I.H.-Y. Chiu and D. Katelouzou, "From Shareholder Stewardship to Shareholder Duties: Is the Time Ripe?," in H. Birkmose (ed.), *Shareholder's Duties* (Kluwer Law International, forthcoming), also available at http://ssrn.com/abstract=2731241.

behavior norms is not a result of catering to bottom-up forces and market demand for corporate governance norms. Rather, it appears to be a regulatory measure rooted in public interest concerns of short-termism and accountability to a broader range of stakeholders.[145] This suggests that the increasing prescription towards shareholder behavior and stewardship addresses other public interest concerns beyond the private proprietary conception of share ownership and investor behavior.

Despite the proposed Shareholder Rights Directive reflecting a broad-based public interest in making institutional shareholders accountable to wider constituents in the exercise of their engagement powers,[146] which is clearly not found in the UK Stewardship Code, the underpinning idea behind these regulatory developments is common. This is the notion that shareholder power is a positive corporate governance attribute that enables investors to act in a twofold way – as a *monitoring mechanism* enforcing shareholder value maximization and as an *accountability mechanism* protecting the interests of other shareholders and the economy as a whole through the promotion of shareholder stewardship. The supposition that compliance with shareholder value maximization as a proxy for aggregate social welfare should be enforced through shareholder engagement and stewardship marks a paradigm shift for corporate law, from contractarianism and agency theory to what can be described as an "investor paradigm" for corporate law. This paradigm is so named because it recognizes the dual role that institutional investors catalytically play in corporate governance today.

On the one hand, as we have already seen, institutional investors are currently more active in exercising direct or indirect (through investing in activist hedge funds) control over their investee companies with positive economic effects. Recent regulatory developments vesting more powers in shareholders recognize the increase in the failure of unfettered managerialism and the influence of institutional investors and are designed to compel managers to act in the shareholders' interests. The mainstream debate has justified the shareholder franchise based on the status of shareholders as residual claimants or as principals vis-à-vis the managers-agents. Yet, none of these suppositions hold to further scrutiny. Shareholders are

[145] *Ibid.*

[146] See, in particular art. 3(f) which states: "Member States shall . . . ensure that institutional investors and asset managers develop a policy on shareholder engagement . . .". Amendments to Shareholder Rights Directive, above n 26 at art. 3(f).

not the only stakeholders with a residual claim,[147] and even though the principal-agent relationship might have some credits and hedge fund activism might provide a form of discipline, especially against the agency problems associated with free cash flow,[148] other internal or external monitoring mechanisms might also lower capital costs.[149] Neither can shareholder franchises be justified on notions of shareholder ownership. The traditional "ownership model" has been already challenged in the 1930s by Berle and Means,[150] and it is almost incontestable among corporate law scholars and practitioners that the ownership of shares is different from the ownership of the corporation's assets.[151]

To understand the changed nature of shareholders, as this is embraced by activist shareholders, one needs to move away from both contractarian accounts of the shareholder franchise on the basis of residual claims or principal-agent relationships and traditional notions of ownership. But is there a better theoretical foundation for promoting shareholder franchise? Paul Edelman, Randall Thomas, and Robert Thompson proposed a positive theory of shareholder voting in which they argue that shareholders, uniquely among corporate constituents, are sensitive to share prices and therefore they "seek to have a vote over issues that are likely to affect share price."[152] Building on this positive theory[153] it can be shown that activist hedge funds are tied closely to the stock price of the corporation and thus it is in their interests that the firm's value be maximized.

Activist hedge funds have the incentives to control the pursuit by managers of self-interested objectives and limit managerial divergence from shareholder wealth maximization. Activist hedge funds also stimulate other institutional shareholders to overcome their rational reticence and

[147] L. Stout, "Bad and Not-So-Bad Arguments for Shareholder Primacy" (2002) 75 *Southern California Law Review*, 1189.

[148] Brav *et al.*, above n 91 at 1731.

[149] But see above nn 69–73 and accompanying text on the diminishing monitoring role of the market for corporate control.

[150] On the traditional ownership model and on how this was challenged by Berle and Means, see Dallas, above n 54 at 21.

[151] In particular, English law has long recognized that the corporation is not owned by any particular group. See *Salomon* v. *Salomon & Co.* [1897] AC 22 HL. As the court in *Short* v. *Treasury Commissioners* [1948] AC 534 HL noted, "shareholders are not, in the eye of the law, part owners of the undertaking. The undertaking is something different from the totality of the shareholding."

[152] Edelman, Thomas, and Thompson, above n 23 at 1382.

[153] An important caveat is that this is not a normative theory about the merits of shareholder activism in promoting corporate or social welfare.

engage in value-enhancing monitoring. Whether activist hedge funds can also account for the firm's other stakeholders depends on the approach we take to the corporation's objectives. For those viewing shareholder value maximization as a means of promoting the public interest, and not as an end to itself, strong shareholder control can serve as a blueprint for an improved, future corporation. Indeed, corporate law scholarship largely recognizes that the interests of the corporation as a whole are closely identified with the profit maximization interests of its shareholders.[154]

Conversely, the emerging investor paradigm recognizes that powers come with responsibilities and, therefore, taps into the major problem with increasing solicitude for shareholders, namely the rise of financialization and short-term shareholder value processes at the expense of other stakeholders. Shareholder stewardship, introduced in the United Kingdom, champions institutional investors as promoters of profit maximization for both their own interests and for society as a whole. The proposed Shareholder Rights Directive even goes a step further by shaping the institutional investors' engagement policy towards non-financial performance and the reduction of social and environmental risks and by compelling institutions to engage with stakeholders in their engagement policies. The United States, however, has not tracked recent developments in shareholder stewardship. Still, the need to mitigate short-termism and trading-focused investment management and the need to rein in any opportunistic activist hedge fund behavior have been recognized and some American commentators argue in favor of a fiduciary duty being introduced and imposed on minority activist shareholders who wield undue influence over the general meeting.[155]

This emerging investor paradigm is largely at odds with dominant assumptions of contractarianism. The nexus of contracts theory, as we have already seen, is based on the premise that the efficiency of the shareholder-management relationship is a function of individual contracting, with the various markets adequately performing a disciplinary function.

[154] For a detailed discussion of shareholder wealth maximization being more desirable than a stakeholder approach, see M.C. Jensen, "Value Maximization, Stakeholder Theory, and the Corporate Objective Function" (2001) 14 *Journal of Applied Corporate Finance* 8. Admittedly, however, both the shareholder primacy and stakeholder theories have shortcomings, the analysis of which are beyond the scope of this chapter. For a detailed examination of the two dominant theories, see A. Keay, *The Corporate Objective* (Cheltenham: Edward Edgar Publishing, 2011).

[155] See, e.g., Anabtawi and Stout, above n 28 at 1255.

Under the contractarian framework, the resulting "optimal" contractual structure of the firm does not find any place for active shareholder control over management and the case for corporate governance reform is largely undermined. At the same time, contractarianism purports particularly to orientate the corporation to the maximization of shareholders' returns, although it views any corporate law reforms that would strengthen shareholder rights as unnecessary. The power of the changing investor landscape and accompanying regulatory developments challenge these assertions. The emerging investor paradigm calls for both shareholder monitoring and shareholder responsibility, bringing together owner control and social accountability.

5.4 Some Concluding Remarks: The Changing Nature of the Public Corporation

This chapter highlights that real-world and policy developments have rendered the contractarian view of the corporation outdated. Of course, contractarianism has never provided a definitive description of the public corporation. Although the description of the corporation as a nexus of contracts is an illuminating analogy, it is neither a historical account nor a normatively correct description of the modern corporation. More importantly for our purposes, despite any general aptness of the contractarian and economic reasoning, it is inappropriate as far as the role of institutional shareholders is concerned. The re-concentration of shareholdings in the hands of institutional investors and the emergence of hedge fund activism challenge the contractarian picture of the management-shareholder relationship, which has for decades provided a legitimizing basis for shareholders' non-intervention. In addition, the contractarian framework cannot provide suitable benchmarks for evaluating the current shareholder-centric policy reforms promoting the shareholder franchise and shareholder accountability. Indeed, these reforms are contrary to the contractarian view of the corporation, which is agnostic to any prescription of having shareholders become directly involved in the firm's internal management and with any accountability obligations this might entail.

The current context provides a promising entry point to reconstruct our approach and understanding of the role of shareholders within the public corporation and shift towards an investor paradigm in corporate law. Theories that separate the world into public and private fail to realize that public and private elements co-exist within the corporation.[156] The modern corporation is not only a point of conflict between private and public theories of the firm, or between shareholders and stakeholders conceptions, but it is also an intersection of "overlapping, intervening, and conditioning authorities, non-traditional rule-makers, mixed norms, and new, not exclusively state-based, enforcement and compliance mechanisms."[157] This conception forces us to more adequately consider the context in which the shareholder-centric policy reforms and the advent of hedge fund activism and institutional investors' "awakening," more generally, are situated.

Still, how can we understand the relations of activist shareholders in and around the corporation? What has been described as an investor paradigm in this chapter provides a basis for understanding the dual role of institutional investors within the internal functioning of the modern corporation. Notions of shareholder engagement and stewardship can have far-reaching implications for the role of institutional investors within the firm's internal management and its impact on other stakeholders, and re-embed the modern corporation within society, its institutions, and values.

[156] Bratton, above n 35 at 442.
[157] Zumbansen, above n 16 at 1473.

6

Regulating for Corporate Sustainability: Why the Public–Private Divide Misses the Point

BEATE SJÅFJELL

6.1 Public or Private? Not the Important Question

The debate on whether the company is a public or private entity is intellectually interesting. The answer to the question may influence the approach one takes to regulating the company. Those seeing it as a public entity may be prepared, to a greater extent, to require it to act for the good of society than those who see it as a private entity. Conversely, those that see it not only as a private entity but even, mistakenly, as the property of the shareholders,[1] may resist the very notion of anything besides returns to shareholders as being the legitimate purpose of the company.

However, we risk that this interesting academic debate – where there will always be different opinions – may serve as a deflection device, keeping bright academic minds occupied with discussing the nature of the company. The positions in the public vs. private debate will tend to be fuelled by political positions as well as theoretical or academic starting points. In a similar way as debates such as the (revealingly or misleadingly named) shareholder vs. stakeholder debate,[2] this may push the contributors into opposing trenches where winning the discussion, or more academically, formulating the best argument becomes paramount. Indeed, while we may say that the stakeholder position has informed the corporate social responsibility (CSR) movement and the shareholder position has led to the still dominant and mainstream corporate governance debate, the

[1] For an eloquent dismantling of the myth, see P. Ireland "Company Law and the Myth of Shareholder Ownership" (1999) 62 *Modern Law Review* 32. See also L. Talbot, *Great Debates in Company Law* (London: Palgrave Macmillan, 2014) where she also touches upon the intense ownership myth debate in Norway in 2013.

[2] Where shareholders are clearly the starting point and "stakeholders" is a denominator for all other interests. See B. Sjåfjell, *Towards a Sustainable European Company Law* (Alphen aan den Rijn, NL: Kluwer Law International, 2009), s. 4.1.2.

public/private debate may perhaps be said to underpin the stakeholder vs. shareholder debate or be the more academic, theoretical variant thereof.[3]

The public/private debate is somewhat more academic in its approach in that determining whether the company is a public or private entity does not necessarily begin from a specific view. This stands in contrast to the shareholder versus stakeholder debate, much of the CSR movement, and of course the corporate governance trend.[4]

However, the public/private question opens up for arriving at a conclusion which would lead to the position that if the company is a private entity, then its societal impact is something we must search for a foundation for including in the discussion. To a certain extent, that basis is in the law itself; which much of the CSR discourse has missed because of the regulatory capture by business lobbyists.[5] Moreover, the idea of internalizing externalities is a further basis for including societal impacts within the scope of a private entity.[6] Conversely, if the company is perceived as a public entity, while that may make the argument for including broader societal considerations easier, we still need to take into consideration the approach the law itself takes today to the relationship between companies and shareholders, creditors, employees, and other interests.

Going into the public/private debate therefore risks exacerbating unnecessarily entrenched positions on the nature, purpose, and responsibility of the company. It also risks enforcing an impression of a more hard-lined dichotomy between public and private, shareholders and other stakeholders, social responsibility and corporate governance, for which there actually is a basis. Accordingly, it may not help, but rather make more difficult, the discussion of the more important question: How do we regulate for corporate sustainability?

Corporate sustainability is achieved when businesses (or more broadly, economic actors) in aggregate create value in a manner that is (a)

[3] See B. Sjåfjell, "Internalizing Externalities in EU law: Why Neither Corporate Governance nor Corporate Social Responsibility Provides the Answers" (2010) 40 *George Washington International Law Review* 977.

[4] In spite of the opposing interests the various approaches wish to promote, all of these tend to (inadvertently) support the notion that the company is a vehicle for shareholders' profits and that all other interests must build up an argument for their own inclusion within the realm of what companies need to care about. *Ibid.*

[5] See the multi-jurisdictional comparative analysis in B. Sjåfjell, A. Johnston, L. Anker-Sørensen, and D. Millon, "Shareholder Primacy: The Main Barrier to Sustainable Companies," in B. Sjåfjell and B.J. Richardson (eds.), *Company Law and Sustainability: Legal Barriers and Opportunities* (Cambridge University Press, 2015) at ch. 3.

[6] See generally Sjåfjell, above n 3.

environmentally sustainable in the sense that it ensures the long-term stability and resilience of the ecosystems that support human life, (b) *socially* sustainable in the sense that it facilitates the respect and promotion of human rights, and (c) *economically* sustainable in the sense that it satisfies the economic needs necessary for stable and resilient societies.

If I were required to take a position on the public/private question, my response would be that the company is a private entity with public obligations.[7] Its existence is founded on its acceptance by society in general as well as from the business participants. This acceptance must be based, and is dependent, on the fulfilment by the company – at least on an aggregate level – of certain societal goals. However, it is the actual impact business has, and not whether it can theoretically be categorized as public or private, that forms the basis for my academic focus on the company as the dominating regulatory form for running business.

The position that the important question is how do we regulate for corporate sustainability is based on the following three points. First, sustainable development cannot be achieved without the contribution of business.[8] The path of "business as usual," which we are on today, is a very certain path towards a very uncertain future. The science on climate change is just one case in point that we are transgressing the planetary boundaries[9] within which we must stay if we wish to preserve the very basis of existence for humanity.[10] The resilience of our entire economic system, on which we

[7] See also the early contributions J. Kay and A. Silberston, "Corporate Governance" and K. Greenfield, "From Rights to Regulation in Corporate Law," both in F.M. Patfield (ed.), *Perspectives on Company Law: 2* (London: Kluwer Law International, 1997).

[8] As the European Commission also states: "[E]nterprises can significantly contribute to the European Union's treaty objectives of sustainable development and a highly competitive social market economy." European Commission, "A Renewed EU Strategy 2011–14 for Corporate Social Responsibility," COM (2011) 681 final at s. 1.2.

[9] Introduced by J. Rockström, W.L. Steffen, K. Noone, Å. Persson, and F.S. Chapin III, Planetary Boundaries: Exploring the Safe Operating Space for Humanity" (2009) 14 *Ecology and Society* 32, available at www.ecologyandsociety.org/vol14/iss2/art32/; confirmed and updated in W. Steffen, K. Richardson, J. Rockström, S.E. Cornell, *et al.*, "Planetary Boundaries: Guiding Human Development on a Changing Planet," *Science*, 13 January 2015, available at www.sciencemag.org/content/347/6223/1259855.abstract.

[10] As the Intergovernmental Panel on Climate Change stated already in 2007: "Unmitigated climate change would, in the long term, be *likely* to exceed the capacity of natural, managed and human systems to adapt." IPCC Core Writing Team, R. K. Pachauri and A. Reisinger (eds.), *Climate Change 2007: Synthesis Report. Contribution of Working Groups I, II and III to the Fourth Assessment Report of the Intergovernmental Panel on Climate Change* (Geneva: IPCC, 2008), p. 65. See the full reports from the Intergovernmental Panel on Climate Change, available at www.ipcc.ch.

have based our societies and the welfare of our generation and those to come, is called into question.[11] And we continue to face the harsh brutality of tens of thousands of people dying daily for poverty-related reasons,[12] which is likely to be exacerbated through the effects of global warming.[13] Sustainable development is a path towards a safe and just operating space for humanity and that is what we need to have as our overarching goal.[14]

Second, business can – with existing knowledge and technology – shift away from business as usual and onto a sustainable path. This means that we should not be content with waiting for technological innovation.[15] There are, however, barriers that prevent business from realizing its enormous potential to contribute to sustainability. Identifying such barriers in the legal infrastructure of companies has been a main focus of the international Sustainable Companies Project.[16]

[11] See, e.g., Carbon Tracker Initiative, *Unburnable Carbon 2013: Wasted Capital and Stranded Assets* (2013), available at http://carbontracker.live.kiln.digital/Unburnable-Carbon-2-Web-Version.pdf. See also D. Hone, "Climate Change and the Carbon Bubble Reality Check, The Energy Collective, 3 May 2013, available at http://theenergycollective.com/davidhone/220316/carbon-bubble-reality-check.

[12] As UN Secretary-General Ban Ki-moon says: "[I]t is clear that improvements in the lives of the poor have been unacceptably slow, and some hard-won gains are being eroded by the climate, food and economic crises." U.N. Millennium Development Goals Report (2010), available at www.un.org/millenniumgoals.

[13] See, e.g., J. von Braun, *The World Food Situation: New Driving Forces and Required Actions* (Washington, DC: International Food Policy Research Institute, 2007), p. 12 ("When taking into account the effects of [unmitigated] climate change, the number of undernourished people in Sub-Saharan Africa may triple between 1990 and 2080 . . .").

[14] See K. Raworth, *A Safe and Just Space for Humanity: Can We Live within the Doughnut?* (Oxford: Oxfam International, 2012), available at www.oxfam.org/sites/www.oxfam.org/files/dp-a-safe-and-just-space-for-humanity-130212-en.pdf. On the EU level, see B. Sjåfjell, "The Legal Significance of Article 11 TFEU for EU Institutions and Member States," in B. Sjåfjell and A. Wiesbrock, *The Greening of European Business under EU Law* (Abingdon: Routledge, 2015), ch. 4. On the international level, see the UN Sustainable Development Goals, available at https://sustainabledevelopment.un.org.

[15] As the 2005 Intergovernmental Panel on Climate Change report noted, there is already a great potential for business to reduce greenhouse gas emissions with existing technology, but there are barriers that prevent this from being put into use. See B. Metz, O. Davidson, P. Bosch, R. Dave, and L. Meyer (eds.), *Climate Change 2007: Mitigation. Contribution of Working Group III to the Fourth Assessment Report of the Intergovernmental Panel on Climate Change* (Cambridge University Press, 2007), available at ipcc.ch/publications_and_data/ar4/wg3/en/contents.html.

[16] The Sustainable Companies Project (2010–2014), led by the University of Oslo, available at jus.uio.no/companies (under Projects). The work of identifying barriers and possibilities continues on a broader scale in the project Sustainable Market Actors for Responsible Trade (SMART; 2016–2020), funded under the EU framework program Horizon 2020, available at jus.uio.no/companies (under Projects).

Third, business is not doing enough on a voluntary basis. A fundamental barrier for businesses shifting voluntarily away from business as usual and onto a path of corporate sustainability is the social norm of shareholder primacy, as has been argued by several commentators and substantiated further through the comparative company law research of the Sustainable Companies Project.[17] This provides the basis for the conclusion that legal reform is necessary. The company law debate we need to have is what such a legal reform should look like and how we can show businesses, policy-makers, and legislators that such reform needs to be adopted.

This chapter briefly summarizes the comparative company law research on barriers to sustainability and the basis for the argument that company law reform is necessary (see Section 6.2). Thereafter, a tentative reform proposal for a first step towards corporate sustainability at European Union (EU) level is presented (see Section 6.3). This chapter closes with some reflections on what future research should look into and on the hope for achieving sustainable policies (see Section 6.4).

6.2 Barriers and Possibilities for Sustainable Companies

The Sustainable Companies Project investigated the barriers to and possibilities for a deeper integration of environmental concerns into the decision-making in companies. We investigated core company law, through an extensive, comparative analysis of the purpose of the company as a matter of law, and the role and duties of the board. We focused on the concept of the interests of the company to find the scope of the board's duty and discretion in its supervision and management of the company. The regulation, or lack thereof, of corporate groups also formed part of our investigation. We also investigated accounting and auditing law, in a similar comparative approach, allowing us to delve deeply into the area of law where broader societal interests, through so-called non-financial or CSR reporting, has made inroads. While the focus of the Sustainable Companies Project was on environmental externalities, the results are to a great extent transferable to social externalities. Indeed, the reform proposal presented in Section 6.3 takes that broader view.

Our results may be summarized as follows: In core company law, the possibilities for a shift away from business as usual and onto a sustainable path are larger than we perhaps beforehand had expected. While

[17] See B. Sjåfjell and B.J. Richardson, above n 5.

the mainstream corporate governance debate tends to regard maximization of shareholder profit as the sole purpose of companies, this is, as a matter of law, to a great extent incorrect, especially understood as society's purpose with companies in aggregate.[18] No company law system insists on boards focusing only on returns for shareholders.[19] All jurisdictions expect boards to ensure environmental legal compliance. We see examples of shareholder value (a legal concept, which we distinguish from the social concept of shareholder primacy) in jurisdictions like the United Kingdom expressly stipulating that broader societal concerns, including environmental protection, should be taken into account.[20] Generally, company law across jurisdictions also allows boards to integrate environmental externalities beyond legal compliance, at least as far as the business case argument allows – that is as far as the case can be made that this is profitable for the company in the long run. Within the current system, company law on a comparative basis provides, perhaps surprising, latitude to the board and by extension the management to shape business in a sustainable manner.[21] However, boards generally do not choose environmentally friendly, low carbon options within the realm of the business case let alone challenge the outer boundaries of the scope to pursue profit in a sustainable manner. This is because of the overriding social norm of shareholder primacy, which, supported by management remuneration incentives and other drivers, dictates that board and senior managers are the "agents" of the shareholders and should maximize returns to shareholders as measured by the current share price.[22] This leads to an extremely narrow, short-term, profit maximization focus.[23]

The resulting general practice of companies is detrimental to those affected by climate change and environmental degradation today and to

[18] See Sjåfjell *et al.*, above n 5.

[19] In some jurisdictions environmental sustainability has begun tentatively to make inroads into the explicit duties of the board. See, e.g., A. Johnston, "Reforming English Company Law to Promote Sustainable Companies" (2014) 11 *European Company Law* 63; T. Lambooy, *Corporate Social Responsibility: Legal and Semi-Legal Frameworks Supporting CSR: Developments 2000–2010 and Case Studies* (Deventer: Kluwer, 2010), pp. 107–146.

[20] C. Villiers, "Mapping Paper: Sustainable Companies UK Report" (2015) 11 *International and Comparative Corporate Law Journal* 105.

[21] Sjåfjell *et al.*, above n 5.

[22] *Ibid.*

[23] This was also identified by the EU Commission as a problem. See B. Sjåfjell and L. Anker-Sørensen, "Directors' Duties and Corporate Social Responsibility (CSR)," in H.S. Birkmose, M. Neville, and K. Engsig Sørensen (eds.), *Boards of Directors in European Companies* (Alphen aan den Rijn, NL: Kluwer Law International, 2013).

the possibility for future generations to fulfil their own needs. It is also damaging to the interests of shareholders with more than a very short-term perspective on their investment, including institutional investors such as pension funds or sovereign wealth funds, as well as companies themselves.[24]

The barrier to sustainability posed by the shareholder primacy norm is exacerbated by the chasm between company law's approach to corporate groups and the dominance and practice of such groups. The parent company's tight control of the group, in practice, is perversely matched by limited legal possibilities for holding the parent company liable for subsidiaries' environmental and social transgressions.[25]

Inspired by ideas based on reflexive theory, the compromise solution between those wishing to regulate companies' environmental and social performance more strictly and those who do not, is asking companies to report on what they are doing. In spite of good intentions and much hard work in this area, reporting requirements are strikingly insufficient. Much reporting remains left to voluntary and discretionary measures, leading to risks of corporate capture, lack of comparability, lack of consistency and uncertainty in benchmarking.[26] Notably, the new EU non-financial reporting requirements, while a step in the right direction, lack the scope and the necessary verification requirements to be a real game changer.[27]

With its company law focus, the Sustainable Companies Project has investigated an area of law that has tended to be ignored in debates on the impact of business and the possible responsibility of business. The exclusion of this area is a part of the explanation for the extremely narrow, short-term focused shareholder primacy drive that is the main barrier preventing sustainable business from being allowed to develop. The company law and corporate governance discourse at the EU level, as well as in many Member States, is dominated by the Anglo-American inspired law and economics influenced mode of thinking. Postulates derived from

[24] As the EU has observed, the financial crisis has "revealed that shareholders in many cases supported managers' excessive short-term risk taking." See Proposal for a Directive of the European Parliament and of the Council amending Directive 2007/36/EC as regards the encouragement of the long-term shareholder engagement [. . .], COM (2014) 213 final at recital 2.

[25] Sjåfjell *et al.*, above n 5.

[26] C. Villiers and J. Mähönen, "Accounting, Auditing and Reporting: Supporting or Obstructing the Sustainable Companies Objective?" in Sjåfjell and Richardson, above n 5.

[27] C. Villiers and J. Mähönen, "Article 11: Integrated Reporting or Non-Financial Reporting?" in Sjåfjell and Wiesbrock, above n 14.

law and economic theories – notably concerning principal-agency issues, the market for corporate control, and the efficient market hypothesis – have made their way into legislative work and policy debates without due consideration of the faults with the assumptions that underline these theories.[28]

We have seen tentative indications of system-critical reflections following the financial crises, with short-termism increasingly being identified as a problem to resolve.[29] Shareholder primacy has not, however, been pinpointed as a part of the problem in a legislative company law and corporate governance context.[30] As for the impact of business on the environment and human rights, the EU has invested considerable effort into trying to find the right mechanisms to encourage responsible behavior by companies.[31] However, a true integration into all areas – which EU Treaty Law requires for environmental protection requirements, including principles of sustainable development – has not been discussed.[32]

Path-dependent legislators have barely started to recognize that the system may be flawed and that the legal infrastructure for companies may, in and of itself, be problematic.[33] The fundamental assumption – that profit

[28] See, e.g., Y. Biondi, "The Governance and Disclosure of the Firm as an Enterprise Entity" (2013) 36 *Seattle University Law Review* 391, with further references; B. Sjåfjell, "More than Meets the Eye: Law and Economics in Modern Company Law," in E. Røsæg, H.B. Schäfer and E. Stavang (eds.), *Law and Economics: Essays in Honour of Erling Eide* (Oslo: Cappelen Akademisk, 2010), pp. 217–35.

[29] See, e.g., the focus in the EU on unrestricted short-termism as a problem in European Commission, *Green Paper – The EU Corporate Governance Framework*, COM (2011) 164 final.

[30] Rather emphasis is on further empowering shareholders in the hope that it will encourage more long-term thinking. See Proposal, above n 24. There is also increasing scholarship on the problem with shareholder primacy as well as growing public concern with it. Jack Welch labelled shareholder primacy as "the dumbest idea in the world." See L. Stout, *The Shareholder Value Myth: How Putting Shareholders First Harms Investors, Corporations, and the Public* (San Francisco: Berrett-Koehler Publishers, 2012) at 6.

[31] See Villiers and Mähönen, above n 26 (on the EU's non-financial reporting initiative).

[32] For a discussion on Article 11 of the Treaty on the Functioning of the European Union, see B. Sjåfjell and A. Wiesbrock, "Why Should Public Procurement Be about Sustainability?" in B. Sjåfjell and A. Wiesbrock, *Sustainable Public Procurement under EU Law* (Cambridge University Press, 2016), ch. 1. For a discussion of what the UN Guiding Principles on Business and Human Rights require, see M.B. Taylor, "Beyond 'Beyond Compliance': How Human Rights Is Transforming CSR," in A. Midtun (ed.), *CSR and Beyond – A Nordic Perspective* (Oslo: Cappelen Akademisk, 2013), pp. 253–4.

[33] Internal Market and Services Commissioner Michel Barnier stated in connection with the presentation of the EU Commission's reform package of 9 April 2014 that "[t]he last years have shown time and time again how short-termism damages European companies and the economy. Sound corporate governance can help to change that." European Commission Press Release, "European Commission proposes to strengthen shareholder engagement and introduce a 'say on pay' for Europe's largest companies" (2014).

for shareholders increases social welfare because shareholders have a residual interest that is only satisfied when all other involved parties have been dealt with fairly and properly – continues to stand strong, in spite of all the criticisms of this simplistic idea.[34]

A general tendency towards compartmentalization has undoubtedly further contributed to company law being ignored in the debate on how to ensure sustainable development.[35] Indeed, the idea that company law can concentrate on enabling the establishment of companies and protecting shareholders and creditors, and much of the unsustainable policy decisions we observe, are supported by this compartmentalization. At the EU level, for instance, each Directorate General of the European Commission focuses only on their core issues. This suggests that each sector can safely concentrate on its own sector objectives, reinforcing the idea that company law can leave issues of ecological sustainability to environmental law. This is contrary to EU Treaty law and to the very essence of sustainable development. Unlike environmental law, which traditionally is very much about anti-pollution or about forbidding or limiting substances, sustainable development is a way of thinking. Sustainable development requires the balancing of the inextricably linked complexity of economic, social, and environmental interests, within the non-negotiable ecological boundaries of our planet. In its essence sustainable development, as an overarching EU Treaty objective, therefore requires a holistic law and policy approach.[36]

Other initiatives are insufficient or even counterproductive, as discussed in detail elsewhere.[37] Legal reform at the EU level is necessary to codify sustainable business as the norm, so that the competitive advantage is given to companies that wish to contribute to sustainable development and taken away from those who do not. Company law has a crucial role to play in the transformation towards sustainability because it provides the legal framework for the internal workings of the company including its decision-making.[38] Based on the research of the Sustainable Companies Project, company law has been identified as a crucial aspect of what may

[34] See, e.g., Sjåfjell, above n 2 at s. 4.3.5; A. Johnston, *EC Regulation of Corporate Governance* (Cambridge University Press, 2010), ch. 2; M. Aglietta and A. Rebérioux, *Corporate Governance Adrift* (Cheltenham, UK: Edward Elgar, 2005).

[35] See also Sjåfjell, above n 3.

[36] B. Sjåfjell, above n 14 at 51.

[37] B. Sjåfjell, "Corporate Governance for Sustainability: The Necessary Reform of EU Company Law," in Sjåfjell and Wiesbrock above n 14 at 97.

[38] *Ibid.*; Sjåfjell and Richardson, above n 5.

be termed the "regulatory ecology" of companies.[39] A thoughtful, well-founded reform is therefore expected to impact not only on the decision-making within the company but also its relationship with its shareholders, its employees, and society at large.

The social norm of shareholder primacy, and its pervasive myth of maximizing returns as the overarching objective of companies as a matter of law, has been allowed to develop because of what company law generally does not expressly address: the societal purpose of companies and the role and duty of the board in that context.[40] This also indicates a way forward. A reform that clearly spells out the societal purpose will set a key issue straight in a principle-based manner, enabling forward-looking sustainable business.

6.3 A Possible Approach to a Sustainable Company Law Reform

Based on the research findings briefly set out above, reforming company law as a first step towards achieving corporate sustainability should address two main points: a redefinition of the purpose of the company, as a matter of law, and of the role and the duties of the board. Combatting shareholder primacy requires more than permitting a sustainability approach, since company law already gives boards surprisingly substantial room to shift away from the path of business as usual and onto a sustainable path. We therefore need firmer rules that set out the direction towards which boards must seek to shift companies. In doing so, this will provide a redefined space for the creation of value, with ample room for creativity and innovation, and enable businesses to reach their full potential. As we are far offtrack from achieving sustainable development,[41] we need to go beyond

[39] On the use of "regulatory ecology" in the company law and sustainability context see B. Sjåfjell and M.B. Taylor, "Planetary Boundaries and Company Law: Towards a Regulatory Ecology of Corporate Sustainability," *Research Paper No. 2015–11* (University of Oslo Faculty of Law, 2015), available at http://ssrn.com/abstract=2610583. This is more commonly discussed under the umbrella of "polycentric regulation," see e.g. J. Black, "Constructing and Contesting Legitimacy and Accountability in Polycentric Regulatory Regimes," (2008) 2 *Regulation and Governance* 137; M.B. Taylor, "The Ruggie Framework: Polycentric Regulation and the Implications for Corporate Social Responsibility" (2011) 5 *Etikk i Praksis Nordic Journal of Applied Ethics* 9.

[40] See Sjåfjell *et al.*, above n 5.

[41] The fifth assessment report of climate change by the Intergovernmental Panel on Climate Change, published in April 2014, reiterates earlier messages from its fourth assessment report in 2007 that it is urgent to begin reducing emissions, otherwise we will not be able to stay below the agreed upon limit of a two-degree temperature rise. IPCC, Climate

stipulating long term, inclusive concepts of the purpose of the company and the interests of the company. What urgently needs to be done is to clarify that while companies in the aggregate may and should have profit as an integrated part of their purpose, this should be achieved within the overarching societal goal of sustainable development.[42]

In the long run, financial sustainability presupposes that business is conducted within these ecological limits. As the impacts of climate change and other environmental degradation take effect, the economy will also be affected. Moreover, as the negative impacts of transgression of the ecological limits become more apparent, legislators will at some point – probably too late – require greater internalization of environmental externalities through stricter environmental regulation, higher taxes on emissions, etc. Businesses that today are allowed to ignore these issues will find themselves forced to change. We can also expect more cases where victims of climate change and other environmental harm sue businesses whose operations have contributed to their loss.

Conversely, the rise of socially responsible investment, green procurement policies and also a shift in private consumer choice towards environmentally friendly products and services may, over time, lead to more demand for responsible businesses – although these drivers today appear to be insufficient.[43] However, the main issue in the long term is that the very basis of our societies, and thereby also our economies, is threatened, making it in everybody's interest, including that of today's business leaders, to participate in the shift away from "business as usual" and onto a sustainable path.

6.3.1 *Redefining the Purpose of Companies and the Duties of the Board*

To encourage the shift away from "business as usual," it is necessary to internalize the fundamental recognition that there are ecological limits that we cannot transgress if we are to achieve sustainability as an overarching

Change 2014: Mitigation of Climate Change. Contribution of Working Group III to the Fifth Assessment Report of the Intergovernmental Panel on Climate Change [O. Edenhofer, R. Pichs-Madruga, Y. Sokona, *et al.*, (eds.)] (Cambridge: Cambridge University Press, 2014). This is but one of the several pressing issues as a case in point for sustainable development.

[42] See also B. Willard, "Better Is Not Good Enough: Toward True Corporate Sustainability" (2014), available at www.greattransition.org/publication/better-is-not-good-enough

[43] See, e.g., concerning responsible investment, B.J. Richardson, "Financial Markets and Socially Responsible Investing" in Sjåfjell and Richardson, above n 5 at 226.

societal goal. In spite of all the information that is publicly available, vital issues such as global warming and the threat to biodiversity still tend to be dealt with as something business can consider within the scope of an overarching pursuit for financial profit. Challenging this approach tends to be dismissed as unrealistic without acknowledging that nature has its own realism, which we ignore at our peril.

However, if we are to achieve a safe operating space for humanity, we cannot continue with incremental improvements; neither can we focus on whichever environmental or social challenges are given the most attention at any one time. The concept of planetary boundaries,[44] state-of-the-art natural science,[45] embodies this fundamental recognition of the non-negotiable ecological limits and should form the space within which all economic and social development is to take place. This concept should therefore be a key issue in a redefined purpose of companies as a matter of company law.

It is estimated that humanity has already transgressed four of the nine planetary boundaries as shown in Figure 6.1 including climate change, biosphere integrity, biogeochemical flows, and land-system integrity.[46] Indeed, the conceptual framework for planetary boundaries itself proposes a strongly precautionary approach, by "setting the discrete boundary value at the lower and more conservative bound of the uncertainty range."[47]

Based on this model, the purpose of companies should be redefined, for example in an EU company law directive, as:

> *The purpose of a company is to create sustainable value within the planetary boundaries while respecting the interests of its investors and other involved parties.*

The fundamental key issues here are the purpose of creating "sustainable value" and the space within which value can be created; that is, "within the planetary boundaries." The concept of "within the planetary boundaries" clearly signals that these are non-negotiable boundaries where the

[44] See Rockström *et al.*, above n 9.

[45] An example of its use is B. Nykvist, Å. Persson, F. Moberg, *et al.*, "National Environmental Performance on Planetary Boundaries: A Study for the Swedish Environmental Protection Agency," *Report 6576* (Swedish Environmental Protection Agency, 2013), available at www.naturvardsverket.se/Documents/publikationer6400/978-91-620-6576-8.pdf.

[46] The other five being global freshwater use, ocean acidification, atmospheric aerosol loading, stratospheric ozone depletion, and cycling of phosphorus and nitrogen. See Steffen *et al.*, above n 9.

[47] Rockström *et al.*, above n 9.

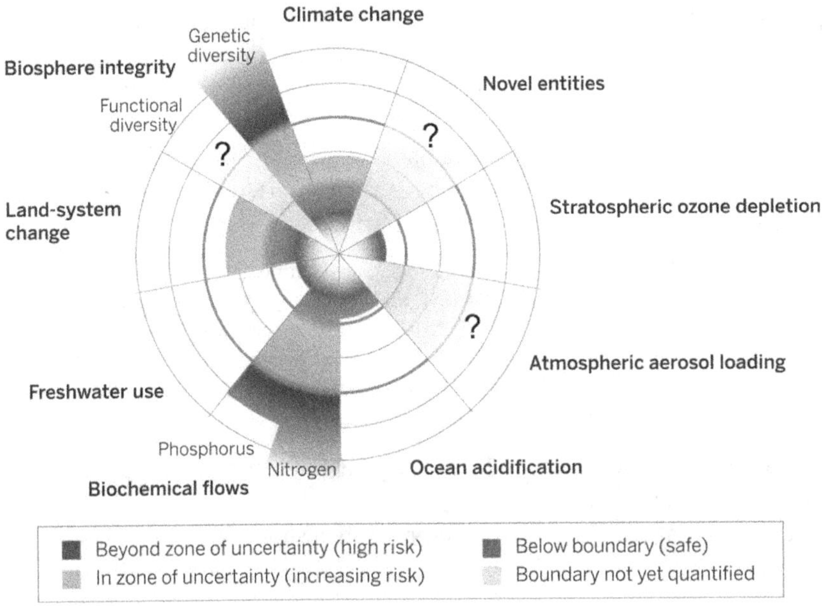

Figure 6.1 Planetary boundaries, 2015
Source: W. Steffen *et al.*

room for trade-offs is limited.[48] At the same time, to develop this idea into a proper legislative proposal, the concept of sustainable value must be given content in the directive's explanatory notes. The basic idea is that "sustainable value" is long term and inclusive and stands in opposition to short-term pursuit of shareholder returns. Protection and promotion of the interest of the shareholders, other investors, and other involved parties, including employees, creditors, and other contractual parties, is encompassed through the formulation that sustainable value is to be sought "while respecting the interest of its investors and other involved parties."[49] Broader societal impact can also be included in the concepts of "sustainable value" and "other involved parties" depending on how this is defined in explanatory notes and implemented, interpreted, and put into

[48] This distinguishes the proposal from the much debated "enlightened shareholder value" in the UK Companies Act, see e.g., Johnston, above n 19 at 63–6, and emphasizes the non-negotiable ecological limits as opposed to what is done in the traditional pluralistic approach of Continental European law. See also Lambooy, above n 19 at 107–46.

[49] Using "investors" rather than "shareholders" recognizes the complex structures of finance through, *inter alia*, debt, equity, or grants.

practice. Yet the ultimate goal remains to achieve not only a safe operating space for humanity but also a safe and *just* space for humanity.[50]

To operationalize this redefined purpose it must be integrated into the duties of the board[51] and companies should be required to draw up a long term, life-cycle based sustainable business plan. As the European Commission has observed, boards have a "vital part to play in the development of responsible companies"[52] and businesses should:

> have in place a process to integrate social, environmental, ethical, human rights and consumer concerns into their business operations and core strategy in close collaboration with their stakeholders, with the aim of: maximising the creation of shared value for their owners/shareholders and for their other stakeholders and society at large; and identifying, preventing and mitigating their possible adverse impacts.[53]

The OECD Guidelines for Multinational Enterprises also support the formulation of such duties.[54]

Therefore, at the EU level, directors' duties should be reformulated as follows:

> *The board of the company is to ensure the life-cycle based creation of sustainable value. To this end, the board shall adopt and regularly revise a long-term business plan for the company, based on a life-cycle assessment of the company's main areas of business.*

A mandatory table of contents of the sustainable business plan should be drawn up as an annex to the directive to encourage proper compliance and comparability between companies. Guidelines, endorsed by the European Commission, should set out how the relevant and sufficient key performance indicators (KPIs) are to be selected according to the sector and concrete business plan of the company.

The operationalization of the board's duty to ensure life-cycle based creation of sustainable value is the sustainable business plan, which should contain the long-term plan for the company.[55] The sustainable business

[50] See Raworth, above n 14.

[51] The duties of the board are arguably the best place in the regulatory ecology of companies. On the significance of boards, see e.g. Sjåfjell and Anker-Sørensen, above n 23. For a further discussion of the concept of regulatory ecology, see Sjåfjell and Taylor, above n 39.

[52] European Commission Green Paper, above n 29 at 5.

[53] European Commission, above n 8 at 6.

[54] OECD, *OECD Guidelines for Multinational Enterprises* (2011), available at www.oecd.org/corporate/mne/48004323.pdf, at 42–6.

[55] A tentative indication is that long-term here would be 15–30 years (or the full time span of the company if it has a shorter time horizon).

plan should outline how the company will achieve life-cycle based value creation within the planetary boundaries. A requirement for such a sustainable business plan, designed thoughtfully, would involve a standardization of a process that companies wishing to achieve long-term sustainable value would need to do anyway. The standardization would contribute to lowering costs and establishing a level playing field.

This proposal, with its life-cycle focus on the products and services that businesses offer, fits well with the integrated product policy of the EU where the life-cycle perspective is identified as the leading principle[56] as it does with the public procurement reform, where life-cycle costing is an important approach to including broader concerns.[57] A full life-cycle analysis to identify and mitigate negative environmental and social impacts would have to be undertaken for any products the company sells or services it offers, either by the company itself or by the manufacturer/supplier.[58] This would be a way of dealing with the pulverization of responsibility for environmental and social impacts that we see today through multinational groups of companies and international supply chains. Any European company would need to draw up its own life-cycle based business plan or substantiate that this was included, for example, within a parent company's sustainable business plan.[59]

The sustainable business plan should further include milestones or objectives to be achieved along the way and KPIs for impacts that are relevant, quantifiable, and that can be reported on annually by a company. The long-term plan should be broken down into shorter time segments,[60]

56 See E.M. Ekern, "Towards an Integrated Product Regulatory Framework Based on Life Cycle Thinking" in Sjåfjell and Wiesbrock, above n 14 at 144–62. See also the European Commission's Joint Research Centre's establishment of the European Platform on Life Cycle Assessment (EPLCA), http://eplca.jrc.ec.europa.eu, and the identification in the EC's 2003 Communication of life cycle assessments as being the "best framework for assessing the potential environmental impacts of products." European Commission, "Integrated Product Policy," COM (2003) 302 final.

57 See D. Dragos and B. Neamtu, "Life-Cycle Costing for Sustainable Public Procurement in the European Union" in Sjåfjell and Wiesbrock, above n 32 ch. 6.

58 This would entail a cradle-to-cradle perspective of a product, including every phase from the sourcing of the materials used in the production through to the production, marketing and selling of the product, to the user phase, and finally to the recycling or waste management of the product, in order to identify all environmental and social impacts.

59 An issue for further research will be how to ensure that such a reform is not circumvented through companies in third countries selling their products to European purchasers.

60 For example, these periods could be fifteen years in length, but broken down into three or five year segments.

requiring a company, at these regular intervals, to undertake a full assessment of its sustainable business plan and consider necessary revisions.

Effective enforcement of these duties would be necessary to ensure that the requirements become more than words on paper and that they are not used as a basis for greenwashing. The drawing up of the business plan itself should be made into an enforceable duty as the first level of enforcement. The qualitative control of the sustainable business plan should be limited to the selection of KPIs to ensure that these core indicators, against which the company is to report, are relevant and sufficient. Such a check, which only needs to be undertaken when the business plan is drawn up or fundamentally revised, should not be overly burdensome with guidelines or standards endorsed by the European Commission to identify the relevant and sufficient indicators.[61]

6.3.2 *Giving Content to the Reporting Requirements*

A general criticism against the preferred compromise solution of requiring companies to report on non-financial issues has been that the reporting requirements are not based on a clear legal duty.[62] Combined with a lack of proper enforcement, the result has tended to be wholly unsatisfactory.[63]

The proposal here would bridge the gap between the internal decision-making in the company and reporting. It would give a clear duty on what to report, in the sense that the business plan requirement would give content to the recently adopted non-financial reporting requirement at the

[61] An issue to be developed further is how this could be undertaken; most likely it can be covered by auditors with sustainability assurance experience. See, e.g., the Sustainability Accounting Standards Board, www.sasb.org.

[62] When the decision-makers in companies are not required to integrate environmental concerns into the decisions of how the core business of the company is to be run and there is no hard law stating that companies must be run in a socially responsible manner, there is a risk that environmental reporting is neither relevant nor reliable, see B. Sjåfjell, "Why Law Matters: Corporate Social Irresponsibility and the Futility of Voluntary Climate Change Mitigation" (2011) 8 *European Company Law* 56.

[63] The ugliest company may tend to use the most makeup. See, e.g., S. Berthelot, D. Cormier, and M. Magnan, "Environmental Disclosure Research: Review and Synthesis" (2003) 22 *Journal of Accounting Literature* 1 at 5, 8, 9, 15, 20, 26, 29, 32, and 34; W.S. Laufer "Social Accountability and Corporate Greenwashing" (2003) 43 *Journal of Business Ethics* 253. However, there are also some positive developments, with companies working seriously on their reporting.

EU level.[64] Under this directive, companies of a certain size are required to include in their management report:

> . . . a non-financial statement containing information to the extent necessary for an understanding of the undertaking's development, performance and position and of the impact of its activity, relating to, as a minimum, environmental, social and employee matters, respect for human rights, anti-corruption and bribery matters.

Companies must further include a "brief description" of the company's "business model," its policies and risks and, where relevant, "its business relationships, products or services which are likely to cause adverse impacts." They must also report on how they will manage those identified risks in addition to "non-financial key performance indicators relevant to the particular business."[65] Reporting is required on a comply-or-explain basis. As a part of the tentative reform proposal presented here, this reporting should be an obligatory part of the management report, linked directly, of course, to the business plan idea presented above, and reporting against the KPIs approved as a part of that plan.

In other words, companies should be required to report annually, in their management report, on the milestones and KPIs identified in the sustainable business plan; that is, on how the company meets its objectives and how the impacts are measured. This would make the current "best practices" model mandatory. The content of this model could then be further developed in guidelines, a first step of which is on its way through the guidelines the EC is developing in relation to the new non-financial reporting directive.[66] This would be the second point of enforcement of the proposed reform – reporting against the KPIs.

Ideally, the accuracy of the information provided in the reports should also be verified. This could be envisaged on the basis of sector guidelines or standards endorsed by the European Commission. This raises another issue: how should the reporting be verified? Would a consistency check by auditors suffice or would a full sustainability assurance be required?[67]

64 Proposal for a Directive of the European Parliament and of the Council amending Council Directives 78/660/EEC and 83/349/EEC as regards disclosure of non-financial and diversity information by certain large companies and groups, COM(2013) 207 final – 2013/0110 (COD), adopted by the European Parliament April 2014. See also Villiers and Mähönen, above n 26 at 175.

65 Proposal for a Directive of the European Parliament, above n 64 at art. 1, amending art. 19(a) of Directive 2013/34/EU.

66 See Villiers and Mähönen, above n 26.

67 See, e.g., the practices of the Sustainability Accounting Standards Board, above n 61.

These requirements could be tightened through subsequent reform, but ideally a full sustainability assurance requirement should be in place from the beginning.

The reform proposal would mandate what is now applied on a comply-or-explain basis. In addition, it would apply to all public companies, instead of the limited scope of application in the current directive.

6.4 Conclusion

This chapter has drawn up the main aspects that should be covered in a reform of EU company law to ensure that European companies become a part of the solution to the convergence of crises that we face with interlinked environmental, economic, and social consequences. While reforming company law will not solve all the problems, it is a missing piece of the sustainability puzzle that needs to be put in its place. It is also a piece that has tended to be ignored in the debate on how to encourage companies to behave in an environmentally and socially friendly manner.

Future research should investigate how such a reform could be operationalized in a way that ensures that the sustainable business plan and the reporting based on it will be reliable, relevant and comparable, and make it easier for companies to make sustainable, long-term choices. While business in Europe is conducted in a variety of forms, the company is the dominant legal form and it is also within this form, and especially its public, listed variant, that we find the strongest push towards short-term profit maximization. The tentative proposal summarized in this chapter therefore concentrates on companies and especially on public companies. Any follow-up on this through legislation should, however, also consider similar reforms for other legal structures for business to avoid a shift from one business form to another. Furthermore, a simplified version should be considered for the smallest companies, ensuring that innovation and entrepreneurship is not hindered, while also nudging the smallest companies towards corporate sustainability.[68]

[68] While one should probably have some differentiation according to size, with perhaps a simpler model for micro companies, the risk of further pulverization of responsibility through setting up micro companies for each little project or product must be considered. One way to achieve these dual goals is to use the simplest model only for small stand-alone companies, and not for subsidiaries of group companies, particularly as the subsidiaries would be covered by the sustainable business plan of the parent company.

This chapter has argued that the most important question for corporate law scholars is how to regulate for corporate sustainability. Certainly, we must hope that the time has come for sustainability as a new normative basis for law and policy.[69] Transformation rather than incremental improvement is necessary. Truly transformative proposals are bound to meet resistance. This does not mean that they are not politically possible because they cannot achieve a sufficient majority. There are a number of signs indicating that we are living in a time where conventional wisdom is questioned and where sustainability issues are discussed in contexts where such topics were previously ignored. With shareholder primacy increasingly being denoted as the "world's dumbest idea," there are indications that management pundits as well as some of the largest companies in the world are moving beyond the detrimental goal of short-term maximization of returns to shareholders.[70] The European Commission's discussion of the circular economy and its Roadmap to a Resource-Efficient Europe also illustrates the growing awareness of the fundamental flaws of business as usual.[71]

Future generations will judge us harshly if we fail to use the window of opportunity that we still have to achieve a peaceful transformation towards sustainability. From a normative perspective, we cannot afford to ignore the overarching societal goal of sustainable development. Nor are we allowed to do so as a matter of EU law. Conversely, whether we call companies private or public entities, at the end of the day, will not really matter all that much.

[69] A compelling argument is made in F. Capra and U. Mattei, *The Ecology of Law: Towards a Legal System in Tune with Nature and Community* (Oakland: Berrett-Koehler Publishers, 2015).

[70] See, e.g., G. Serafeim, "The Role of the Corporation in Society: An Alternative View and Opportunities for Future Research," *Working Paper No. 14–110* (Harvard Business School, 2013), available at ssrn.com/abstract=2270579; C.M. Christensen and D. van Bever, "The Capitalist's Dilemma" (2014) *Harvard Business Review* 60, discussing the flawed metrics with which a company's success is measured.

[71] European Commission, "Towards a Circular Economy: A Zero Waste Programme for Europe" (2014) COM/2014/0398 final; European Commission, "Roadmap to a Resource Efficient Europe" (2011) COM/2011/0571 final.

PART III

Rights or Duty Bearer?

7

The Constitutional Rights of Corporations in the United States

BRANDON L. GARRETT

7.1 Introduction

What are the constitutional rights of a corporation in the United States? The US Supreme Court has recognized that corporations may litigate rights under the First Amendment, Fourth Amendment, Fifth Amendment, Sixth Amendment, and Seventh Amendment, the Due Process Clauses of the Fifth and Fourteenth Amendments, and the Equal Protection Clause of the Fourteenth Amendment. Corporations can litigate a long list of key constitutional rights. However, the items on the list should not give the impression that corporate persons litigate in the same way that individual persons do. The substance and scope of particular rights are far more limited than others, and the mechanisms for litigating them vary as well. Moreover, corporations may not litigate, for example, the Self-Incrimination Clause of the Fifth Amendment, the Privileges and Immunities Clause, or liberty rights under the Due Process Clauses of the Fifth and Fourteenth Amendments. In this chapter, I will discuss what, if any, commonality can be observed in the reasoning behind these various rulings, and the special concerns regarding potential conflicts between individual and corporate constitutional rights that have been front and center in the most controversial recent rulings regarding corporate rights relating to political spending (*Citizens United*), religious rights of conscience (*Hobby Lobby*) and self-incrimination (*Braswell*).

Many of the most important constitutional rights can be litigated by corporations and organizations of all types. Corporations and other types of organizations have long exercised a range of constitutional rights, including: the Contracts Clause,[1] Due Process Clauses,[2] Fourteenth Amendment Equal Protection Clause,[3] First Amendment, Fourth Amendment,[4] Fifth Amendment Takings and Double Jeopardy Clause,[5] Sixth Amendment,[6] and Seventh Amendment right.[7] Does that mean that the complete extension of all constitutional rights to corporations is inevitable? Justice John Paul Stevens in dissent in *Citizens United* made light of that possibility: "Under the majority's view, I suppose it may be a First Amendment problem that corporations are not permitted to vote, given that voting is, among other things, a form of speech."[8] Corporations cannot vote, as the Court has ruled they are not citizens under the Fourteenth Amendment.[9] Indeed, the Supreme Court ruled that corporations lack citizenship in Chief Justice John Marshall's far earlier decision in *Bank of the United States v. Deveaux*.[10] There are other important constitutional rights that corporations cannot litigate. Corporations currently lack Fifth Amendment self-incrimination rights,[11] Article IV Privileges and Immunities Clause rights,[12] and liberty rights under the Due Process Clauses of the Fifth and Fourteenth Amendments.[13]

Perhaps there is some line that can be drawn to explain why corporations can litigate many but certainly not all constitutional rights. Some constitutional rights are individual-centered and for the reason that they are "personal," they have been found unsuitable for litigation as rights of

[1] *Trustees of Dartmouth College* v. *Woodard*, 17 US (1 Wheat.) 518 (1819).

[2] *Minneapolis & St Louis Railway* v. *Beckwith*, 129 US 26 (1889) (recognizing corporations receive protection for "enjoyment of property," including to challenge "legislation injuriously affecting it").

[3] *Metro Life Insurance Co.* v. *Ward*, 470 US 869 at 881, and footnote 9 (1985) (citing "well established" Equal Protection Clause rights of corporations); *Santa Clara County* v. *Southern Pacific Railroad Company*, 118 US 394 at 396 (1886).

[4] *Marshall* v. *Barlow's, Inc.*, 436 US 307 at 325 (1978) (Fourth Amendment right to be free from warrantless search).

[5] *United States* v. *Martin Linen Supply Co.*, 430 US 564, at 565, 575 (1977) (assuming corporate double jeopardy clause rights); *Russian Volunteer Fleet* v. *United States*, 282 US 481 at 489 (1931) (takings clause).

[6] *Southern Union Co.* v. *United States*, 132 S. Ct. 2344 (2012).

[7] *Ross* v. *Bernhard*, 396 US 531 at 536, 542 (1970).

[8] *Citizens United* v. *FEC*, 558 US 310 at 424–5 (2010) (Stevens, J., dissenting).

[9] *Paul* v. *Virginia*, 75 US (8 Wall.) 168, at 177 (1869) ("The term citizens ... [in the Fourteenth Amendment] applies only to natural persons . . . not to artificial persons created by the legislature.").

[10] *Bank of the United States* v. *Deveaux*, 9 US (5 Cranch) 61 (1809).

[11] *Hale* v. *Henkel*, 201 US 43 at 74–5 (1906).

[12] *Bank of Augusta* v. *Earle*, 38 US (13 Pet.) 519, at 586–7 (1839).

[13] *Northwestern National Life Insurance Co.* v. Riggs, 203 US 243 at 255 (1906).

corporations. Courts have unsurprisingly not recognized a right of corporations, since they are not individuals nor citizens, to vote, or serve on juries, run for public office, marry, procreate, or travel.[14]

Whether any such line will hold in the future, where many types of injuries can be characterized as economic, and where companies may sometimes be allowed to assert third-party claims on behalf of individuals, remains a hotly disputed question. Recent cases, particularly the *Hobby Lobby* ruling, although not resolved on constitutional grounds, raise the question whether the Supreme Court will permit corporations to litigate even the most personal constitutional rights, such as rights of religious conscience, on behalf of others, such as individual owners. That is a specter that many find troubling and for good reasons that I will develop in this chapter.

7.2 Early Corporate Constitutional Rights Rulings

In the earliest US Supreme Court case directly addressing the integrity and purposes of the corporate form, Chief Justice John Marshall wrote in *Dartmouth College v. Woodward*, how corporate charters are protected from alteration by state legislation by the Contract Clause of the Constitution.[15] Chief Justice Marshall famously called a corporation "an artificial being, invisible, intangible, and existing only in contemplation of law."[16] However, far from existing as a mere legal fiction, Chief Justice Marshall also placed great emphasis on the ability of corporations to realize the "charitable or other useful" and "beneficial" goals of their creators.[17]

Corporate constitutional litigation rose in importance as the US industrialized states adopted general incorporate laws, and as the post-Civil War Amendments resulted in more and more powerful constitutional rights applicable to the states. Following Reconstruction, the Supreme Court held that corporations are not citizens under the Privileges or Immunities Clause of the Fourteenth Amendment.[18] In contrast, the Court noted that it did not wish to hear argument in *Santa Clara County* v. *S. Pac. R.R.* in 1886

[14] A.J. Sepinwall, "Citizens United and the Ineluctable Question of Corporate Citizenship" (2012) 44 *Connecticut Law Review* 575 at 604.

[15] *Trustees of Dartmouth College*, above n 1.

[16] *Ibid.* at 636.

[17] *Ibid.* at 637–8.

[18] *Paul*, above n 9 at 177 ("The term citizens . . . [as used in the Fourteenth Amendment] applies only to natural persons . . . not to artificial persons created by the legislature . . . ."). The Court had earlier held the same as to the Article IV Privileges and Immunities Clauses. See *Bank of Augusta*, above n 12 at 586–7.

on the question whether the Equal Protection Clause of the Fourteenth Amendment extended to corporations, since the Justices were "are all of opinion that it does." That assumption has since been reaffirmed. The Court in 1985 called the principle that corporations have Equal Protection Clause rights "well established."[19]

In other still more marginal references to corporate constitutional rights, the Court assumed in *Russian Volunteer Fleet* v. *United States* in 1931 that the Takings Clause of the Fifth Amendment extended to a Russian corporation, entitling it to just compensation.[20] The Supreme Court assumed in 1977 in *United States* v. *Martin Linen Supply Co.*, that it violated the Double Jeopardy Clause for corporations prosecuted for criminal contempt to be subjected to an appeal following an acquittal after the deadlocked jury's inability to reach a verdict.[21] Corporations have also asserted challenges based on structural provisions of the Constitution, challenging statutes or regulations as violating separation of powers principles or the enumerated powers of Congress. In such cases, such as *Northern Pipeline Co.* v. *Marathon Pipe Line Co.*, in which a company raises a separation of powers issue as a defense in litigation, courts have entertained the challenges without comment.[22] The sections that follow explore some of the most significant areas of corporate constitutional litigation.

7.3 Due Process Rights

Corporations have long exercised due process rights in litigation of great public importance, particularly in challenges to statutes seeking to regulate commerce and the economy. In 1893, in *Noble* v. *Union River Logging*

[19] *Santa Clara County*, above n 3 at 396 "[t]he court does not wish to hear argument on the question whether the [Equal Protection Clause] . . . applies to these corporations. We are all of the opinion that it does." Reaffirming that language, see *Southern Railway Co.* v. *Greene*, 216 US 400 at 412 (1910); *Metro Life Insurance*, above n 3 at 881, and footnote 9. But see *Wheeling Steel Corp.* v. *Glander*, 337 US 562 at 576–7 (1949) (Douglas, J., dissenting) (noting that "[t]here was no history, logic, or reason given [in Santa Clara] to support [the] view"); *Connecticut General Life Insurance Co.* v. *Johnson*, 303 US 77 at 85 (1938) (Black, J., dissenting) ("I do not believe the word 'person' in the Fourteenth Amendment includes corporations."). See also M.J. Horwitz, "Santa Clara Revisited: The Development of Corporate Theory" (1985) 88 *West Virginia Law Review* 173 at 173–4; H.J. Hovenkamp, "The Classical Corporation in American Legal Thought" (1988) 76 *Georgetown Law Journal* 1593 at 1649.

[20] *Russian Volunteer Fleet*, above n 5 at 489.

[21] *Martin Linen Supply*, above n 5.

[22] See, e.g., *Northern Pipeline Co.* v. *Marathon Pipe Line Co.*, 458 US 50 (1982).

Railroad, the Court first extended due process protections to a corporation.[23] In the decades to come, the Due Process Clause would come into its own, used by corporations to challenge progressive-era social and economic regulations.[24] Those rulings focused on property rights of corporations, as well as a substantive due process right to contract and a focus on the motives of economic legislation among other methods used; in contrast, the Court held in 1906, that corporations may not litigate liberty rights under the Due Process Clause, since it protects "the liberty of natural, not artificial persons."[25]

The Due Process Clause also regulates personal jurisdiction of individuals, and corporations, when facing a civil lawsuit. Corporations that do business across state and international boundaries can present difficult questions concerning "where" a corporation is and is capable of fairly being sued for its activities in a jurisdiction, and where it is "at home" and perhaps susceptible of being sued for any reason at all.[26] Typical of a "realist" view of the status of corporations was language in the famous *International Shoe* decision regarding personal jurisdiction, which did not dwell on the formal status of incorporation, "[s]ince the corporate personality is a fiction, although a fiction intended to be acted upon as though it were a fact."[27] Instead, the Court focused its due process analysis on the "activities" and "contacts" of a corporation with a state, whether "it enjoys the benefits and protection of the laws of that state," and whether jurisdiction over such business activity is "reasonable."[28]

The Court's due process punitive damages decisions have all involved corporations challenging jury verdicts. The Court's rulings do not ask whether corporations have standing to challenge arbitrary jury awards. The Court nevertheless does come close to considering corporate-specific factors when assessing excessiveness of punitive damages awards.[29] (Do corporations have Eighth Amendment rights to be free from cruel and unusual punishment? The Court has not reached that question.[30])

23 *Noble* v. *Union River Logging Railroad*, 147 US 165 (1893).

24 *New State Ice Co.* v. *Liebmann*, 285 US 262 at 278 (1932).

25 *Northwestern National Life Insurance*, above n 13 at 255.

26 A.R. Stein, "The Meaning of 'Essentially at Home' in Goodyear Dunlop" (2012) 63 *South Carolina Law Review* 527.

27 *International Shoe Co.* v. *State of Washington*, 326 US 310 at 316 (1945).

28 *Ibid.* at 316–18.

29 *Phillip Morris USA* v. *Williams*, 549 US at 354; *State Farm Mutual Automobile Ins., Co.* v. *Campbell*, 538 US 408 at 423–4 (2003).

30 *Browning-Ferris Industries of Vermont, Inc.* v. *Kelco Disposal, Inc.*, 492 US 257 at 276, and footnote 22 (1989) (but see at 285 suggesting that the Excessive Fines Clause applies to corporations).

7.4 First Amendment

Speech might appear to be a right that could only be properly exercised by individuals, who are, after all, the persons capable of speaking their mind. Indeed, it was in its first decision recognizing corporate free speech rights under the First Amendment, that the Court suggested that certain "purely personal" constitutional rights cannot be exercised by corporations.[31] Taking such a view when writing separately in a subsequent First Amendment case involving corporations, Chief Justice Rehnquist explained:

> Extension of the individual's freedom of conscience decisions to business corporations strains the rationale of those cases beyond the breaking point. To ascribe to such artificial entities an "intellect" or "mind" for freedom of conscience purposes is to confuse metaphor with reality . . . The insistence on treating identically for constitutional purposes entities that are demonstrably different is as great a jurisprudential sin as treating differently those entities which are the same.[32]

Times have changed. More recently, the constitutional speech rights of corporate persons have become a subject of popular and political debate in the wake of the Supreme Court's 2010 decision in *Citizens United* v. *Federal Election Commission*,[33] in which the Court ruled in favor of a non-profit corporation that brought a challenge to the Bipartisan Campaign Reform Act of 2002, which had barred corporations and unions (but not media corporations) from making direct contributions or from using independent expenditures for "electioneering communication" or speech expressly advocating election or defeat of a political candidate.[34] As Robert Sprague and Mary Ellen Wells put it: "To say that *Citizens United's* holding is controversial is an understatement."[35]

The general and foundational doctrine has remained constant since the 1970s. As noted, the Court had recognized First Amendment rights of corporations, beginning in 1978 in *First National Bank of Boston* v. *Bellotti*,[36] and it had also long extended First Amendment protection to

[31] *First National Bank of Boston* v. *Bellotti*, 435 US 765 at 778, and footnote 14 (1978).

[32] *Pacific Gas & Electric Co.* v. *Public Utilities Commission*, 475 US 1 at 33 (1986).

[33] *Citizens United*, above n 8.

[34] *Ibid.* See also 2 USC § 441b(b)(2); 2 USC § 431(9)(B)(i).

[35] R. Sprague and M.E. Wells, "The Supreme Court as Prometheus: Breathing Life into the Corporate Supercitizen" (2012) 49 *American Business Law Journal* 507 at 508.

[36] *First National Bank of Boston*, above n 31. For earlier cases not reaching the issue, see, e.g., *Pipefitters* v. *United States*, 407 US 385 at 400–1 (1972); *United States* v. *Automobile Workers*, 352 US 567 at 591 (1957) ("[r]efus[ed] to anticipate constitutional questions").

commercial speech. In *Bellotti*, the Court noted that speech does not lose First Amendment protection "simply because its source is a corporation."[37]

It is the details of the corporate First Amendment doctrine that have sharply changed, together with the practical importance of the litigation. In subsequent cases involving political speech, such as *FEC* v. *National Right to Work Committee*, the Court found that a federal campaign statute restricting which persons could be solicited to contribute to segregated corporate funds, "reflect[ed] a legislative judgment that the special characteristics of the corporate structure require particularly careful regulation."[38] Similarly, in *Austin* v. *Michigan Chamber of Commerce*, the Court held that business organizations could be regulated, based on "the compelling state interest of eliminating from the political process the corrosive effect of political 'war chests' amassed with the aid of the legal advantages given to corporations."[39]

In *Citizens United*, the Court did not discuss what a corporation is: whether it is a pure creature of state law, a "real entity" that can exercise all or most of the legal rights of an individual person, or an aggregate entity that helps groups of people realize their interests. The Court emphasized that despite not being "natural persons," corporations have First Amendment rights, which had certainly been established in prior rulings.[40] The Court briefly noted: "The Court has recognized that First Amendment protection extends to corporations," followed with a lengthy citation to decisions reaching back to the 1930s.[41] So much was relatively uncontroversial.

What was more controversial and striking was that the Supreme Court rejected its earlier approach seeking to distinguish among types of corporations in the interest of protecting individual speech from the corrupting influence of big money in politics. Following its earlier approach in *Austin*, the Court might have narrowly ruled that as a non-profit organization, *Citizens United* was the type of entity that people donate money to promote their speech, and therefore it should be given an exception from the relevant provisions.[42] The Court rejected the "anti-distortion" rationale of *Austin*, suggesting that it is irrelevant that money from the marketplace may not come from the speaker, and reasoning that all speakers make use of money from the marketplace.[43] The Court rejected the exemption of

[37] *First National Bank of Boston*, above n 31 at 777, 784.

[38] *FEC* v. *National Right to Work Committee*, 459 US 197 at 207–8 (1982).

[39] *Austin* v. *Michigan Chamber of Commerce*, 494 US 652 at 666 (1990).

[40] *Citizens United*, above n 8 at 310.

[41] *Ibid.* at 342.

[42] *Ibid.* at 937–8 (Stevens, J. dissenting).

[43] *Ibid.* at 905.

media corporations, reasoning they are no different, and can even be controlled by business corporations.[44] The Court ruled: "There is no precedent supporting laws that attempt to distinguish between corporations which are deemed to be exempt as media corporations and those which are not."[45]

Justice Stevens' *Citizens United* dissent instead emphasized how "[t]he financial resources, legal structure, and instrumental orientation of corporations raise legitimate concerns about their role in the electoral process."[46] Justice Stevens asked who is speaking, noting, "It is an interesting question 'who' is even speaking when a business corporation places an advertisement that endorses or attacks a particular candidate."[47] The Court addressed the question whether shareholders might object to corporate speech by noting that "[s]hareholder objections" can be "raised through the procedures of corporate democracy."[48] Whether such mechanisms actually address the flow of corporate money into politics, was not of real concern to the Court. After all, once money is equated with speech, adding corporate money to the mix adds still more speech. If more is better, with spending and with speech, then the First Amendment ruling can be seen as following from the Court's increasingly money-driven view of speech.

Even apart from that business-friendly interpretation of what is First Amendment protected speech, the Court's analysis of corporate constitutional litigation, with a concern that there be no discrimination or attempt to distinguish between types of corporations, introduces a novel analysis. Perhaps corporate constitutional rights are now all or nothing, where either all types of organizations can be regulated or none. First Amendment challenges to a range of business regulation could potentially be supported by such reasoning, and the *Hobby Lobby* case discussed next suggests the type of expanded corporate constitutional rights litigation that we may continue to see in the future.

7.5 Religious Rights?

In *Burwell* v. *Hobby Lobby Stores, Inc.*, three for-profit closely held and family owned corporations challenged contraceptive coverage under the Affordable Care Act of 2010 (ACA).[49] In its decision, the Supreme Court

44 *Ibid.* at 906.
45 *Ibid.* at 352.
46 *Ibid.* at 930 (Stevens, J., concurring in part and dissenting in part).
47 *Ibid.* at 972.
48 *Ibid.* at 370.
49 *Burwell* v. *Hobby Lobby Stores, Inc.*, 134 S. Ct. 2751 (2014).

stated that since corporations protect those "associated with a corporation in one way or another," a for-profit firm can assert free-exercise rights and can itself claim to have sincere "religious beliefs."[50] Several lower courts had addressed whether the ACA burdens a First Amendment religious exercise right: the Seventh and Tenth Circuits have entertained the claim, while the DC Circuit found "no basis for concluding a secular organization can exercise religion."[51] The Court avoided the First Amendment issue entirely, relying on statutory rights under the RFRA of 1993, while similarly evading the question of corporate third-party standing: could the views of the owners of these companies be ascribed to the entity itself, and then litigated by the entity? Apparently so, but the Court did not explain why.

Writing for the majority in *Hobby Lobby*, Justice Alito stated that as a matter of statutory interpretation, "[t]he plain terms of RFRA make it perfectly clear that Congress did not discriminate in this way against men and women who wish to run their businesses as for-profit corporations in the manner required by their religious beliefs."[52] Justice Ruth Bader Ginsburg in dissent disagreed that this was a correct reading of RFRA's text, which uses the term "persons" but does not detail which types of entities have standing to raise religious exercise objections to regulations. Justice Ginsburg argued: "the exercise of religion is characteristic of natural persons, not artificial legal entities." The majority in *Hobby Lobby* did not address the separate claims brought by the individual owners themselves; the notion that the owners could sue on behalf of legally separate corporations would raise still more problematic issues of third-party standing.

Throughout the majority opinion, Justice Alito emphasized that both the owners "and their companies" "sincerely believe" that provided contraceptive coverage violates "their religious beliefs." On thinnest ground

[50] *Ibid.* at 2768, 2774, 2778–9.

[51] *Hobby Lobby Stores, Inc.* v. *Sebelius*, 723 F.3d 1114 at 1135 (10th Cir. 2013) ("We see no reason the Supreme Court would recognize constitutional protection for a corporation's political expression but not its religious expression."); see also *Grote* v. *Sebelius*, 708 F.3d 850 (7th Cir. 2013) (holding that the plaintiffs, a family and its private business, had a likelihood of success under the Religious Freedom Restoration Act (RFRA) and would not be forced to follow the contraception mandate in the ACA); but see *Gilardi* v. *US Department of Health & Human Services*, 733 F.3d 1208 at 1214 (D.C. Cir. 2013) ("When it comes to the free exercise of religion, however, the Court has only indicated that people and churches worship. As for secular corporations, the Court has been all but silent."); *Conestoga Wood Specialties Corp.* v. *Secretary of Health & Human Services*, 724 F.3d at 385 (3d Cir. 2013) (determining that for-profit, secular corporations cannot exercise religion).

[52] *Burwell*, above n 49 at 2759.

of all, Justice Alito cited to the *Braunfeld* v. *Brown* decision in 1961 as an example in which the Court supposedly "recognized" that "a sole proprietorship that seeks to make a profit may assert a free exercise claim." That was the only effort to suggest that the Court had found standing to assert free exercise claims by a for-profit. That case involved five merchants, sole proprietors, challenging a Sunday business closing law. A sole proprietorship is nothing like a corporation; it is unincorporated, run by a single person, and is not in any way separate from that single owner. Moreover, the *Braunfeld* case never discussed the fact that any of the merchants were sole proprietors, and neither did another 1961 case, *Gallagher* v. *Crown Kosher Super Market of Mass.*, which included a corporation and five individual challengers, and where the Court did not reach the question of standing.[53] That case had no reason to discuss standing, and not only because the decisions pre-dated modern Article III standing jurisprudence, but also because – in contrast to the misleading way that Justice Alito quoted from the case – the Court in *Braunfeld* dismissed the free exercise claims of the merchants finding insufficient injury where a law made business "more expensive" for them. The Court in *Gallagher* then simply relied on the reasoning in *Braunfeld* without addressing standing.[54]

The reasoning connecting the beliefs of the owners with that of the corporation was not carefully explained. Justice Alito emphasized that the purpose of a corporation "is to provide protection for human beings" adding that "[a] corporation is simply a form of organization used by human beings to achieve desired ends."[55] Justice Alito then discussed corporate constitutional rights in a quite odd passage, particularly troubling for its potential implications in cases in which a court reaches the substance of a constitutional claim.[56] That reasoning suggests that a corporation may claim a constitutional right so long as individuals might indirectly benefit from the litigation, regardless of whether there is any direct injury to the corporate litigant itself. Such an approach ignores the corporate form and would undo Article III standing (and in the process, calling into question the occasions in which the Court has denied standing to, for example, non-profit organizations.)

[53] *Gallagher* v. *Crown Kosher Super Market of Massachusetts*, 366 US 617 (1961).

[54] *Braunfeld* v. *Brown*, 366 US 599 at 609 (1961); *Gallagher*, above n 53 at 629. ("Since the decision in that case rejects the contentions presented by these appellees on the merits, we need not decide whether appellees have standing to raise these questions.").

[55] *Burwell*, above n 49 at 2768.

[56] *Ibid.*

In the majority opinion, Justice Alito then recited examples of other constitutional rights that corporations may litigate; perhaps *Hobby Lobby* was more of a constitutional case than the majority was formally letting on, when deciding just the statutory issue. After all, the majority opinion took pains to note that the Fourth Amendment protects corporations – and that this protection can simultaneously protect privacy interests of employees. The Supreme Court has, as discussed, ruled that under the Fourth Amendment, corporations have somewhat more limited rights, however, and "neither incorporated nor unincorporated associations can plead an unqualified right to conduct their affairs in secret."[57] Justice Alito then cited to the Takings Clause, stating that it protects corporations from "seizure of their property without just compensation" and in doing so, it also protects the financial stake of the owners.[58]

The great leap in *Hobby Lobby* occurred where Justice Alito concluded that protecting free-exercise rights of corporations also protects "the religious liberty of the humans who own and control those companies."[59] That reasoning assumes that corporations and individuals can have common "beliefs" just as they can have common property or privacy interests. A corporation itself is injured if its premises are searched as part of a civil or criminal investigation targeting the corporation itself, or if its property is taken without compensation. A separate corporation lacks the relevant free-exercise injury, since it lacks "religious liberty" as a for-profit corporation (Justice Alito would have had to do hard work to justify such a claim, beyond citing to views of the owners). In contrast, a non-profit religious organization, functioning in effect as an association, exists to permit religious exercise of members:[60] as the Court puts it, "[f]or many individuals, religious activity derives meaning in large measure from participation in a larger religious community."[61] For the Court to suggest that a for-profit company is no different than a non-profit or an association or a religious entity, and that these distinctions are "quite besides the point," ignores the relevance of the corporate form entirely.[62]

57 *United States* v. *Morton Salt Co.*, 338 US 632 at 652 (1950).

58 *Burwell*, above n 49 at 2768.

59 *Ibid.*

60 R.C. Schragger and M. Schwartzman, "Against Religious Institutionalism" (2013) 99 *Virginia Law Review* 917.

61 *Corp. of Presiding Bishop of the Church of Jesus Christ of Latter-Day Saints* v. *Amos*, 483 US 327 at 342 (1987).

62 *Burwell*, above n 49 at 2768.

To be sure, at times the Court suggested that its holding was limited to for-profit and closely held corporations, taking pains to emphasize that for-profit companies may pursue "worthy objectives" like charitable causes or the public interest, in addition to profit-seeking.[63] The Court stated that any contrary argument "flies in the face of modern corporate law."[64]

That statement was particularly perverse. Nothing could be more fundamental to modern corporate law than the complete separation of the investors and owners from the legal entity itself. While undoubtedly modern corporations can pursue a range of "worthy objectives," the notion that the objectives of investors or owners can be imputed to corporations is foreign to modern corporate law. The Supreme Court has often recognized the underlying principle of legal separateness. As the Court put it in *J.J. McCaskill Co.*, "Undoubtedly a corporation is, in law, a person or entity entirely distinct from its stockholders and officers."[65] Similarly, as the Court stated in *Cedric Kushner Promotions, Ltd.* v. *King*, "incorporation's basic purpose is to create a distinct legal entity, with legal rights, obligations, powers, and privileges different from those of the natural individuals who created it, who own it, or whom it employs."[66] Contrary to the majority's statement in *Hobby Lobby*, there is a "sharp line" between non-profits, religious organizations, and for-profits, and the Court attempted to blur those lines in ways that have very troubling implications for corporate law generally.[67] Far from being "quite beside the point," legal separateness is central to the purpose of creating a corporation.

The *Hobby Lobby* ruling also runs counter to the Supreme Court's own prior statements regarding third-party suits by shareholders, although to be sure, the Court in *Hobby Lobby* delicately avoided the topic of public companies (calling free-exercise litigation by "corporate giants" an "unlikely" event[68]), as well as the question whether the owners of the closely held corporations in the case could separately sue. State incorporation law protects rights of individuals with a stake in a corporation by permitting shareholders standing to themselves litigate injuries to the corporation in derivative lawsuits, brought not on their own behalf, but on behalf of the corporation. In federal court, such actions are regulated to ensure that

63 *Ibid.* at 2771–2.
64 *Ibid.* at 2772.
65 *J.J. McCaskill Co.* v. *United States*, 216 US 504 at 514 (1910).
66 *Cedric Kushner Promotions, Ltd.* v. *King*, 533 US 158 at 163 (2001).
67 *Burwell*, above n 49 at 2772.
68 *Ibid.* at 2774.

the plaintiff really was a shareholder at the relevant time, to ensure fair and adequate representation of other shareholders, among the requirements imposed by Rule 23.1 of the Federal Rules of Civil Procedure.[69] The Supreme Court considered such rules for shareholder suits in *Franchise Tax Board* v. *Alcan*, suggesting without reaching the question that even if there is Article III standing, the "prudential requirements of the standing doctrine" might counsel against permitting standing by a corporation's investors, if under state law those shareholders may not pursue an action where the management have declined to do so in exercise of good-faith business judgment.[70]

7.6 Constitutional Criminal Procedure Rulings

Federal prosecutors in the United States benefit from a strict standard for corporate criminal liability. Quoting a criminal law treatise, the Supreme Court approved a statutory respondeat superior standard for corporate criminal liability in a 1909 ruling, in *New York Central & Hudson River Railroad Co.* v. *United States*.[71] The Court explained:

> If, for example, the invisible, intangible essence or air which we term a corporation can level mountains, fill up valleys, lay down iron tracks, and run railroad cars on them, it can intend to do it, and can act therein as well viciously as virtuously.[72]

The Court explained there might be some crimes that cannot be committed by corporations, but a range of statutory regulatory offenses can readily be applied to corporations. Doing so helps to make the regulation more effective:

> It is a part of the public history of the times that statutes against rebates could not be effectually enforced so long as individuals only were subject to punishment for violation of the law, when the giving of rebates or concessions inured to the benefit of the corporations of which the individuals were but the instruments. This situation, developed in more than one report of the Interstate Commerce Commission, was no doubt influential in bringing about the enactment of the Elkins law, making corporations criminally liable.[73]

69 Federal Rules of Civil Procedure r. 23.1.
70 *Franchise Tax Board of California* v. *Alcan Aluminum Ltd.*, 493 US 331 at 336 (1990).
71 *New York Central & Hudson River Railroad Co.* v. *United States*, 212 US 481 (1909).
72 *Ibid.* at 493.
73 *Ibid.* at 495.

The Supreme Court concluded in still stronger language, that to give corporations "immunity" from responsibility for crimes, "because of the old and exploded doctrine that a corporation cannot commit a crime would virtually take away the only means of effectually controlling the subject-matter and correcting the abuses aimed at."[74]

In criminal prosecutions, as Professor William Stuntz put it in the context of antitrust, mail fraud, or tax evasion cases, "the damning documents may be everything – there is no equivalent to crime scene evidence, and witnesses are typically involved in the crime."[75] Yet based on the Supreme Court's early rulings, the Fourth Amendment to the Constitution made such searches prohibitively difficult. In its 1886 decision in *Boyd* v. *United States*, the Court held that a person did not need to respond to a subpoena for customs invoices, since it sought "a man's private papers."[76] Yet those customs documents were not particularly "personal" or private papers; they were invoices needed to show whether a company was illegally importing goods into the country. That case also involved an individual person, and not a corporate defendant. With the rise of more modern federal agencies designed to regulate commerce, the Court without extensive discussion abandoned the earlier ruling on document subpoenas by 1906, in its *Hale* v. *Henkel* ruling, stating that a corporation has Fourth Amendment rights, and must comply with reasonable subpoena requests.[77]

As the Supreme Court put it in 1946 in *Oklahoma Press Publishing Co.* v. *Walling*, "corporations are not entitled to all of the constitutional protection which private individuals have in these and related matters."[78] The Court noted that historically corporations had been subject to "visitorial power" and in a rare instance of reasoning across corporate constitutional rights, the Court noted that entities lack the Fifth Amendment privilege against self-incrimination (as discussed in the next section).[79]

In perhaps the best known of this line of Fourth Amendment cases involving subpoenas for corporate records, in *United States* v. *Morton Salt Co.*, the Supreme Court treated as unsettled whether corporations had Fourth Amendment rights, stating "It is unnecessary here to examine the question of whether a corporation is entitled to the protection of the Fourth

[74] *Ibid.* at 496.

[75] W.J. Stuntz, "Commentary, O.J. Simpson, Bill Clinton, and the Transsubstantive Fourth Amendment" (2001) 114 *Harvard Law Review* 842 at 858–61.

[76] *Boyd* v. *United States*, 116 US 616 (1886).

[77] *Hale* v. *Henkel*, 201 US 43 at 70 (1906).

[78] *Oklahoma Press Publishing Co.* v. *Walling*, 327 US 186 (1946).

[79] *Ibid.* at 205.

Amendment."[80] But the Court emphasized that "corporations can claim no equality with individuals in the enjoyment of a right to privacy."[81] Further, the Court was tolerant of a quite broad federal search by the Federal Trade Commission, permitted even if it "was caused by nothing more than official curiosity," the FTC could satisfy itself that the company was "consistent with law and the public interest."[82]

The Supreme Court has also created exceptions – albeit very limited exceptions – to the search warrant requirement of the Fourth Amendment for "pervasively regulated business,"[83] and for "closely regulated" industries that have been "long subject to close supervision and inspection."[84] Most recently, in *United States* v. *Burger* in 1987, the Court held that an automobile junkyard could be subject to warrantless regulatory searches, but reaffirmed that it continues to follow the test recognizing a select few narrow pervasively regulated industries.[85] In the *Dow Chemical* case about a search of a business premises (aerial surveillance without a warrant), the Court noted that a manufacturing site lacks the same privacy protections as the area outside a private home, but did note that "[t]he businessman, like the occupant of a residence, has a constitutional right to go about his business free from unreasonable official entries upon his private commercial property."[86]

Corporations may not take the Fifth Amendment and refuse to incriminate themselves like individuals may do. The Supreme Court held in its 1906 decision in *Hale* v. *Henkel* that a corporation agent may not assert a corporation's Fifth Amendment right not to incriminate, in response to a government subpoena. The Court explained that "the corporation is a creature of the state" and in addition, "[w]hile an individual may lawfully refuse to answer incriminating questions unless protected by an immunity statute, it does not follow that a corporation, vested with special privileges and franchises, may refuse to show its hand when charged with an abuse of such privileges."[87] The ruling focused on the inability of individuals to assert the corporation's Fifth Amendment rights to justify not testifying,

[80] *Morton Salt*, above n 57.
[81] *Ibid.* at 651.
[82] *Ibid.* at 652.
[83] *United States* v. *Biswell*, 406 US 311 at 316 (1972).
[84] *Colonnade Catering Corp.* v. *United States*, 397 US 72 at 74, 77 (1970).
[85] *New York* v. *Burger*, 482 US 691 (1987).
[86] *Dow Chemical Co.* v. *United States*, 476 US 227 (1986).
[87] *Hale* v. *Henkel*, 201 US 43 at 74–5 (1906).

explaining that the right not to testify is "purely personal."[88] The Fifth Amendment "respects a private inner sanctum of individual feeling and thought" and seeks to protect it from state compulsion.[89]

And as the Supreme Court put it decades later in *United States* v. *White* in 1944, "[w]ere the cloak of the privilege to be thrown around these impersonal records and documents, effective enforcement of many federal and state laws would be impossible."[90] The Court also made clear that corporate officers could not resist process, since the records are corporate in nature.[91] The Court then ruled in *Fisher* v. *United States* in 1976 that the contents of business records are not ordinarily regarded as privileged, since they are created voluntarily and without state compulsion.[92]

More controversially, in 1988, the Supreme Court ruled in *Braswell* v. *United States* that the president of a company could be held in contempt for refusing to produce corporate records, since as custodian, he was not being asked to testify. The Court reiterated that giving corporations Fifth Amendment rights "would have a detrimental effect on the Government's efforts to prosecute 'white-collar crime,' one of the most serious problems confronting law enforcement authorities."[93] Thus, in some respects, the Fifth Amendment rule as to entities led to an erosion of rights of individual members of the organization. In the more recent case of *United States* v. *Hubbell* the Supreme Court said that if officials do not know of the precise location of documents, providing a response to a subpoena might be self-incriminating, since the very act of production would disclose "the mental and physical steps necessary" to provide that "accurate inventory."[94] However, that act of production defense still does not apply if it is a corporate officer being asked to produce the records.

88 *Ibid.* at 69–70.

89 *Bellis* v. *United States*, 417 US 85 at 91 (1973) ("We have recognized that the Fifth Amendment 'respects a private inner sanctum of individual feeling and thought' . . ." (quoting *Couch* v. *United States*, 409 US 322 at 327 (1973)).

90 *United States* v. *White*, 322 US 694 (1944).

91 *Wilson* v. *United States*, 221 US 361 at 383–4 (1911); *Dreier* v. *United States*, 221 US 394 (1911); *In re Harris*, 221 US 274 (1911); *Essgee Co. of China* v. *United States*, 262 US 151 at 158 (1923).

92 *Fisher* v. *United States*, 425 US 391 (1976).

93 *Braswell* v. *United States*, 487 US 99 (1988). For criticism of that reasoning, see Note, "Organizational Papers and the Privilege Against Self-Incrimination" (1986) 99 *Harvard Law Review* 640 at 648 ("Because the fifth amendment is concerned with the integrity of the process of law enforcement, its effect on the success of prosecution should be relatively unimportant.").

94 *United States v. Hubbell*, 530 US 27 (2000).

The Supreme Court in its 2012 decision in *Southern Union* v. *United States*, held that a criminal fine imposed on a corporation for environmental violations itself violated the Sixth Amendment rights of the corporation, where the fine was imposed in excess of the statutory maximum based on facts not charged to the jury. Companies can be fined, but not jailed. However, the *Southern Union* Court noted that "[w]hile the punishments at stake in those [prior] cases were imprisonment or a death sentence, we see no principled basis . . . for treating criminal fines differently." The Court added, "Criminal fines, like these other forms of punishment, are penalties inflicted by the sovereign for the commission of offenses. Fines were by far the most common form of noncapital punishment in colonial America." The Court added that fines are particularly important in prosecutions of "organizational defendants who cannot be imprisoned." The Court noted that in 2011, "a fine was imposed on 9.0% of individual defendants and on 70.6% of organizational defendants in the federal system." The ruling will put somewhat more of a burden on prosecutors to factually support fine calculations in corporate criminal cases, although as I have developed in a book, many of the largest corporate prosecutions are settled out of court, and on highly favorable terms.[95] Constitutional rights may over time provide corporations with still additional defensive weapons in criminal litigation.

7.7 Conclusion

Legal scholars have long found the Supreme Court's lack of engagement with theoretical questions concerning the nature of the firm disturbing, calling the Court's rulings "ad hoc," "right-by-right," "arbitrary," "sporadic," inconsistent and not coherent.[96] As the Court emphasized in *Belloti*,

[95] B.L. Garrett, *Too Big to Jail: How Prosecutors Compromise with Corporations* (Cambridge, MA: Harvard University Press, 2014), Ch.8.

[96] See, e.g., J.M. Krannich, "The Corporate 'Person': A New Analytical Approach to a Flawed Method of Constitutional Interpretation" (2005) 37 *Loyola University of Chicago Law Journal* 61 at 62 (calling the Court's approach "ad hoc" and "arbitrary," "fundamentally flawed," and inconsistent even within the same constitutional amendments); T. Bennigson, "Nike Revisited: Can Commercial Corporations Engage in Non-Commercial Speech?" (2006) 39 *Connecticut Law Review* 379 at 399 (describing a "right-by-right" approach); C.R. O'Kelley, Jr., "The Constitutional Rights of Corporations Revisited: Social and Political Expression and the Corporation After First National Bank v. Bellotti" (1979) 67 *Georgetown Law Journal* 1347 at 1348 (calling the Court's approach "ad-hoc," "sporadic," and noting "the artificial nature of a corporation is an inherent source of difficulty in developing an all-encompassing rationale").

"[c]ertain 'purely personal' guarantees, such as the privilege against compulsory self-incrimination, are unavailable to corporations and other organizations because the 'historic function' of the particular guarantee has been limited to the protection of individuals."[97] But the Court increasingly does not adhere to any fixed test for what corporations can or cannot assert, perhaps because constitutional rights can be characterized as specific and personal or alternatively, at a more general and impersonal level.

As Justice Felix Frankfurter famously remarked, "The history of American constitutional law in no small measure is the history of the impact of the modern corporation upon the American scene."[98] Corporate litigation has long reshaped the content of constitutional rights, from the early Marshall Court rulings, to Reconstruction, the *Lochner* era, modern Commerce Clause jurisprudence and recent rulings like *Citizens United.* When the corporation is the litigant, judges may ask different constitutional questions, examine different facts, and perhaps reach different answers. Understanding the contours of the approach across very different areas, from civil procedure, to criminal procedure, to speech, can help us understand where corporate constitutional litigation may go in the future and what consequences those rulings will have upon the US Constitution.

97 *First National Bank of Boston*, above n 31 at 778, and footnote 14.

98 F. Frankfurter, *The Commerce Clause Under Marshall, Taney and Waite* (Columbia: University of North Carolina Press, 1937), p. 63.

8

Understanding Corporate Criminal Liability

IAN B. LEE

8.1 Introduction

The aim of this chapter is to explore the rationale for the institution of corporate criminal liability. Of particular interest is the question as to what corporate punishment achieves that other forms of public action, such as taxation, regulation, and the imposition of civil liability, do not.

From a law and economics perspective, a widely held view has been that the application of punishment to corporations via the criminal law serves no purpose that could not be served equally well (and, perhaps, at lower cost), by other forms of public action. Many scholars writing from this perspective have concluded that corporate criminal liability is, in fact, inefficient. In contrast, a small number of academic philosophers have argued that corporations, among other groups, are moral agents. As such, they can be deserving of blame and, potentially, punishment.

This chapter discusses these two familiar approaches to the task of understanding corporate criminal liability and identifies their limitations. Beyond this, I put forward two alternative understandings of the rationale for corporate criminal liability. The first is based on the utility of the criminal law as an instrument for shaping social and moral norms. The second is based on an understanding of collective responsibility that focuses not on the autonomous moral agency of groups, but on the moral relationship of individuals to the groups with which they identify; I suggest that we think of a collectivity, not as a quasi-person, but as a team.

Before proceeding further, it may be useful to mention two common but fallacious arguments for corporate criminal liability. First, one sometimes encounters the argument that corporate criminal liability is implied by the concept of corporate legal personality. The latter view mistakenly supposes that "legal personality" has a natural content consisting of a predetermined set of rights and obligations, so that one can say, "if X is a legal person, that entails right A and obligation B." This supposition is misguided insofar as it mistakes the label attached to a bundle of legal rights and obligations for the reason for their existence. The law establishes that when certain formalities have been accomplished, property may be acquired, held, and alienated, and liabilities incurred, in the name of a corporation; we call this "legal personality." The term is a shorthand label for the particular legal rules, rather than the reason for the rules.

A related argument is that corporate criminal liability is the counterpart of the privileges associated with corporate legal personality, such as the corporation's civil capacity, limited liability, and perpetual existence. This argument rests on the problematic assumption that civil capacity, limited liability, and continuity of existence are private benefits calling out for compensation, rather than being socially desirable, in their own right, as a matter of public policy. It appears, for instance, that the policy rationale for the corporation's civil capacity lies in the social desirability of facilitating economic activity by enabling capital-owners to make irrevocable commitments of resources to a business venture.[1] There might similarly be good reasons for it to be possible to enter a criminal conviction against a corporation, but these must be identified. It is no more adequate to view corporate criminal liability as a quid pro quo than as a natural entailment of corporate legal personality.

This chapter explores four possible paths toward an understanding of the institution of corporate criminal liability. Two conventional approaches and their limitations are described in Section 8.2. The third and fourth approaches, which I put forward as superior alternatives to the conventional understandings, are discussed in Section 8.3.[2] In Section 8.4, I offer concluding remarks.

8.2 Conventional Approaches

In the legal literature, two approaches to understanding corporate criminal liability predominate. On the one hand, the application to the corporate context of the neoclassical economic understanding of the criminal law invites the conclusion that corporate criminal liability is inefficient

[1] M.M. Blair, "Locking in Capital: What Corporate Law Achieved for Business Organizers in the Nineteenth Century" (2003) 51 *UCLA Law Review* 387.

[2] Section 8.2 draws on the descriptive summary in I.B. Lee, "Corporate Criminal Responsibility as Team Member Responsibility" (2011) 31 *Oxford Journal of Legal Studies* 755 at 758–65. The theory of "team member responsibility" developed in that article is consistent with the "alternative approaches" outlined in Section 8.3.

and therefore socially undesirable. This approach is discussed in Section 8.2.1. On the other hand, some legal commentators argue that corporate criminal liability is connected with the notion, developed most notably by Peter French and Philip Pettit, that the corporation is an autonomous moral agent. I discuss this approach in Section 8.2.2.

8.2.1 *Neoclassical Economic Perspective*

It is possible to summarize the neoclassical economic perspective on corporate criminal liability very simply.[3] The purpose of legal liability is to compel individual actors to internalize the social costs of their behavior. The social utility of criminal liability, as opposed to civil liability, resides in the value of incarceration and other non-monetary penalties as a means of ensuring cost internalization by impecunious individuals.[4] On this view, it is highly significant that corporations cannot be incarcerated and that criminal sanctions against corporations are typically monetary; if the penalties are in any event monetary, there is little point in corporate liability being criminal rather than civil.

8.2.1.1 Corporate Liability

According to the neoclassical economic view, the function of laws that create liability, including both tort law and criminal law, is to attach a price to behaviors that produce net negative externalities.[5] For instance, assuming 100 percent detection, a law imposing liability upon an actor in an amount equal to the social cost of the activity (net of any social benefit) aligns the actor's incentives with the interests of society. In the real world, of course, some socially costly activities go undetected. Given that rational actors will discount the nominal liability amount by the probability of non-detection, an upward adjustment to the former is needed so as to ensure that actors will internalize the full net external cost of their act.

A corporation is not an individual. What is referred to in casual conversation as the "actions of a corporation" are in reality actions taken by individuals in the context of an incorporated business. For instance, such actions

[3] See, e.g., D.R. Fischel and A.O. Sykes, "Corporate Crime" (1996) 25 *Journal of Legal Studies* 319; V.S. Khanna, "Corporate Criminal Liability: What Purpose Does It Serve?" (1996) 109 *Harvard Law Review* 1477.

[4] Fischel and Sykes, above n 3 at 322.

[5] G.S. Becker, "Crime and Punishment: An Economic Approach" (1968) 76 *Journal of Political Economy* 169.

might include a policy decision taken by the board of directors to deploy the corporation's resources in a particular manner, or an operational decision taken by a mid-level manager. The function of imposing liability on a corporation is to influence such actions; the underlying assumption is that the structure of rewards and sanctions within the corporation is such that the pain imposed on a corporation is felt by the responsible individuals.[6]

Many economic theorists of the firm believe that market forces lead rational individuals to create corporate arrangements in which managers and the board of directors have strong incentives to maximize corporate profits.[7] From this belief, it follows that society has reason to be concerned that managers and boards may cause corporations to pursue profits regardless of the cost for society.[8] But it also follows that the behavior of managers and boards of directors will be highly responsive to corporate liability; monetary sanctions affecting the corporation's bottom line will cause corporate managers and boards of directors to internalize the social costs of their decisions.

8.2.1.2 Criminal versus Civil Liability

It does not follow, however, that corporate liability should be criminal. The conventional economic view is that the difference between criminal and civil liability resides in the availability of distinctive sanctions under the criminal law, especially imprisonment. Imprisonment is useful when the external costs of an activity (multiplied to take into account the probability of non-detection) exceed the actor's resources. In short, the prospect of becoming the defendant in a civil suit is likely to have little impact on the choices of a pauper. The risk of losing his or her liberty might have more.

Imprisonment is not an available sanction when the defendant is an "artificial person." Instead, a corporation convicted of an offence is most likely to be ordered to pay a fine. Given, however, that the sanctions will be pecuniary, there is no reason for liability to be criminal rather than civil.[9]

In fact, when the defendant is a corporation, civil liability seems preferable from an economic perspective. Criminal prosecution contains procedural and substantive safeguards, especially the reasonable doubt standard,

[6] Fischel and Sykes, above n 3 at 321.

[7] See, e.g., F.H. Easterbrook and D.R. Fischel, *The Economic Structure of Corporate Law* (Cambridge: Harvard University Press, 1991).

[8] See, e.g., L.E. Mitchell, *Corporate Irresponsibility: America's Newest Export* (New Haven: Yale University Press, 2001); R. Reich, *Supercapitalism* (New York: Knopf, 2007).

[9] Fischel and Sykes note that punitive damages can be used in the civil system to compensate for the probability of non-detection. Fischel and Sykes, above n 3 at 331.

the apparent purpose of which is to protect individuals from unjustified incarceration. Where only money and not liberty is at stake, there is no good reason to burden the cost-internalization process with these safeguards.[10] In other words, the institution of corporate criminal liability compares unfavorably with civil liability as a means of behavior modification.

8.2.1.3 Stigma

One common way of expressing the difference between a criminal (monetary) punishment and an award of civil damages is that a criminal fine carries "stigma." It may appear that stigma is a non-monetary sanction that, unlike incarceration, can usefully be inflicted upon a corporation by criminal law.[11]

However, stigma is a false hope in constructing a defense of corporate criminal liability from a neoclassical perspective. I leave to one side the common criticisms of stigma that it is difficult for a court or policy-maker to calibrate stigma (unlike a fine or damages)[12] and that stigma inflicts a deadweight loss (like imprisonment, but unlike a fine or damages).[13] More fundamentally, stigma is a reputational sanction; it affects the corporate bottom line through the reduced willingness of potential contracting counterparties to transact. The desire to avoid its impact on profitability is the source of the motivation of corporate actors to avoid doing things that will incur stigma. But precisely because the prospect of stigma operates on the behavior of managers through its effect on corporate profitability, stigma is less useful as a substitute for monetary sanctions in the case of corporate as opposed to individual defendants.

Consider that, in the case of individuals, where the level of damages necessary to achieve cost internalization would exceed the defendant's resources, the fact that criminal convictions carry stigma allows fines to be set at a somewhat lower amount in the knowledge that the defendant also receives a non-monetary penalty in the form of stigma. In contrast, when the accused is a corporation, there is a limit to the total amount of economic harm that can be visited upon it without driving it out of business. Stigma can be part of the package of harm, but when it is present the upper bound of the range of possible monetary sanctions is simply reduced accordingly.

10 *Ibid.* at 332.

11 For discussion, see J.C. Coffee, Jr., "'No Soul to Damn, No Body to Kick': An Unscandalized Inquiry into the Problem of Corporate Punishment" (1981) 79 *Michigan Law Review* 386 at 424–34.

12 Khanna, above n 3 at 1504.

13 *Ibid.* at 1503.

8.2.1.4 Limitations of the Neoclassical Perspective

The foregoing analysis leads to the conclusion that corporate criminal liability is an inefficient instrument of behavior modification. Corporate liability should be civil, not criminal, so that the cost-internalization mechanism is not burdened by procedural and other hurdles intended to protect individuals from wrongful incarceration.

It is tempting to try to avoid this conclusion by identifying direct behavior-modification mechanisms that are potentially useful in relation to corporate defendants and that are available within the criminal, but not the civil system. Stigma, previously discussed, is one example; probation might be another. I do not believe that this is a promising strategy. It is not clear, for instance, that corporate probation offers an advantage over administrative regulation backed by civil remedies.

A more significant limitation of the neoclassical analysis concerns its underlying assumption that laws operate only on the prices individuals face rather than on their preferences. It is axiomatic within neoclassical analysis that individuals have stable preferences and that they maximize their utility (the satisfaction of their preferences) within the constraints imposed by their resources and the prices they face. The role of legal liability, in this model, is to modify individuals' behavior by changing the prices they face: the greater the sanction imposed for engaging in particular conduct, the greater its price and the less an individual will engage in the conduct.

But it is important to remember that assumption of fixed preferences is a methodological device employed for the convenience of analysts rather than an empirical truth. It is not that preferences *are* fixed as an empirical matter, but rather that economic analysis typically treats preferences as exogenous. Preferences might just as easily be treated as endogenous, if the evolution in people's preferences is the phenomenon one wishes to study.[14] It may be, for instance, that the criminal law has as one of its purposes to shape the preferences of members of society, and not only to attach prices to their behavior.[15]

Another limitation of the standard neoclassical analysis is that it focuses exclusively on legal mechanisms of behavioral regulation, ignoring

[14] See, e.g., R.H. Frank, "If Homo Economicus Could Choose His Own Utility Function, Would He Want One with a Conscience?" (1987) 77 *American Economic Review* 593. In a sense, it is obvious that people's preferences change: hence, the truism that consumers, or voters, are "fickle."

[15] K.G. Dau-Schmidt, "An Economic Analysis of the Criminal Law as a Preference-Shaping Policy" (1990) 1990 *Duke Law Journal* 1.

non-legal mechanisms such as moral and social norms. In Section 8.3.1, I shall consider whether the prosecution and punishment of corporations may be understood in terms of the law's preference-shaping function and the law's impact upon non-legal norms.[16]

8.2.2 *Corporate Moral Agency Perspective*

A different strategy is pursued by some academic philosophers. Rather than focusing on what corporate criminal liability achieves, this literature seeks to generate a conception of corporate moral responsibility. Its objective, in other words, is to ascertain the conditions under which the ascriptions of blameworthiness entailed by criminal liability make sense in relation to corporate defendants. The key move is to show that corporations and, in general, certain types of groups possess "non-eliminatable . . . agen[cy],"[17] which is to say that it can be sensible to speak of the acts and intentions of the group in a manner that does not reduce to the acts and intentions of individuals.

8.2.2.1 Corporate Intentionality

A leading example of this strategy is Peter French's *Collective and Corporate Responsibility*.[18] French's argument proceeds in two stages. First, he distinguishes between two types of groups: those which possess an identity apart from their several members ("conglomerates") and those which do not ("aggregates"). He posits three features that distinguish conglomerates from aggregates: the existence of internal decision-making procedures, the enforcement of standards of conduct on the part of individuals within the group, and the immutability of the identity of the group despite a change in the identity of the individuals playing any given roles within the group.[19]

Second, with respect to conglomerates, French develops a conception of group intentionality that is not reducible to the intentions of

[16] I reach the opposite conclusion from Dau-Schmidt: he argues that since corporations do not have preferences to be shaped, criminal liability should be imposed only on individuals. I shall suggest that despite the fact that corporations do not have preferences, corporate criminal liability may be of use in shaping other people's preferences. The position may be compared with that advanced in D.M. Kahan, "Social Meaning and the Economic Analysis of Crime" (1998) 27 *Journal of Legal Studies* 609.

[17] P.A. French, "The Corporation as a Moral Person" (1979) 16 *American Philosophical Quarterly* 207 at 211.

[18] P.A. French, *Collective and Corporate Responsibility* (Columbia University Press, 1984).

[19] *Ibid.* at 13–14.

individuals. The crucial element is what French calls the "Corporation's Internal Decision Structure" (its "CID Structure") – in essence, the set of offices and procedures that constitute the "rule of recognition" for corporate decisions.[20] The CID Structure enables an observer (at least in theory) to determine when a decision is "of the corporation." French further supposes that every corporation has a "basic policy," a notion which he does not develop in detail but which one surmises is to be gleaned from a global examination of the decisions that have emanated from the corporation's CID Structure, or perhaps by examining some subset of them (for example, policy directives so labeled by the corporation). French asserts, finally, that when a particular corporate decision is consistent with the corporation's basic policy, it may fairly be said that the corporation "intended" the decision.

More recently, Philip Pettit has advanced a similar argument. Pettit's claim is that "group agents" (a term that might be compared with the conglomerates of French's analysis, and that includes corporations)[21] are "responsible" in the sense that they are suitable candidates for approval or blame, apart from any such judgment that may attach to the individual members of the group.

According to Pettit, a group of individuals is an agent when its members act on a common intention that the group acts as if it were an agent – when they "each intend that together they mimic the performance of a single unified agent."[22] A group agent is capable of acting intentionally, in the sense of forming beliefs and "action-suited desires," and then acting in such a way that its desires are realized given its beliefs.

To show that group agency is not reducible to individual agency, and is in that sense autonomous, Pettit draws upon the discursive dilemmas familiar to social choice theorists. A well-known result in social choice theory is that, when the decisions of a group are submitted to majority voting, they are liable to be internally inconsistent. In forming a group, individuals face a choice between tolerating this inconsistency, on the one hand, and establishing a constitution whereby the group acts consistently but its acts are detached from the judgments of its constituent members, on the other hand. When the latter choice is adopted, the individuals have constituted the group as an autonomous agent.

20 *Ibid.* at 41. Also French, above n 17 at 213.
21 P. Pettit, "Responsibility Incorporated" (2007) 117 *Ethics* 171 at 172.
22 *Ibid.* at 179.

8.2.2.2 Beyond Intentionality

Intentionality plays a special role in some philosophical justifications of individual criminal liability. For instance, in one account, intentionality is significant because of the perceived need for a non-instrumental justification of the application of physical coercion by the state: the significance of intentionality is that, if the act that attracts liability is intentional, then the punishment results, in a sense, from the defendant's own will rather than being inflicted upon him.[23] In another philosophical account, intentional trespasses against the person or property of another are criminally culpable wrongs, because culpability consists of one individual treating another as a means to his ends, in violation of their equal freedom.[24]

It is far from clear that intentionality should have the same importance in a theory of corporate liability. There is no need to characterize the punishment of corporation as the product of "its own will." Moreover, the culpability of a corporation cannot obviously be grounded in a principle prohibiting one individual from treating another as a means to his ends. A case has not been made (and it is not obvious) that any such duty subsists between corporations (or more generally intentional agents that are not human beings) and individual human beings.

In a theory of corporate transgression, concepts other than intentionality must assume greater importance. French and Pettit pursue different strategies for supplementing intentionality. French's approach is to expand the basis of corporate accountability beyond intentional acts, by developing two weaker principles, which he labels the "extended principle of accountability" (EPA)[25] and the "principle of responsive adjustment" (PRA).[26] Under EPA, a person is morally accountable for unintended effects the occurrence of which he "was willing to have occur as the result . . . of his actions."[27] For instance, French argues that McDonnell-Douglas Corp. was morally responsible in respect of the crash of one of the aircrafts it manufactured because it was "willing to manufacture and market" the aircraft despite "its knowledge" that the aircraft's design exposed passengers to a "higher probability" of life-threatening failure than competing aircraft.[28]

[23] A. Brudner, *The Unity of the Common Law: Studies in Hegelian Jurisprudence* (University of California Press, 1995); A. Brudner, *Punishment and Freedom* (Oxford University Press, 2009).

[24] A. Ripstein, "Beyond the Harm Principle" (2006) 34 *Philosophy and Public Affairs* 216.

[25] French, above n 18 at 134.

[26] *Ibid.* at 156 and following.

[27] *Ibid.* at 134.

[28] *Ibid.* at 138.

Under PRA, a person becomes morally accountable for an "untoward event" caused by it, if it does not subsequently take measures to prevent the event's recurrence.[29] The refusal to "adjust one's harm-causing ways . . . associat[es] oneself, morally speaking, with the earlier untoward event."[30] For example, after an Air New Zealand passenger jet crashed into the side of a mountain, a commission of inquiry identified several organizational defects that contributed to causing the disaster. Although it could not be said that the airline had intended the disaster or even had willingly assumed the possibility of its occurrence,[31] French concluded that Air New Zealand was morally responsible in respect of the disaster because, afterward, it did not act to correct the defects identified.[32]

Pettit's strategy is simpler. He argues that group agents do not only act intentionally, but are also capable of forming "evaluative beliefs," which is to say beliefs about propositions of value.[33] Group agents can make value judgments, in other words. A group agent does so whenever the group endorses a proposition of value presented for its consideration by its members.[34] Because a group agent is "capable of making a judgment on what is good and bad and right and wrong" and of acting in consequence, it is "as fit as any individual human being to be held responsible for what it does."[35]

8.2.2.3 Assessment of the Corporate Moral Agency Approach

French and Pettit have surely advanced our understanding of corporate criminal liability and, in particular, of why corporations may deserve the blame that distinguishes criminal punishment from civil liability and taxation. For Pettit, it is the capacity to make value judgments that supplies a basis on which the resulting act may deserve blame: specifically, the corporation's act is blameworthy when the underlying value judgments were wrong. For French, it is the willingness to accept an unwarranted harm or,

[29] *Ibid.* at 156.

[30] *Ibid.*

[31] *Ibid.* at 154.

[32] *Ibid.* at 161.

[33] Pettit, above n 21 at 186–7.

[34] *Ibid.* at 187.

[35] *Ibid.* at 192. According to Pettit, the capacity to make value judgments distinguishes humans and group agents from robots and non-human animals – even though the latter are capable of acting intentionally in the sense of forming desires and beliefs and acting in pursuance of them, they cannot make value judgments. *Ibid.* at 178, 185. Similarly, although French appears to concede that non-human animals can act intentionally, they are, unlike corporations, incapable of "responsive adjustment" and are therefore not moral persons. See French, above n 18 at 166.

alternatively, the failure to make responsive adjustments in the wake of an unintended harm that engages the corporation's moral responsibility.

Nevertheless, I have reservations about both authors' approaches. In relation to French, I worry that the appropriateness and coherence of moral judgments about the behavior of corporations is assumed, rather than argued for.

Consider, for instance, French's account of the responsibility incurred by the McDonnell Douglas Corp. Self-consciously, French does not treat it as sufficient that the corporation's design choice exposed passengers to a risk of harm. Instead, the critical fact is that the design of the MD aircraft carried a greater risk than that of competing aircraft manufactured by the company's rivals. French's account assumes, in other words, the existence of an implicit principle of moral behavior that the manufacturers of aircraft should not produce and sell aircraft that expose passengers to a greater risk of death than competing aircraft. The existence of such a principle strikes me as debatable.[36] More fundamentally, the question arises, and is not answered by French, as to why a corporation owes moral duties to individuals, such as a duty not to harm them in particular ways, at all.

Similarly, in French's account of the responsibility of Air New Zealand, the relevant choices of the airline were not described in neutral terms as elements of the causal chain leading to the disaster, but – borrowing the commission of inquiry's label – as organizational "defects" which the airline had an obligation to remedy once it was made aware of them.

What distinguishes a defect from an innocent causative act is not explained by French. Yet, there must be a distinction. For not every harm caused by someone can give rise to an obligation of that person to prevent its recurrence. Business people knowingly and repeatedly harm competitors in the marketplace.[37] I harm a law student by giving him a D on an assignment, and I repeat this harm, but I do not wrong him, if I give him a D on the next assignment, too. What makes a harm wrongful is not that it is intentional or that it is knowingly repeated, but that it violates a duty owed by one person to another. In the absence of a duty, there is no wrong in causing or in knowingly repeating a harm.

In the final analysis, I worry that what French has succeeded in showing is simply that, *assuming that there is such a thing as corporate wrongdoing*, if a corporation commits a wrongful act, then it is all the more reprehensible

[36] The Concorde was known to be less safe than its subsonic competitors. Was it immoral to operate flights on the Concorde?

[37] Ripstein, above n 24 at 217.

if it was committed knowingly or if the corporation does not take steps to prevent doing it again. What is missing, however, is a theory of corporate wrongdoing.

At first glance, Pettit's account does not suffer from this gap. He combines an undemanding conception of intentionality (such that even robots possess it) with the notion that corporations (unlike robots) encounter and must dispose of competing "propositions of value." The capacity to make value judgments supplies a basis on which the resulting act can be wrongful, in the sense of deserving blame. One supposes, although Pettit does not say so, that an act can be blameworthy even if the relevant propositions of value were not explicitly considered: the criticism in such cases is that the corporation could have and ought to have taken them into account.

Like French, Pettit constructs corporate responsibility – the responsibility of the corporation as an entity – so that it is detached from any responsibility of its members in respect of the act. By hypothesis it is the entity, and not necessarily any individual, that acted, had the capacity to consider value judgments, and so on. The fact of the corporation's responsibility does not imply the responsibility of any member. An entity may be blamed and yet each of the members be blameless.

A disadvantage of constructing the entity's agency so that it is independent of the agency of any of its human members is that it is not clear why the entity is a member of *our* moral community. A corporation, in Pettit's understanding, differs from a robot only in that it makes value judgments. I am not certain that it is fair to assume that anyone or anything that makes value judgments is a member of our moral community, such that moral rights and duties subsist between us and them the violation of which would be the kind of "bad value judgment" that rightly attracts blame.

The corporate moral agency approach seems to be most persuasive if we are prepared to assume that certain acts (such as endangering life) are morally wrong regardless of the type of intentional actor, but on this assumption we would also pass judgment on robots and on non-human animals committing the same acts. If we instead assume that wrongdoing is relational, and conceptualize it as a violation of duties owed by one member of a moral community to the other members, then the group agency approach seems incomplete insofar as it takes for granted that moral duties subsist between group agents and individuals.

My misgivings about the strategy of emphasizing the independent moral agency of corporations as a route to understanding corporate criminal liability lead me to explore a different approach. Section 8.3.2 considers whether, even if corporate criminal liability is a form of collective responsibility, the latter should be understood, not as the responsibility of an autonomous group entity, but as the responsibility of the members of the group.[38]

8.3 Alternative Approaches

In this section, I consider two alternative understandings of corporate criminal liability. The first strategy situates corporate criminal liability within a criminal justice system that serves not only to deter and incapacitate (that is, not only to price harm-causing behavior) but also to instruct, through the declaration and denunciation of violations of social and moral norms.

The second strategy focuses on the notion of group responsibility, and accordingly may be compared with the argument developed by French and Pettit. These authors' philosophical arguments in favor of corporate responsibility are hampered, in my view, by a self-imposed and unnecessary obstacle: French and Pettit seek to detach group responsibility from the responsibility of the constituent individuals. They construct the group as an $(N + 1)$ person distinct from each of the N persons who compose it, and whose responsibility may be incurred irrespective of the responsibility, or lack thereof, of any of the individual members. The problem with this approach is that it necessitates a theory of the rights and duties that subsist between group agents and individual agents and the violation of which constitutes wrongdoing. Such a theory is elusive. I propose that we discard French and Pettit's notion that collective responsibility is the responsibility of a quasi-person in favor of the notion that collective responsibility is the responsibility of the members of a team.

8.3.1 Law and Norms

Like taxation and civil liability, criminal liability seeks to ensure that there is a consequence to the offender for doing a particular act – that a "price" is paid; however, a punishment differs from a tax and civil liability in that

[38] Pettit appears to take a step back from the disconnection between the group's responsibility and that of its members when, very briefly and near the end of the paper, Pettit suggests that the members of a group incur "membership responsibility" – they are complicit in the wrongs of the group agent if they remain members without protest. See Pettit, above n 21 at 194. It is this idea, which is very much peripheral to Pettit's argument and which he does not develop, that I shall pursue in Section 8.3.2.

it communicates that the reason for the consequence is the wrongfulness of the act. The purpose of communicating the wrongfulness of the act is to reach the moral sensibility of the wrongdoer and of others – their consciences and not only their self-interest. In this section, I conceptualize this purpose in terms of state intervention in the market for norms.

I begin with a brief overview of moral and social norms as non-legal sources of behavioral regulation, and of the role of the criminal law in supporting and influencing the content of norms by declaring norms violations. I then suggest that the punishment of a corporation declares that a norm was violated in the course of the corporation's business. I do not suppose corporations to be educable moral beings: punishment does not seek to reach corporate moral consciousness. Instead, I suggest that the goal of corporate punishment is to support and influence the moral and social norms observed by individuals: third parties and members of the corporation.

8.3.1.1 Norms and the Criminal Law

Moral and Social Norms No society relies exclusively, or even primarily, on legal rules and sanctions to regulate the behavior of its members. Most people do not make most choices with one eye on the legal requirements and the other eye on the probability of detection and punishment for noncompliance with those requirements. We are not "rational fools."[39]

People's actions are guided, not only by legal incentives, but also by "norms" that may be of two types. I use the term "social norm" to refer to the influence on behavior of a normative belief on the part of people whose esteem the actor values; that is, where a person does something because people whose esteem she values think that she ought to. I use the term "moral norm" to refer to the behavioral influence of a person's belief that she herself ought to act in a particular way.[40] That is, where a person does something, not because she looks forward to the consequences of her act, and not out of a desire for the esteem of others, but because she believes that it is the right thing for her to do, the latter motivation has its source in an internalized moral norm.

Within the category of social norms, it is useful to distinguish between two ways in which such norms might influence a person's conduct. The

[39] A. Sen, "Rational Fools: A Critique of the Behavioral Foundations of Economic Theory" (1977) 6 *Philosophy and Public Affairs* 317.

[40] For a similar distinction between moral and social norms, see also E. Elhauge, "Sacrificing Corporate Profits in the Public Interest" (2005) 80 *New York University Law Review* 733.

distinction turns on whether the esteem of observers is intrinsically or instrumentally valued. An individual might comply with a social norm in order to obtain enhanced exchange opportunities or she might comply with the same norm because she values the esteem of the relevant observers for its own sake. Where a person's motivation is of the second type, I shall speak of an "internalized social norm." Where it is of the first type, the avoidance of social sanctions is indistinguishable from self-interest. Even a sociopath will comply with a social norm if this will help her to get a job; however, a sociopath does not act upon internalized social norms. A whole person, in contrast, cares what (at least some) others think of her, and when she violates an internalized social norm and exposes herself to the disapproval of these same others, she experiences the negative emotion of shame.

The Significance of Punishment Given their conceptualization as a source of order distinct from the law of the state, it is common to think of social norms as arising spontaneously, without state intervention. One influential theoretical account describes a mechanism in which, on the assumption that members of a community desire the development of norms against antisocial conduct, observers confer esteem upon others who impose informal sanctions (for example, admonishment) for antisocial behavior.[41] The process of norms development can be analogized to a market in which "norms entrepreneurs" offer their sanctioning services to observers in exchange for the latter's esteem.

However, the state need not (and does not) simply stand aside and let norms markets do their work unimpeded. The state might attempt to obstruct the operation of a dysfunctional norm by prohibiting the subject behavior, or by prohibiting or otherwise impeding the social sanctions that attach to violation of the norm.[42] Collective action problems might also act as a drag on the spontaneous development of beneficial norms, creating a role for the state.

For instance, a norm of "protecting children from unnecessary injury in vehicular accidents" might be expected to arise spontaneously, but the translation of this abstract principle into concrete norms about specific

[41] R. McAdams, "The Origin, Development and Regulation of Norms" (1997) 96 *Michigan Law Review* 338; see also E. Posner, *Law and Social Norms* (Cambridge: Harvard University Press, 2000). In Posner's model, the individuals who impose informal sanctions thereby signal their suitability as transactional counterparties and benefit from increased exchange opportunities.

[42] See, e.g., McAdams, above n 41 at 349.

conduct – requiring the use of a rear-facing car seat until the age of twelve months, a forward-facing seat until three years, and a booster until the age of seven years – requires an investment of research likely exceeding the resources and motivation of any individual norms entrepreneur.[43]

The state may also seek to influence the content of norms by labeling particular conduct as wrongful. It is conventional to assume that prohibitory law carries "moral weight" with citizens.[44] This may be because public officials (such as legislators) are believed to have a good sense of what does or does not attract the community's respect or opprobrium and to be responsive to the community's opinion.[45] That is, officials are believed to be reliable sources of information about social norms. It may also be that citizens give weight to society's opinion in forming their moral views. If so, then the state's designation of certain conduct as discreditable can be expected to shape both social norms and the moral norms followed by individuals.

This is one way of understanding why the criminal law does not only visit a consequence upon a wrongdoer but also *labels* the consequence a "punishment."[46] Punishment represents the punisher's declaration that the act was wrong – it violated social norms and, perhaps moral norms. In the case of criminal punishment, the assumption is that legislatures that enacted the prohibition, and the judge who administers the punishment, are viewed by defendants (and potential defendants) as credible sources of insight into the relevant social and moral norms. The punishment will then occasion guilt (for violating a moral norm), shame (for violating a social norm), or both, on the part of the accused, and will serve as a reminder to other members of society of the existence and content of the relevant norms.

8.3.1.2 Corporate Punishment

In principle, there are two categories of consumers of the information about norms contained in a criminal punishment: the defendant and third parties. On the one hand, it is typically considered important that the defendant understand that the reason why she is going to prison, or being

[43] Regarding the relationship between law and norms in the context of child car restraints, see also *ibid.* at 407–8.

[44] C. Sunstein, "On the Expressive Function of Law" (1995) 144 *University of Pennsylvania Law Review* 2021 at 2031; see also Kahan, above n 16; J. Hampton, "The Moral Education Theory of Punishment" (1984) 13 *Philosophy and Public Affairs* 208; Dau-Schmidt, above n 15.

[45] Robert Ellickson, "The Market for Social Norms" (2001) 3 *American Law and Economics Review* 1 at 40.

[46] See McAdams, above n 41 at 398.

made to pay a fine, is that she committed a wrong (transgressed a moral or social norm). On the other hand, the punishment of a wrongdoer also advertises the existence of the norm to citizens at large.

When the defendant is a corporation, matters are somewhat different. For the reasons discussed in Section 8.2.2, I am wary of speaking of the "corporation's wrongdoing." Moreover, I am reluctant to characterize the corporation as a being capable of valuing esteem for its own sake or internalizing moral norms.[47] It may be that the corporation is not fully described by the expression "nexus of contracts," and that a collectivity is more than an aggregate of individuals. But it is one thing to depart from strict methodological individualism; it is another, less defensible matter to indulge in anthropomorphism. Philip Pettit shows that there is a way of conceptualizing corporate (and other group) moral agency, in the sense of that one can speak of the group's judgments (not reducible to the judgments of the constituent individuals) on matters of moral value. This is not the same thing as showing that corporations and other groups are educable moral beings. I proceed on the basis that corporations "have no soul to damn."[48]

Instead, I suggest in this part that corporate punishment operates upon the social and moral norms observed by natural persons. First and more straightforwardly, it speaks to third parties; it asserts to citizens at large the existence and content of the norm violated by the corporation. Second, punishment may seek to reach the social and moral faculties of the corporation's "members," by which I mean individuals who identify with the corporation as a collective venture. Depending on the corporation and the circumstances, these may be its shareholders, its employees, its customers, or others.

Third Parties In general, the punishment of wrongdoing does not only seek to convey a lesson to the wrongdoer but also serves to instruct society about the limits of acceptable conduct and, thereby, reinforce and shape the content of social norms. Accordingly, even assuming that the corporation is not a candidate for salvation (or damnation), corporate punishment may yet provide useful normative guidance to the human members of society. Indeed, when civil, tax, or regulatory liability is the legal response to the violation of social norm, it may send the wrong message: that society attaches a price to the behavior rather

[47] See Dau-Schmidt, above n 15.

[48] Baron Thurlow quoted in Coffee, above n 11 at 386.

than requiring its members to abstain from it altogether.[49] For example, when a corporate fraud results in civil liability rather than criminal punishment, it may weaken the force, for individuals, of moral and social norms against fraud.

Given my assumption that corporations do not act upon internalized norms, we may anticipate an objection to the notion that corporate punishment is useful for the moral guidance of individuals. It is not unknown in human history for societies to seek to reinforce moral and social norms by putting animals on trial, or by "punishing" the instruments of crime. Is that what corporate punishment is – the punishment of an instrument of crime? Knowing that many laypersons are susceptible to the anthropomorphic fallacy in relation to corporations, do lawmakers enact laws that treat corporations as if they were human beings, so as to teach individuals valuable lessons about appropriate human-to-human behavior? If this is what corporate criminal liability amounts to, the institution is an offence against the intelligence of the community, even if it is perhaps not an offence against the community's welfare: there is such a thing as a useful delusion.[50]

I would like, however, to suggest a different account of corporate criminal liability that captures its usefulness as a pedagogical device for citizens at large, without insulting the latter's intelligence. Organizational (including corporate) liability is useful where it can be established that a norm was violated by one or more individuals within an organization, but where the identity of the individual wrongdoers cannot be established. In our legal system, a heavy burden of proof must be discharged before a human being can be convicted of a crime – presumably, because of the risk of wrongful incarceration. Sometimes this burden cannot be met, even if it is clear that one or more individuals within the corporation committed a crime, because the responsible individuals cannot be identified. Punishing the organization allows society to declare and denounce the violation of the norm by unnamed individuals within the organization, thereby reminding outsiders of its existence and content – in circumstances where the violation would otherwise go unpunished.

[49] Kahan, above n 16. See also L. Friedman, "In Defense of Corporate Criminal Liability" (1999) 23 *Harvard Journal of Law and Public Policy* 833.

[50] But see Khanna, above n 3 at 1531 ("citizens might find imposing criminal liability on artificial entities farcical, and this response may decrease the criminal label's effect for other types of crimes").

Let me offer the following illustration. Suppose that the Chief Executive Officer and her deputy are suspected of authorizing a fraudulent corporate tax declaration. Each points the finger at the other; both are equally credible. There is, from the perspective of the trier of fact, a 50% probability that the CEO was responsible, and a 50% probability that it was her deputy. Both must be acquitted, for the guilt of neither individual is proved beyond a reasonable doubt (nor even on a balance of probabilities) – even though there is no question that one or the other of them committed a serious crime.[51] In these circumstances, the prosecution and punishment of the corporation communicates to the public the message that one or more individuals within the organization violated a social or moral norm. The message is truthful, not delusional.

Members of the Corporation I have assumed that the corporation is not an educable moral being; it follows that the criminal law does not seek to engage *its* moral or social conscience. However, the criminal law might serve to influence the social and moral norms observed by the human beings who participate in the corporation.

Corporate theory urges us to view the corporation as a nexus of contracts. It urges us to recognize that the behavior of corporations is the vector sum of the behaviors of countless numbers of individuals – investors, employees, customers, suppliers, and so on – who participate in the business and transact with one another through the corporate person. Not all of these transactions are alike: for instance, some are punctual (a consumer buys an MP3 player; a student accepts a short-term contract to provide casual labor) while others create an ongoing relationship (an employee invests in the acquisition of firm-specific skills).[52]

In the next section, I hypothesize that there are some individuals whose relationship with the corporation is such that they identify with it as a collective enterprise. I call these individuals the corporation's "members." The members' behavior generates local social norms which can be a goal of corporate criminal liability to influence.

I must defer to the end of the next section an explanation of the manner in which corporate criminal liability might seek to influence the norms

[51] Compare *Cook* v. *Lewis* [1951] SCR 830. [The defendant hunters act carelessly, firing in the plaintiff's direction. The plaintiff is struck by one of them; it cannot be provided which of the defendants fired the shot that caused the plaintiff's injury.]

[52] M.M. Blair and L.A. Stout, "A Team Production Theory of Corporate Law" (1999) 85 *Virginia Law Review* 247 at 248.

observed by the members of the corporation, because I first need to explain my understanding of the corporation as a collective enterprise, and what it means for someone to be a member of the corporation. That is the task of the next section.

8.3.2 *Collective Responsibility as Membership Responsibility*

Our task in this chapter is to explain the rationale for punishing a corporation rather than imposing civil damages or taxation upon it. We saw in Section 8.2.2 that some philosophers have sought the answer to this question in a type of collective responsibility. More specifically, they have defended a conception of a collectivity as a moral entity separate from any of the associated individuals. That entity, they argue, may deserve blame and therefore, potentially, punishment in its own right.

In this section, I explore a different understanding of corporate punishment, one that rests on a different conception of collectivities. I argue that collectivities should be thought of as teams, constituted by the self-identification of their members with the group. The fact of self-identifying as the member of a collectivity makes each member a stakeholder in the success or failure of the collective enterprise. In particular, the punishment of a corporation visits shame or guilt upon certain individuals associated with the corporation (its "members"). It is not the corporation as an entity, but rather these individuals who experience the guilt and shame associated with criminal punishment. Therefore, it is to these individuals' conduct and circumstances that we must look for the reasons why punishment is justified.

8.3.2.1 A Collectivity, Defined

Sometimes a group is more than the sum of its constituent individuals. What differentiates a collectivity from a mere collection of individuals? I want to distinguish between two approaches to answering this question.

One approach seeks to find in certain groups the characteristics of individual agents. This is French and Pettit's approach. For both of these authors, a key element is an "identity" that remains stable despite changes in group membership: that is, a statement referring to the group has the same meaning before and after a change in its membership.[53] Another crucial distinguishing characteristic of a collectivity is an institutional framework for making decisions.[54]

[53] French, above n 18 at 13. Pettit, above n 21 at 172.

[54] See, e.g., *ibid.* French's definition includes additional elements, notably the existence of "enforced standards of conduct" applicable to group members (i.e., group norms).

This chapter defends a different manner of thinking about what distinguishes collectivities from mere collections of individuals. I suggest that we think of a collectivity as being constituted and maintained by the self-identification of its members with the group. In this definition, the key concept is neither the group's *identity* nor its institutional features but the *self-identification* of its members with the group. One might say that a collectivity exists when its members view themselves as a collectivity.

This understanding of what constitutes a collectivity draws on Amartya Sen and Elizabeth Anderson's conceptualization of the rationality of cooperative action in prisoner's dilemmas.[55] In a series of articles foreshadowing the literature on law and norms, Sen had argued that rational individuals sometimes consciously act in ways that do not maximize the attainment of the actor's self-interest, even where the latter term is defined broadly so as to include the impact on one's own welfare or the welfare of others for whom one has sympathy. For instance, in a prisoner's dilemma, the choice of a cooperative outcome might be described in terms of commitment.[56] The choice of a lower individual payoff, Sen argued, might somehow be "more sophisticated" than that choice of a higher individual payoff, although the latter is exclusively recommended by the standard conception of rationality.[57]

Sen's argument left a gap in that he did not explain in what sense it is rational for a person to act in accordance with a commitment rather than his or her self-interest or sympathy.[58] In what sense is the prisoner's choice of a lower payoff rational?[59] Anderson sought to supply the missing link by supposing that the "parties to [the] prisoner's dilemma identify with one another as common members of a social group." They "regard [themselves] as acting in concert with the other parties, as a single body" and, so, regard "the object of their choice to be a single joint strategy. They . . . thereby

[55] E. Anderson, "Unstrapping the Straitjacket of 'Preference': A Comment on Amartya Sen's Contributions to Philosophy and Economics" (2001) 17 *Economics and Philosophy* 21.

[56] It is not a case of sympathy, assuming that neither prisoner's welfare is dependent upon the other's; that is, neither prisoner feels better off just because the other feels better off.

[57] Example of the distinction between sympathy and commitment: "If the knowledge of torture of others makes you sick, it is a case of sympathy; if it does not make you feel personally worse off, but you think it is wrong and you are ready to do something to stop it, it is a case of commitment." Sen, above n 39 at 326.

[58] Anderson, above n 55.

[59] Conventional attempts to account for the choice of the cooperative strategy seek to modify the payoffs, for instance by introducing repeated play and reputational effects, so that the cooperative strategy yields a higher individual payoff than the uncooperative strategy. Thus, conventional arguments do not rationalize the choice of a lower payoff; they show that what looks, at first glance, like the lower payoff is in reality the higher payoff when all of the consequences of both choices are taken into account.

constitute themselves as members of a single collective agent."[60] Anderson did not claim that individuals confronted with a prisoner's dilemma necessarily approach the matter this way, but only that they might, and that, if they did, they would not be acting irrationally.

One may think of this as a conception of collectivities as teams. What makes a group of individuals a team is not that the group has a decision-making process, or that outsiders would view it as being fundamentally changed in the event of a change in membership. Rather, the question is whether the individual members are guided by their common interest and sometimes pursue the latter at the expense of their personal interests. To the extent that they do, they constitute themselves a team; they constitute themselves a collective enterprise.

If the members regard themselves as isolated individuals, that is what they are. If, however, each member does not approach every occasion for choice from the perspective of what would maximize her individual utility but, at least sometimes, asks what would serve the group's collective interest, then the group constitutes a collectivity.[61]

8.3.2.2 Collective Guilt and Shame

The successes and failures of a collective enterprise are a source of positive or negative emotions for the members of the enterprise: the members feel honor or pride about their collective accomplishments, and shame or guilt about their collective failures. When the national team experiences success in international sports competition, their compatriots feel pride. If a soldier commits an atrocity while on patrol, all service members, especially the members of the wrongdoer's unit, may experience shame, if not guilt.

Because my topic is punishment, I shall focus here on shame and guilt rather than honor and pride. There are at least two ways of understanding the sentiment of shame or guilt experienced by the members of a collectivity for the wrongdoing of one or a few of their number.

[60] Anderson, above n 55 at 28.

[61] In the language of norms, we would say that a collectivity exists when individuals are guided by an internalized norm that they ought to pursue the collective interest. Commitment and norms do not have exactly the same conceptual architecture: norms are typically conceptualized as sources of esteem or self-esteem, from which individuals are assumed to derive utility; in contrast, commitment is a second-order preference, which is to say a ranking on the basis of which individuals evaluate and critique their preferences. This difference is not significant for purposes of this chapter.

Contribution to Wrongdoing One possibility is that the members experience guilt, the feeling of having acted as they should not. In the case of some members, this may be because of a specific act of assistance to the immediate wrongdoer. But even where a wrongdoer seems to have acted alone, the efforts of many, if not necessarily all, members may contribute to creating a context in which the wrongdoing was foreseeable, or at least made more likely.[62]

Compare, for instance, two auditing firms. In one, the prevailing ethos is: "think straight, talk straight." In the other, the ethos is: "above all, produce profits for the firm."[63] In each firm, the relevant slogan has attained the status of a local social norm: it guides the actions of the members, and the actions of the members reinforce the norm. If, in the second firm, dishonest but profitable conduct were widespread, it would be understandable if each of the members of the firm, and not only those directly responsible for the dishonest acts, experienced guilt, to the extent that each of them contributed to creating the climate within which a few people might become disposed toward dishonesty.[64]

In the terminology of norms, the nature of teamwork is such that the members are partly motivated by intragroup social norms, and these norms are in turn generated by the behavior of the members. We are all influenced by peer pressure, and at the same time our behavior generates the underlying peer norms. Whether the resulting norms are commendable or reprehensible, we had a hand in their creation and it is reasonable that we experience pride or guilt at the resulting behavior of our teammates.

Crisis of Identification The feeling of having acted as one should not may be distinguished from another emotion, often described in terms of shame. Psychologists suggest that shame is associated with a diminished sense of one's self.[65] This is one way of describing, in the context of a

[62] G. Fletcher, "Liberals and Romantics at War: The Problem of Collective Guilt" (2002) 111 *Yale Law Journal* 1499 at 1541–2.

[63] K. Brown and I.J. Dugan, "Andersen's Fall from Grace is a Sad Tale of Greed and Miscues," *Wall Street Journal*, 7 June 2002. The first slogan was the motto of the founder of Arthur Andersen LLP, recited by incoming junior auditors. Later, an Andersen partner said, "produce profits for the firm" became the dominant value.

[64] Fletcher, above n 62 at 1541–2 ("those who generate a climate of moral degeneracy bear some of the guilt for the criminal actions that are thereby endorsed").

[65] J.P. Tangney, R.S. Miller, L. Flicker, and D.H. Barlow, "Are Shame, Guilt and Embarrassment Distinct Emotions?" (1996) 70 *Journal of Personal and Social Psychology* 1256 at 1265 ("when shamed, [participants] felt more isolated, diminished, and inferior to others."); R. Smith, J.M. Webster, G.W. Parrott, and H.L. Eyre, "The Role of Public Exposure in Moral and Nonmoral

collectivity some members of which have committed a wrong, the conflict experienced by each of the others between her solidarity with the group and her regret at what some of them have done. We may interpret in this vein Ronald Dworkin's assertion that "as an American citizen he was ashamed of the Vietnam War – even though he opposed it."[66]

This conflict is not a purely emotional phenomenon. It also presents a forward-looking ethical dilemma, for one's choice to identify, or to continue to identify, as members of the team, is a decision that engages one's conscience. Consider Bernhard Schlink's description of the emotional and ethical dilemma experienced by Germans too young to have contributed directly to the Holocaust:

> [Members of the postwar generation must cope with] learning that the beloved parents, or admired teachers and professors, or respected pastors and other figures of love and authority had a dark past, had been involved in crimes. How do you deal with that? You realize that in a way you are entangled in the guilt of those whom you love or keep solidarity with . . . What should I do when I learn that someone I love is guilty? Do I have to break with this person? Can I keep this person in my life? These questions are universal.[67]

The children of the wartime generation have no causal responsibility for what their parents did – they did not even contribute to the norms that influenced their parents' behavior. The shame of the postwar generation is not for what they themselves did; instead, it points to a forward-looking ethical question for the members of that generation: "Are we right to continue in solidarity with the nation and the intertemporal community which we share with our parents?"

More generally, when a team member commits a wrong in the name of the team, the other members are right to ask themselves: is it right for us to remain members of the team?

The notion that collective success and failure are shared is antithetical to French and Pettit's understanding according to which the group's

Shame and Guilt" (2002) 83 *Journal of Personal and Social Psychology* 138. I hope that it will not be a source of confusion for the reader that, earlier in this chapter, "shame" was used to describe the emotional consequence of violating a social norm. In using the term again here, I am supposing that the emotion of shame can have different sources: it can arise because of a feeling of social disapproval (from violating a norm) or from the conflict between solidarity and regret described in this section.

[66] Quoted in J. Raikka, "On Disassociating Oneself from Collective Responsibility" (1997) 23 *Social Theory and Practice* 93.

[67] Interview remarks in S. Davis, "An Interview with Bernhard Schlink," *Cardozo Life*, Fall 2009, p. 36. The wartime generation feels guilt; the postwar generation feels shame.

successes and failures are those of a separate collective agent and are detached from the accomplishments or failures of any individual member of the group; yet, it seems to be a more natural understanding of collective life.

8.3.2.3 Corporations as Collectivities

If our conception of collective responsibility as team-member responsibility is to shed light on the significance of corporate punishment, we must next show that corporations are collectivities – that they are teams. Such a demonstration begins with the observation that corporate law theorists commonly describe the firm as a vehicle for the coordination of team production. For instance, Easterbrook and Fischel write:

> Much production is performed in teams. Teams of employees sweep the floor, teams of engineers design new products, teams of managers decide whether and where to build new plants. So long as no monitor can determine what each member's marginal contribution to the team's output is, each member will be a less than perfect representative of the interests of the team as a whole. Unless one person receives all the rewards of success and penalties of failure, his incentives are not properly aligned with those of the venture as a whole. "Let George do it" is a predictable response when any given employee gets some of the benefits of George's hard work and does not get all of the benefits of his own hard work.[68]

According to the conventional contractarian wisdom, various monitoring and bonding devices arise within firms to combat the divergence of interests between the individual members of the team and the team as a whole.[69] However, one normally wants team members to devote more than the bare minimum of effort that will prevent their incurring contractual penalties or dismissal from the team; to accomplish this goal, strategies beyond bonding and monitoring are necessary, such as the cultivation of a sense of mutual loyalty.[70] This is why Sen argued that commitment to an organization is "central to the problem of work motivation . . . To run an organization entirely on incentives to personal gain is pretty much a hopeless task."[71] Successful production requires, in other words, that the

[68] Easterbrook and Fischel, above n 7. See also Blair and Stout, above n 52.

[69] *Ibid.* See also M.C. Jensen and W.H. Meckling, "Theory of the Firm: Managerial Behavior, Agency Costs and Ownership Structure" (1976) 3 *Journal of Financial Economics* 305.

[70] I.B. Lee, "Efficiency and Ethics in the Debate about Shareholder Primacy" (2006) 31 *Delaware Journal of Corporate Law* 533 at 550.

[71] Sen, above n 39 at 333–5.

participants be motivated (at least in part) by loyalty toward the team; that they identify, in other words, as the members of a collective enterprise.

Indeed, certain features of the corporation can be well understood only if the corporation is characterized as a collective entity.[72] Most obviously, the manner in which the board's mandate is formulated under corporate law – as a duty to pursue the "best interests of the corporation" – presupposes that there is such a thing as a collective corporate interest.[73]

Who are the members of the corporation as a collective enterprise? Recall that a collectivity is constituted by the self-identification of its members with the group. The preceding discussion of team production suggests that the employees of a corporation may well identify as members of the collective enterprise carried on within the corporation.

The situation of shareholders is surprisingly ambiguous. In principle, shareholders could identify as members of a collectivity: after all, they possess, collectively, the power to select the corporation's board of directors[74] and the latter are often understood to be carrying on the corporation's business in the shareholders' collective interest. The premise of many shareholder proposals on corporate social responsibility matters, moreover, is that the proponents believe themselves to be morally implicated by policies and practices undertaken in the name of the corporation.[75] As shareholders, the proponents do not see themselves as bystanders, but as participants in the corporation's collective enterprise.

However, many shareholders do not view themselves as the members of a collective entity, but instead, consistently with their portrayal under conventional contractarian analysis, as the separate suppliers of an input.[76] Some shareholders do not view themselves even in these terms, but instead consider themselves to be mere speculators on security price movements.[77] So one cannot say that shareholders, in general, are the members of the corporation as a collective enterprise. The most one can say is that *some* shareholders in *some* corporations identify as the members of a collective enterprise.

[72] I.B. Lee, "Citizenship and the Corporation" (2009) 34 *Law and Social Inquiry* 129.

[73] *Ibid.* at 147.

[74] See, e.g., Delaware General Corporation Law § 211(b).

[75] See I.B. Lee, "Corporate Law, Profit Maximization and the 'Responsible' Shareholder" (2005) 10 *Stanford Journal of Law, Business and Finance* 31 at 64.

[76] See U. Rodrigues, "The Seductive Comparison of Shareholder and Civic Democracy" (2006) 63 *Washington and Lee Law Review* 1389 at 1399.

[77] See Mitchell, above n 8 at 134.

8.3.2.4 Significance of Corporate Punishment

The relevance of the punitive or condemnatory nature of the criminal law, as applied to corporations, now comes into focus. When someone commits a wrong in the course of the corporation's business, society should punish the *corporation*, and not only the direct individual wrongdoer, and it should *punish* the corporation, and not only levy a tax on the corporation, because the corporation's members are not moral strangers to the behavior. Punishment visits guilt upon the members who contributed to the wrong, including those whose behavior generated the organizational norms that motivated the wrongdoer; and it gives all of the members food for thought as they evaluate their continued attachment to the corporate team.

The purpose of corporate punishment may also be articulated in instrumental terms. Within the conception of the criminal law as an instrument of socialization, the shame and guilt occasioned by criminal punishment serve to shape an individual's moral norms and to contribute to the functioning or alter the content of social norms. Of particular interest in the context of corporate criminal liability is the situation where deviant organizational norms have contributed to the occurrence of wrongdoing. In such cases, the punishment of the corporation draws attention to the gap between moral norms or society's norms and the norms prevailing within the organization; it facilitates the operation of the social sanctions that act upon the members of organizations; indirectly, therefore, it shapes organizational norms by changing the attitudes and behavior of the members.

8.4 Conclusion

I have outlined four possible theoretical understandings of corporate criminal liability. First, from a neoclassical perspective, it appears that corporate criminal liability achieves nothing that could not be achieved by means of civil, tax, or administrative liability. However, this analysis does not demonstrate the undesirability of corporate criminal liability as much as it reveals the limitations of the neoclassical perspective in the criminal law context.

Second, an influential, though far from abundant, philosophical literature argues that corporations are intentional agents and, as such, can incur moral responsibility for their acts. However, a gap remains between the demonstration that it is possible, without abusing the English language, to describe a corporate act as "intentional" and a conception of corporate wrongdoing. The latter is needed to explain why a given corporate act, whether or not intentional, should attract criminal punishment rather than civil liability or taxation.

In my view, the third and fourth approaches, although less orthodox, are more promising. The third approach draws upon the notion that the criminal law regulates behavior not only directly, by attaching a price to particular actions, but also indirectly, by facilitating the operation and influencing the content of non-legal norms. Corporate criminal liability can serve the latter function when a non-legal norm is violated by one or more individuals in the context of an incorporated venture, or when such a venture is characterized by deviant local norms.

The fourth approach views the condemnation of a collectivity as a source of shame or guilt for the members of the group. The members of a corporation are not bystanders relative to the wrongdoing of their fellow member. Like the members of any other team, each of them experiences guilt if and to the extent that his or her contributions to the enterprise created conditions conducive to the wrongdoing. And regardless of what the other members individually have done, each of them experiences shame – a tension between their solidarity with the corporate enterprise and what the wrongdoer has done on their collective behalf. On this view, the condemnation intrinsic in criminal punishment is not directed at the corporation as an autonomous moral person, for its own misdeeds, but rather at the individual members of the corporate enterprise.

In articulating the third and fourth approaches, I have tried to define and occupy a middle ground between the neoclassical and corporate agency approaches. On the one hand, these approaches depart from the strict individualism of the neoclassical approach: not all groups are mere aggregates of individuals. In particular, it must be recognized that collectivities come into existence and are maintained by virtue of the mutual commitment of their members, and that, within collectivities, cooperative norms compete with self-interest as sources of individual motivation. But it is equally important, on the other hand, to try to avoid the pitfalls that come with treating collectivities as if they were "persons" in their own right.

9

Human Rights and Business: Expectations, Requirements, and Procedures for the Responsible Modern Company

KARIN BUHMANN

9.1 Introduction

Conventionally, lawyers consider human rights to be rights held by individuals with corresponding duties to be held by States. That perception accords with the international human rights regime that has evolved since the late nineteenth century and with the conventional state-centrist structure of post-Westphalian international law. However, recent decades have witnessed a surge in social expectations and policy debates that argue or even assume that businesses have responsibility for their human rights impact. This has translated into a series of regulatory instruments, ranging from private codes of conduct and contractual obligations to policy, incentive-based regulation, international soft law, and increasingly statutory requirements for firms to report on their human rights policies or impact.

Over the past decades, business enterprises have gained increased influence and power. In particular, multinational enterprises have grown not just in numbers and size, but also in political and economic power. In line with the view that with power comes responsibility, this development has led to expectations that firms assume responsibilities beyond the conventional economic aspects of trade and production. Such expectations have challenged the conventional division of political tasks and legal obligations between the private and public sector. Much of this blurring of boundaries between public and private and even between national and international influence and regulation is a side effect of globalization – not only of trade and the world economy, but also of information flows leading to enhanced knowledge among consumers of the conditions under which goods have been made. Simultaneously there has been increased privatization of many sectors and services from the provision of water to health services. Many of these issues and processes entail human rights aspects, ranging from working conditions, child labor, and forced labor to the impact of mining and large-scale agricultural projects on the access to food, land, work, shelter, and health of local communities and from the impact of industry and toxic emissions on access to water to short-term government requirements for private local health services in exchange for corporate concessions.

Media and civil society have shared these human rights implications leading to pressure from consumers, investors, and companies interested in acquiring other business entities. Much of this pressure reflects social expectations that business enterprises respect human rights. This stands in contrast to international law doctrine on human rights obligations, which focuses only on the state. However, state duties matter little in social expectations, which hold firms to account for their human rights impact through economic decisions and reputational damage. While the legal license to operate may remain unaffected, the effect on the "social license to operate" (a term originating from the extractives sector and literature)[1] can be seriously affected.

Much of the background for the evolution of expectations that businesses are responsible for human rights can be traced to the Corporate Social Responsibility (CSR) debate. CSR and the emerging Business & Human Rights (BHR) regime differ in some ways, especially through the BHR insistence on the role of the State and a State-Business nexus, but they also build on and feed into each other. Indeed, the United Nations (UN) mandate that led to the formulation of the UN *Protect, Respect and Remedy* Framework on Business and Human Rights[2] ("UN Framework") in 2008 referred to "corporate responsibility and accountability for transnational corporations (TNCs) and other business enterprises with regard to human rights."[3] This anchored the mandate within the larger CSR debate that had fuelled much of the concern with businesses' social impact in the years before.

[1] J. Prno and D.S. Slocombe, "Exploring the Origins of 'Social License To Operate' in the Mining Sector: Perspectives From Governance and Sustainability Theories" (2012) 37 *Resources Policy* 346; J.R. Owen and D. Kemp, "Social Licence and Mining: A Critical Perspective" (2013) 38 *Resources Policy* 29; R.J. Burke, G. Martin, and C.L. Cooper, *Corporate Reputation: Managing Opportunities and Threats* (London: Ashgate, 2011).

[2] Report of the Special Representative of the Secretary-General on the Issue of Human Rights and Transnational Corporations and Other Business Enterprises, John Ruggie, *Protect, Respect and Remedy: A Framework For Business and Human Rights*, UN Doc. A/HRC/8/5 (2008).

[3] Commission on Human Rights, *Human Rights and Transnational Corporations and Other Business Enterprises*, UN Doc. E/CN.4/2005/L.87 (2005), at para. 1(a).

The intersection of business issues and human rights also takes on a particularly international or global perspective for several reasons. These include the multinational character of many business activities, the globalization of information flows and civil society activity to draw attention to the plight of victims of business-related human rights abuse, and the international and transnational character of emergent soft and hard law, spanning from the UN to the OECD,[4] the World Bank's IFC performance Standards,[5] and private codes such as the ISO's 26000 Social Responsibility Guidance Standard[6] to national and regional disclosure requirements and the capacity of certain remedial institutions to assess business conduct across territorial borders. Yet despite emerging statutory requirements and a juridification of CSR across international and national, public and private, hard and soft law,[7] the role of business in promoting human rights remains largely informed by ethics or morals and political considerations. The transnational character of this issue and its basis in moral norms or political needs may cause confusion and uncertainty among businesses. The fact that many TNCs have activities in several countries, of which some may be common law and others civil law states, adds to the confusion.

Against this background, this chapter explores the nature of the company's human rights responsibilities. It begins, in Section 9.2, by offering an explanation and examples to illustrate why human rights matter to companies. It then traces the evolution of the increasing responsibility of companies for human rights against the backdrop of the CSR debate before evolving into its own regime. Section 9.3 explores the UN Guiding Principles on Business and Human Rights, which detail corporate responsibilities for human rights. Section 9.4 discusses the corporate duty to protect human rights, before turning to examine, in Section 9.5, the due diligence process for human rights, likely one of the most important aspects of the modern company's obligations to promote human rights. Section 9.6 concludes.

[4] See in particular, Organisation of Economic Cooperation and Development, *OECD Guidelines for Multinational Enterprises* (2011).

[5] International Finance Corporation, *IFC Performance Standards on Environmental and Social Sustainability* (2012).

[6] ISO 26000 Social Responsibility Guidance Standard, available at www.iso.org/iso/iso_catalogue/management_standards/social_responsibility.htm. ISO 26000 SR was developed over a five-year period between 2005 and 2010 based on a multi-stakeholder process comprising industry, government, labor, consumers, nongovernmental organizations, academics, and others.

[7] K. Buhmann, "Corporate Social Responsibility and Public Law: Towards Juridification and Coherence through UN Guidance on Business & Human Rights" (2016) 11 (3) *International and Comparative Corporate Law Journal* 194–228.

9.2 Why Human Rights Matter to Businesses

The general idea that businesses should take responsibility for their impact on human rights or should actively act to help human rights becoming fulfilled is closely related to ideas of CSR. In recent years, business responsibilities have become subject to soft (nonbinding) or hard (binding) legal regulations. The CSR, business ethics, and soft and hard legal elements are often closely related and even integrated. For example, private CSR codes on working conditions and minimum age for employees draw, on the one hand, on consumers' and businesses' concern with CSR, and, on the other hand, on international human rights and labor standards, treaties, and declarations as the normative foundation and source of operational principles for business conduct. A company's human rights code or CSR code may be "soft law" in its own right, but when integrated into a legally binding business contract turns into "hard law."

The international human rights regime, which was mainly developed in the twentieth century, in great part within the auspices of the UN, focuses on states as duty holders. The international economic regime developed during the same period of time, much of which has evolved in international or regional organizations distinct from the UN, has provided firms with extensive rights to make economic profits. Some firms have agreed with civil society organizations that businesses should take responsibility for their adverse impact or human rights whereas others have insisted that responsibility for human rights belongs to states, arguing that states could put new or revised rules in place or regulate business conduct if they are concerned with adverse business impacts.

Yet social expectations that businesses do not infringe on human rights of their employees, host or neighboring communities, suppliers or even users have been growing as well. Allegations that firms cause human rights abuse, for example by employing child labor or not ensuring decent working conditions for employees, may lead to significant reputational damage for the firm. Social expectations are often coupled with social or market-based sanctions, which may be potentially considerable in financial terms.[8] These sanctions may be highly significant to a company, despite often being hidden as general operational costs.[9]

[8] E.B. Kapstein, "The Corporate Ethics Crusade" (2001) 80 (5) *Foreign Affairs* 105.

[9] J.G. Ruggie, *Just Business: Multinational Corporations and Human Rights* (New York: W.W. Norton & Company, 2013), pp. 136–8.

9.3 From CSR to the "Corporate Responsibility to Respect Human Rights"

9.3.1 The Evolution of CSR

In many ways, the push for corporate responsibility for human rights derives from the greater recognition of companies' general responsibilities toward society. CSR encompasses both a general idea, harbored by many social actors, and a series of academic theories or sub-sets of theories, particularly within studies of business ethics, organization and management, economics and accounting, and business strategy. The general idea is that companies[10] have a responsibility to avoid or at least reduce their adverse impact on society, understood broadly to encompass both social and environmental dimensions, and/or to maximize their positive impact. This responsibility has been viewed as independent of legal obligations – indeed often complementary and additional to legal obligations – and initially was thought of as voluntary in nature.[11] Yet the purely "voluntary" nature of CSR is increasingly complemented by public soft or reflexive law or informed by standards derived from international law.[12]

In 2011, to align better with developments at the UN and at the OECD, the EU redefined the term CSR simply as being businesses' responsibilities for their impacts on society.[13] These responsibilities include both the obligation to comply with applicable national law and the obligation to act in accordance with international human rights and labor law,[14] which often serve as the normative source for social expectations on business. Where national law does not live up to international legal standards in terms of

[10] This chapter uses the term company in a broad sense. The usage corresponds to similar broad usage of the term "corporation" deployed in UN human rights instruments on business and human rights. The term does not require a particular form of incorporation but is synonymous with enterprise, firm, and corporation. Indeed, those terms as well as business are deployed interchangeably.

[11] The "beyond-the-law" aspect was indicated in the EU's first definition of CSR, presented in 2001 in a Green Paper, and the basis for a Communication. See European Commission, *Promoting a European Framework for Corporate Social Responsibility*, COM (2001) 366 at 8; European Commission, *Communication from the Commission Concerning Corporate Social Responsibility: A Business Contribution to Sustainable Development*, COM (2002) 347 at para. 21.

[12] K. Buhmann, "Public Regulators and CSR: The 'Social Licence to Operate' in Recent United Nations Instruments on Business and Human Rights and the Juridification of CSR" (2015) *Journal of Business Ethics* 1.

[13] European Commission, "A renewed EU Strategy 2011–2014 for Corporate Social Responsibility" COM (2011) 681 final at s. 3.1.

[14] Report of the Special Representative, above n 2, at para. 54.

the letter of the law or its implementation, businesses have the responsibility to self-regulate.

Moreover, the changing definition of CSR now includes explicit references to a series of specific issues, including human rights. For instance, the 2011 European Commission Communication states that to fully meet their CSR, enterprises should have in place a process to integrate social, environmental, ethical, human rights and consumer concerns into their business operations and core strategy in collaboration with stakeholders, with the aim of maximizing the creation of shared value for their owners/shareholders and for their other stakeholders and society at large. It also requires companies to identify, prevent, and mitigate possible adverse impacts.[15]

The EU's expanded definition of CSR reflects economic and organizational literature that has proven popular among both business practitioners and scholars, as well as international soft law instruments that have recently been either developed or revised. Thus, the reference to "creation of shared value" is a direct reference to the "creating shared value" idea propounded by Harvard Business School scholars Michael Porter and Michael Kramer.[16] The list of issues to be integrated into business operations and strategies corresponds to many of those included in the OECD's Guidelines for Multinational Enterprises.[17] The reference "to steps to identify, prevent and mitigate adverse impact" corresponds both to the human rights due diligence process defined in the UN Framework and Guiding Principles and the due diligence process prescribed by the OECD's Guidelines as a result of the 2011 revision. The latter explicitly sought to streamline the Guidelines with the UN Guiding Principles but do not limit the due diligence requirement to human rights.[18] Moreover, the EU's 2011 Communication introduced a reference to "smart mix regulation," a term that had also been applied earlier by the UN Guiding Principles and noted that the EU would be introducing a proposal for mandatory

[15] European Commission, above n 13.

[16] M.E. Porter and M.R. Kramer, "Creating Shared Value" (2011) *Harvard Business Review* 63; M.E. Porter and M.R. Kramer, "Strategy & Society: The Link between Competitive Advantage and Corporate Social Responsibility" (2006) *Harvard Business Review* 78.

[17] The OECD Guidelines for Multinational Corporations are recommendations from states addressed to businesses concerning responsible action in the areas of human rights, labor/industrial relations, environment, consumer concerns, anti-corruption, science and technology, competition, and taxation.

[18] The Guidelines' due diligence recommendations do not apply to the chapters on science and technology, competition, and taxation. See Organisation of Economic Cooperation and Development, above n 4 at "Commentary to General Principles," para. 14.

non-financial reporting. In sum, the EU's 2011 Communication reflects a strong receptiveness to the emerging BHR regime, even beyond traditional human rights issue areas. We shall revert to the issue of due diligence below.

In the area of theory, CSR has inspired a large number of contributions to a literature that is not necessarily consistent within and across fields. Business ethics scholars claim that social responsibility is based on morals or utilitarian or instrumental arguments.[19] Some business ethicists claim that businesses need to engage in public policy implementation or indeed take over what they term as "political" tasks because the state has failed[20]; whereas some organizational scholars have come to recognize that the state indeed is present and may influence CSR through a range of explicit or implicit means.[21] Certain scholars promote CSR as a strategic modality for firms to combine profits and contributions to society as a matter of strategy creating "shared value"[22] or contribute to poverty alleviation and growth among the poorest,[23] whereas others have little faith in the ability of CSR to go beyond window-dressing or "green-wash"[24] or to contribute to development.[25] Much of the debate has turned on the idea of a "business case" for CSR, which however still remains to be fundamentally proven.[26]

Although one specific substantive definition of CSR does not exist, and although CSR is much more than human rights, the private sector's responsibility for its impact on human rights is seen by many actors as part of CSR. Partly due to the political sensitivity of human rights in some

[19] A.B. Carroll, "A Three-Dimensional Conceptual Model of Corporate Performance" (1979) 4 (4) *Academy of Management Review* 497; A.B. Carroll, "Corporate Social Responsibility: Evolution of a Definitional Construct" (1999) 39 (3) *Business & Society Review* 264; J.D. Rendtorff, *Responsibility, Ethics and Legitimacy of Corporations* (Copenhagen: Copenhagen Business School Press, 2009).

[20] A.G. Scherer and G. Palazzo, "The New Political Role of Business in a Globalized World: A Review of a New Perspective on CSR and Its Implications for the Firm, Governance and Democracy" (2011) 48 (4) *Journal of Management Studies* 899.

[21] D. Matten and J. Moon, "'Implicit' and 'Explicit' CSR: A Conceptual Framework for a Comparative Understanding of Corporate Social Responsibility" (2008) 33 (2) *Academy of Management Review* 404.

[22] Porter and Kramer, above n 16.

[23] C.K. Prahalad, *The Fortune at the Bottom of the Pyramid: Eradicating Poverty Through Profits* (Upper Saddle Hill, NJ: Prentice Hall, 2004).

[24] R.B Reich, *Supercapitalism* (New York: Knopf, 2007).

[25] M. Prieto-Carron, P. Lund-Thomsen, A. Chan, A. Muro, and C. Bhushan, "Critical Perspectives on CSR and Development: What We Know, What We Don't Know, and What We Need To Know" (2006) 82 (5) *International Affairs* 977.

[26] A.B. Carroll and K.M. Shabana, "The Business Case for Corporate Social Responsibility: A Review of Concepts, Research and Practice" (2010) 12 *International Journal of Management Reviews* 85.

states, partly perhaps because human rights remain primarily obligations of states, corporate responsibilities for human rights and labor rights are often referred to as "social issues" in CSR instruments or strategies. This was the case in the so-called "Triple Bottom Line: People, Planet, Profit" proposed by sustainable management expert John Elkington in 1998,[27] which spurred CSR-reporting in many companies in Europe and beyond. The human and labor rights informed understanding of social issues as part of CSR remains reflected in the widely used CSR reporting tool Global Reporting Initiative (GRI) and its fourth-generation G4 reporting guidelines, revised in 2015,[28] as well as in CSR policies and strategies of many companies.

9.3.2 *The Evolution of the BHR Regime*

While the CSR debate has been characterized by broadness in terms of issue areas (including human and core labor rights) that firms may address at their discretion, a particular current has focused on human rights and evolved into what is now arguably a particular regime of its own. This BHR regime has evolved around instruments developed under the UN system, but it is not limited to those. However, the course toward the UN Framework and the UNGPs was not straightforward. The significance of the agreement that led to those instruments and the debate surrounding the treaty debate are best understood against the backdrop of previous efforts.

In the 1970s, the UN Commission on TNCs initiated an attempt to formulate a Code of Conduct for TNCs.[29] The UN Code project was abandoned in the beginning of the 1990s, however, partly due to opposition and divergence of investment-related interests among certain governments. The text of the UN Draft Code of Conduct on TNCs,[30] agreed during the late 1980s, contained duties for TNCs to respect host countries' development goals, observe their domestic law, respect fundamental human

[27] J. Elkington, *Cannibals with Forks: The Triple Bottom Line of 21st Century Business* (Gabriola Island, BC: New Society Publishers, 1998).

[28] Global Reporting Initiative, "G4 – Sustainability Reporting Guidelines" (2015), available at www.globalreporting.org/standards/g4/Pages/default.aspx

[29] Established by the Economic and Social Council resolution 1913 (LVII) of 5 December 1974.

[30] Draft Code of Conduct on Transnational Corporations. Last version of the proposed draft code: UN Doc. E/1990/94, 12 June 1990.

rights, and observe consumer and environmental protection objectives.[31] Related responsibilities were covered by the successfully adopted 1976 OECD Guidelines for Multinational Corporations (revised most recently in 2011) and the 1977 ILO Tripartite Declaration of Principles concerning Multinational Enterprises and Social Policy. The OECD Guidelines were drafted with the objective of providing a degree of home state guidance for TNCs incorporated in OECD member states whereas the ILO's Tripartite Declaration seeks to engage TNCs in complying with ILO social policy conventions and recommendations even where the host state is not bound by these or does not enforce them.

At the end of the 1980s and during the 1990s, societal concern with business impact on the environment and involvement with or complicity in human rights violations grew. This was spurred by specific incidents such as events in Nigeria relating to Shell's oil production. "Political consumerism" and ethical investment became an issue, along with the prevalence of child labor in some exporting industries in developing countries, growing awareness of negative social and environmental impact of logging in parts of Asia, Latin America, and Africa, and the practices of the late-apartheid regime in South Africa. In 1984, a gas leak in Bhopal in India in a plant run by American-owned Union Carbide Corporation caused the death of 15,000 individuals.

Reports of substandard working conditions at apparel and textile facilities in Vietnam, Bangladesh, and Indonesia, which supplied to companies located elsewhere, led to consumer concerns and pressure on investors and states to cease activities that might support abusive regimes. Several multinational corporations, including Nike, Reebok, Nestlé, and Shell, were the targets of boycott campaigns organized by NGOs in response to the alleged negative impact on the environment and on human rights or labor rights that was associated with the actions of these companies and

[31] For discussions of the human rights aspects of the Draft Code of Conduct, see A.E. Mayer, "Human Rights as a Dimension of CSR: The Blurred Lines Between Legal and Non-Legal Categories" (2009) 88 *Journal of Business Ethics* 561; P. Redmond "Transnational Enterprise and Human Rights: Options for Standard Setting and Compliance" (2003) 37 *The International Lawyer* 69; C.F. Hillemans, "UN Norms on the Responsibilities of Transnational Corporations and Other Business Enterprises with Regard to Human Rights" (2003) 10 *German Law Journal* 1065; J. Bendell, "Barricades and Boardrooms: A Contemporary History of the Corporate Accountability Movement," *Technology, Business and Society Programme Paper No. 13* (United Nations Research Institute for Social Development, 2004), at 12–13; P. Lansing and A. Rosaria, "An Analysis of the United Nations Proposed Code of Conduct for Transnational Corporations" (1991) 14 *World Competition* 35.

their production and sourcing practices. Lawyers and civil society organizations started relying on the Alien Tort Claims Act in the United States for cases that involved severe allegations of corporate complicity in human rights violations.

In several reports during the second half of the 1990s, the UN Human Rights Commission's Sub-Committee on Prevention of Discrimination and Protection of Minorities addressed the impact of TNCs on the enjoyment of human rights, labor rights, and the right to development. A 1995 Report argued that TNCs were assuming power resembling that of states and that as a corollary, TNCs share a responsibility for development and human rights, especially in poor states.[32] A 1996 report proposed a "New International Regulatory Framework" for corporate governance, based on public international law. The report argued that a uniform system applicable across borders was necessary to avoid powerful economic actors' abuses of weak governance or economic differences between states.[33] On this basis, a 1998 report argued that economic non-state actors must be regulated by public international law.[34] These reports offered a public law model of corporate responsibility and corporate governance in a human rights context.

At the 1999 World Economic Forum meeting in Davos, then Secretary-General of the UN, Kofi Annan, delivered a speech that called on business leaders to join the UN in "a global compact of shared values and principle, which will give a human face to the global market"[35] and help realize the UN's goal of social progress with respect to human rights, labor standards, and the environment. The unprecedented support generated by the

[32] Sub-Commission on Prevention of Discrimination and Protection of Minorities, *The Realization of Economic, Social and Cultural Rights: The Relationship Between the Enjoyment of Human Rights, in particular, International Labour and Trade Union Rights, and the Working Methods and Activities of Transnational Corporations*, UN Doc. E/CN.4/Sub.2/1995/11 (1995).

[33] Sub-Commission on Prevention of Discrimination and Protection of Minorities, *The Impact of the Activities and Working Methods of Transnational Corporations on the Full Enjoyment Of Human Rights, in Particular Economic, Social and Cultural Rights and the Rights to Development, Bearing in Mind Existing International Guidelines, Rules and Standards Relating to the Subject-Matter*, UN Doc. E/CN.4/Sub.2/1996/12 (1996).

[34] Sub-Commission on Prevention of Discrimination and Protection of Minorities, *The Realization of Economic, Social and Cultural Rights: The Question of Transnational Corporations*, UN Doc. E/CN.4/Sub.2/198/6 (1998).

[35] Kofi Annan's address to the World Economic forum can be found in "Secretary-General Proposes Global Compact on Human Rights, Labour, Environment, in Address to World Economic Forum in Davos," UN Press release SG/SM/6881, 1 February 1999, available at www.un.org/News/Press/docs/1999/19990201.sgsm6881.html

speech led to the establishment of a multi-stakeholder process, known as the Global Compact, in which the UN worked with selected civil society organizations, firms, and CEOs to develop principles for responsible business conduct.[36] The principles cover four issue areas: human rights, labor, the environment, and corruption[37] and draw directly from international law declarations including the Universal Declaration of Human Rights and the ILO's Declaration on Fundamental Principles and Rights at Work.

In parallel with the establishment of the Global Compact, an expert Working Group under the UN Commission on Human Rights developed a document that eventually became known as the Draft UN Norms.[38] While some business organizations welcomed guidance on their human rights responsibilities, others were opposed and the draft Norms were eventually rejected by the UN Human Rights Commission and declared to be without legal standing.[39] In 2005, the Commission returned to efforts to further clarify the relationship between business and human rights and appointed John Ruggie as Special Representative on BHR.[40] Ruggie, a professor of International Affairs at Harvard, had been involved in the setting up of the Global Compact and was not a newcomer to either the human rights and business topic or the UN's cooperation with business.

During his tenure, Ruggie and his team of experts engaged in a series of multi-stakeholder consultations and expert meetings that resulted in the UN *Protect, Respect and Remedy* Framework in 2008, followed by the UNGPs, which were endorsed by the Human Rights Council in June 2011.[41] Both are structured around three pillars: (1) The State Duty to Protect;

[36] For details on the process, see K. Buhmann, *Normative Discourses and Public–Private Regulatory Strategies for Construction of CSR Normativity: Towards a Method for Above-National Public–Private Regulation of Business Social Responsibilities* (Copenhagen: Multivers Publishing, 2014), chapter 4.

[37] For a full list of the Global Compact principles, see UN Global Compact, The Ten Principles of the UN Global Compact, available at www.unglobalcompact.org/what-is-gc/mission/principles

[38] United Nations Sub-Commission on the Promotion and Protection of Human Rights, *Norms on the Responsibilities of Transnational Corporations and Other Business Enterprises with Regard to Human Rights* (2003).

[39] Human Rights Commission, Decision 2004/116, UN Doc. E/CN.4/2004/L.73/Rev.1 (2004).

[40] Commission on Human Rights, above n 3 at paras. 2–3, 5.

[41] Report of the Special Representative of the Secretary-General on the issue of human rights and transnational corporations and other business enterprises, John Ruggie, *Guiding Principles on Business and Human Rights: Implementing the United Nations "Protect, Respect and Remedy Framework,"* UN Doc. A/HRC/17/31 (2011); endorsed in Resolution 17/4 adopted by the Human Rights Council, UN Doc. A/HRC/RES/17/4 (2011) [hereinafter "UNGP"].

(2) The Corporate Responsibility to Respect; and (3) Access to Remedy (all explained in more detail below). Those three pillars draw inspiration from the classic three-pronged distinction between State obligations with regard to human rights: Protect, Respect, and Fulfill.[42] For pragmatic reasons and with a focus on reducing harm to victims, the UN Framework and UNGPs, however, focus on the "protect" and "respect" aspects, leaving it to firms to decide whether to actively contribute to fulfilling human rights.

The processes leading to both the UN Framework and the UNGPs were unusual for a UN process in the human rights area. In accordance with the text of the mandate resolution, business organizations and business representatives were consulted to a much higher degree than what is common for UN human rights law making.[43] As part of the consultation, it was explained to businesses that it was in their interest to understand their human rights impact and pay attention to social actors' expectations.[44] The UN Framework process did not result in binding rules for businesses, but it did arguably contribute to the breakthrough that was reached with the UN Human Rights Council's decision in 2008 to "welcome" the UN Framework and to extend the mandate for another three years, which led to the Council's adoption of the UNGPs in 2011. While the UN Framework and UNGPs are not perfect, they laid the ground for work that may take global protection of human rights from business impact further, including through the current treaty process and other binding measures.

Currently, the UNGPs are the most comprehensive and recent instrument to offer guidance on how businesses should respect human rights.[45] They also advise states on how to implement processes to ensure that businesses respect human rights. The UNGPs have further had ripple effects on complementary international guidelines. Thus, the UN Global Compact refers to the UNGPs and the UN Framework in its detailed guidance on

[42] C. Tomuchat, *Human Rights: Between Idealism and Realism* (Oxford: Oxford University Press, 2014).

[43] J.H. Knox, "The Ruggie Rules: Applying Human Rights Law to Corporations," in R. Mares (ed.), *The UN Guiding Principles on Business and Human Rights* (Antwerp: Brill, 2012); K. Buhmann, "Development of the 'UN Framework': A Pragmatic Process Towards a Pragmatic Output," in R. Mares (ed.), *The UN Guiding Principles on Business and Human Rights* (Antwerp: Brill, 2012).

[44] K. Buhmann, "Business and Human Rights: Analysing Discursive Articulation of Stakeholder Interests to Explain the Consensus-based Construction of the 'Protect, Respect, Remedy UN Framework'" (2013) 1 *International Law Research* 88.

[45] Additional guidance has been developed by the UN's Office of the High Commissioner for Human Rights. See United Nations Office of the High Commissioner for Human Rights, *The Corporate Responsibility to Respect Human Rights: An Interpretive Guide* (2012).

human rights as an issue for businesses. Similarly, the ISO 26000 Social Responsibility Guidance Standard was strongly influenced by the UN Framework and draft UNGPs in regard to human rights, labor, and due diligence issues. Moreover, the OECD's Guidelines for Multinational Enterprises were revised in 2011 to ensure coherence with the UNGPs as were the social performance guidelines required by the International Finance Corporation.

9.4 The Corporate Duty to Respect Human Rights

9.4.1 The UNGPs Set the Baseline

Primary guidance on what is required of companies to respect human rights is therefore currently found in the UN Framework and the UNGPs, which in turn consist of three pillars. The first pillar is the state duty to protect. This is based on states' "horizontal" human rights obligations to protect individuals or communities against human rights abuses by third parties, such as companies. The second pillar is the corporate responsibility to respect. This responsibility is based on the recognition that societies and stakeholders often expect firms not just to comply with applicable law but to go beyond the law by respecting international human rights law where the national legal framework or its implementation offers a lower degree of human rights respect and protection. Finally, the third pillar, access to remedy, focuses on providing remedies for victims of business-related human rights abuse either at the operational level (that is within the business) or at the state level.

Company responsibilities for human rights may therefore arise through the imposition of state measures or may be imposed on the company directly. In terms of which human rights companies must respect, the UNGPs set out salient human rights principles that it derives from the International Bill of Rights and the International Labour Organization's (ILO) Declaration on Fundamental Principles and Rights at Work. The International Bill of Rights is comprised of the Universal Declaration of Human Rights, the International Covenant on Economic, Social and Cultural Rights, and the International Covenant on Civil and Political Rights. The principles concerning fundamental rights set out in the ILO's Declaration on Fundamental Principles and Rights at Work include freedom from discrimination, the right to collective bargaining and freedom of association, the elimination of child labor, and the abolition of slavery, involuntary, and forced labor.

The obligations in these instruments outline the standards for businesses' respect of human rights and thus provide a benchmark against which the human rights impacts of companies will be measured. The baseline expectation that firms observe those standards therefore makes understanding and respect of these standards relevant to firms. This can be either on legal compliance grounds or on economic grounds based on risks of economic sanctions administered by consumers, investors, and other stakeholders.

The UNGPs' focus is that businesses should "do no harm." Thus, emphasis is on how firms can avoid infringing human rights. In addition to avoiding harm, businesses may contribute to the promotion or fulfillment of human rights optionally. For example, businesses may set up health clinics that help provide for access to health services, or finance schools or offer vocational training that helps individuals gain access to education. In those instances, a core challenge for the firm is to consider the institutional sustainability: how to ensure that obligations are not simply shifted from the state to the private sector and how to preserve access to human rights-related important goods or services such as schools or health clinics, if or when the firm pulls out of the area or sector. A strategic take on this can involve collaboration with the local or central host country government to ensure capacity building and financial flows to keep the services going.

9.4.2 *The Contours of the Corporate Responsibility to Respect*

While "doing no harm" outlines in broad strokes the basic responsibilities of companies in relation to human rights, the UNGPs go farther by providing further details. The UNGPs emphasize three operational types of steps for firms to discharge the responsibility: a policy commitment to human rights, undertaking human rights due diligence, and ensuring remedy.

Yet the obligations for business are not simply couched in Pillar 2. Under Pillar 1, states are obliged to take proper steps to prevent or punish abuses by the private sector through regulation, policy-making, investigation, and enforcement. Moreover, under Pillar 3, both states and businesses are expected to provide and enhance access to remedies, thus ensuring that business-related human rights abuse is redressed even where solid efforts are made to avoid such impact.

Because of their focus on two essentially different types of organizations – public and private – Pillars 1 and 2 are often treated as distinct and much of the emerging literature looks at Pillar 2.[46] However, for purposes of

[46] See, e.g., D. De Felice, "Challenges and Opportunities in the Production of Business and Human Rights Indicators to Measure the Corporate Responsibility to Respect" (2015) 37 *Human Rights Quarterly* 511; B. Fasterling and G. Demuijnck, "Human Rights in the Void?

implementation of the UNGPs, the two pillars have several closely connected elements. These relate particularly to the ways in which governments may promote the "corporate responsibility to respect" by requiring or recommending specific business activities. From the perspective of the UNGPs, Human Rights Due Diligence (HRDD) and communication-based transparency (including human rights reporting) may be subject to statutory obligations on companies or to social expectations. Even when subject to statutory obligations, HRDD and/or reporting may in practice have to deal with social expectations.

As noted, the corporate responsibility to respect is comprised of both the obligation to comply with applicable law and a responsibility to respect social expectations. There is an implicit connection between the two in that the boundary between what is a compliance obligation and what is social expectation may be narrow. From a legal perspective, the responsibility to observe social expectations may be perceived as weaker than the obligation to comply with applicable law. Yet, social expectations may be met with social or market-based sanctions, which may be highly significant to a company, although in practice they are often hidden as general operational costs and therefore not explicit.[47]

What is perhaps the greatest weakness of the responsibility to respect social expectations is the inherent problem in defining what that "responsibility" really is. Increasing the persuasive power of the "corporate responsibility to respect" may require strengthening the call or drive for companies to obtain knowledge of the relevant social expectations in a given context and to make them raise the bar high rather than set it low. Where the "corporate responsibility to respect" connects to statutory compliance, there is often a close connection to the state's duty to protect found under the first pillar of the UNGPs. Such a connection may also be present, however, in relation to social expectations. This may particularly be the case where a home state seeks to govern businesses beyond its own jurisdiction through encouraging or requiring measures that will make companies consider human rights extraterritorially, for example in terms of social expectations.

Nevertheless, beyond social expectations, the key obligation that arises out of the "corporate responsibility to respect" is the obligation for companies to engage in human rights due diligence; that is, to identify,

Due Diligence in the UN Guiding Principles on Business and Human Rights" (2013) 116 *Journal of Business Ethics* 799; T.E. Lambooy, "Corporate Due Diligence as a Tool to Respect Human Rights" (2010) 28 (3) *Netherlands Quarterly of Human Rights* 404.

[47] Ruggie, above n 9 at 136–8.

prevent, and mitigate adverse human rights impacts and offer reparations where it occurs. The process – and the way it differs from the concept of due diligence – as it is applied in the context of corporate transactions constitutes the remainder of this chapter.

9.5 Human Rights Due Diligence

9.5.1 What is Human Rights Due Diligence?

The due diligence concept applied by the UNGPs differs from most other corporate due diligence. It is focused first and foremost on risks caused by the firm to society as opposed to risks to the firm. It entails a process that continues as long as the activity to which it is related continues and may continue beyond its end if a remedy is required. The UNGPs apply the term "impact" to distinguish between business-related human rights abuse and states' violations. According to the UNGPs, human rights due diligence includes assessing actual and potential human rights impacts, integrating and acting upon the findings, tracking responses, as well as communicating how impacts are addressed. It should cover not only adverse human rights impacts that the firm may cause or contribute to through its own activities but also those which may be directly linked to its operations, products, or services by its business relationships. While it may vary in complexity with the size of the business enterprise, the risk of severe human rights impacts, and the nature and context of its operations, the process should be open-ended in recognition of the fact that human rights risks may change over time as the firm's operations and operating context evolve.[48]

Under Pillar 1 of the UNGPs, states are generally encouraged to consider whether provisions for human rights due diligence by businesses should be introduced as part of measures to honor the state's duty to protect.[49] This may form part of states' guidance to firms on how to respect human rights throughout their operations, which is also encouraged by the UNGPs.[50] The UNGPs explicitly note that steps taken by states to protect against human rights abuses by firms owned or controlled by the state, or otherwise closely connected to state agencies through support and services, should include requiring human rights due diligence where appropriate.[51]

[48] UNGP, above n 41 at 16 (Principle 17).
[49] *Ibid.* at 9–10 (Principle 4 and Commentary).
[50] *Ibid.* at 8 (Principle 3(c)).
[51] *Ibid.* at 9 (Principle 4).

The UNGPs' due diligence concept has been adopted by the OECD's Guidelines for Multinational Enterprises not only in its new human rights chapter but also in many of the areas covered by the Guidelines, including labor/industrial relations, environment, and anti-corruption.[52] With the possibility of emerging unified jurisprudence among the 42 National Contact Points,[53] which are state-based remedy institutions, and the significance of states' due diligence obligations under international law to avoid violating their own obligations, the potential complementarity between firms' human rights due diligence and states' obligations have been noted to be of considerable interest to the promotion and protection of human rights.[54]

Turning to the actual details of how human rights due diligence is conducted, it should be first noted that this process ideally begins when a project idea is conceived and continues throughout the process until completion of the project. It focuses first and foremost on risks to society, particularly individuals and communities. Due to the reputational and other damage that a firm may suffer as a result of alleged or proven human rights abuse, human rights due diligence may also serve as a form of risk management for the firm. The due diligence process involves the creation of mechanisms that allow the firm to assess actual and potential human rights impacts, integrate, act upon the findings, track responses, and communicate how impacts are addressed.[55] The firm should further adopt a policy commitment to human rights, made preferably by top management, and integrate it throughout the firm. Experts and stakeholders, including in particular potential or actual victims, should be involved in the identification of human rights impacts and elaboration of steps to prevent abuse. If prevention is not possible – for example, because adverse impacts have already occurred – impacts need to be mitigated and findings should feed into learning in order to reduce future risks. When abuse has occurred, culturally appropriate remedies should be available.

[52] Organisation of Economic Cooperation and Development, above n 4 at "General Policies, II.A.10 and Commentary para. 14."

[53] K. Buhmann, "Business and Human Rights: Understanding the UN Guiding Principles from the Perspective of Transnational Business Governance Interactions," *Research Paper No. 20/2014* (Osgoode Legal Studies Transnational Business Governance Interactions, 2014).

[54] H. Cantu-Rivera, "Human Rights Due Diligence: A Developing Concept For Human Rights and Environmental Justice?," *Paper for 3rd UNITAR-Yale Conference on Environmental Governance and Democracy* (UNITAR-Yale Conference on Environmental Governance and Democracy, 2014).

[55] See UNGP, above n 41 at 16–20 (Principles 17–21).

9.5.2 *Due Diligence and Policy Coherence*

The UNGPs emphasize that states need to strive toward policy coherence. Policy coherence entails that public policies are consistent across diverse departments, sectors, and national policies, such as the requirements of national export funding agencies and effects of those who benefit from their funding. States should also work toward greater policy coherence at the international level, because they retain their international human rights law obligations when they participate in international economic and other organizations.[56] The UNGPs recognize that a "poor understanding" of the human rights implications of both corporate and securities law as well as policy is a common occurrence. States need to provide guidance to companies to clarify what is expected of them and to guide them, particularly with regard to human rights due diligence.[57]

The due diligence concept already occurs in several human rights relevant contexts in which public regulators seek to govern CSR-related issues, typically outside their own territory or jurisdiction. Policy coherence is, obviously, highly significant in this context. The revision of the OECD's Guidelines for MNEs to include the UNGPs' due diligence approach demonstrates awareness of the significance of policy coherence across states, sectors, and issues. The OECD Guidelines are recommendations addressed by governments to MNEs operating *in* or *from* adhering countries.[58] That territorial scope makes companies potentially subject to grievances in front of home state National Contact Points for actions committed even in non-OECD states.

Issues of relevance to human rights (and the risk of adverse business impacts) often do not come labeled as such. Social and environmental business impacts may have human rights elements to them and economic activities may affect human rights in a number of ways that do not fit squarely with the general "headings" that are expressed by international human rights standards such as those in the International Bill of Rights.[59]

[56] *Ibid.* at 11–12 (Principle 8 and Commentary).

[57] *Ibid.* at 8 (Principle 3).

[58] Besides OECD countries, some non-OECD countries, including Argentina, Brazil, and Egypt adhere to the Guidelines.

[59] Recent elaborations in the Human Rights Committee's General Comments of the implications for business enterprises testify to this. See UN Committee on Economic, Social and Cultural Rights, "General Comment No. 15: The Right to Water" (2002).

9.6 Conclusion

Human rights have become of concern to businesses as a result of social expectations that have fueled the development of an emerging international regime of business responsibilities for human rights. The international regime is affecting national law as well as private or public–private regulation of business. Often based on international human rights standards, the social expectations for practical purposes do not distinguish between legal obligations or actions beyond the law. Firms are simply judged on their observance of, as a typical minimum, the standards contained in the International Bill of Rights and the ILO's core labor conventions. A measure of "translation" may be required for the firm to understand and appreciate the impacts of these standards on the firm. Although the standards were formulated to target states, the UNGPs have done much to act as a translator for business.

It has become clear that the UNGPs represent a watershed moment on clarifying the relationship between business and human rights. Not only do they unequivocally answer the question whether companies have obligations to respect human rights, but they also detail what those obligations are and specify what companies must do to meet those obligations.

Nevertheless, efforts are currently underway to draft an international UN treaty regulating business and human rights. Treaty proponents hope to further clarify the relationship between business and human rights and impose an even greater set of responsibilities on companies relating to human rights. Thus, the human rights due diligence obligations from the UNGPs may be only the tip of the iceberg and businesses can expect further detailed requirements on human rights obligations in years to come.

10

A Balancing Approach to Corporate Rights and Duties

MARTIN PETRIN

10.1 Introduction

Despite its age, the longstanding debate surrounding corporate rights and duties remains unresolved. Until today, the type and scope of corporate rights and duties, as well as the manner by which they are assigned, are both contested and evolving. The questions at stake are manifold. For instance, should we view corporations as aggregates of individuals, which would suggest that the corporate entity should be given the rights that their shareholders or other controlling individuals possess? Should corporations be criminally liable, and if so, does it matter whether misconduct can be attributed to individuals at a certain hierarchical level? Or, are corporations capable of bearing social or "moral" responsibility for societal issues, namely in the form of corporate social responsibility (CSR)?

In order to elucidate these and similar issues, this chapter first traces the roots of the corporate rights and duties debate in Section 10.2. It will survey traditional theories that explain the nature of legal entities and, turning to contemporary corporate law, discuss the nexus of contracts approach, focusing in particular on these theories' implications for corporate rights and duties. This chapter then, in Section 10.3, moves on to demonstrate how traditional and modern corporate theories influence the law and academic discussion on the rights and duties of corporate entities, highlighting also how this has led to various problems.

Finally, Section 10.4 outlines an alternative approach to conceptualizing corporations, which aims to provide a more useful and transparent method by which to ascertain corporate rights and duties. In short, this chapter argues that instead of relying on the theories of the firm that are currently used – old and new – a better way going forward is to engage in a balancing approach, which seeks to assign rights and duties by reference to corporations' social and economic function, purpose, and effects.

10.2 Theory of the Firm and Corporate Rights and Duties

Legal scholars have long attempted to explain, in theoretical terms, the precise nature of legal entities. The resulting theories have often been tied to the question of how and to what extent legal entities should be given rights and duties. Today, this debate continues and is in significant parts still based on ancient conceptions of the firm, which remain very much alive. Thus, for a deeper understanding of current law and jurisprudence that govern what corporations are allowed and required to do, knowledge of the relevant theories is paramount. Against this background, the following sections will provide an overview of the most influential theories of the firm, emphasizing their treatment of rights and duties.

10.2.1 Fiction Theory and Aggregate Theory

During the nineteenth century, a growing number of legal scholars became consumed by the idea that the nature of "juristic persons" and their status within the broader legal framework could be "scientifically" explained, which in turn would clarify which rights and duties these entities could bear.[1] One of the most important theories to emerge from this period was the Roman law inspired "fiction theory," which emphasized the artificial character of legal entities such as states, municipalities, and corporate entities.

The fiction theory dominated English and American corporate law for the first part of the nineteenth century.[2] For example, in the landmark decision of *Trustees of Dartmouth College* v. *Woodward*, US Supreme Court Chief Justice Marshall characterized the corporation as an "artificial being, invisible, intangible, and existing only in contemplation of law."[3] Emphasizing the state's role in the formation of corporations, he also noted that these entities only possess those properties that they are conferred upon by their charter.

[1] See, e.g., R. Harris, "The Transplantation of the Legal Discourse on Corporate Personality Theories: From German Codification to British Political Pluralism and American Big Business" (2006) 63 *Washington & Lee Law Review* 1421 at 1422–3.

[2] See W.W. Bratton, "The New Economic Theory of the Firm: Critical Perspectives from History" (1989) 41 *Stanford Law Review* 1471 at 1502–6; M.J. Horwitz, "Santa Clara Revisited: The Development of Corporate Theory" (1985) 88 *West Virginia Law Review* 173 at 184. In Anglo-American law, the fiction theory was also known as the "grant theory" or "concession theory," although it is worth noting that some scholars have distinguished the latter theory from the traditional fiction theory.

[3] *Trustees of Dartmouth College* v. *Woodward*, 17 US (1 Wheat.) 518 at 636 (1819).

In Germany, jurist Friedrich Carl von Savigny played the most prominent role in helping to further develop and popularize the fiction theory.[4] His account of the fiction theory is particularly illuminating. Along with other fiction theorists, he argued that legal persons only have recognized rights and duties as a consequence of an act of the state,[5] which meant that they were purely artificial or fictitious in nature.[6] Further exploring the fiction theory's implications for rights and duties of legal entities, Savigny contended that given their artificial personality, these entities could only bear a limited set of rights and duties, which mostly related to property.[7] Furthermore, apart from instances of strict liability, legal entities – in contrast to the individuals acting for them – could not incur civil or criminal liability. Given their artificial nature, they were perceived as being incapable of developing the requisite state of mind, such as negligence or intent.[8]

During this period, the fiction theory also competed with the "aggregate" or "contractualist" theory, which was particularly popular in nineteenth century England[9] and emerged more clearly and became dominant in the United States during the latter half of the same century.[10] This theory asserted that corporations and other legal entities were aggregations of human individuals whose relationships were structured by way of mutual agreements.[11] As such, both a legal entity's legal rights and duties were often seen, in an indirect or derivative manner, as simply those of its shareholders or other individuals that made up the entity. In other words, under the aggregate theory, rights and obligations held by individuals could be construed to reflect upon the legal entity itself.[12]

[4] The central work is F.C. von Savigny, *System des heutigen römischen Rechts* (Berlin: Bei Deit und Comp, 1840), vol. II.

[5] *Ibid.* at 275.

[6] *Ibid.* at 236.

[7] *Ibid.* at 238–9, 314.

[8] *Ibid.* at 317.

[9] N.H.D. Foster, "Company Law Theory in Comparative Perspective: England and France" (2000) 48 *American Journal of Comparative Law* 573 at 585.

[10] See J.C. Coates, "State Takeover Statutes and Corporate Theory: The Revival of an Old Debate" (1989) 64 *New York University Law Review* 806 at 815–18.

[11] See, e.g., Bratton, above n 2 at 1489.

[12] For example, in *San Mateo* v. *Southern Pacific Railroad*, 13 F 722 (C.C.D. Cal. 1882) the court stated that the beneficiaries of constitutional and other legal rights would always be the individuals behind a corporation, never the entity itself. As will be shown later in this chapter, this theory has recently once more risen to prominence through two landmark US Supreme Court decisions.

10.2.2 *Real Entity Theory*

The practical shortcomings of the fiction theory (with its limits on corporate liability, which proved increasingly difficult to reconcile with the needs of modern society) led to the development of the Germanic "real entity theory" in the late nineteenth century.[13] The real entity theory (or "organic theory") was based on a very different premise. Legal entities were not seen as fictions, but rather as "real" beings that represented "social organisms with heads and extremities."[14] Although it was admitted that legal entities technically gained their personality through acts of the state, the theory's proponents argued that juristic personality formed and existed independently or "naturally," and that therefore the law simply confirmed a preexisting reality already in place by its own virtue.[15]

The real entity theory included two important features. First, in contrast to the fiction theory, it was "pro-liability."[16] Higher-ranking officials or executive bodies, referred to as "organs," could commit torts and crimes in their official capacities. These acts would be imputed to the legal entity, resulting in both the entity's and the responsible individual's liability to third parties.[17] Importantly, therefore, entity liability depended on the seniority of the person within the entity committing the offense. Second, because of its understanding of legal entities as non-artificial, organic beings, the real entity theory contended that these entities could have any right that they were capable of exercising, which was usually defined in the negative as rights that did not require human qualities.[18]

In the early twentieth century, the real entity theory, together with the discourse over its clash with the fiction theory, was "transplanted" from Germany to England and the United States, where it gained traction, challenging both the fiction and aggregate theories.[19] The real entity

[13] One of the leading proponents was German scholar Otto von Gierke. See O. von Gierke, *Die Genossenschaftstheorie und die deutsche Rechtsprechung* (Berlin: Weidmann, 1887). For a helpful discussion of the theory's broader background and impact, see Harris, above n 1 at 1427–30; M. Gelter, "Taming or Protecting the Modern Corporation? Shareholder–Stakeholder Debates in a Comparative Light" (2011) 7 *New York University Journal of Law & Business* 641 at 665–6.

[14] O. von Gierke, *Deutsches Privatrecht* (Leipzig: Duncker & Humboldt, 1895), vol. I, pp. 470, 472.

[15] Gierke, above n 13 at 611; Harris, above n 1 at 1424.

[16] M.M. Hager, "Bodies Politic: The Progressive History of Organizational 'Real Entity' Theory" (1989) 50 *University of Pittsburgh Law Review* 575 at 588.

[17] Gierke, above n 13 at 743–60.

[18] For example, legal entities were thought to be incapable of assuming parenthood.

[19] Harris, above n 1 at 1435.

theory was not as successful in the common law as in the civil law, where it defeated the fiction theory for the most part and was even elevated to statutory law. Nevertheless, from the early twentieth century onward, the real entity theory also increasingly influenced courts and gained considerable prominence in the common law. Among others, the theory's rejection of the notion of corporate artificiality can be credited with the recognition of corporate tortious liability and certain aspects of corporate law, including the decline of *ultra vires* theory and a strengthened limited liability principle.[20]

10.2.3 Nexus of Contracts

Despite the reality–fiction–aggregate debate and its persistent presence in both the common law and civil law, some scholars began to argue that theories of the firm should emphasize economic aspects rather than only the *nature* of legal entities. The American legal realist movement that blossomed around the 1920s and similar movements in Europe[21] paved the way to new academic theories of the firm, beginning from around the 1970s, that placed their focus on functional aspects of the corporate form.

The most notable development to emerge from this period is the nexus of contracts theory of corporations, in some jurisdictions now regarded as the dominant corporate law theory.[22] The nexus of contracts model, however, still contains elements of both the traditional aggregate and fiction theories. This becomes evident in the theory's portrayal of the firm as a construct of various explicit and implicit contracts between a firm's constituencies[23] and its characterization as an "aggregate of various inputs acting together to produce goods or services."[24] Additionally, the theory also embraces the view that firms are legal fictions, with the fiction forming

[20] See Horwitz, above n 2 at 186–8; R.S. Avi-Yonah, "Citizens United and the Corporate Form" (2010) *Wisconsin Law Review* 999 at 1018–19; see also Chapter 1.

[21] See K. Grechenig and M. Gelter, "The Transatlantic Divergence in Legal Thought: American Law and Economics vs. German Doctrinalism" (2008) 31 *Hastings International & Comparative Law Review* 295 at 348–53.

[22] The theory is often traced back to R. Coase, "The Nature of the Firm" (1937) 4 *Economica* 386. In addition, other scholars with notable pioneering works in this area include Oliver Williamson, Armen Alchian, Harold Demsetz, Michael Jensen, and William Meckling.

[23] See, e.g., S.M. Bainbridge, *The New Corporate Governance in Theory and Practice* (Oxford: Oxford University Press, 2008), p. 28; F.H. Easterbrook and D.R. Fischel, *The Economic Structure of Corporate Law* (Cambridge, MA: Harvard University Press, 1991), p. 12.

[24] Bainbridge, above n 23 at 28.

the nexus that is at the center of a complex web of explicit and implicit contracts.[25]

Modern theories of the firm are almost exclusively preoccupied with the corporate governance problems that arise between shareholders and corporate managers and assume that non-corporate laws will regulate corporate responsibility vis-à-vis non-shareholder third parties. Therefore, perhaps surprisingly, the nexus of contracts theory – and contemporary corporate law and theory generally – have little to say about corporations' rights and duties.[26] One notable exception is the nexus of contracts theory's stance on the question for whose benefit corporations operate. According to this aspect of the theory, shareholders are the primary beneficiaries of corporate activities and, consequently, managers should normally – and unless shareholders direct them otherwise – maximize shareholders' wealth without regard to other stakeholders' interests.[27] Contractarians also tend to deny the firm's ability to bear social or moral duties and responsibilities based on its fictional character, which they see as precluding the firm from assuming such obligations.

If the nexus of contracts model would be used without any adjustments to define which rights and duties legal entities should have, it would lead to untenable results. Taken literally, the nexus itself as a mere web of contractually connected individuals could not bear any rights or be liable. Indeed, the atomistic nexus model would demand that rights and duties are those of the various individuals or constituencies that act for or as part of the nexus. In this sense, the contractarian model's partial proximity to the old aggregate and fiction theories becomes once more apparent.

10.3 Impact on Corporate Rights and Duties

Focusing on constitutional law, tort and criminal law, and CSR, this section highlights how the corporate theories discussed above influence today's theory and practice of corporate rights and duties. As it turns out, the traditional fiction, reality, and aggregate theories retain a strong presence and

25 S.M. Bainbridge, "Abolishing Veil Piercing" (2001) 26 *Journal of Corporation Law* 479 at 485.

26 As one scholar recently observed, "orthodox corporate theory . . . has relatively little to say about the corporation itself and even less to say about corporate responsibility." L. Johnson, "Law and Legal Theory in the History of Corporate Responsibility: Corporate Personhood" (2012) 35 *Seattle University Law Review* 1135 at 1163.

27 See, e.g., S.M. Bainbridge, "Director Primacy: The Means and Ends of Corporate Governance" (2003) 97 *Northwestern University Law Review* 547 at 548.

influence the law in a number of ways.[28] The nexus of contracts theory, outside of the academic realm, does not appear to have directly shaped the law governing corporate rights and duties. However, it is an important point of reference and basis for those that oppose CSR-type obligations of businesses, which also makes it important for the purposes of this chapter.

10.3.1 Constitutional and Statutory Rights

The real entity theory and its counterparts, the fiction and aggregate theories, have made their mark on constitutional law. This is particularly pronounced in the United States. Over the course of the nineteenth and twentieth centuries, a number of Supreme Court cases held that a corporation was akin to a real person and therefore entitled to constitutional rights such as commercial speech, protections against unreasonable searches and seizures, and freedom of the press, among others. Conversely, in other cases decided during this period, the firm's fictional nature prevailed.[29] It is also worth noting that apart from the constitutional arena, questions surrounding corporate rights have arisen in the statutory context, where – as in the case of constitutional law – it may be equally unclear whether specific rights or duties, such as privacy, apply to a legal entity or not.[30]

Recently, two landmark cases have once more shown the effect of corporate theories on corporate rights. In *Citizens United* v. *Federal Election Commission*, the Supreme Court struck down statutory provisions limiting corporate election contributions based on the real entity and aggregate theories.[31] *Citizens United* raised the question as to whether corporations should be granted political speech rights, thus allowing them to

[28] In addition to the following sections of this chapter, the continuing effect of traditional theories on corporate theory and practice is noted for example in V. Harper Ho, "Theories of Corporate Groups: Corporate Identity Reconceived" (2012) 42 *Seton Hall Law Review* 879 at 896; J.M. Krannich, "The Corporate "Person": A New Analytical Approach to a Flawed Method of Constitutional Interpretation" (2005) 37 *Loyola University of Chicago Law Journal* 61 at 61, 67, 84, 90. See also M. Petrin, "From Nature to Function: Reconceptualizing the Theory of the Firm" (2013) 118 *Penn State Law Review* 1, which explored this section's topic and the theme of this chapter from a pre-*Hobby Lobby* perspective (on said case, see below text accompanying n 37–40).

[29] For an overview of the case law, see P.I. Blumberg, "The Corporate Entity in an Era of Multinational Corporations" (1990) 15 *Delaware Journal of Corporate Law* 283 at 299–318; Krannich, above n 28 at 90–100.

[30] In *FCC* v. *AT&T, Inc.*, 131 S. Ct. 1177 (2011), for example, the Supreme Court held that a corporation as an artificial entity could not claim a statutory "personal privacy" interest in law enforcement records.

[31] *Citizens United* v. *FEC*, 558 US 310 (2010).

use their general treasury funds to influence election campaigns.[32] The Court was asked to decide whether, from a constitutional standpoint, corporate political speech differed from that of individual political speech such that the former should be more limited. The majority opinion suggested that, for the most part, there was no difference between humans and corporations in this regard. While the Court did not expressly state that corporations are real persons or that they solely represent their shareholders – thus warranting First Amendment rights given to individuals – the decision's wording suggests and was widely read as relying on the aggregate and real entity theories.[33] The Court analogized corporations with "associations of individuals"[34] and appeared to generally treat the corporation as being on the same or similar footing as individuals. Conversely, the dissenting opinion argued that corporations are vastly different from natural persons and should generally not be given political speech rights. The dissent noted that corporations are "legal fiction[s]" that "have no consciences, no beliefs, no feelings, no thoughts, no desires."[35] By doing so, the dissent invoked the core idea of nineteenth-century fiction theory, even using language that is strikingly similar to eighteenth-century fiction theory proponent Edward Thurlow's famed observation that corporations have no "conscience . . . no soul to be damned, and no body to be kicked."[36]

In the 2014 decision in *Burwell* v. *Hobby Lobby Stores, Inc.*,[37] the US Supreme Court once again returned to corporate rights. This time, the Court was faced with determining the scope of corporations' religious rights, based on a statute that specifies the constitutional right to free exercise of religion. In particular, the Court had to address whether a corporation

[32] The case arose when non-profit corporation Citizens United sought to confirm certain portions of a law that regulates financing of political campaigns that were unconstitutional as applied to its documentary on then-Senator Hillary Clinton.

[33] See, e.g., Avi-Yonah, above n 20 at 1040–2; Harper Ho, above n 28 at 922–3; D.A.H Miller, "Guns, Inc.: Citizens United, McDonald, and the Future of Corporate Constitutional Rights" (2011) 86 *New York University Law Review* 887 at 930; J. MacLeod Heminway, "Thoughts on the Corporation as a Person for Purposes of Corporate Criminal Liability" (2011) 41 *Stetson Law Review* 137 at 138; A. Tucker, "Flawed Assumptions: A Corporate Law Analysis of Free Speech and Corporate Personhood in Citizens United" (2010) 61 *Case Western Reserve Law Review* 497 at 505, 515.

[34] *Citizens United*, above n 31 (Scalia J. concurring).

[35] *Ibid.* at 466 (Stevens J., concurring in part and dissenting in part).

[36] J.C. Coffee, "'No Soul to Damn: No Body to Kick': An Unscandalized Inquiry into the Problem of Corporate Punishment" (1981) 79 *Michigan Law Review* 386 at 386 (quoting Baron Thurlow).

[37] *Burwell* v. *Hobby Lobby Stores, Inc.*, 134 S. Ct. 2751 (2014). On this decision, see generally L. Johnson and D. Millon, "Corporate Law after Hobby Lobby" (2014) 70 *Business Lawyer* 1.

could choose not to provide health-insurance coverage for certain methods of contraception – despite a governmental requirement mandating otherwise – in order to preserve the company's controlling shareholders' religious beliefs.

In its characterization of the corporate form, the Supreme Court returned to some of the familiar reasoning previously seen in *Citizens United*, although it now relied most heavily on the aggregate theory. It referred to corporations as "legal fictions," but noting that "the purpose of this fiction is to provide protection for human beings."[38] On this basis, the Court found that a "corporation is simply a form of organization used by human beings to achieve desired ends."[39] Consequently, it concluded that "[w]hen rights, whether constitutional or statutory, are extended to corporations, the purpose is to protect the rights of these people."[40] Based on this assessment, the majority held that the purpose of extending constitutional and statutory rights to corporations was to protect the rights of individuals that are associated with such entities, including shareholders, officers, and employees. Consequently, the Court concluded that protecting corporations' free-exercise rights was necessary in order to protect the religious liberty of the humans who own and control them.

Unfortunately, *Hobby Lobby* leads to more questions than it answers. For instance, on a fundamental level, it is not clear why the Court found that the established separation between the legal entity and individuals should not apply when it comes to corporate rights. More importantly, particularly for businesses, it is also unclear from the Court's reasoning why its holding should not apply to corporate duties as well. On this understanding, however, the legal obligations of corporations could in future cases also be imputed to those who control them, meaning that shareholders (or directors, officers, employees) could become liable for their firm's debts and other obligations. Given this potential flipside to the Court's conception of incorporate entities, *Hobby Lobby* may turn out to be only a pyrrhic victory for businesses and their owners.

10.3.2 Tort and Criminal Law

Tort law and criminal law are further areas that reflect the influence of legal entity theories, here in the shape of corporate duties in the form of liability. On the one hand, in Continental Europe, tort law as applied to

[38] *Hobby Lobby*, above n 37 at 2768.
[39] *Ibid.*
[40] *Ibid.*

legal entities remains almost wholly captured by the real entity theory. In the case of corporations, normally, only torts committed by the company's higher-ranking officials can incur the company's liability. Although vicarious liability for lower-level employees is recognized, establishing the legal entity's responsibility in several jurisdictions still requires, at least in theory, that a higher-level "organ" acting for the entity was negligent in exercising her duties in selecting, supervising, or monitoring such employees.[41]

The real entity theory's effects are also visible in Anglo-American law. In the United Kingdom, the organic approach still retains "a lingering grip" on the civil liability of corporations[42] and governs, among others, the attribution of knowledge and conduct to legal entities through the theory of the "directing mind."[43] In the United States, the distinction between a legal entity's senior officials and lower-level employees, although of lesser importance for tort law overall, manifests itself in the area of punitive damages. The law in some states rejects pure corporate vicarious liability for punitive damages and, instead, provides that punitive damages can only be awarded upon a showing of involvement by certain higher-level corporate officials – such as directors, officers, or "managing agents" – that control and represent the corporation itself.[44] As one court has explained, by confining liability to situations involving individuals that are seen as the corporation's alter ego, the law aims to punish a corporation for misbehavior that reflects "the corporate 'state of mind' or the intentions of corporate leaders."[45] This conception is reminiscent of the real entity theory's idea that only misconduct by "organs" can be attributed to a company.

Criminal liability of legal entities, on the other hand, is under the influence of both the real entity and fiction theory. Courts and scholars in many jurisdictions have long adhered to the traditional axiom that legal entities lacked the capability of incurring *mens rea* and could not be criminally liable. Instead, only individuals acting on behalf of a company could be subject

[41] This is true, for example, under German, Swiss, and Austrian law. See M. Petrin, "The Curious Case of Directors' and Officers' Liability for Supervision and Management: Exploring the Intersection of Corporate and Tort Law" (2010) 59 *American University Law Review* 1661 at 1690, footnote 151.

[42] B. Hannigan, *Company Law* (Oxford University Press, 2012), p. 77.

[43] *Stone & Rolls Ltd.* v. *Moore Stephens* [2008] EWCA (Civ) 644, [2009] 1 AC 1391.

[44] See C.R. Green, "Punishing Corporations: The Food-Chain Schizophrenia in Punitive Damages and Criminal Law" (2008) 87 *Nebraska Law Review* 197 at 200.

[45] *Cruz* v. *Homebase*, 99 Cal Rptr 2d 435 at 439 (Cal. Ct. App. 2000).

to criminal punishment.[46] Still today, many civil law countries typically do not recognize general corporate criminal liability, with the narrow exception of certain statutory liabilities.[47] Conversely, in the United Kingdom, a corporation's criminal liability is often premised on the principles of the real entity theory. According to the classic "directing mind" or "identification" theory, which was adopted in the House of Lords' *Lennard's case*[48] and corresponds to the real entity theory, only criminal offences committed by individuals that can be regarded as physical embodiments of the company can be attributed to the company.[49] Although the introduction of the UK's Corporate Manslaughter and Corporate Homicide Act has mitigated some of the harsh effects of the identification doctrine, the Act's provisions still require a breach of duty on the part of senior management and remain reminiscent of the real entity theory.[50]

Under US law, a mixed picture of corporate criminal liability emerges. While corporations' vicarious liability for criminal conduct is broadly recognized for strict liability offenses, there are splits among both jurisdictions and legal scholars when it comes to offenses requiring *mens rea*.[51] On the one hand, federal courts hold that corporations may become vicariously

[46] See G. Geis and J.F.C. DiMento, "Empirical Evidence and the Legal Doctrine of Corporate Criminal Liability" (2002) 29 *American Journal of Criminal Law* 341 at 342–8; V.S. Khanna, "Corporate Criminal Liability: What Purpose Does It Serve?" (1996) 109 *Harvard Law Review* 1477 at 1490.

[47] See, e.g., G.O.W. Mueller, "Mens Rea and the Corporation: A Study of the Model Penal Code Position on Corporate Criminal Liability" (1957) 19 *University of Pittsburgh Law Review* 21 at 28–32; P.S. Abril and A. Morales Olazábal, "The Locus of Corporate Scienter" (2006) *Columbia Business Law Review* 81 at 106.

[48] *Lennard's Carrying Co.* v. *Asiatic Petroleum Co.* [1915] AC 705. Another notable case is *H.L. Bolton (Engineering) Co. Ltd* v. *T.J. Graham & Sons Ltd.* [1957] 1 QB 159, in which Lord Justice Denning used the reality theory's organic approach in establishing corporate liability. Although a civil case, other courts have often relied on *Bolton* in the criminal context.

[49] The individuals triggering corporate liability are normally directors, officers, or other senior employees. *Tesco Supermarkets Ltd.* v. *Nattrass* [1972] AC 153. A broader definition of which persons can represent the corporation in this context was suggested in *Meridian Global Funds Management Asia Ltd.* v. *Securities Commission* [1995] 2 AC 500 (PC).

[50] The Act may impose criminal liability on organizations if the management or organization of their activities causes a person's death and the conduct of senior management is a substantial element in the breach of their duties in this respect. Corporate Manslaughter and Corporate Homicide Act 2007, s. 1. Although the UK Law Commission has recently considered law reform to abolish the identification doctrine, it was ultimately decided not to move forward with proposals on corporate criminal liability.

[51] See P.I. Blumberg, K.A. Strasser, N.L. Georgakopoulos, and E.J. Gouvin, *Blumberg on Corporate Groups* (New York: Aspen Publishers, 2005), vol. III, pp. 106–7 and footnote 6; Green, above n 44 at 200; B. Thompson and A. Yong, "Corporate Criminal Liability" (2012) 49 *American Criminal Law Review* 489 at 494–5; MacLeod Heminway, above n 33 at 141–2.

liable for criminal acts committed by employees of any hierarchical level. Under this approach, criminal liability does not require any involvement by senior corporate officials. On the other hand, a considerable number of states follow the approach incorporated in the American Law Institute's Model Penal Code (MPC). The MPC's rules generally provide that a corporation may incur criminal liability if "the commission of the offense was authorized, requested, commanded, performed or recklessly tolerated by the board of directors or by a high managerial agent acting on behalf of the corporation within the scope of his office or employment."[52] The MPC's approach represents a variation of the English identification theory and as such continues to embody an outflow of traditional real entity theory.[53]

The real entity theory and the fiction theory's application in tort and criminal law yields unfortunate results. The real entity theory – as used in various contexts in both tort and criminal law – and its application mean that a corporation can only be liable if the injured party can show that someone akin to an "organ" of the company committed or was otherwise involved in the offense. Especially in larger and decentralized organizations, this tends to be difficult to prove for outsiders. Conversely, insofar as the fiction theory is still adhered to (in the criminal law context), its application has the effect that corporate liability is impossible or severely restricted. In sum, in both instances, corporations' exposure to civil and criminal liability may be limited, resulting in equally limited recourse by third parties injured by corporate activities.

10.3.3 Corporate Social Responsibility

A final example of the impact of corporate theory on rights and duties can be found in the area of CSR, which focuses on the imposition of corporate duties to stakeholders other than shareholders, such as employees, communities, or governments.[54] The question to what degree corporate

[52] Model Penal Code § 2.07(1)(c) (Proposed Official Draft 1962). According to the MPC's definition in § 2.07(4)(c), a "high managerial agent" is an officer or agent that has "duties of such responsibility that his conduct may fairly be assumed to represent the policy of the corporation."

[53] See E. Colvin, "Corporate Personality and Criminal Liability" (1995) 6 *Criminal Law Forum* 1 at 9–11.

[54] On the (potential) differences between CSR and stakeholder theory, see generally J.M. Conley and C.A. Williams, "Engage, Embed, and Embellish: Theory Versus Practice in the Corporate Social Responsibility Movement" (2005) 31 *Journal of Corporation Law* 1; D. Millon, "Two Models of Corporate Social Responsibility" (2011) 46 *Wake Forest Law Review* 523.

directors and managers can or should engage in acts that depart from shareholder wealth – and indeed the broader questions of the corporate purpose – remains controversial. US corporate law, perhaps apart from corporate constituency statutes,[55] fails to provide clear guidance on this point.[56] In the United Kingdom, the Companies Act 2006 now includes a statutory duty of directors to "promote the success of the company," which includes an obligation to have regard to the impact of the company's operations on employees, the community, and the environment.[57] Nevertheless, this language still leaves room for varying interpretations and lacks a degree of clarity that would put the corporate purpose debate to rest.

Given the law's ambiguities, scholars have frequently attempted to solve the controversy by developing arguments that draw from theories of the firm. Merrick Dodd's classic account of corporate citizenship and CSR rejected the fiction theory's implications and was already inspired by real entity theory.[58] "If the unity of the corporate body is real," Dodd theorized, "then there is reality and not simply legal fiction in the proposition that the managers of the unit are fiduciaries for it and not merely for its individual members, that they are . . . trustees for an institution rather than attorneys for the stockholders."[59] Thus, with corporations viewed this way, businesses and corporate managers can pursue societal interests and have duties to other constituencies besides shareholders.

Building upon this foundation, other CSR scholars and stakeholder theorists have justified consideration of broader stakeholder interests

[55] These statutes generally allow or require directors of public corporations to consider the welfare and other interests of non-shareholder groups in the course of making corporate decisions. However, they are regarded as largely ineffective in practice.

[56] See, e.g., C.M. Bruner, "The Enduring Ambivalence of Corporate Law" (2008) 59 *Alabama Law Review* 1385; B. Choudhury, "Serving Two Masters: Incorporating Social Responsibility into the Corporate Paradigm" (2009) 11 *University of Pennsylvania Journal of Business Law* 631 at 633. One of the most recent Delaware decisions concerning this point is *eBay Domestic Holdings, Inc.* v. *Newmark*, 16 A 3d 1 (Del. Ch. 2010), in which the court noted that directors are obliged to promote the value of the corporation for the benefit of its shareholders. Nevertheless, the case does not appear to change Delaware's stance on the corporate purpose and the specific facts and language of the case suggest that directors are not precluded from taking into account non-shareholder constituencies' interests.

[57] Companies Act 2006, s. 172.

[58] See E.M. Dodd, "For Whom Are Corporate Managers Trustees?" (1932) 45 *Harvard Law Review* 1145 at 1146, 1160. Dodd opposed Adolf Berle's view that managers hold their powers in trust for shareholders as the sole beneficiaries of corporate activities. See A.A. Berle, "Corporate Powers as Powers in Trust" (1931) 44 *Harvard Law Review* 1049.

[59] Dodd, above n 58 at 1160.

by characterizing the firm by reference to its "real" character,[60] with one scholar arguing that "CSR is most easy to justify in all its forms on the basis of the real theory of the corporation and is likely to remain practiced for the future."[61]

On the other spectrum of the debate, prominent law and economics scholars and other shareholder theorists have drawn upon both the fiction theory and the nexus of contracts theory to support their opposing view of CSR.[62] Opining that a corporation is not real but rather a legal fiction and a nexus of contracts, these theorists conclude that the corporation is incapable of having social or moral obligations. As we have already noted earlier, characterizing the firm as a mere nexus of contracts lends itself to the argument that corporations cannot have societal duties to the public at large.[63]

10.4 Toward a Balancing Approach

As the previous sections have shown, century-old theories on the nature of the firm still pervade important areas of contemporary law, leading to outcomes that can be inconsistent with other legal or economic principles and broader policies. However, as evidenced by the long-standing and seemingly "endless"[64] debate on corporate theories, the nature of the corporate form cannot be conclusively proven and explained. Indeed, albeit interesting, it appears that the question "what is the firm?" – the focal point of traditional approaches to seeking to conceptualize the firm – is largely insignificant and should not be relied on by legislators, courts, or academics. In reality, the choice of a particular theory and its interpretation are a

60 See, e.g., W. Bradford, "Beyond Good and Evil: The Commensurability of Corporate Profits and Human Rights" (2012) 26 *Notre Dame Journal of Legal Ethics* 141 at 148; S.K. Ripken, "Corporations Are People Too: A Multi-Dimensional Approach to the Corporate Personhood Puzzle" (2009) 15 *Fordham Journal of Corporate & Financial Law* 97 at 117.

61 R.S. Avi-Yonah, "The Cyclical Transformations of the Corporate Form: A Historical Perspective on Corporate Social Responsibility" (2005) 30 *Delaware Journal of Corporate Law* 767 at 780–2. Conversely, David Millon previously noted that today's stakeholderism debate is mostly conducted based on aggregate theories of corporate personhood rather than real entity conceptions. D. Millon, "The Ambiguous Significance of Corporate Personhood" (2001) 2 *Stanford Agora* 39 at 43–6.

62 See Bradford, above n 60 at 147 (explaining that these scholars are "grounded in a theory of the firm which regards a corporation as a legal creation designed and managed solely to generate profits for its stockholders").

63 D.R. Fischel, "The Corporate Governance Movement" (1982) 35 *Vanderbilt Law Review* 1259 at 1273.

64 M. Radin, "The Endless Problem of Corporate Personality" (1932) 32 *Columbia Law Review* 643.

function of convictions, values, and policy goals that may well be arbitrary. Even the now dominant nexus of contracts theory, reminiscent in part of the aggregate and fiction theories, fails to convincingly support its one claim that is of greatest interest for this chapter, namely that shareholders should be the firm's sole beneficiaries.

Given these shortcomings, this section explores a new way to conceptualize the firm. The following sections will outline a "balancing" or "functional" approach that suggests that the firm should be defined not by its nature, but rather by its function. This approach, it is argued, is better suited than current corporate theories to deciding matters relating to corporate rights and duties.

10.4.1 Corporate Characteristics

Corporations are economic creatures. Apart from special types of corporations, these entities, with their limited liability and asset partitioning functions,[65] are designed and operate with a view to generating profits. As such, *prima facie*, a legal entity's *rights* should reflect its core economic function and purpose. For instance, with regards to constitutional and statutory rights, the economic core function makes it justifiable to protect corporate commercial speech in order to increase sales of goods and services. Beyond this, corporations may also be given other rights, such as rights to privacy, political speech, and even religious rights if there is a sufficiently strong link to the entity's economic goals. For example, a kosher food company might claim that certain provisions violate its right to religious exercise, or a business could make the case that corporate privacy rights are necessary to protect its confidential documents and trade secrets. Where such a link is not present, the entity may still assert a specific non-economic right,[66] but, as will be further explained later, there should be a differentiation based on the entity's function and purpose, namely whether we deal with for-profit businesses or entities that pursue other goals.[67] A case in point is Hobby Lobby Stores, Inc., one of the companies at the center of the

[65] On the asset partitioning theory of corporations and other legal entities, see H. Hansmann and R. Kraakman, "The Essential Role of Organizational Law" (2000) 110 *Yale Law Journal* 387.

[66] Unless one assumes, as some commentators have argued, that any speech by for-profit corporations is economically motivated commercial speech. See, e.g., Tucker, above n 33 at 521.

[67] See Section 10.4.2.

US Supreme Court's controversial *Hobby Lobby* decision.[68] This company, albeit grounded in Christian values, focuses its business on the sale of crafting supplies, not in the dissemination of religious views. While Hobby Lobby as a corporation is free to pursue any non-economic mission that its shareholders approve of, there is no firm basis in the view that its activities in this regard should be legally protected.[69]

Economic considerations further dictate important corporate *duties*. For instance, economic analysis suggests that in many cases it is efficient to hold corporations liable for torts and criminal acts committed by their agents or that otherwise flow out of their business activities. Holding the corporation liable in these cases enhances loss prevention, helps to internalize costs, and facilitates efficient risk allocation.[70] In particular, the concept of loss internalization demands that the full effects of corporate activities, including negative effects in the form of pollution, injuries, and others, must be internalized, that is reflected in the price of corporate goods and services. Only if the true cost to society is reflected in goods and services will there be an optimal volume of production. Yet, full cost internalization can only be achieved if the corporation is liable for crimes and torts of employees and other individuals at all hierarchical levels. However, this stands in contrast to a number of contemporary legal rules in both criminal and tort law, which, as explained above, still reflect the spirit of the real entity theory and require acts or involvement by senior officials as a prerequisite to corporate liability.[71] Conversely, the approach as proposed herein looks to economic theory and the effects of corporations, suggesting that the full costs of torts and crimes should be internalized, regardless of the actors' status within the corporation.

10.4.2 *Beyond an Economic Function*

In addition to the corporation's economic side, legal entities also serve a *social* function and purpose and can have wide-ranging societal effects. Thus, legal entities are commonly used for non-economic goals and the law allows for and supports such use as evidenced by, for instance,

[68] On this case, see Section 10.3.1.

[69] Of course, the individuals that control Hobby Lobby and similar companies are protected in exercising their own religious rights. After all, they are separate from the companies that they control.

[70] See Petrin, above n 41 at 1703.

[71] See Section 10.3.2.

non-profit corporations and, in the United States, the new class of Benefit Corporations.[72] Moreover, corporations have considerable effects on society, both in positive and negative ways. These social aspects, which are often intertwined with economic effects, need to be included in a contemporary concept of the firm and should also inform the way in which corporate rights and duties are ascertained.

In terms of rights, it is self-evident that legal entities that primarily or exclusively pursue non-economic interests will need to be granted rights that pertain to their respective social, political, cultural, religious, or other goals. Still, such rights are not without boundaries but have to be balanced against potential effects of the entity's exercise of a right. Thus, as an example, *Citizens United*[73] could have entailed weighing the necessity and benefits of granting political speech rights to the plaintiff, a non-profit corporation, against potential negative impacts in the form of a distortion of the electoral process or undue political influence.

Conversely, when it comes to for-profit companies, the case for granting rights other than those that pertain to their economic functions is much less clear-cut, given that such rights would normally not relate to the company's core. For instance, from a functional viewpoint, the need to give these types of corporations the right to exercise religion is difficult to rationalize, although there is a possibility that certain entities could make a convincing case that adherence to religious beliefs or practices is in fact an essential part of their business. Similarly, the less closely a free speech right relates to an economic goal, the weaker the case will be for extending the right to a for-profit business. Under this approach, then, for-profit firms would have a weaker case for the right to engage in political speech that is ideologically motivated, whereas there would be a stronger case for protecting firms' political speech that is aimed to have an impact on its own profits.

In determining to what extent for-profit entities should bear duties, the social effects of firms also play an important role. In this respect, social considerations are in line with economic analysis that supports broad corporate responsibility for torts and crimes flowing from business activities. Conversely, the question of whether corporations have or should have societal duties is more complex and touches upon a much-contested issue.

[72] See generally on Benefit Corporations, J.F. Sneirson, "Green is Good: Sustainability, Profitability, and a New Paradigm for Corporate Governance" (2009) 94 *Iowa Law Review* 987 at 1017–19.

[73] On this case, see Section 10.3.1.

In this regard, the approach proposed in this chapter does not directly endorse either side. Nevertheless, based on the growing impact that businesses have on society at large, a balancing view incorporates the idea that social considerations should be taken into account in assessing the duties of businesses.[74] In line with the idea of a balancing approach, the degree to which a corporation owes duties to third parties can be seen as being dependent on its impact as measured by negative externalities. The stronger an entity's "footprint" is in this regard, the more extensive its duties to affected stakeholders or society at large should be. For example, a corporation that operates in an industry that is prone to extensive pollution should have a corresponding duty toward affected stakeholders, which may go beyond adherence to positive laws and regulations.

10.4.3 Summation: Balancing Economic and Social Functions

In short, balancing corporate rights and duties refers to an approach that defines the firm by its economic and social functions, purpose, and effects, which includes elements of an economic and social inquiry into the role of legal entities. It is this inquiry, and not the question of the nature of the firm, that should inform our conception about firms and define corporate rights and duties. Given the dominant function and purpose of corporations, economic considerations are the starting point of this approach. They protect a firm's economic rights and further act as a basis for justifying duties and rules that support the internalization of business risks.

At the same time, the social element factors into a rights and duties analysis in three ways. First, it helps to define the types of non-economic rights a legal entity should be granted. Second, the social element is used in the analysis of a legal entity's duties. The notion that companies should have regard to the interests of third parties and the public at large also ties in with the economic consideration that they should be liable for torts and crimes that result from their activities. Third, the social element can act to counterbalance a firm's rights. In particular, the social functions and purpose of a firm may temper rights that relate to a corporation's economic function and purpose.

[74] See also K. Greenfield, "Defending Stakeholder Governance" (2008) 58 *Case Western Reserve Law Review* 1043 at 1059–62, who has drawn a connection between corporate disasters and corporate duties to act responsibly toward third parties.

10.5 Conclusion

Theories that define corporations, and legal entities more generally, retain a strong presence and affect various contemporary areas of the law. However, despite the considerable efforts undertaken to explain the nature of the firm, the notion of a corporation as real, fiction, or otherwise fails to provide convincing answers and often only further complicates attempts to solve legal issues. In lieu of traditional approaches, the approach outlined in this chapter provides a more useful and sound framework by which to think about corporations and other business entities and their rights and duties. Ascertaining and assigning rights and duties by balancing a corporation's core economic and social aspects against its impacts on economic and social factors allows courts and legislatures to replace judgments and intuition with tangible and measureable variables to conduct their analysis. This allows for a far more transparent and goal-oriented approach than the status quo. Given the increasing intersections between corporate, economic, and a variety of societal issues, reorienting the underpinnings of corporate theory represents an important step closer to a better understanding of the modern company and its rights and duties.

PART IV

Governing the Modern Company

11

Corporate Law Reform in the Era of Shareholder Empowerment

WILLIAM W. BRATTON

11.1 Introduction

At some point during the last decade, everyone in corporate law woke up to a change in the fact pattern: shareholders are no longer disempowered. The awakening came with a jolt, for shareholder disempowerment had been corporate legal theory's mainspring assumption for three quarters of a century, taking normative pride of place as the problem corporate law needed to solve. Yet suddenly shareholders were pushing managers around without the benefit of a law reform assist.

The unexpected turn of events upends corporate law's prevailing paradigm, referred to in this chapter as the "shareholder paradigm." The paradigm makes three assertions: (1) management agency costs are chronically excessive due to structural barriers that disempower shareholders; (2) fundamental law reform is needed to correct the power imbalance; and (3) reform holds out no cognizable negative effects.

The real world emergence of empowered shareholders denudes all three assertions of force. According to the first assertion, events in practice show that market forces have stronger agency cost-reductive capabilities than the shareholder paradigm assumes, rebutting its diagnosis of structural impediment. The change in the fact pattern shifts the description back to that found in Jensen and Meckling's original agency cost model, which predicts that market and corporate actors endogenously reduce agency costs in a dynamic interaction.[1] Events in practice similarly undercut the second assertion: with shareholders empowered in fact as a result of market operations, fundamental law reform no longer is required. The third assertion, which disavows the possibility that law reform designed to empower

[1] M.C. Jensen and W. Meckling, "Theory of the Firm: Managerial Behavior, Agency Costs and Ownership Structure" (1976) 3 *Journal of Financial Economics* 305.

shareholders could hold out negative effects, always followed from an unsound premise. It assumes that the stock price, the vehicle through which empowered shareholders convey to management their views about the state of the business, holds out a reliable means of information transmission. But that is not the case: shareholders come to the business policy table disabled by information asymmetries, necessitating a degree of management insulation. Perhaps the possibility of suboptimal outcomes stemming from shareholder inputs plausibly could be dismissed as *de minimis* in the past. Now that shareholders wield power, the possibility must be confronted: shareholder empowerment poses a trade-off, not a win–win.

Plainly, corporate law's conceptual framework must be reconsidered and rearticulated. Discussions have begun, but have tended to proceed from extreme positions. Prominent shareholder opponents contend that shareholder empowerment means unproductive emphasis on short-term goals at the expense of long-term shareholders, proceeding immediately to the conclusion that excessive short-term shareholder influence requires legal constraint.[2] Their interlocutors favor sticking with the old disempowerment-centered paradigm as if nothing had changed. They assert that those who complain about short-term shareholder influence really seek management insulation, a bad outcome in a world where management agency costs still need constraining and further shareholder empowerment would have beneficial effects.[3] It is a binary, either/or debate posing a choice between two views of the world. There is no apparent middle ground: if one side is right, the other side is wrong; it must be one or the other.

In fact, it is neither one nor the other. The binary framing is misdirection, and the back-and-forth between shareholder partisans and shareholder opponents assists us little in addressing questions arising as a result of the shift in the corporate balance of power. The questions go to matters of degree – the magnitude of the new shareholder empowerment; they go to matters of impact – the effects of shareholder empowerment both on management agency cost reduction and on corporate business plans and results; and they go to matters of means – the mechanisms by

[2] See, e.g., L.E. Strine, Jr., "Can We Do Better By Ordinary Investors? A Pragmatic Reaction to the Dueling Ideological Mythologists of Corporate Law" (2014) 114 *Columbia Law Review* 449; Wachtell, Lipton, Rosen, and Katz, "Petition for Rulemaking Under Section 13 of the Securities Exchange Act of 1934," March 7, 2011, available at www.sec.gov/rules/petitions/2011/petn4-624.pdf.

[3] See L.A. Bebchuk, "The Myth that Insulating Boards Serves Long-Term Value" (2013) 113 *Columbia Law Review* 1637 at 1651; M.J. Roe, "Corporate Short-Termism – In the Boardroom and in the Courtroom" (2013) 68 *Business Lawyer* 978 at 1006.

which shareholder instructions are formulated and then transmitted to business policy. Only once the questions are answered, we will know whether shareholder empowerment implies healthy agency cost reduction, unproductive short-termism, neither, or both.

As yet, answers are in short supply. We know that there has been a change in the market and institutional structures within which power is allocated between managers and shareholders. We await more information about the new relational equilibrium's incidents and effects as events unfold in practice. Meanwhile, we are left in a state of uncertainty.

Corporate law's conceptual framework needs to be revised and restated for this uncertain environment, with attention directed to the interaction between market correction and costly trade-offs. Corporate governance operates in a system in which markets and hierarchies interact. The system is dynamic and capable of endogenous adjustment, lowering costs without requiring exogenous intervention. But the system is also imperfect and does not automatically hold out first-best results based on market transactions. As the system is dynamic and responds to market demands, its adjustments should enjoy the positive presumption ordinarily accorded to private ordering. But because the system is imperfect, structural changes require careful evaluation, for they inevitably involve trade-offs.

It follows that this is not a time for law reform. Evaluation of recent changes is at an early stage: shareholder–manager relations have arrived at a new equilibrium and the magnitude of the implicated trade-offs is only beginning to be quantified. Meanwhile, the situation is dynamic; the facts on the ground continue to develop even as we try to figure out where we were last week. A reform-driven, structural shift in the balance of power between shareholders and managers in *either* direction could have perverse effects on management decision-making and corporate productivity. An increase in shareholder power could have the negative effect of triggering destructive short-termism, while a decrease in shareholder power could revive the agency cost problem. Accordingly, all sides in current debates should face the same burden of proof and be required to surmount a presumption against law reform and in favor of the status quo.

This may not sound like much, for the burden of proof ordinarily falls on the law reform proponent. But the proposition is radical in the corporate law context, where, under one or another paradigm and for at least eight decades, law reform constraining management power has enjoyed presumptive favor.

This chapter takes this universal burden of proof to corporate law's competing policy agendas, taking a fresh look at a selection of contested issues – antitakeover regulation, shareholder agenda control, triennial director elections, and barriers to hedge fund activist intervention. Each law reform proposition is put to the trade-off test. None survive inspection.

11.2 Structural Reform to Empower Shareholders

Given their druthers, shareholder proponents would roll back the corporate law of takeovers to its posture as of 1980, when management's defensive arsenal lacked such weapons as poison pills and statutory supermajority votes. They would then continue back a century more to the late nineteenth century and remove management's agenda control over mergers and charter amendments.[4] This section considers these propositions in turn.

11.2.1 Antitakeover Regulation

The shareholder paradigm's most fundamental precept is that antitakeover regulation is a bad thing. Although no one actually expects to see antitakeover regulation rolled back, shareholder proponents continue to highlight it as a salient problem,[5] for the hostile takeover is thought to be the great missing piece in the agency cost-control puzzle.

Let us hypothesize a rollback. The primary means to the end would be poison pill abolition, for a poison pill taken together with a staggered board provides more practical protection against hostile offers than any single or combined state antitakeover statute. Of course, absent a pill, antitakeover statutes do have some bite, so we must repeal them simultaneously.

What would we have accomplished? Market forces would certainly bear on managers with a harder, more immediate edge. But forceful trade-off questions arise. Control threats force managers to focus the business plan on the market price of the stock, which can result in suboptimal decision-making.[6] An antitakeover rollback would much exacerbate the problem. Commitments to long-term contributors to firm output would be harder to sustain. At the same time, the benefits of a harder disciplinary edge due to a hostile takeover threat become less and less clear-cut when one

[4] See W.W. Bratton and J.A. McCahery, "Regulatory Competition, Regulatory Capture, and Corporate Self-Regulation" (1995) 73 *North Carolina Law Review* 1861 at 1928–36.

[5] See, e.g., Roe, above n 3 at 20; Bebchuk, above n 3 at 12.

[6] See W.W. Bratton and M.L. Wachter, "The Case Against Shareholder Empowerment" (2010) 158 *University of Pennsylvania Law Review* 655 at 696–704.

takes a closer look at the mergers and acquisitions (M&A) market. Such is the effect of a quarter century of market correction.

Back around 1980, when the market for corporate control was first held out as the system's built-in corrective, corporate governance was in its infancy. Boards of directors were stocked with insiders and seen, justifiably, as ineffectual rubber stamps. Some managers did prefer empire building to shareholder value enhancement.[7] And, when a hostile tender offer was made, the target managers had no incentive to negotiate and sell. All of that has changed, thanks to independent directors, equity compensation, and side payments to exiting managers.[8] Even poison pills are acknowledged to have a positive aspect. They permit the governance system to operate so as to procure the best price for the selling shareholders by forcing the acquirer to deal with the independent directors on the target board.[9] It is not clear that competitive bidding in an unstructured control market assuredly gets selling shareholders to the same place of bargaining advantage.

Selling shareholders have little of which to complain in any event. Merger volume remains high. Indeed, since the close of the takeover era, merger volume has repeatedly reached new records without a need for hostile impetus. Figure 11.1 shows annual public company acquisitions from 1981 to 2013, tracking both numbers of companies acquired and the total consideration paid, stated in billions of inflation-adjusted dollars. The market matches the hostile takeover era's 1988 peak year by 1995 in consideration paid and by 1996 in numbers of targets. It goes on to surpass everything that came before and during the tech boom of the late 1990s. These days, most deals are friendly most of the time, and, while hostility may have been an important motivation of total M&A activity before and during the 1980s, it is not the *sine qua non* of a vigorous market. Given willing sellers, a friendly platform works fine.[10] Hostility persists in the M&A market less as a fundamental transactional distinction than as a secondary strategy choice determined by cost–benefit calculations at the acquiring firm.[11]

[7] See M.C. Jensen, "Agency Costs, Free Cash Flow, Corporate Finance, and Takeovers" (Papers & Proceedings 1986) 76 *American Economic Review* 323.

[8] See Bratton and Wachter, above n 6 at 675–87.

[9] M. Kahan and E.B. Rock, "How I Learned to Stop Worrying and Love the Pill: Adaptive Responses to Takeover Law" (2002) 69 *University of Chicago Law Review* 871 at 911.

[10] *Ibid.* at 878–80.

[11] See G.W. Schwert, "Hostility in Takeover: In the Eyes of the Beholder?" (2000) 55 *Journal of Finance* 2599 at 2600.

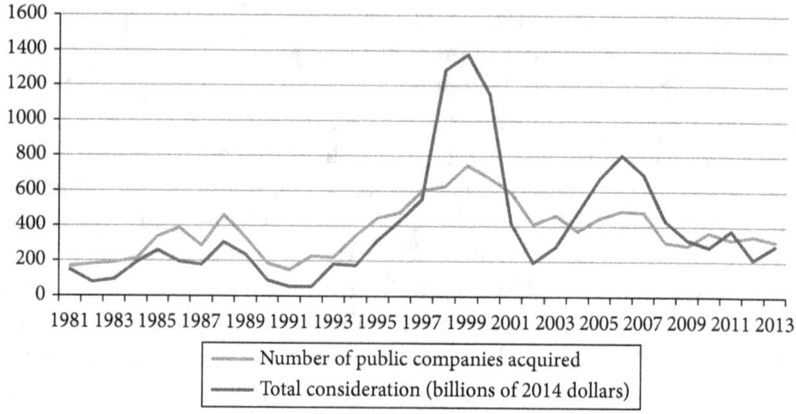

Figure 11.1 Public company acquisitions, 1981–2013
Source: Mergerstat

Merger premiums, which have gone up since the 1980s,[12] are substantial; so substantial as to arrogate all of the merger gain to the selling shareholders. Studies of announcement period price effects bear out this assertion with a stark allocational picture. Target shares consistently go up while bidder shares go down.[13] The figures imply consistent losses to bidder shareholders. Other studies yield more moderate results, but confirm that acquirer shareholders do no better than breakeven.[14]

It is accordingly unsurprising that today's managers, with substantial equity stakes in their companies, are willing to sell. Even managers who initially defend against hostile offers eventually tend to do so.[15] Data on hedge fund engagements yield a powerful further confirmation. Hedge funds get their best returns when their interventions push targets into

[12] See B.E. Eckbo, "Corporate Takeovers and Economic Efficiency," *Working Paper No. 391/2013* (European Corporate Governance Institute, 2013), available at http://ssrn.com/abstract=2530440, at 27.

[13] See G. Andrade, M. Mitchell, and E. Stafford, "New Evidence and Perspectives on Mergers" (2001) 15 (2) *Journal of Economic Perspective*, 103 at 109–10; S.B. Moeller, F.P. Schlingemann, and R.M. Stulz, "Wealth Destruction on a Massive Scale? A Study of Acquiring Firm Returns in the Recent Merger Wave" (2005) 60 *Journal of Finance* 757 at 770.

[14] Eckbo, above n 12 at 28–9.

[15] See L.A. Bebchuk, J.C. Coates IV, and G. Subramanian, "The Powerful Antitakeover Force of Staggered Boards" (2002) 54 *Stanford Law Review* 887 at 933.

mergers, whether sale of the whole or a part.[16] Significantly, these mergers occur without the benefit of a push in the form of a hostile tender offer. Today, a smaller, cheaper push gets the job done because the target managers are willing to sell, so willing as to make activism profitable.

Meanwhile, the absence of a vigorous takeover corrective no longer implies continued, unremedied slack. The same hedge funds that push companies into mergers also challenge management decisions on financial and operational matters. Any residual disciplinary deficit is checked by the private equity buyout, which reappeared at the front line of corporate governance in the mid-1990s. In this sector, voluntary sales have disciplinary consequences. Buyout firms act as aggressive blockholders, closely monitoring management performance and imposing performance targets.[17]

Finally, let us take a look back at the 1980s merger market and ask whether it actually conformed to the picture drawn under the shareholder paradigm. The paradigm assumes that hostile takeovers belong to an identifiable class of mergers that create value by separating poor managers from valuable assets. Economists have been testing merger and governance data for a quarter century in an attempt to verify this assumption. But confirming data became more elusive as more tests were run[18]; any

[16] See A. Brav, W.J. Jiang, F. Partnoy, and R. Thomas, "Hedge Fund Activism, Corporate Governance, and Firm Performance" (2008) 63 *Journal of Finance* 1729 at 1730; M. Schor and R.M. Greenwood, "Investor Activism and Takeovers" (2009) 92 *Journal of Financial Economics* 362 at 372; N. Gantchev, "The Costs of Shareholder Activism: Evidence from a Sequential Decision Model" (2013) 107 *Journal of Financial Economics* 610 at 623–26.

[17] B.R. Cheffins and J. Armour, "The Eclipse of Private Equity," *Law Working Paper No. 082/2007* (European Corporate Governance Institute, 2007), available at http://ssrn.com/abstract=982114, at 9.

[18] See M. Becht, P. Bolton, and A. Roell, "Corporate Governance and Control," *Finance Working Paper No. 002/2002* (European Corporate Governance Institute, 2002), available at http://ssrn.com/abstract=343461, at 46 (describing the empirical results as "surprisingly sketchy").

For an early paper showing that disciplinary energies are concentrated on poorly performing firms, see R. Morck, A. Shleifer, and R. Vishny, "Alternative Mechanisms for Corporate Control" (1989) 79 *American Economic Review* 842. Subsequent searches for correlation between post-merger turnover and pre-merger performance yield less satisfying results. See K.J. Martin and J.J. McConnell, "Corporate Performance, Corporate Takeover, and Management Turnover" (1991) 46 *Journal of Finance* 671 at 672; O. Kini, W. Kracaw, and S. Mian, "Corporate Takeovers, Firm Performance and Board Composition" (1995) 1 *Journal of Corporate Finance* 383 at 386; O. Kini, W. Kracaw, and S. Mian, "The Nature of Discipline by Corporate Takeovers" (2004) 59 *Journal of Finance* 1511 at 1512; A. Agrawal and J.F. Jaffe, "Do Takeover Targets Underperform? Evidence from Operating and Stock Returns" (2003) 38 *Journal of Financial and Quantitative Analysis* 721 at 723–24.

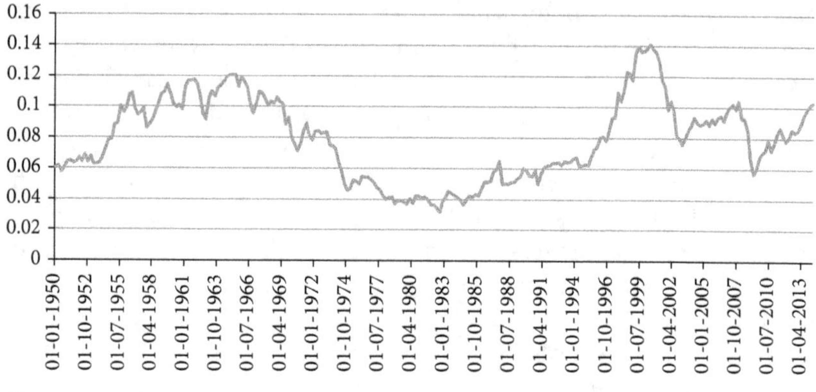

Figure 11.2 S&P/Gross National Product, 1950–2013

statistical connection between management performance, market price, and takeover probability became clouded by endogenous complicating factors. The most recent work does establish a connection between low market prices and takeover probability, but only that. Whether the low price stems from poor performance by management or market mispricing remains an open question.[19]

Consider in this regard Figure 11.2, which tracks a ratio that puts the Standard & Poor's (S&P) 500 Average in the numerator and Nominal Gross National Product in the denominator. When the ratio is low, equities are cheap relative to the output of the overall economy. And, when equities are cheap, hostile takeovers make particularly good cost–benefit sense. The chart shows that equities were at rock bottom during the 1980s – it was the best time to acquire going concern assets through control block purchases via the stock market during the six decades after 1950. The 1980s hostile acquirers were, literally, snapping up bargains. It remains an open question whether the bargain pricing stemmed from mismanagement or external, macroeconomic factors, or both. Whatever the answer to that question, the increase of the ratio after 1990 invites us to attribute the waning of the hostile takeover to changed economic conditions rather than to regulatory developments.

[19] A. Edmans, I. Goldstein, and W. Jiang, "The Real Effects of Financial Markets: The Impact of Prices on Takeovers" (2012) 67 *Journal of Finance* 933 at 939–45.

There is, in short, no firm basis for the shareholder paradigm's assertion that the 1980s hostile takeover boom reflected a market response to a chronic mode of mismanagement that somehow persists today in the wake of antitakeover regulation. Holmstrom and Kaplan's characterization of 1980s takeovers resonates better. They describe the takeover wave as a reaction to an external shock caused by deregulation, globalization, and new technologies, an adjustment that saw the financial markets taking the lead over management as agents of change. Significantly, Holmstrom and Kaplan do not take the additional step of asserting that the financial markets possess this comparative advantage as a permanent proposition. A different economic environment, they say, could trigger a shift away from the markets.[20]

To sum up, it is not safe to assume that antitakeover regulation leaves in its wake a persistent, salient quantum of unaddressed agency costs. Nor is there any basis whatever for assuming that shareholders as a group are being deprived of significant takeover premiums that would be generated absent antitakeover regulation. It follows that the case for dismantling antitakeover barriers comes down to stock market discipline for its own sake. The 1980s cannot be brought back.

11.2.2 Shareholder Agenda Control

Corporate charters can only be amended given prior approval by the board of directors. The shareholders, who have no power of initiation, act as second-level ratifiers of board decisions. The same regime of board agenda control obtains with mergers. A slight shift in these process rules could substantially alter the balance of power between managers and shareholders. If shareholders could initiate charter amendments, a hostile acquirer could solicit proxies to remove a poison pill; then, after winning the proxy fight, it could proceed directly to acquire 51% of the shares and control. Alternatively, if shareholders could initiate mergers, a potential acquirer could draft a merger agreement and then use a proxy contest to ram it through. Finally, an activist hedge fund could initiate a proposal to reincorporate a target in a shareholder-friendly state like North Dakota,[21]

[20] See B. Holmstrom and S.N. Kaplan, "Corporate Governance and Merger Activity in the United States: Making Sense of the 1980s and 1990s" (2001) *Journal of Economic Perspective* 121 at 122–23, 139.

[21] See, e.g., W.B. Chandler III, "Thoughts on the North Dakota Publicly Traded Corporations Act of 2007" (2008) 84 *North Dakota Law Review* 1051.

thereby stripping management of the insulation afforded by the corporate law of a state like Delaware.

Agenda access, then, could materially enhance shareholder power. Even so, it amounts to more of a background fixture in corporate politics than a present point of policy debate[22] – a change so fundamental as to be thought unattainable as a practical political matter. This assumption appears to be holding even as power shifts in the shareholders' direction.

There is also an irrelevance argument: agenda access is a point of theoretical and political salience that would make little difference in practice.[23] Many other national systems hold out access, requiring the proponent to collect consents from a threshold percentage of shareholders. Actual usage in these other countries is rare. This suggests that agenda access, while a point of theoretical and political salience, would make little difference in practice.[24] Shareholders in the United States seem to be following suit. They shy away from exercising their new nuclear options – no vote majorities against corporate directors are less likely to occur with the proliferation of majority voting.[25] Other shareholder-favorable governance improvements, like proxy contest expense reimbursement,[26] are now open to shareholder-initiated implementation, but little advantage of this new access portal has been taken.[27] At the same time, many of the results that agenda access would be expected to facilitate already exist. Managers now voluntarily dismantle staggered boards that are safely embedded in corporate charters[28]; hedge fund activists shake loose merger gains without any need for shareholder agenda control.

The question is whether the irrelevance argument changes anything in the analysis of the policy question in chief. It need not. The irrelevance

[22] It has been discussed only sporadically. See J.N. Gordon, "Shareholder Initiative: A Social Choice and Game Theoretic Approach to Corporate Law" (1991) 60 *University of Cincinnati Law Review* 347 at 376–81; Bratton and McCahery, above n 4 at 1925–47; A. Ferrell and L. Bebchuk, "A New Approach to Takeover Law and Regulatory Competition" (2001) 87 *Virginia Law Review* 111; P. McGinty, "Replacing Hostile Tenders Offers" (1996) 144 *University of Pennsylvania Law Review* 983.

[23] M. Kahan and E.B. Rock, "Symbolic Corporate Governance" (2014) 94 *Boston University Law Review* 1997 at 1999–2021.

[24] *Ibid.* at 2005–09 (discussing proxy access in the United States).

[25] See generally S.J. Choi, J.E. Fisch, M. Kahan, and E.B. Rock, "Does Majority Voting Improve Board Accountability?," *Research Paper No. 15-31* (University of Pennsylvania Institute for Law and Economics, 2015), available at http://ssrn.com/abstract=2661560

[26] Delaware General Corporation Law §§ 112, 113.

[27] Kahan and Rock, above n 23 at 2018–21.

[28] See M. Cremers, L.P. Litov, and S.M. Sepe, "Staggered Boards and Firm Value, Revisited" (2013), available at http://ssrn.com/abstract=2364165, at 40–3.

point has contradictory implications. On the one hand, one presumably might as well go ahead and enact the change in the theory that some good might come of it but no harm. Real world shareholders are not about to use access to choke real world companies with bad business plans, and if, despite this projection, patterns of shareholder intervention veered off into destructive directions, contra-directed market correction can be expected. On the other hand, given market correction, why bother putting through a risky reform of which no one is likely to take advantage? Shareholder-directed market correction already reduces agency costs, operating against a background that accords management with substantial insulation. The historic barriers to shareholder directives, however tall, no longer matter very much. Meanwhile, pressure on management intensifies even as the barriers remain in place, holding out the possible perverse effects.

The contradictory possibilities in the end return us to the issue's original statement, in which the case for a wide portal for shareholder intervention stands or falls depending on the paradigm holding sway. Under the shareholder paradigm, the case is robust. Given a one-way picture of management agency cost reduction, shareholder control holds out immense gains. Under a trade-off approach, the case quickly fails. An access portal holds out a constant threat of intervention against the business plan. A salient risk of negative consequences follows, not only a more pronounced tendency to manage the market price but also imposition of specific schemes based on inadequate information. Given the recent pattern of market correction of management agency costs, there is no persuasive case for taking the risk.

Significantly, the question concerning countervailing costs cannot be finessed by implementing access on a company-by-company opt-in basis and avoiding an across-the-board mandate. An opt-in could continue the present system of board agenda control and be made conditioned on the prior consent of the board of directors. But it is hard to imagine that many boards would ever consent. If, in contrast, the power to opt-in were vested in the shareholders, bypassing the board, the opt-in by itself would effectively accomplish shareholder agenda control, amounting to a minor procedural step in a larger substantive campaign.

11.3 Reform to Insulate Managers

Proposals also have been advanced in recent years which would insulate managers from shareholder pressure. Hedge fund activism is the immediate motivation. This new form of blockholder intervention is the leading edge of the shift in power in the shareholders' favor. To be sure, blockholding has been held out for decades as an effective cure for agency problems. A holder of a big block, say 20 to 30% of a company's stock, has every incentive to monitor its managers[29] even as its holding's magnitude makes exit impracticable and binds it to the company's long-term welfare.[30] The hedge fund activists destabilized this inherited picture, for they do not fit the mold of the patient, loyal, locked-in blockholder. They assemble smaller blocks; they hold for shorter periods; and they do not necessarily seek or attain insider status. But they have had a disciplinary impact and so have been welcomed into the shareholder paradigm.[31] They also have loud opponents, who accuse them of being short-termers – their median 23-month holding period[32] does not qualify them as long-term investors in their detractors' eyes. The detractors have a point, a point the hedge funds do not dispute. They make no pretense of investing for an indefinite long term as they trade in and outs – their business model precludes it.

11.3.1 Proposals

Management defenders pursue a multifaceted campaign to contain the hedge funds. There is, for example, a proposal to narrow the filing window under section 13(d) of the 1934 Act.[33] This requires parties acquiring more than 5% of a reporting company's stock to file a public disclosure of their ownership and intentions. The section 13(d) filing date is a key moment in any activist hedge fund campaign involving acquisition of more than 5% of a target's stock. Prior to reaching the filing threshold, the activist acquires target stock by stealth, without having to pay a premium stemming from the market's knowledge of its presence. Public disclosure drives up the target's stock price, opening the door for market freeriding as stock watchers pile into target stock to take advantage of a positive price bump. To the extent the activist is still buying the stock, publicity lowers its profit

[29] A. Shleifer and R. Vishny, "Large Shareholders and Corporate Control" (1986) 94 *Journal of Political Economy* 461.

[30] See, e.g., A. Bhide, "The Hidden Costs of Stock Market Liquidity" (1993) 34 *Journal of Financial Economics* 31; P. Aghion, P. Bolton, and J. Tirole, "Exit Options in Corporate Finance: Liquidity Versus Incentives" (2004) 8 *Review of Finance* 327.

[31] See R.J. Gilson and J. Gordon, "The Agency Costs of Agency Capitalism: Activist Investors and the Revaluation of Governance Rights" (2013) 113 *Columbia Law Review* 863 at 865–7.

[32] See W.W. Bratton, "Hedge Funds and Governance Targets: Long-Term Results," *Research Paper No. 10-17* (University of Pennsylvania Institute for Law & Economics, 2010), available at http://ssrn.com/abstract=1677517, at 9–11.

[33] 15 USC § 78m(d) (2012).

from the engagement. The rules under section 13(d) hold out an important assist. They accord the holder a space of 10 days within which to file from the date of acquisition of the share that puts it over the 5% threshold, giving the activist an extra 10 days for stealth purchasing. The 10-day filing window, which dates from the statute's enactment in 1968, has become controversial accordingly.

Management advocates now pressure the SEC to revise its rule. In a famous petition,[34] the Wachtell Lipton firm laid out the case for a shorter window, arguing that filing easily can be effected in a day and that stock purchases should be prohibited for an additional day thereafter.[35] The resulting debate poses policy concerns traditional to securities regulation against putative governance benefits stemming from activism. A shorter window would indeed assure equality of access to information, enhancing transparency.[36] Ordinarily, it would be safe to assume that earlier disclosure of this market information would make investors better off. But here disclosure trades off against intervention, which in turn holds out the benefits because it makes managers more accountable and reduces agency costs.[37] The resolution of the trade-off question turns on an evaluation of the effects of hedge fund intervention.

There are also more fundamental, structural proposals. Consider in this regard the triennial board election. State corporate codes mandate annual meetings of shareholders, and annual meetings are now occasions for hedge fund intervention in the form of credible albeit uninvited candidates for election as directors. Classified boards respect the yearly election mandate even as they extend directors' terms and stagger their election – although only a subset of directors is up for election in a given year, there is still a shareholders' meeting and an occasion for contest. Triennial elections hold out enhanced insulation – all directors would have three-year terms and the board as a whole would enjoy immunity from electoral confrontation with the shareholders for three full years. Immunity would extend to hostile tender offers: armed with a poison pill, a three-year board can forestall the closing of a hostile offer for the duration of its term.

The triennial board election is accordingly a radical suggestion. But, as is not the case with shareholder agenda access, here optionality would

[34] Wachtell, Lipton, Rosen, and Katz, above n 2.

[35] *Ibid.* at 5.

[36] *Ibid.* at 2.

[37] L.A. Bebchuk and R.J. Jackson, Jr., "The Law and Economics of Blockholder Disclosure" (2012) 2 *Harvard Business Law Review* 39 at 47.

mitigate any potential negative effects. With an opt-in based on a charter amendment, no company would be forced to abandon annual elections and conversion would require a favorable shareholder vote. Presumably, such a proposal would be attractive only to shareholders of a company experiencing losses manifestly attributable to myopia or activist intervention. Indeed, in the present environment it is difficult to imagine a shareholder relations-conscious management group proposing a triennial election scheme, much less any collection of public shareholders approving one.

The triennial election thus emerges as a more benign reform than does shareholder agenda control because actual approval and implementation are all that much more unlikely. But that is not much of a defense. Optionality by itself does not justify a reform initiative that potentially disrupts the existing shareholder-management equilibrium. So the question is better posed this way: Are we presently facing a short-termism crisis so severe as to justify a revision of a process mandate under which corporations have operated for more than a century? Once again, the answer to this question depends on one's appraisal of hedge fund activism.

11.3.2 Inputs from Financial Economics

The question is whether activist hedge funds do economic good. The answer is complicated. A pattern emerges from a growing collection of empirical studies: activist intervention clearly is good for the stock price; evidence on its impact on corporate operations, while slightly positive, is shakier. A cautious conclusion is supported: activist intervention triggers stock market gains that persist over time and does not appear to result in any harm to operations.

The studies produce a consistent result as regards target stock prices: activist intervention causes an immediate increase that lasts for at least a year. The magnitude of the bump varies with the study: 7–8%,[38] 10.2%,[39] 3.39%,[40] 3.5%,[41] or 6%.[42] Some of the studies show that positive cumulative abnormal returns continue to rise during the period following the

[38] Brav *et al.*, above n 16 at 1729.

[39] A. Klein and E. Zur, "Entrepreneurial Shareholder Activism: Hedge Funds and Other Private Investors" (2009) 64 *Journal of Finance* 187 at 188.

[40] C.P. Clifford, "Value Creation or Destruction? Hedge Funds as Shareholder Activists" (2008), available at http://ssrn.com/abstract=971018, at 4–5.

[41] Schor and Greenwood, above n 16 at 366–8.

[42] L.A. Bebchuk, A. Brav, and W. Jiang, "The Long-Term Effects of Hedge Fund Activism" (2015) 115 *Columbia Law Review* 1085 at 1122.

activists' first appearance: an additional 6.5% over eighteen months[43] and an additional 11.4% over one year.[44] Other studies tune these numbers more finely.[45]

Positive, albeit smaller, numbers are reported regarding operations. One study reports an increase in target return on assets (ROA) of 1.22% over one year.[46] Over two years, the ROA of experienced activist targets exceeds that of comparable companies by 1.2%; the targets' cash flows exceed those of the comparables by 1.8%.[47] There is also a showing of increases in the ratio of earnings before interest, taxes depreciation and amortization (EDITBA) taken over assets, and the ratio of EDITBA taken over sales of, respectively, 0.9 to 1.5% and 4.7 to 5.8%.[48] But results are mixed – another study reports no significant change in ROA.[49] Still another study on patents finds a positive association between hedge fund stock ownership and patent quality – the larger the block held, the bigger the effect.[50] There is also evidence of stepped up CEO turnover and cuts in executive compensation.[51]

Activist opponents remit us to other numbers. For example, the studies find step ups in amounts of dividends and stock repurchases, increases in debt to asset ratios, decreases in cash balances, R&D, and capital expenditures.[52] Bonds issued by targets underperform when compared to those issued by comparable companies[53] and employees suffer plant closings and

43 Schor and Greenwood, above n 16 at 366–8.

44 Klein and Zur, above n 39 at 188.

45 N.M. Boyson and R.M. Mooradian, "Experienced Hedge Fund Activists," *Working Paper* (American Finance Association Chicago Meetings, 2012), available at http://ssrn.com/abstract=1787649, at 3 (dividing activists into experienced and inexperienced and showing that experience yields positive results).

46 Clifford, above n 40 at 4–5.

47 *Ibid.* at 20.

48 Brav *et al.*, above n 16 at 1730.

49 Schor and Greenwood, above n 16 at 370–1. But cf. A. Brav, W. Jiang, and H. Him, "Hedge Fund Activism: A Review" (2010) 4(3) *Foundations and Trends in Finance* 185 at 229–30 (suggesting that this may be due to selection bias).

50 Y. Wang and J. Zhao, "Hedge Funds and Corporate Innovation" (2014), available at http://ssrn.com/abstract=2191744, at 2–3.

51 Brav, Jiang, and Him, above n 49 at 230.

52 Klein and Zur, above n 39 at 189; Brav *et al.*, above n 16 at 1730; Schor and Greenwood, above n 16 at 370–1.

53 Y. Allaire and F. Dauphin, "'Activist' Hedge Funds: Creators of Lasting Wealth? What Do the Empirical Studies Really Say?" (2014), available at http://ssrn.com/abstract=2460920, citing H. Aslan and H. Maraachlian, "Wealth Effects of Hedge Fund Activism" (2009), available at www.efa2009.org/papers/SSRN-id1428047.pdf

layoffs.[54] The greatest return to activism, moreover, has been shown to lie in the sale of the target.[55] It is held to follow that activism is about short-term gain and not improvement of long-term performance.

Hedge fund proponents have responded with a second generation of studies that purport to confirm that activist intervention adds long-term value. Bebchuk, Brav, and Jiang ran five-year post-engagement ROA and Tobin's Q figures for a set of engagements from 1994 to 2007.[56] The industry adjusted ROA figures rise steadily from −0.028 in the engagement year to −0.009 in the fifth year. The Tobin's Q figures rise from −1.507 in the engagement year to −0.984 in the fifth year.[57] The authors claim, justifiably, a "clear pattern" of improvement,[58] "facilitated" by the activists.[59] The story trails off at this point, however. The authors have little success in explaining how it is that activist engagements can be deemed to cause improvements stretching across five years, having failed to identify an operations-based transmission mechanism.[60] And, while their regressions show statistical significance,[61] economic significance remains questionable.[62]

Indeed, if one puts aside the consistent results confirming a significant and enduring stock price increase at the time of engagement, none of the figures on the corporate-level results of hedge fund activism impress as regards magnitude. The transmission mechanism is clear only when discreet actions result from the engagement – the CEO gets fired; money is borrowed; or the target is merged. When attention turns to performance improvements over the long term, the causal mechanism is not at all clear.

At the same time, there is no aggregate evidence of significant harm to going concerns. Results on leverage and shareholder payouts show no back-door return to the leveraged restructuring craze of the 1980s. Nor should one be troubled by the finding that most of the gain yielded by activism comes from mergers and asset sales. The deals are voluntary. The

[54] A. Brav, W. Jiang, and H. Kim, "The Real Effects of Hedge Fund Activism: Productivity, Asset Allocation, and Industry Concentration" (2015), available at http://ssrn.com/abstract=2022904, at 31.

[55] See Schor and Greenwood, above n 16 at 378.

[56] Bebchuk, Brav, and Jiang, above n 42 at 1103–5.

[57] *Ibid.* at 1105.

[58] *Ibid.* at 1117.

[59] *Ibid.* at 1136–7.

[60] See *ibid.* at 1119–21 (asserting that the improvements are not the result of stock-picking).

[61] *Ibid.* at 1107–8.

[62] *Ibid.* at 1089–90.

activists are positioned neither to dictate their terms nor to extract special benefits. Indeed, it has been shown that a better deal results when there is an activist hedge fund in the target shareholder population.[63] Finally, mergers make a positive productivity contribution to the economy as a whole.[64]

Even as the studies strenuously try to explain the stock price bump that accompanies activist engagement as a reflection of productivity gains incident to discipline, there is an alternative possibility. The bump could result from informational correction. Hedge funds take large positions in companies only after extensive analysis – they amount to a contemporary variant on the traditional "value investor."[65] When a hedge fund's position becomes public, it is possible that the market's valuation of the target is adjusted upward to reflect value thus signaled.

The studies take pains to show that stock picking does not drive the gains. They compare hostile to passive hedge fund engagements and show that hostility, which implies a forced change in the direction of the target's business plan, triggers bigger gains.[66] They also show that in the rare case of hedge fund defeat and withdrawal, the price bump is reversed.[67] And they point out that an investor looking for a signaling yield would move on quickly once its position became public, rather than hanging around for a year or two as do the hedge funds.[68] All of these points are well-taken.

But one wonders whether it has to be all one or all the other. To insist that hedge fund activism is solely about discipline and agency cost reduction is to cabin it inside the shareholder paradigm, ignoring the matters on the other side of the trade-off, information asymmetry, and myopia. Nothing in the numbers precludes the possibility that activists could be aggravating management's myopic tendencies. At the same time, it has been forcefully suggested that activist intervention ameliorates information asymmetries, by providing a channel through which credible information about fundamental value is dispersed into the market, ameliorating myopia.[69]

63 See J. Huang, "Hedge Funds and Shareholder Wealth Gains in Leveraged Buyouts" (2009), available at http://ssrn.com/abstract=1086687

64 Eckbo, above n 12 at 3.

65 W.W. Bratton, "Hedge Funds and Governance Targets" (2007) 95 *Georgetown Law Journal* 1375.

66 Brav, Jiang, and Him, above n 49 at 231.

67 *Ibid.* at 232.

68 *Ibid.*

69 A. Edmans, "Blockholder Trading, Market Efficiency, and Managerial Myopia" (2009) 64 *Journal of Finance* 2481 at 2482–4.

11.3.3 Resolution

Financial economics weighs in for the hedge fund activists on both sides of the trade-off. The stock price bump is the mainspring result, and it, to some extent, reflects the intervention's impact on the business. But it is important to look also at the informational side and activist interventions enrich the market's base of information. Meanwhile, there are no cognizable showings of harm. If, as is appropriate in the present environment, the burden of proof falls on the activists' opponents, then the case for section 13(d) reform and for triennial boards fails accordingly.

11.4 Conclusion

The presumption against law reform mooted and applied in this chapter is not intended to be universally preclusive. This chapter's commendation follows from current events rather than from some reflexive conservatism.

Shareholders are putting the corporate franchise to unprecedented uses. There is a steady stream of new initiatives. For example, Section 11.3.1 above posits that shareholder agenda control could prove irrelevant due to disuse, pointing, among other things, to the fact that shareholders have not been making use of a new statutory access point that facilitates proxy access. Right now this is a fair point. A year from now it could ring hollow. Shareholder-sponsored amendments to mandate proxy access have shown up on more than hundred corporate proxy statements already in 2015.[70] If this new crop of proposals does well, more will follow and shareholder-catering managers will begin adopting proxy access voluntarily.

At that point, shareholder proponents will go on to something else. There is a growing cadre of professional governance intermediaries, actors at proxy advisory services along with the actors at investment institutions who set the agenda and direct the voting. The intermediaries have a common interest: maintaining and promoting an active reform agenda that progressively enhances shareholder power, which also enhances the intermediaries' sphere of influence. Trade-off possibilities are dismissed as the intermediaries herd from one agenda item to another.

We will not know where we are until the stampede stops. In such circumstances, law reform is not only unnecessary but potentially destructive.

[70] See Wachtell, Lipton, Rosen, and Katz, "The Unintended Consequences of Proxy Access Elections" (Corporate Governance Update, March 2015).

12

Board Accountability and the Entity Maximization and Sustainability Approach

ANDREW KEAY

12.1 Introduction

Undoubtedly the accountability of boards is regarded as a critical issue in corporate governance. The OECD has stated that "[t]he corporate governance framework should ensure the strategic guidance of the company, the effective monitoring of management by the board, and the board's accountability to the company and the shareholders."[1] In the report of the Cadbury Committee on the Financial Aspects of Corporate Governance[2] (commonly referred to as "the Cadbury Report"), delivered in 1992, the central issue for corporate governance was said to be: how to strengthen the accountability of boards of directors to shareholders.[3] It has been said that good corporate governance is able to be best achieved by holding directors accountable for their behavior and decisions.[4] It has been argued that accountability of directors is at the heart of corporate governance[5] and a cornerstone of good corporate governance.[6] Good corporate governance is able to be best achieved by focusing on the accountability of directors,

1 Organisation for Economic Co-Operation and Development, "OECD Principles of Corporate Governance" (2004), available at www.oecd.org/dataoecd/32/18/31557724.pdf, at 24.

2 Cadbury Committee on the Financial Aspects of Corporate Governance, *Report of the Committee on the Financial Aspects of Corporate Governance* (London: Gee, 1992).

3 *Ibid.* at para. 6.1.

4 J. Solomon and A. Solomon, *Corporate Governance and Accountability* (Chichester: John Wiley & Sons, 2004), p. 14; E. Makuta, "Towards Good Corporate Governance in State-Owned Industries: The Accountability of Directors" (2009) 3 *Malawi Law Journal* 55 at 56.

5 A. Belcher, *Directors' Decisions and the Law* (Abingdon: Routledge, 2014), p. 183.

6 A. Young, "Frameworks in Regulating Company Directors: Rethinking the Philosophical Foundations to Enhance Accountability" (2009) 30 *Company Lawyer* 355 at 356.

and it can be argued that accountability of directors is the basis for the success of all other principles of corporate governance.[7]

The issue of accountability has been raised as a major issue at very important points of time over the years and particularly following scandals like Enron and Worldcom in the early days of this century. Certainly the Cadbury Committee was established shortly after scandals involving UK companies, such as Polly Peck and Maxwell Communications. According to the Cadbury Report, its purpose was "to review those aspects of corporate governance specifically related to financial reporting and accountability."[8] It also stated that while boards have to be free to take their companies forward, in doing so they must operate within a framework of effective accountability, and this is the essence of any system of good corporate governance.[9] One of the leading problems in corporate governance is the fact that what accountability involves and how it is worked out in practice has not been identified and thought through properly.

The fact that the accountability of boards is essential to corporate governance means that the nature of corporate governance is an important matter. There are various theories of corporate governance and these are tied to theories devised to identify and articulate what is to be the objective of a company. A recent approach that does this is the entity maximization and sustainability theory (EMS). This holds essentially that the directors are to endeavor to maximize the wealth of the corporate entity by increasing the overall long-run market value of the company as a whole and at the same time to ensure that the life of the company is sustained, that is, it survives. It provides an alternative to other theories such as the shareholder value and stakeholder theories. This chapter focuses on EMS in relation to board accountability, and because of space limitations its aim is to explore perhaps the primary issue as far as board accountability is concerned:[10] to whom is the board accountable?

This chapter develops in the following way. First, there is a brief explanation of what board accountability involves. Second, there is a short discussion of the essence of the EMS theory. In the third and main part of this chapter, there is an examination of the question to whom the board should

[7] Makuta, above n 4. While the commentator was writing about the corporate governance of State Owned Enterprises, it is argued that the comment is as applicable to the normal commercial public company.

[8] *Cadbury Report*, above n 2 at para. 1.2. However, the Report's definition of "corporate governance" did not include an express reference to "accountability" (para. 2.5).

[9] *Ibid.* at para. 1.1.

[10] This is the same for accountability in any areas of society: J. Lerner and P. Tetlock, "Accounting for the Effects of Accountability" (1999) 125 *Psychology Bulletin* 255 at 259.

be accountable in an EMS framework. Finally, there are some concluding remarks.

12.2 Board Accountability

As noted at the beginning of this chapter, accountability has been mentioned frequently in the corporate governance literature and relied on as a critical factor in corporate governance.[11] It has also been used in definitions of corporate governance. Nevertheless, there have been few attempts to explain what it actually means, certainly in the context of corporate governance. This is not the case in other areas of law and society, such as in public administration, politics and even administrative law, where there have been several helpful contributions.[12] A recent study[13] has argued that accountability in relation to boards is concerned with a number of elements and is a process that involves several stages. These stages must be preceded by boards accepting responsibility for what they do and the need to be answerable.[14] Unless boards realize and acknowledge that accountability constitutes an essential part of corporate governance then there cannot be worthwhile and effective accountability. Boards could always take action to stymie many of the accountability mechanisms that are in place if they wished to do so. This element does not, of itself, require any action, necessarily, but involves a mindset that should exist within a board.

It has been argued that there are four stages to accountability[15]:

- The first stage entails the board providing accurate information concerning its decisions and actions, so that the ones to whom the account

[11] For a detailed discussion of the issue, see A. Keay, *Board Accountability in Corporate Governance* (Abingdon: Routledge, 2015).

[12] For instance, see A. Sinclair, "The Chameleon of Accountability: Forms and Discourses" (1995) 20 *Accounting, Organizations and Society* 219; R. Mulgan, "'Accountability': An Ever Expanding Concept?" (2000) 78 *Public Administration* 555; M. Dubnick, "Accountability and Ethics: Reconsidering the Relationships" (2005) 6 *International Journal of Organization Theory and Behavior* 405; J. Koppell, "Pathologies of Accountability: ICANN and the Challenge of 'Multiple Accountabilities Disorder'" (2005) 65 *Public Administration Review* 94; M. Bovens, "Two Concepts of Accountability" (2010) 33 *West European Politics* 946; M. Dubnick and K. Yang, "The Pursuit of Accountability: Promise, Problems and Prospects" (2010), available at http://chapters.ssrn.com/abstract=1548922, at 3.

[13] A. Keay and J. Loughrey, "The Framework for Board Accountability in Corporate Governance" (2015) 35 *Legal Studies* 252.

[14] Canadian Democracy and Corporate Accountability Commission, "Canadian Democracy and Corporate Accountability: An Overview of Issues" (2001) at iii.

[15] Keay and Loughrey, above n 13.

is being given are informed as to what has been done. This part constitutes disclosing and reporting, and certainly candid reporting is an essential element of it.[16] Inter alia, this addresses the problem of information asymmetry.

- The second stage involves a board explaining and justifying its actions, omissions, risks, and dependencies for which it is responsible.[17] Often this is seen as the primary aspect of accountability and is the stage that is focused on in much of the accountability literature. It has been referred to as constituting explanatory accountability[18] and it includes the notion of being answerable, a key element of accountability.[19] This explanatory stage, together with the disclosure stage, produce transparency, as they lay bare what has occurred; it provides truthful information about the board's actions. The element of justification provides a check on the decision-making of the board, and acts in such a way as to move the balance between director accountability and director power somewhat toward the former.
- The third stage is constituted by the questioning and evaluating of the reasons provided by the board for what it has done. This allows for analysis of the actions of boards.
- Fourth, the final stage is that there is the possibility, but not the requirement, of the imposition of consequences. This might simply constitute feedback and may not necessarily entail negative consequences being imposed, but on many occasions it is likely that it will.[20]

12.3 Entity Maximization and Sustainability Theory

Jonathan Macey has said, in relation to the two leading governance theories, that no company can sustain the abstract goal of shareholder wealth maximization or the broad stakeholder model.[21] Thus, EMS was

[16] A. Licht, "Accountability and Corporate Governance" (2002), available at http://ssrn.com/abstract=328401, at 29.

[17] AccountAbility, "AA1000 Framework Standards for Social and Ethical Accounting, Auditing and Reporting" (1999), available at www.accountability.org/images/content/0/7/076/AA1000%20Overview.pdf, at 8.

[18] J. Uhr, "Redesigning Accountability: From Muddles to Maps" (1993) 65 *Australian Quarterly* 1 at 4.

[19] A. Quinn and B. Schlenker, "Can Accountability Produce Independence? Goals as Determinants of the Impact of Accountability on Conformity" (2002) 28 *Personality and Social Psychology Bulletin* 472 at 472; Mulgan, above n 12 at 569.

[20] This could involve censure or, in the most extreme case, removal of directors.

[21] L.A. Cunningham, "Convergence in Corporate Governance" (1999) 84 *Cornell Law Review* 1166 at 1172.

constructed to offer another alternative when addressing the issue of the ultimate objective of the company, and the basis for corporate governance development.[22] It has two elements to it. First, putting it simply, there is a commitment to maximize the wealth of the entity. Management should seek to develop the total wealth-creating potential of the enterprise that they oversee.[23] The second part is to sustain the company as a going concern, that is, to ensure its survival[24]; it will remain as a going concern.

A critical aspect of the model is that there is a focus on the company as an entity or enterprise, that is, "an institution in its own right."[25] The model assumes that the company has interests that are independent of any stakeholder, including shareholders, or group of stakeholders who affect the company or are affected by it. This model is company focused, and while the company owes something to each of its investors, it is owned by nobody[26] and it is not a composite of all of the individual products of each cooperating resource[27]; it is an end in itself, and it is not an instrument of anyone but a living and developing enterprise[28] that is autonomous[29] and has a life of its own. As Margaret Blair and Lynn Stout have said, once the shareholders have formed a company and selected a board, they have "created a new and separate entity that takes on a life of its own and could,

[22] For a full discussion of the theory, see A. Keay, *The Corporate Objective* (Cheltenham: Edward Elgar Publishing, 2011).

[23] See M. Blair, *Ownership and Control* (Washington, DC: The Brookings Institute, 1995), p. 239.

[24] The French Viénot Report in 1995 stated something that is similar: Viénot I Report, "The Boards of Directors of Listed Companies in France" (1995) at 8, and referred to in E. Pichet, "Enlightened Shareholder Value: Whose Interests Should be Served by the Supports of Corporate Governance" (2008), available at http://ssrn.com/abstract=1262879, at 16.

[25] W. Suojanen, "Accounting Theory and the Large Corporation" (1954) 29 *The Accounting Review* 391 at 392.

[26] C. Handy, "What is a Company for?" (1993) 1 *Corporate Governance: An International Review* 14 at 16.

[27] This was acknowledged as far back as 1972 and mentioned in the classic work on team production: A. Alchian and H. Demsetz, "Production, Information Costs and Economic Organizations" (1972) 62 *American Economic Review* 777 at 781–3. It would be impossible to find a single way of aggregating the interests of all stakeholders over time: S. Marshall and I. Ramsay, "Stakeholders and Directors' Duties: Law, Theory and Evidence" (2012) 35 *University of New South Wales Law Journal* 291.

[28] Handy, above n 26 at 17.

[29] This is the vision of the company in France: M. Viénot, "Rapport sur le Conseil d'Administration des Sociétés Cotées" (1995) 8 *Revue de Droit des Affaires Internationales* 935, referred to in A. Alcouffe and C. Alcouffe, "Control and Executive Compensation in Large French Companies" (1997) 24 *Journal of Law and Society* 85 at 91.

potentially, act against their interests."[30] The theory means that the directors are not under the direct control of the shareholders or any other stakeholder group. This allows the directors to make decisions which are best for the entity and not any shareholder or stakeholder. So, in making any decisions the directors must ask: what will benefit the company? Under EMS the company is not run for the benefit of the shareholders or any other stakeholders, but for itself. This is akin to sole traders who own and run a business, and they do so for their own benefit. As with a sole trader's operations, the company's operations will usually benefit others.

12.4 To Whom is the Board Accountable in EMS?

As mentioned at the outset, one of the primary issues with board accountability is ascertaining to whom the board is accountable and it is on that point that the balance of this chapter focuses. In shareholder value theory the board is said to be accountable to the shareholders of the company and this involves the board being accountable for, inter alia, maximizing shareholder wealth. A good instance of this approach was provided by the Cadbury Committee when it stated:

> Boards of directors are accountable to their shareholders and both have to play their part in making that accountability effective. Boards of directors need to do so through the quality of the information which they provide to shareholders, and the shareholders through their willingness to exercise their responsibilities as owners.[31]

In another popular theory, stakeholder theory, the board is said to be accountable to all of the company's stakeholders. But, what this means is unclear. In EMS theory, the directors owe their duties to the company entity. Thus it could be argued that it follows the board is accountable to the company. But what does that actually mean? Can it mean that the board is accountable to the board acting as the company? Stephen Bainbridge, as part of his director primacy theory, seems to think so as he says that board members will monitor each other and, presumably, be accountable to each other.[32] Thus the board is accountable to itself. Bainbridge asserts that the board is a small, close-knit group that works together over a significant

[30] M. Blair and L. Stout, "A Team Production Theory of Corporate Law" (1999) 85 *Virginia Law Review* 247 at 277.

[31] *Cadbury Report*, above n 2 at paras. 3.2–3.4.

[32] S. Bainbridge, *The New Corporate Governance* (New York: Oxford University Press, 2008), pp. 100–4.

period of time and this permits them to see how each other behaves. He goes on to say that appropriate norms develop and the board members can monitor whether they are adhering to them.[33] The commentator sees the board as a Platonic guardian.[34] But, it is contended that it is not rational to say that the directors as a board are accountable to the board acting for the company. While the board would be accounting to the company in the larger scheme of things, in reality it is accounting to itself. There must be accountability to some persons or body that is independent of the board, as any accountee (the one accounted to) in the accountability process must be independent of the accountor (the one who does the accounting).[35] So, let us rule out the board being accountable to itself. Therefore, what are the options? There appear to be two clear ones.

12.4.1 An Accounting Council

The first option is rather novel as far as Anglo-American companies are concerned. Such companies, unlike those in many countries, only have one board as part of their governance structure. One option is to introduce another board or body, to be known as "the accountability council" ("the council") that acts on behalf of the company and is the body to which the board accounts. The council would bear some general similarity to the supervisory board that is used in two-tier board systems such as in Germany. In Germany, the role of the supervisory board (*Aufsichtsrat*) is to monitor the management of the company and safeguard the company's interests.[36] The German Corporate Governance Code 2012 provides that the supervisory board is to "advise regularly and supervise the management board in the management of the enterprise. It must be involved in decisions of fundamental importance to the enterprise."[37] The council that is considered in this chapter would not have such a broad role or as extensive powers as the *Aufsichtsrat* for its only remit would be to act as

[33] *Ibid.*

[34] S.M. Bainbridge, "Director Primacy in Corporate Takeovers: Preliminary Reflections" (2002) 55 *Stanford Law Review* 791 at 795.

[35] See M. Elliott, "Ombudsman, Tribunals, Inquiries: Re-Fashioning Accountability Beyond the Courts" (2012), available at http://ssrn.com/abstract=2133879, at 2; Bovens, above n 12 at 957.

[36] Stock Corporation Act 2010 (*Aktiengesetz*), s. 111.

[37] German Corporate Governance Code 2012, available at www.ecgi.org/codes/documents/cg_code_germany_15may2012_en.pdf, at para. 5.1.1.

the accountee to the board. In this respect, it would be acting directly on behalf of the company.

Unlike in the German system where the *Vorstand* (the management board) is constituted solely by executive type directors, it is suggested that it would be preferable to retain the present constituency of the board in one-tier systems. That is, the board would continue to be comprised of both executive directors and non-executive directors. Monitoring would continue to be undertaken by the non-executive directors, and not, as in the German system, by a supervisory board. The retention of non-executives on the management board would mean that there would not be the same need for the council to monitor or be kept as informed as the supervisory board has to be in a two-tier system. However, the council would have to be empowered to seek information from the board and this is likely to mean that it is better informed and is able to posit more and better-informed questions of the board when compared to the general meeting under the present arrangements in Anglo-American corporate governance. It would be solely a review body. Of course, the council would not be prevented from acquiring information elsewhere than directly from the board and taking independent and external advice on what is presented to it. The members of the council would be subject to a duty to act in the best interests of the company. How this might work is set out below.

In corporate governance systems with dual boards the management board is generally accountable to the supervisory board,[38] so the existing system could remain in companies with two-tier boards, to ensure accountability if EMS is practiced[39]; the supervisory board would act as accountee (that is, the one to whom an account is given). This board does already act as accountee and usually has the power to dismiss the members of the board of directors.[40] Also, the supervisory board may bring company actions against the members of the board of directors, just as shareholders

[38] A. Belcher and T. Naruisch, "The Evolution of Business Knowledge in the Context of Unitary and Two-Tier Board Structures" (2005) *Journal of Business Law* 443 at 451; S. Goo and F. Hong, "The Curious Model of Internal Monitoring Mechanisms of Listed Companies in China: The Sinonisation Process" (2011) 12 *European Business Organizations Law Review* 469 at 476.

[39] An exception is China as the board of directors is accountable to the shareholders and not the supervisory board. See Company Law 2005, Art. 46.

[40] Stock Corporation Act 2010, s. 84(3). See, R. Ghezzi and C. Malberti, "The Two-Tier Model and the One-Tier Model of Corporate Governance in the Italian Reform of Corporate Law" (2008) 5 *European Company and Financial Law Review* 1 at 13; J. Warchol, "The Balance of Power in Polish Company Code Regulations" (2011) 8 *European Company and Financial Law Review* 174 at 191.

may, using derivative proceedings.[41] To whom is the supervisory board accountable? This is not stated in legislation or codes, but as this board is selected, in the German framework, by the shareholders and employees one might think that the board is accountable to these two stakeholder groups. These groups have the power to decline to reelect board members.

If the proposal concerning the creation of the council were able to be implemented in relation to Anglo-American companies, then the powers of the council would have to be established. It is not possible, given space limitations, to flesh out all of the powers that should be granted to the council, although I would not envisage there would be a huge number. Here are a few. First, it should be awarded the power to remove directors. Second, it should be required to make a report to the general meeting prior to meetings of that body, and especially before the Annual General Meeting (AGM). Third, the council should be entitled to require at any time a report from the board on the affairs of the company. This should ensure that the council has sufficient and detailed information to allow for questioning and evaluation of the board's explanations of what it has done or not done. Fourth, the council should be permitted to inspect and examine the books and records of the company, or appoint special experts to carry out such inspection and examination. Fifth, it should be able to call a shareholders' meeting whenever the interests of the company so require.

The council itself will also need to be accountable. It is probably appropriate that it is accountable to the general meeting. The problem with this is that it might be thought that the shareholders will take action according to their own interests and this would not appeal to other stakeholders of the company. Although it could be said that the shareholders might not be as influential in the proposed system as they would in the present system, it is still a matter of concern. More is to be said about this issue later, but suffice it to say that the shareholders should be under a duty to act in the best interests of the company when dealing with the accounting of the council.

The safeguard in this option for non-shareholders is that it has been proposed that in an EMS approach a broader range of people could institute derivative actions against defaulting directors and others.[42] This would include being able to initiate a derivative action against the council if it

[41] K. Hopt and P. Leyens, "Board Models in Europe – Recent Developments of Internal Corporate Governance Structures in German, the United Kingdom, France and Italy" (2004) 1 *European Company and Financial Law Review* 135 at 142.

[42] A. Keay, "The Ultimate Objective of the Public Company and the Enforcement of the Entity Maximization and Sustainability Model" (2010) 10 *Journal of Corporate Law Studies* 35.

fails to act in the best interests of the company or contravenes any other mandate imposed on it. Ordinarily in most systems, such as the United Kingdom, derivative actions are only available to shareholders. But it has been argued that the range of persons who would be entitled to institute these proceedings could be widened.[43] There are jurisdictions where the right to bring derivative actions is granted to persons other than shareholders.[44] It might make sense to limit derivative actions to shareholders if a shareholder value approach is implemented, but if an EMS approach is taken it makes sense to give the right to anyone who has an interest in the company to bring proceedings.[45] In articulating their team production approach to corporate law, Margaret Blair and Lynn Stout argue that the shareholders in bringing derivative actions act as proxies for all those with claims on the company.[46] But, while such proceedings are designed to obtain some relief for the company, it might be argued that shareholders do not take proceedings in relation to actions of the board unless they are convinced that either they will benefit from the proceedings, at least indirectly, or the action of the board is likely to harm them in the short term or even in the long term. It is probable that whether or not shareholders would be prepared to institute derivative proceedings will very much depend on what the directors have done. Some actions that the directors take, in contravention of EMS, might well lead shareholders to reason that the action taken would end up, indirectly, adversely affecting the shareholders, so they will consider proceeding. But other board actions that might not be said to fulfill the EMS demand will not adversely affect shareholders, and might even benefit them, and in such cases no shareholder is likely to take proceedings to ensure that the wrong is corrected.

It is implicit in the EMS model that all those who have effectively invested in the company should be entitled to take action to safeguard the wealth of the company entity, in which they have a potential distinct interest, albeit one that is not vested or able to be calculated. As a consequence, there needs to be an enforcement mechanism that is more encompassing. If what is proposed above were to be put into effect then the fact that one

[43] *Ibid.*

[44] Examples are Canada, South Africa, and Singapore.

[45] One commentator accepts the need for it in relation to creditors: R.B. Campbell, Jr., "Corporate Fiduciary Principles for the Post-Contractarian Era" (1996) 23 *Florida State University Law Review* 561 at 606.

[46] Blair and Stout, above n 30 at 293. David Millon doubts this, see D. Millon, "New Game Plan or Business as Usual? A Critique of the Team Production Model of Corporate Law" (2000) 86 *Virginia Law Review* 1001 at 1013.

is broadening the range of those who can bring proceedings could mean that there is an increase in the chances of a company's interests being protected, because it leads to the knowledge of more people being brought to consider the company's position and some stakeholders might well have greater knowledge than the shareholders. It is envisaged that the present situation that exists in many countries where a person who wishes to institute a derivative action is required first to seek court approval to proceed would remain and it would enable a court to determine if the applicant is a person who is entitled to bring such an action and has a substantial and good faith claim.

It has also been argued that besides private persons being able to instigate derivative actions power should be given to an appropriately staffed and funded public authority to be able to file derivative proceedings where this power does not presently exist, as is the case in the United States and the United Kingdom.[47] The argument is based, inter alia, on the following grounds. It could foster greater accountability of directors, deter improper activity, enhance the public interest, and protect all kinds of investors.[48] Such a power could bolster the confidence of all stakeholders in the system.

Perhaps the leading benefit of the introduction of the council is that it is likely that it could be a more effective body as far as requiring an account to be given and taking the role away from the general meeting might avoid the problem of individual, or groups of, shareholders only being concerned about their own interests. Thus, the council might have greater credibility as an accountee body than the general meeting in the eyes of stakeholders, the government and the public. What would be important to ensure is that the role of the council would not overlap significantly with that of the non-executive directors, so that confusion as to who does what is avoided as is the incurring of unnecessary cost.[49]

Perhaps one of the major issues with this option relates to the constitution of the council. The establishment of the council might provide an opportunity to widen the involvement of stakeholders in the governance process, something argued for many years by pluralists. The argument has been put that a board of directors should be representative of all of

[47] A. Keay, "The Public Enforcement of Directors' Duties: A Normative Inquiry" (2014) 43 *Common Law World Review* 89.

[48] *Ibid.*

[49] Clearly there is confusion in China where companies have both a supervisory board and non-executive directors on the management board.

the stakeholders in a company.[50] The problem with this has been that it is difficult to see how it would work. It would also be difficult to find a way of having all stakeholders involved in the appointment of the council,[51] and all stakeholders being represented. To be realistic it is likely that it would not be acceptable to many in government and even less so to those engaged in commercial life. Nevertheless it might well be possible to have the councils in public companies appointed in accordance with the approach adopted in Germany in relation to large public companies where half of the members of the *Aufsichtsrat* are appointed by the shareholders and the other half by the employees with the Chair being appointed by the shareholders. The Chair has a casting vote in the event of a tie.

While there have been many criticisms aimed at the governance process in the German system, overall it seems to have worked reasonably well. Also, employees are a major group in a company's performance and contribute firm-specific capital.[52] In fact having representation of workers on a board is seen by many as something that is desperately needed.[53] Admittedly in many, if not most, countries that practice the Anglo-American system of corporate governance, and particularly the United States and the United Kingdom, the idea of workers sitting on a council would not be well received by all and would probably be given a cool reception by many. Shareholder groups are likely to be against it. The proposal is not going to be an attractive proposition to many shareholders as they are not going to be the direct accountees of the board and they might be concerned about the fact that the council is constituted by some who are nominated by employees, and whose interests might diverge from those of some shareholders. In 1997, Sally Wheeler observed that the notion of employee representation at board level in the United Kingdom,

[50] For example, K. Greenfield, "Saving the World with Corporate Law" (2008) 57 *Emory Law Journal* 947 at 978; F. Post, "A Response to 'The Social Responsibility of Corporate Management: A Classical Critique'" (2003) 18 *Mid-American Journal of Business* 25 at 32.

[51] This was also the opinion of the Viénot Report in France. It said that if board members were appointed to represent certain interest groups it would not be desirable. The result could well be to make the board a focus for conflicts between such groups instead of collectively representing the interests of all shareholders as it is supposed to. See Viénot I Report, above n 24, available at www.ecgi.org/codes/documents/vienot1_en.pdf, at 13–14.

[52] M. O'Connor, "The Human Capital Era" (1993) 78 *Cornell Law Review* 899; Blair, above n 23; L. Zingales, "In Search of New Foundations" (2000) 55 *Journal of Finance* 1623.

[53] Aspen Institute Business and Society Program, "Unpacking Corporate Purpose: A Report on the Beliefs of Executives, Investors and Scholars" (2014), available at www.aspeninstitute.org/sites/default/files/content/upload/Unpacking%20Corporate%20Purpose%20May%202014.pdf, at 47.

and other countries, was not likely to happen given the then capitalist agenda,[54] and the same can probably be said today. There continues to be resistance to worker participation in a number of circles. It was evident recently when proposals to have worker representatives on the remuneration committee of UK boards[55] were speedily dismissed. There have been several arguments against employee involvement in the United Kingdom, such that it would circumscribe open discussion. But while that argument might have, to some degree, application to the council, it is not likely that free discussion would be hampered as much as it might be at the board level where ideas receive their genesis and where arguments are likely to be more vigorous and extensive, especially on issues of policy and strategy. The council is a review body and, while it might see its fair share of arguments, there is probably less room for debate about policy and strategy.

The council does not need to be large, although it must be of sufficient size to ensure that it is reasonably wide in representation. Given the fact that gender has been an issue in the management of companies, it might be appropriate to set some sort of minimum level for female members.[56] This, together with the inclusion of employee representatives, should go some way to addressing the criticism often directed at boards in the United States and the United Kingdom that they are made-up, on the whole, by middle-aged, well-connected white males with similar socioeconomic and educational backgrounds.

It is emphasized that what is proposed is not a "carbon copy" of the German system, and really there are few changes needed to the present

[54] S. Wheeler, "Works Councils: Towards Stakeholding?" (1997) 24 *Journal of Law and Society* 44 at 46.

[55] Trades Union Congress, "Worker Representatives Can Curb Excess Pay at the Top" (2012), available at www.tuc.org.uk/economic-issues/economic-analysis/worker-representatives-can-curb-excess-pay-top; *Executive and Remuneration Bill*, Bill No. 105, presented by Thomas Docherty (House of Commons, 2013–14), available at www.publications.parliament.uk/pa/bills/cbill/2013-2014/0105/14105.pdf; Department of Business, Innovation and Skills, "Executive Remuneration Discussion Chapter: Summary of Responses" (January 2012), available at www.gov.uk/government/uploads/system/uploads/attachment_data/file/31381/12-564-executive-remuneration-discussion-chapter-summary-responses.pdf. The Trades Union Congress has been calling for employee representation on remuneration committees since the 1990s. See M. Carley, "Discussions about Whether Workers should Help Set Executive Pay" (2011) EIROnline, available at www.eurofound.europa.eu/eiro/2011/10/articles/uk1110029i.htm

[56] See, e.g., the practice in Germany: Act on Equal Participation of Women and Men regarding Leadership Positions within the Sectors of Private Economy and Public Service ("Gesetz für die gleichberechtigte Teilhabe von Frauen und Männern an Führungspositionen in der Privatwirtschaft und im öffentlichen Dienst") (2015).

setup that exists in one-tier board systems. The constitution of the board would be the same, and the shareholders still appoint the directors and retain some monitoring roles.

A disadvantage of the changes proposed would be some increase in costs, as the council members would have to be paid a fee and expenses and there would need to be some administrative support provided to the council. The council would only need to meet infrequently, say twice yearly, as the non-executives on the board should be able to monitor the managers and they will be attending regular board meetings, so it is not likely that the overall cost would be substantial, given the fact that the proposal only covers public companies. Nevertheless, smaller public companies could find the cost onerous, so it might be appropriate to limit the proposal to public companies of a particular size by establishing some minimum criteria that must exist in relation to a company before a council must be established.

12.4.2 The General Meeting

The second option is that the board is accountable to the general meeting, which obviously is a similar situation to that which applies in many jurisdictions already. But it must be emphasized that in this role as accountee, as in all of its roles, the general meeting is acting as and for the company.[57] Like the board, the general meeting is entitled in this capacity to define the will of the company.[58] In no way does the board or the general meeting express the will of the shareholders,[59] nor do they act for the shareholders; they act for the company itself. Generally speaking, the shareholders cannot interfere in the exercise of the powers that are given to the board under the articles of association (bylaws) except in very limited circumstances.[60] But that does not impede the general meeting from acting as the accountee of the board. In this capacity, it would not be interfering in the exercise of the powers of the board directly as it would only be acting as a review body

[57] L. Sealy and S. Worthington, *Sealy and Worthington's Cases and Materials in Company Law* (Oxford: Oxford University Press, 2013), p. 179. Certain powers may be reserved for the general meeting to be exercised on behalf of the company: *John Shaw & Sons Ltd.* v. *Shaw* [1935] 2 KB 113 at 134.

[58] R. Flannigan, "Shareholder Fiduciary Duties" (2014) *Journal of Business Law* 1 at 9.

[59] *Ibid.* at 5.

[60] *John Shaw & Sons Ltd.* v. *Shaw*, above n 57 at 134; *NRMA* v. *Parker* (1986) 4 ACLC 609 at 613–14; *Auer* v. *Dressel*, 118 NE 2d 590 at 594 (1954). Also, see, *Automatic Self-Cleansing Filter Syndicate Co. Ltd.* v. *Cunninghame* [1906] 2 chapter 34 at 44; *Ashburton Oil NL* v. *Alpha Minerals NL* (1971) 123 CLR 614.

and only be able to do those things permitted by the relevant companies legislation, the articles of association, and possibly any code that operates. Stephen Bottomley states that accountability is in fact one reason for the dual division and separation of the decision-making powers in the company between the board and the general meeting.[61]

Under this second option, when the shareholders are acting in the general meeting they are acting for the company and carrying out an accountability role. This option, where the shareholders alone are placed in a position to scrutinize what the board has done will not appeal to many, and certainly those attracted to EMS, on the basis that it is not reasonable and fair. At the general meeting the shareholders might well be biased and there might well be a tendency to be concerned only about how their own interests individually, or as a member of a group of shareholders, will be served and these interests might well not be consistent with those of the company, and contrary to EMS, and are certainly not likely to be consistent with all or even some of the wider interests that contribute to the enhancement of the company's wealth. Given past performance, shareholders might be overly concerned with favoring what gives them short-term gains. Furthermore, shareholders can have serious conflicts of interest with other shareholders arising from their other relationships with the company, from their investments in derivatives or securities issued by other companies, from their investments in other parts of the company's capital structure, and from their short-term investment focus.[62] If the general meeting has to be the body that effectively acts as accountee is there not a danger in some companies of it only being concerned to benefit some of the members or to produce short-term benefits? So, for instance, if the directors did act in such a way as to benefit shareholder interests alone, and did not consider the interests of the company, then it is unlikely that the shareholders will, in an accounting role, question what the directors have done. If the members in general meeting are said to be acting on behalf of the company (the accountee), cannot it be said that they should be putting aside their own selfish interests and acting in what are the best interests of the company?

To address this issue are we able to say that the shareholders owe a duty to act in the best interests of the company? It must be noted at the outset that what is being mooted here is a duty imposed on the shareholders in general meeting and not a duty on shareholders across the board

[61] S. Bottomley, *The Constitutional Corporation* (Aldershot: Ashgate, 2007), p. 73.

[62] I. Anabtawi and L. Stout, "Fiduciary Duties for Activist Shareholders" (2008) 60 *Stanford Law Review* 1255 at 1261.

and in everything that they do. Arguably, the concern about shareholder bias would not be as strong if the shareholders, like the directors, were subject to fiduciary duties[63] and had to act in the best interests of the company, with this meaning the company entity and not the shareholders as a whole. But the problem with this is that the general position that is usually posited as being taken around the world is that, unlike directors, shareholders may use the rights in their shares, such as the power to vote, as they wish and they do not owe duties. Most commentators in the United States, as opposed to those in other jurisdictions such as the United Kingdom, generally accept that controlling shareholders are regarded as owing a fiduciary duty.[64] But where there is no control exerted by a majority shareholder, as the case is with most public companies (a majority is only usually obtained by organizing a broad coalition of shareholders), the shareholders are entitled to vote in general meetings in a selfish manner.[65] In this respect it has been said, as far as US companies are concerned, that, "American public shareholders are uniquely blessed by the freedom to do what they will . . . [S]hareholders owe the corporation no legal duties."[66] This is generally accurate in the US save where controlling shareholders are concerned.[67] Moreover, it is generally said to be the position in the United Kingdom in relation to any company. The comment of Jessel MR exemplifies this approach when he said that "those who have the rights

[63] The roots of fiduciary duties are explained in the old English case of *Bishop of Woodhouse* v. *Meredith* (1820) 1 Jac & W 204 at 213.

[64] See, e.g., *Kahn* v. *Lynch Communications Systems Inc.*, 638 A 2d 1110 (1994); *Ivanhoe Partners* v. *Newmont Mining Corp.*, 535 A 2d 1334 at 1344 (1989); *Linge* v. *Ralston Purina Co.*, 293 NW 2d 191 (Iowa S. Ct. 1980); *Donahue* v. *Rodd Electrotype Co. of New England*, 367 Mass. 578, 328 NE 2d 505 (1975); Z. Cohen, "Fiduciary Duties of Controlling Shareholders: A Comparative View" (1991) 12 *University of Pennsylvania Journal of International Business Law* 379. R. Karmel, "Should a Duty Be Imposed on Institutional Shareholders?" (2004) 60 *Business Lawyer* 1 at 2; D. Donald, "Shareholder Voice and Its Opponents" (2005) 5 *Journal of Corporate Law Studies* 305 at 320 and following. Note the robust rejection of a duty existing by P. Dalley, "The Misguided Doctrine of Stockholder Fiduciary Duties" (2004) 33 *Hofstra Law Review* 175; P. Dalley, "Shareholder and (Director) Fiduciary Duties and Shareholder Activism" (2008) 8 *Houston Business and Tax Law Journal* 301.

[65] R. Gilson and J. Gordon, "Controlling Shareholders" (2005) 152 *University of Pennsylvania Law Review* 785 at 786. See also M. de Jongh, "Shareholders' Duties to the Company and Fellow Shareholders" (2012) 9 *European Company Law* 185, discussing the Dutch approach.

[66] D. Hoffman, "The 'Duty' to Be a Rational Shareholder" (2006) 90 *Minnesota Law Review* 537 at 537.

[67] D. Block, N. Barton, and S. Radin, *The Business Judgment Rule* (New York: Aspen Law and Business, 1996), pp. 368–9.

of property are entitled to exercise them, whatever their motives may be for such exercise – that is as regards a court of law as distinguished from a court of morality or conscience, if such a court exists."[68]

But is this in fact the position at law. Are shareholders in general meeting subject to fiduciary duties? If not, should they be? It is not intended to discuss in any depth what fiduciary duties are as it is a complex subject that has been considered on many occasions,[69] and the concept is rather elusive. The original notion of fiduciary duty is a product of equity concerning the duty of a person in a discretionary position of trust to serve the interests of another person.[70] What the courts have said about those subject to fiduciary duties is that loyalty is the distinguishing obligation of such persons.[71] The fundamental aspect of loyalty is that a fiduciary acts for proper purposes and without self-interest and in another person's interests.[72] According to Millett LJ in the English Court of Appeal in *Bristol and West Building Society* v. *Mothew*[73]: "[t]he principal is entitled to the single-minded loyalty of his fiduciary . . . he may not act . . . for the benefit of a third person without the informed consent of his principal."[74] Millett LJ said, in this case, that fiduciary duty is restricted to duties that are peculiar to fiduciaries and if they are breached it leads to different consequences from the breach of other duties.[75] Certain relationships have been identified as being fiduciary in nature, such as solicitors/attorneys (in relation to their clients), partners, trustees, agents (but not always), and company directors.

[68] Cohen, above n 64 at 381.

[69] For instance, A. Scott, "The Fiduciary Principle" (1949) 37 *California Law Review* 539; P. Finn, *Fiduciary Obligations* (Sydney: Law Book Co, 1977); D. DeMott, "Beyond Metaphor: An Analysis of Fiduciary Obligation" (1988) *Duke Law Journal* 879; R. Cooter and B. Freedman, "The Fiduciary Relationship: Its Economic Character and Legal Consequences" (1991) 66 *New York University Law Review* 1045; P. Finn, "Fiduciary Law and the Modern Commercial World," in E. McKendrick (ed.), *Commercial Aspects of Trusts and Fiduciary Obligations* (Oxford: Clarendon Press, 1992); M. Conaglen, "The Nature and Function of Fiduciary Loyalty" (2005) 121 *Law Quarterly Review* 452; J. Edelman, "When Do Fiduciary Duties Arise?" (2010) 126 *Law Quarterly Review* 302; A. Stafford and S. Ritchie, *Fiduciary Duties* (Bristol: Jordans, 2014).

[70] See *Re Smith & Fawcett Ltd.* [1942] chapter 304 at 306, 308; *Hospital Products Ltd* v. *United States Surgical Corp.* (1984) 156 CLR 41.

[71] *Bristol and West Building Society* v. *Mothew* [1998] 1 chapter 1 at 18.

[72] A. Scott, "The Fiduciary Principle" (1949) 37 *California Law Review* 539 at 540.

[73] *Bristol and West Building Society*, above n 71.

[74] *Ibid.* at 18.

[75] *Ibid.* at 16.

As foreshadowed earlier, traditionally shareholders are not recognized as being under fiduciary duties.[76] But people other than those who fall into traditional relationships can be subject to fiduciary duties. Paul Finn stated, in a comment that was adopted by the English Court of Appeal, that a person "is not subject to fiduciary obligations because he is a fiduciary; it is because he is subject to them that he is a fiduciary."[77] A person is, therefore, a "fiduciary" when it is determined that particular duties are owed.

It only seems proper that when shareholders are, like directors on the board, acting for the company, they should be required to focus on the company's best interests and have a duty to the company. And often, of course, their interests will coincide with the company's, although perhaps not always.

It is my view that there are some reasonably weighty arguments from case law in favor of the contention that shareholders do owe a duty to their company to act in the interests of the company when they are congregating as the general meeting of the company. These arguments follow from an analysis of the case law in the United Kingdom and other Commonwealth jurisdictions,[78] the thrust of which is often seen as providing that only two limitations are placed on shareholders in how they vote. First they must act in good faith for the benefit of the company in voting on a motion to alter the company's constitution,[79] and second they must not commit a fraud on the minority in exercising their votes. The concept of a fraud on the minority is one that has been developed over the years by the courts. It is not easily subject to clear exposition and there is no obvious principle that can be extrapolated from the cases,[80] but it does cover the situation where the majority expropriates either the assets of the company or the interest of the minority in the company for the use of the majority. In such cases, this action is not able to be ratified by the general meeting.

[76] Most of the discussion in recent times has been concerning making intermediaries who invest on behalf of pension funds, etc. in companies subject to fiduciary duties. See Law Commission of England and Wales, *Fiduciary Duties of Investment Intermediaries*, Consultation Chapter No. 215 (October 2013), available at http://lawcommission.justice.gov.uk/docs/cp215_fiduciary_duties.pdf

[77] *Bristol and West Building Society*, above n 71 at 18.

[78] For an examination of some of the pertinent issues, see Flannigan, above n 58; Keay, above n 11 at chapter 4.

[79] The leading case in the United Kingdom and much of the Commonwealth is usually regarded as *Allen* v. *Gold Reefs of West Africa Ltd.* [1900] 1 chapter 656 (CA).

[80] See *Clemens* v. *Clemens Bros. Ltd.* [1976] 2 All ER 268 at 282.

So, while the case law has not developed clearly and logically, it is possible to see a line of United Kingdom and Commonwealth cases that indicate that a middle way has been adopted, one that does not involve the embracing of a duty to the company and one that does not allow shareholders to act completely freely in all situations. Why shareholders are only required to rein in their selfishness in the situations mentioned above and not more broadly is unclear. It is contended that it is correct to say that there is a lack of uniformity in the English and Commonwealth jurisprudence on the obligations of shareholders.[81] However, due to space limitations, I am not able to pursue those arguments or elaborate on them in this chapter. I will accept for present purposes that there is law that says that shareholders can always please themselves when exercising their votes in general meetings save in the circumstances mentioned earlier.

What I want to suggest is that whatever is the state of the law there is a solid normative argument that supports the fact that a duty should exist when shareholders are in a general meeting and acting as the company. The recognition of a duty would, quite rightly, acknowledge the legal status of the company entity and the fact that the general meeting must act on its behalf and for its independent interests. The following reasons are given in support of this normative argument.

First, it makes sense that if the members of the board are subject to duties the members of the general meeting, when acting for the company, are also subject to duties. For just as the board acts for the company when making decisions within its authority, so the general meeting acts for the company when involved in the making of decisions within its authority. Shareholders can use their votes in meetings to indulge in opportunism, just as directors can, and this could involve voting for the company to take a particular course of action that could produce some personal gain for shareholders, but to the detriment of the company. Shareholder opportunism could also lead, inter alia, to externalizing the cost of providing benefits to shareholders. As Iman Anabtawi and Lynn Stout have said: "there is no reason to assume that activist shareholders are somehow impervious to the same temptations of greed and self-interest that are widely understood to face corporate officers and directors."[82]

There will be occasions where shareholders can vote for their own interests, such as where there is debate over the power to compulsorily

[81] Cohen, above n 64 at 384.

[82] Anabtawi and Stout, above n 62 at 1262.

dispose of, or expropriate, shareholders' shares,[83] and where the corporate entity has no interest in what is decided. This is something that was recognized by the Privy Council in *Citco Banking Corp NV* v. *Prusser's Ltd.*[84] But clearly it has been accepted in several decisions that the company is a distinct entity that is separate from the shareholders,[85] so consideration must be for its interests and not those of the shareholders when the general meeting is acting as the company.

Second, in the establishment of the company the expectation is that the shareholders, when part of the general meeting, will seek to enhance the wealth of the company and only seek to benefit reflectively[86] because that is why they have become involved in the company.

Third, if the shareholders were under a duty to the company to act in its best interests that would go some way to assuaging the concerns of many non-shareholders who are connected with the company, for they might feel that the shareholders do get too much out of the company enterprise and have too much influence over it.

Fourth, the case law in the United Kingdom and the Commonwealth has essentially focused on the actions and voting of majority shareholders, but it is becoming clear that minority shareholders can play a part in destabilizing a company.[87] There appears to be more minority shareholder opportunism occurring in public companies as shareholders become more powerful and more diverse.[88] This can lead to corporate loss. So, these shareholders, as well as majority shareholders who are the ones whose role has been circumscribed to some degree, should also be required to act in the best interests of their company when voting at a general meeting.

Fifth, the proposal would not lead to a major change in practical application of the law. As mentioned earlier, imposing a duty to the company on shareholders in a general meeting would not be that radical as the substance of the law would remain largely intact.[89] It is submitted that more than the foundations have been laid for the duty in the extant law.

83 See *Peters American Delicacy Co. Ltd.* v. *Heath* (1939) 61 CLR 457 at 481. An exception might be in the type of case where shareholders are using their shares to allow themselves to assist a competitor as this potentially would be damaging the company.

84 *Citco Banking Corp NV* v. *Prusser's Ltd.* [2007] UKPC 13; [2007] BCC 205 at para. 18.

85 *John Shaw & Sons Ltd.* v. *Shaw*, above n 57.

86 Flannigan, above n 58 at 23.

87 This is particularly applicable to hedge funds.

88 Anabtawi and Stout, above n 62 at 1294.

89 Flannigan, above n 58 at 30.

The approach is a natural extension of corporate law principles,[90] and it acknowledges that on incorporation a new entity enters the stage and it is independent of the shareholders' existence. Finally, if shareholders are subject to a duty, they might be encouraged to be engaged in the life of the company and more diligent in seeking information and monitoring, so that they can make informed decisions.[91]

Naturally if a duty owed by shareholders existed then any breach would need to be enforced and this causes one to ask: who will do the enforcing? The shareholders in breach could be subject to an action by the company, and this would be brought by the board, acting for the company. It all might seem rather incestuous in that the board is accountable to the shareholders (acting as the company) and if the shareholders do not exercise their duties properly, in the eyes of the board, the board can then bring an action. A danger with this scenario is that a board might not like what the general meeting has done and will seek to engage in litigation to hamper or deny the effect of what the general meeting has decided. For instance, if the general meeting decided to remove director X and X had sufficient support at board level an action could be commenced by the board, on behalf of the company, against certain shareholders who carried the vote for removal on the basis that the shareholders have not acted in the best interests of the company. Naturally in this type of situation it would be a matter for the courts to decide whether the shareholders had fulfilled their duties or not.

But what would happen if a member or, more likely, a group of members were to act other than in the interests of the company? The company would have an action against them for breach of duty. The board could take the action, but if the miscreant shareholders controlled the board or were able to influence the board and no action were brought, then a shareholder who believed that the shareholders in general meeting were not acting in the best interests of the company could seek to continue a derivative action on behalf of the company, as could other parties interested in the company, along the lines discussed earlier when considering the option of creating a council as a second board. The concern that some might emit is that shareholders could seek to use the right to enforce an alleged breach of duty by other shareholders, if the board does nothing, to fight again, in a different forum, battles that they lost in the general meeting. Certainly

90 Anabtawi and Stout, above n 62 at 1296.

91 It is acknowledged that the imposition of a duty could cause some shareholders to steer clear of meetings to avoid the application of the duty to them.

this is something that a court would have to be careful to police, and it could do that at the hearing that will decide whether permission should be given for the continuation of the derivative action. Particularly, the court would have to consider the bona fides of the shareholder who is bringing the action. That problem could exist if a large number of shareholders, or even all of them, voted to do something that was not in the best interests of the company. Theoretically a stakeholder could seek to take derivative proceedings against all of the shareholders as a group, but this is not likely to be possible. Perhaps the way to proceed would be for a group of leading shareholders to be sued.

So in sum if we say that the general meeting is to act as accountee to the board, the board is still accountable to the company. The general meeting is acting as and for the company just as the board is when it acts as accountee to the managers who must account to the company. As an accountee body the general meeting is given the task of reviewing what the board has done or not done.

12.5 Conclusion

Clearly the accountability of boards is a critical issue in corporate governance. Thus any approach to corporate governance must engage with it seriously. In this chapter, I have sought to consider one of the primary issues when it comes to board accountability, namely to whom are boards accountable, and I have done so in relation to EMS theory, which constitutes a particular approach to corporate governance.

I have argued that the board must be accountable to the company entity and there are two options that could be implemented to ensure that this takes place. The board is accountable either to an accountability council or to the general meeting of shareholders. Both have certain allure. The former has many attractions, the least not being that it takes direct accountability away from the shareholders, and this is likely to sit well with non-shareholder stakeholders and the public, and it provides for greater inclusion in corporate governance. But it is likely to encounter stiff opposition in many jurisdictions.

Accountability of the board to the general meeting also has attractions. However, it is probably only going to work if the shareholders are, in the general meeting, subject to a fiduciary duty to act in the best interests of the company in order to ensure that the shareholders do not act opportunistically and against the company's interests.

13

The Corporation and the Question of Time

LYNN STOUT

13.1 Introduction

What is a corporation? Non-lawyers often find this question quite difficult. But from a legal perspective, the answer is more straightforward: a corporation is a legal entity that can operate in perpetuity.

The twin characteristics of legal personality and perpetual life are elemental to the corporate form.[1] So elemental, perhaps, they are sometimes taken for granted and deemphasized by commentators who focus on other characteristics often found in corporate entities, such as centralized professional management, transferable shares, or limited personal liability for shareholders.[2] Yet these other characteristics are not nearly so fundamental to corporations. A sole proprietor or a partnership, for example, can hire professional managers as easily as a corporation can. Many corporations do not have freely transferable shares (unlisted companies often restrict share sales, and non-stock companies, including most non-profits, have no shares at all). And limited shareholder liability is a bit of a legal afterthought to the corporate form. Although incorporated entities have been around for centuries, shareholders in British public corporations did not enjoy limited liability until the Limited Liability Act of 1865 and shareholders in California corporations did not receive limited liability until 1931.[3]

Yet for as long as we have had incorporated entities – a category that includes not only business corporations but also non-profits and

[1] A.A. Schwartz, "The Perpetual Corporation" (2012) 80 *George Washington Law Review* 764; L.A. Stout, "The Corporation as Time Machine: Intergenerational Equity, Intergenerational Efficiency, and the Corporate Form" (2015) 38 *Seattle University Law Review* 685.

[2] Schwartz, above n 1 at 768–77.

[3] M.I. Weinstein, "Limited Liability in California 1928–1931" (2005) 7 *American Law and Economics Review* 439.

municipalities – they have been treated as "legal persons" that can own property, enter contracts, and incur liabilities in their own names, just as natural persons can.[4] Moreover, these corporate persons have an important and unique capacity that clearly distinguishes them from natural persons and unincorporated business forms: they can exercise their rights in perpetuity. As political scientist David Ciepley has put it, corporations are "sempiternal" – once created, a corporate entity can, in theory, live forever.[5]

13.2 What Personhood and Perpetuity Can Do

The essential combination of legal personhood and perpetual life gives corporate entities a unique and economically important ability to commit resources to projects that require long and indeterminate time frames: founding universities, building cathedrals, opening continents, creating artificial intelligence. To understand why corporations are singularly suited to these sorts of enterprises, let us examine the implications of legal personhood and perpetual life in greater detail.

Legal personhood permits a corporation to own property in its own name. This has important economic consequences, because it allows corporate entities to "lock in" their assets and protect them from natural persons who might want to seize those assets for themselves.[6] Corporate assets can be insulated from natural persons' cupidity because corporate entities typically are controlled by boards of directors whose members are precluded by their fiduciary duty of loyalty from taking corporate assets for their personal use, whether directly or through unfair "interested" transactions.[7] Unable to extract the corporation's assets for themselves, directors are more likely to keep the assets committed to the corporate project.[8] This is especially true for corporations without shareholders – such as many non-profits – or those with disbursed and relatively powerless shareholders – such as many public companies. Conversely, as this brief explanation suggests, asset lock-in disappears when shareholders have power to demand

[4] D. Ciepley, "Beyond Public and Private: Toward a Political Theory of the Corporation" (2013) 107 *American Political Science Review* 139.

[5] D. Ciepley, "The Corporate Roots of the Liberal Democratic State" (2014) (unpublished manuscript) (draft on file with author).

[6] M.M. Blair, "Locking in Capital: What Corporate Law Achieved for Business Organizers in the Nineteenth Century" (2003) 51 *UCLA Law Review* 387.

[7] M.M. Blair and L.A. Stout, "A Team Production Theory of Corporate Law" (1999) 85 *Virginia Law Review* 247.

[8] *Ibid.*

the distribution of corporate assets, for example, when a controlling shareholder can easily replace a board that refuses to pay large dividends.[9]

Legal personality that permits asset lock-in can have enormous economic importance. This is because locking in corporate assets reassures important corporate stakeholders – employees, customers, creditors, not to mention other equity investors – that it is safer to make what economists call "specific" investments in the corporate project, meaning investments that would lose much of their value if the project were suddenly abandoned. Thus employees, for example, become more willing to acquire skills uniquely suited to the corporation's business, and customers become more willing to rely on its products or services.[10] These specific investments by corporate stakeholders help the corporate project succeed.

Of course, many large-scale projects require not only significant stakeholder investments, but also significant and often uncertain amounts of time. Consider a plan to create a new software operating system or to design and build a new type of commercial aircraft. Such a project can take years or decades. There is a real risk the natural persons who begin it might not last to complete it; they might die, fall ill, lose interest, or pursue other opportunities. Here is where another important advantage of legal personhood comes into play. Unlike natural persons, legal persons can exist in perpetuity, a possibility of tremendous value in protecting an enterprise from being abandoned before it succeeds. Corporations can not only lock in their assets, but also keep those assets at work for as long as they need to be – even if it is centuries. Individual shareholders, CEOs, and directors may come and go; the corporation and its project endure.

The combination of asset lock-in and perpetual life accordingly gives corporations an ability to pursue large-scale, long-term projects that humans or other business forms (such as partnerships and proprietorships) cannot. Over the centuries, corporate entities have pursued just such projects: constructing monasteries, cathedrals, and universities during the Middle Ages; opening continents to commercial trade during the seventeenth century (the Hudson's Bay Company, first chartered in 1670, is still in operation); designing commercial space transport; and self-driving cars in the twenty-first century.

[9] L.A. Stout, "The Toxic Side Effects of Shareholder Primacy" (2013) 161 *University of Pennsylvania Law Review* 2003.

[10] Blair and Stout, above n 7.

13.3 Corporations as Vehicles for Intergenerational Equity and Efficiency

This description of what corporations are and what they do is quite different from the way many commentators, especially non-experts, talk about corporations. Corporations are often described in vague, oversimplified terms as aggregations of people, as their shareholders' "property," or even simply as vehicles for making money. (Each of these notions is referenced in the varying judicial opinions written in the Supreme Court's recent *Hobby Lobby* case.)[11] Such characterizations may be at best impoverished, and at worst misleading. As legal persons (a phrase also employed in *Hobby Lobby*), corporations are unique and powerful institutions capable of pursuing projects that are likely to affect the lives not only of their current shareholders and other stakeholders, but also of multiple future generations of shareholders and stakeholders.

In other recent writings, I explore the implications of this reality.[12] In particular, I argue that the corporation can be understood as a legal technology designed to permit a current human generation to aggregate, preserve, and invest resources in projects that may not generate benefits until long after the current generation is gone. Preserving and investing resources for the future this way often serves intergenerational equity. (It is hard to justify allowing those alive today to consume all the resources of the planet, leaving nothing for those who follow.) It also serves intergenerational efficiency, by encouraging investment in projects whose possibly distant future benefits nevertheless outweigh their present costs.

Of course, non-profit corporations, like the Nature Conservancy or the New York Metropolitan Museum of Art, rely largely on the altruism of the living to attract investments to benefit those not yet born. For-profit business corporations, however, can benefit future generations without relying on altruism, by harnessing a current generation's self-interest to attract investments in the future. This is possible because, when a for-profit corporation's shares are traded on a reasonably efficient market, the present generation can be compensated immediately for investing in the future to the extent that expected future profits are incorporated into today's share price.[13] If the market believes Google will succeed in developing commercially viable self-driving cars, Google's current shareholders will

[11] *Burwell* v. *Hobby Lobby Stores, Inc.*, 134 S. Ct. 2751 (2014).

[12] See generally Stout, above n 1.

[13] *Ibid.* at 703.

be rewarded for Google's investment with a higher share price today even though those shareholders may have passed away, or at least sold their shares, before any actual profits from selling self-driving cars appear.

History demonstrates that corporate entities have, in fact, often benefited multiple future generations in exactly this fashion. European and American universities founded centuries ago are educating students and undertaking important research today. The Massachusetts Bay Company, a commercial venture, colonized New England. In the nineteenth century, corporations built the railroads that opened the Western United States and Canada, and, in the twentieth century, they built the electrical grids that still power our cities. This chapter was written using voice recognition technology IBM first began working on in 1960s. Thanks to their unique capacity to commit large amounts of capital to long-term, uncertain projects, corporations may be more responsible than any other institution, with the possible exception of political democracy, for economic growth and technological progress in the Western world.

This perspective on corporate entities, which recognizes their critical role in the sweep of economic history, suggests how narrow-minded it can be to view the corporation merely as the property of its current shareholders. Even stakeholder theory, which teaches that corporations should be run to benefit not just shareholders, but also employees, customers, suppliers, and creditors,[14] typically fails to capture the full significance of perpetual corporate life. Assuming humanity escapes extinction, the multiple generations of people who will live in the future likely dramatically outnumber the people who happen to be alive today. In considering how corporations benefit or harm either shareholders or stakeholders, should we not consider their impact on future shareholders and stakeholders too? After all, from a utilitarian perspective, by weight of sheer numbers, the interests of multiple future generations likely outweigh the interests of the cohort who happen to be alive today.

13.4 The Problem of Measuring Perpetual Performance

Focusing our attention on corporations' unique status as sempiternal legal persons accordingly offers a variety of insights into the fundamental nature and purpose of corporate entities. At the same time, however, recognizing the importance of corporations' temporal dimension – which

[14] E.R. Freeman, "Stockholders and Stakeholders: A New Perspective on Corporate Governance" (1993) 25 *California Management Review* 88.

must be measured on a chronological scale far longer than that of a mortal human being – also raises a number of challenging theoretical problems. One of the most important of these problems is how to measure corporate performance.

Today's business world is obsessed with performance metrics. This obsession is reflected in Section 162(m) of the US tax code, which requires public companies to tie executive pay to objective performance measures to ensure full deductibility. It underlies SEC rules requiring companies to generate quarterly financial statements emphasizing quantitative data. It can be seen in organizations like the International Organization for Standardization (ISO) and the Sustainability Accounting Standards Board (SASB), which are working on developing objective measures of companies' social and environmental performance. It can be found in the omnipresent business school dogma that "if you can't measure it, you can't manage it."[15]

Yet measuring the performance of an entity with perpetual life raises difficult problems indeed. A corporation's "performance" depends not only on what it is doing today, but also what it will be doing tomorrow, next year, next decade, and possibly next century. Unfortunately, the further we look into the future, the more uncertain our predictions become. Investors, financial analysts, and business leaders use a number of statistical techniques to deal with risk, known as probabilistic variation, like the risk involved in tossing a coin or throwing dice. They have not yet figured out how to deal well with uncertainty, which exists whenever we do not know the probabilities of possible future outcomes and may not even know the possible future outcomes themselves.[16] Whether and when China will come to dominate the world economy is not only a risky bet, but an uncertain one.

Uncertainty makes it impossible to accurately predict – much less measure – a company's destiny. Different people have different opinions and often disagree. Indeed, disagreement is what makes an active stock market.[17] It does not matter whether one adopts a traditional shareholder primacy perspective that focuses only on shareholders' returns, or whether one takes a broader, stakeholder-oriented view that also considers the

[15] L. Ryan, "If You Can't Measure It, You Can't Manage It: Not True," *Forbes*, 10 February 2014.

[16] N.N. Taleb, *The Black Swan: The Impact of the Highly Improbable* (New York: US Random House, 2010).

[17] L.A. Stout, "Are Stock Markets Costly Casinos? Disagreement, Market Failure, and Securities Regulation" (1995) 81 *Virginia Law Review* 611.

corporation's impact on other groups. In either case, the deeper we look into the crystal ball, the murkier the future becomes. To use the language of economics, a company's future performance – whether we measure returns to shareholders only, or costs and benefits for others as well – is inevitably to some degree *unobservable*. We cannot predict what will happen, and even if we think we can, we cannot prove to others that our predictions are correct unless and until they are eventually fulfilled. To scramble two of Keynes's most famous quotes, in the long run, we cannot defeat the dark forces of time and ignorance.

13.5 The Temptation and Danger of Observable Metrics

Nevertheless, in the face of uncertainty, many investors, academics, policymakers, and business leaders continue to place their faith in so-called objective performance metrics. Unable to observe a company's long-term fate, they fixate on what can be observed: the company's recent past performance as measured by quantifiable measures like last year's dividends, the last quarter's accounting profits, or changes from yesterday's share price.

Consider the popular investment performance measure Total Shareholder Return (TSR). TSR measures dividends and share price appreciation over some time period – for example, the last quarter or the last year – adding these numbers together to create a measure of economic returns to shareholders during the period in question. TSR is, thus, a backward-looking measure and typically a relatively short-term measure as well. But it is also objective, quantifiable, and relatively easy to observe. As a result, it is a favorite performance metric among investors, executives, and lawmakers. The Securities Exchange Commission, for example, recently proposed that public companies be required to provide investors with graphic illustrations of how a company's annual TSR compared to the TSRs of peer companies.[18]

This sort of emphasis on relatively recent and short-term results is in obvious tension with the corporate entity's fundamentally future-oriented and long-term time frame. Commentators sometimes try to resolve this tension by claiming that, because an efficient stock market should punish managers who adopt strategies that harm long-term results, short-term

[18] Securities Exchange Commission, "SEC proposes rules to require companies to disclose the relationship between executive pay and a company's financial performance" (29 April 2015), available at www.sec.gov/news/pressrelease/2015-78.html

metrics are merely a convenient means to the ultimate end of better long-term corporate performance.[19]

This facile assertion is rejected, however, by a growing cohort of legal academics, judges, management consultants, corporate lawyers, business journalists, and business and economics professors who argue that markets are not always perfectly efficient, and that corporate strategies based on short-term metrics can harm long-term investors as well as stakeholders and society.[20] For example, managers might inflate reported profits by cutting accounting expenses like payroll or research and development, or try to raise share price by selling off vital assets or leveraging to disgorge cash through dividends or share repurchases. According to those who worry about corporate "short termism," these strategies can temporarily increase accounting profits or TSR.[21] However, they can also end up harming long-term performance, and even put the firm's survival at risk.[22]

13.6 The Tension between Natural Persons' Short-Term Interests and Corporate Entities' Long-Term Interests

The dangers inherent in relying on metrics of recent corporate performance are only magnified by the fact that corporations, as legal entities, necessarily make decisions and act through natural persons. These natural persons – the directors, shareholders, and executives who collectively control the company – are, in an economic sense, the entity's agents. But they are agents who often find that focusing on short-term metrics, even if harmful to the corporate entity, serves their personal interests quite well. Consider that the average director of an S&P 500 company serves on its board less

[19] R. Anderson IV, "The Long and Short of Corporate Governance" (2015) 23 *George Mason Law Review* 19.

[20] *Ibid.* at 30–45; L.A. Bebchuk, "The Myth That Insulating Boards Serves Long-Term Value" (2013) 113 *Columbia Law Review* 1637; J.B. Jacobs, "'Patient capital': Can Delaware Corporate Law Help Revive It?" (2011) 68 *Washington and Lee Law Review* 1645; A. Rappaport, *Saving Capitalism from Short-termism: How to Build Long-term Value and Take Back Our Financial Future* (New York: McGraw-Hill, 2011).

[21] L.A. Stout, *The Shareholder Value Myth: How Putting Shareholders First Harms Investors, Corporations, and the Public* (San Francisco: Berrett-Koehler Publishers, 2012), p. 63.

[22] Aspen Institute Business & Society Program's Corporate Values Strategy Group, "Overcoming Short-Termism: A Call for a More Responsible Approach to Investment and Business Management" (2009), available at www.aspeninstitute.org/sites/default/files/content/docs/pubs/overcome_short_state0909_0.pdf, at 3; The Conference Board, "Is Short-term Behavior Jeopardizing the Future Prosperity of Business?" (2015), available at www.wlrk.com/docs/IsShortTermBehaviorJeopardizingTheFutureProsperityOfBusiness_CEOStrategicImplications.pdf

than nine years[23]; the average American worker remains with an employer for less than five years[24]; and the average shareholder in a public company holds its stock for less than six months.[25] Short-term corporate performance may be the only kind of corporate performance these natural persons care about.

In contrast, both the corporate entity and the multiple future generations of human shareholders and stakeholders who stand to benefit from its activities have a large stake in the long run. Their time frame is not months or years but decades or centuries. The welfare of these multiple future generations necessarily depends on the decisions and actions of the directors, shareholders, and executives who collectively control the corporation's assets today. If the natural persons who control a corporation sacrifice long-term goals to focus on short-term metrics that serve their personal interests, and the company's future performance suffers as a result, the present generation of shareholders and managers has inflicted agency costs (as an economist would put it) on future generations of shareholders and/or stakeholders.

There is some evidence that, at least in the United States, such agency costs may be a real problem. Over the past quarter century, US law and business practice has shifted dramatically in ways that encourage today's corporate directors and executives to focus on "maximizing" metrics like TSR.[26] For example, as already mentioned, in 1993 the US tax code was changed to encourage public companies to tie executive pay to objective performance measures. In 1992, the SEC amended its proxy regulations to make it easier for institutional investors like pension funds and hedge funds – which typically hold shares for only a year or two – to influence corporate boards. Meanwhile, a generation of business leaders and regulators has been taught that corporations should "maximize shareholder value" and that objective metrics are essential to hold directors and executives accountable to this goal.[27]

[23] Spencer Stuart Board Index 2014, available at www.spencerstuart.com/~/media/PDF%20 Files/Research%20and%20Insight%20PDFs/ssbi2014web14Nov2014.pdf

[24] United States Department of Labor, Bureau of Labor Statistics, Employee Tenure Summary (18 September 2013), available at www.bls.gov/news.release/tenure.nr0.htm

[25] Stout, above n 21 at 66.

[26] E.D. Rock, "Adapting to the New Shareholder-Centric Reality" (2013) 161 *University of Pennsylvania Law Review* 1907; Stout, above n 9.

[27] D. West, "The Purpose of the Corporation in Business and Law School Curricula" (2011), available at www.brookings.edu/~/media/research/files/papers/2011/7/19%20corporation %20west/0719_corporation_west.pdf

Contrary to what traditional shareholder primacy theory would predict, these supposedly shareholder-friendly changes in business law and practice have not increased shareholders' returns from holding public equity. Indeed, average returns have declined slightly in recent decades.[28] Meanwhile, we have seen dramatic drops in both the number, and the life expectancy, of US public corporations. The number of US listed companies declined from nearly 9,000 in the mid-1990s to just over 5,000 today,[29] while the life expectancy of S&P 500 firms has decreased even more dramatically, from around 50 years in the middle of the twentieth century to only about 15 years.[30]

Of course, correlation is not causation. Moreover, the normative implications of having fewer and more short-lived public companies can be debated. Nevertheless, the empirical phenomena of declining investor returns, declining public companies, and reduced corporate life expectancy are all consistent with concerns raised by commentators who argue that an undue emphasis on quarterly earnings, share price, and similar metrics is driving US companies to pursue short-term business strategies – selling assets, taking excessive risks, neglecting important stakeholders, failing to reinvest – that are harming long-term results.[31]

13.7 An Alternative: The Corporation as System

These issues raise the question whether there is another way to assess corporate performance that avoids the risks associated with demanding that managers "maximize shareholder value"? Must we choose between either abandoning any attempt at managerial accountability or using objective metrics in ways that may threaten corporate entities' abilities to pursue large-scale, long-term projects that benefit future generations?

In fact, there is a way to avoid both these unpleasant options.[32] This alternative path does not require us to abandon the use of backward-looking

[28] L.A. Stout, "On the Rise of Shareholder Primacy: Signs of Its Fall and the Return of Managerialism (In The Closet)" (2013) 36 *Seattle University Law Review* 1169 at 1178.

[29] D. Strumpf, "U.S. Public Companies Rise Again," *Wall Street Journal*, 5 February 2014.

[30] S. Denning and P. Noonan, "On Steve Jobs and Why Big Companies Die," *Forbes*, 19 November 2011.

[31] Aspen Institute Business & Society Program's Corporate Values Strategy Group, above n 22 at 3.

[32] The ideas presented in the following Sections 13.7 through 13.9 were developed in close collaboration with Professor Tamara Belinfanti of New York Law School. The author and Professor Belinfanti are currently working together on a law review article that explores the relevance of system theory to corporations in greater detail.

metrics like accounting profits or TSR. Rather, it requires us to use such metrics *wisely*: not as ends in themselves, but as means for assessing the general health of a corporate system that is operating over long periods of time in an uncertain world.

Many contemporary discussions of corporate governance treat quantitative measures like profits or share price appreciation as objectives in and of themselves, "outputs" that corporate directors and executives ought to be "maximizing." In other words, these metrics are viewed as the ultimate goal of the corporate entity. This approach fails to recognize that corporations are sempiternal legal entities that are uniquely suited to, and are often expressly created to, pursue large-scale, long-term projects under highly uncertain conditions. This reality means that however nice it might be in theory to describe maximizing profits or share price over some period of time as the corporate goal, in practice we cannot know in advance *what future results will be or even how long the corporation will exist*. The corporation may succeed – or fail – next year, next decade, or next century. Indeed, in many cases, the corporation may have been founded in the hope it will operate indefinitely.

As discussed in greater detail below, when we do not know how long or how well the corporation is going to operate, there is no way to calculate the sum of its outputs – whether they be accounting profits, share price appreciation, or something else. But we do know that, whatever we want the corporation to do, it can only do it as long as the corporation survives. The most fundamental measure of corporate performance may be, first and foremost, *continued corporate functioning*.

The idea of continued functioning as a corporate objective may seem odd to readers who are accustomed to glossing over the significance of corporate personhood or to thinking of corporate entities merely as aggregations of living people or as their current shareholder's property. It makes sense, however, to engineers, biologists, ecologists, computer scientists, medical doctors, and management theorists familiar with systems thinking and with the performance assessment methodologies commonly applied to systems.[33]

[33] F. Capra and P.L. Luisi, *The Systems View of Life: A Unifying Vision* (Cambridge University Press, 2014); J. Gharajedaghi, *Systems Thinking: Managing Chaos and Complexity* (Burlington, MA: Butterworth-Heinemann, 1999); D.K. Hitchens, *Advanced Systems Thinking* (Norwood, MA: Artech House, 2003); D.H. Meadows, *Thinking in Systems: A Primer* (White River Junction, VT: Chelsea Green Publishing, 2008).

13.7.1 An Introduction to Systems Thinking

Systems theorists define a "system" as a set of independent but interrelated elements or parts comprising a unified whole that serves a function or purpose.[34] For example, a coffee brewing machine is a system. Its fluid reservoir, filter, heating element, supply of ground beans, etc. operate together over time to produce coffee. Systems thinking is a staple of many disciplines. This is because, just as a coffee machine can be viewed as a system, so too can ecosystems, organisms (including human beings), and computer programs. As a result, systems thinking is common in fields ranging from biology[35] to engineering[36] and to computer science.[37]

Systems thinking offers many basic lessons that can help us better understand corporate entities and how to measure their performance. This is because, just as a coffee machine can be understood as a system, so too can the corporation that manufactures and sells the machine. The company's financial and physical assets, employees, and managers operate together, over time, to produce profits – as well as jobs, tax revenues, and coffee machines. Thus systems thinking offers some basic lessons on how we might view corporate entities. Indeed, the field of study known as management science explicitly applies a systems approach for analyzing and improving operational efficiency in industries and organizations.[38]

One of the most basic lessons of systems analysis is that a corporation, like any system, is more than the sum of its parts. The disconnected pieces of a coffee machine do nothing but occupy space. Only when the parts are fitted together properly, can the machine make coffee. Similarly, a corporation must bring together physical assets, financial resources, intellectual capital, and human labor, so that these different parts interact with and affect each other, before it can produce innovative products, investment returns, employment opportunities, and tax revenues. Both the coffee

[34] Meadows, above n 33 at 11.

[35] Capra and Luisi, above n 33; Meadows, above n 33.

[36] Hitchens, above n 33; N.G. Leveson, *Engineering a Safer World: Systems Thinking Applied to Safety* (Cambridge, MA: MIT Press, 2011).

[37] H.J. Rosenblatt and T.J. Cashman, *Systems Analysis and Design* (Boston, MA: Course Technology Cengage Learning, 2014).

[38] S. Beer, *Management Science: The Business Use of Operations Research* (Garden City, NY: Doubleday, 1967); D.C. Heinze, *Management Science: Introductory Concepts and Applications* (Cincinnati, OH: South-Western Publishing Co., 1982); P. Senge, *The Fifth Discipline: The Art and Practice of the Learning Organization* (New York: Doubleday/Currency, 1990).

machine and the corporation operate as integrated systems that perform functions and their parts cannot perform in isolation.

A second basic lesson implicit in systems thinking is that systems typically operate over uncertain periods of time – a coffee machine is designed to make coffee not only this morning, but also tomorrow morning, next week, and hopefully on into the uncertain future. Similarly, the typical business corporation is created to operate – generating profits, jobs, and consumer products – indefinitely. This means that system behavior must also be analyzed over time. As we are about to see, this has important implications for how to think about measuring system performance.

A third basic lesson of systems thinking is that in order to continue operating over time, all the essential parts or elements of the system, and the connections between those parts or elements (the system's "subsystems"), must be and must continue to be functioning. If the coffee machine's heating element breaks or becomes disconnected from the rest of the machine, the machine can no longer make coffee. Similarly, if a corporation stops making profits, loses its employees or customers, or fails to invest in developing new products, it will stop functioning. The health of the systems depends on the continued health of each of its essential subsystems.[39]

13.7.2 Measuring Performance in a System

Applying basic principles of systems thinking to corporate entities raises intriguing possibilities about how we can best measure corporate performance. In particular, it suggests that we can measure corporate performance using the same sorts of methodologies commonly employed by systems thinkers assessing the performance of systems. These methodologies go by a variety of labels depending on the field in which they are applied, including system analysis (computer science), operations analysis (engineering and management), cybernetics (control engineering and social science), and medicine (human biology). Whatever the field, systems thinkers tend to assess system performance in similar ways.

In particular, systems thinkers typically do not assess a system's performance by observing whether it is currently "maximizing" any single measurable output. (There is only so much coffee one wants to drink in a single day). Rather, they look first to whether the system is operating in a fashion that will allow it to continue to do so – that is, whether the system

[39] Meadows, above n 33.

is operating sustainably. Typically this means looking at the health of each of the system's essential subsystems and whether they are operating within necessary parameters. To continue to function, the coffee machine must operate in a temperature range that is neither too hot nor too cold; it must get a certain amount of electrical current but not too much. Similarly, a corporation that makes coffee machines must have a certain amount of employee turnover but not too much; must invest a certain amount in developing new products; and must provide decent returns to its investors, but not disgorge so much cash that it cannot retain employees or develop new products.

Systems analysis treats the health and functioning of a system's essential subsystems as *incommensurables*. There is a limit to how much we can safely improve the performance of one part of the system at the expense of another. For example, maximizing a coffee machine's energy efficiency by turning off the heating element leads to unacceptably cold, weak coffee. Maximizing coffee temperature overloads the electrical circuits and leads to system breakdown (and a burned tongue). Similar principles of subsystem incommensurability can be applied to corporations. Maximizing profits by cutting all current research and development expenditures can cause the corporate entity to eventually fail. So, too, can maximizing current R&D expenditures at the expense of profitability.

Only when we have determined that each necessary subsystem is healthy, can we conclude that a system can perform sustainably. And only at this point does the systems thinker turn to looking for incremental tweaks that can improve the performance of some subsystem without threatening another essential subsystem. (Systems theorists do not talk about maximizing: they talk about "optimizing within constraints.") For example, a corporate systems thinker might look for ways to increase profits without unduly harming employee loyalty or sacrificing R&D investment. Systems thinkers in different fields have developed a variety of methodologies (systems analysis in computer science, operational analysis in engineering and management) and mathematical modeling techniques (nonlinear programming, multiobjective optimization functions) for assessing and improving the performance of ongoing systems this way.[40]

Systems thinking accordingly cautions against focusing all our attention on any single performance metric. When corporate operation involves

[40] US Department of Commerce, Office of Chief Information Officer, "Operational Analysis and Performance Reporting" (Undated), available at www.ocio.os.doc.gov/ITPolicyandPrograms/dev01_003715; Hitchens, above n 33 at 314.

multiple subsystems, we need to pay attention to the health and sustainability of each. Thus, along with monitoring metrics like accounting profits and share price appreciation, systems thinking suggests that a sensible corporate manager should also look at employee turnover, customer satisfaction surveys, supplier costs, research budgets, and so forth. Only when the manager is assured that each of the corporation's essential parts is in good shape, can she safely turn to the secondary task of trying to find room for marginal improvements in corporate performance.

Viewing the corporation as a system accordingly offers an interesting and novel perspective on how to use metrics like accounting profits or share price appreciation to assess corporate performance. In brief, *these metrics are not ends in themselves*. It makes no sense to talk about trying to "maximize" such numbers; the corporation is intended to operate into an indefinite and uncertain future and the sum of those numbers over time is unobservable. Current profits and share price should be treated not as the ultimate corporate objective, but as sources of information about whether essential corporate subsystems are operating within acceptable parameters, so that the corporation is likely to be able to operate sustainably into the future.

13.8 Corporate Purpose and the Shareholder Primacy Paradigm

Readers at this point might fairly raise the question: but if maximizing profits or share price should not be treated as the ultimate corporate objective, what should be? Among its many other insights, a systems approach to the corporate entity sheds light on this question as well.

For the past three decades, most corporate scholars in the Anglo-American world have subscribed to some version of the philosophy known as shareholder primacy.[41] According to this philosophy, corporations exist for one purpose and one purpose only, to "maximize shareholder value." A few theorists adopt what David Millon has labeled "radical" shareholder primacy, and treat maximizing shareholder value as equivalent to maximizing either current accounting profits or dividends plus share price appreciation.[42] Many more subscribe to what Millon calls "traditional" shareholder primacy, which gives a nod to the corporate entity's

[41] H. Hansmann and R. Kraakman, "The End of History for Corporate Law" (2001) 89 *Georgetown Law Journal* 439; D. Millon, "Radical Shareholder Primacy" (2014) 10 *University of Saint Thomas Law Review* 1013.

[42] Millon, above n 41 at 1013.

perpetual existence by holding that corporate managers should maximize shareholder value "in the long run."[43] Delaware Chancellor William Allen famously championed traditional shareholder primacy in his dicta in *Katz* v. *Oak Industries* that "it is the obligation of directors to attempt, within the law, to maximize the long-run interests of the corporation's stockholders."[44]

Shareholder primacy, whether radical or traditional, has not gone unchallenged. Influential theorists have proposed alternative models of corporate purpose that leave more room for managers to consider how corporations affect not only shareholders but also other corporate stakeholders like employees or customers[45] and how they benefit or harm third parties or society at large.[46] Nevertheless, shareholder primacy has continued to dominate both the academic literature and business practice in many large public firms.

Why has the philosophy of shareholder primacy proven so influential? Commentators who are not well-versed in corporate law sometimes argue for shareholder primacy on the basis of emotionally powerful but legally incorrect assertions such as "shareholders own corporations" (as legal persons, corporate entities own themselves) or "corporate directors are shareholders' agents" (as a matter of law, directors are not agents but fiduciaries who owe duties to both shareholders and the corporate entity itself and controlling shareholders also owe fiduciary duties to other shareholders and to the entity).[47] Similarly, shareholders are sometimes described as the sole "residual claimants" in corporations, another erroneous claim contradicted by both corporate law and modern options theory.[48]

Sophisticated commentators typically defend shareholder primacy on a quite different basis: namely, that to hold corporate directors and executives accountable, it is essential to have a single, measurable corporate objective. For example, in a recent opinion piece in the *New York Times*, Stephen Bainbridge asserted that "the most basic" reason why maximizing

[43] *Ibid.* at 1014; Schwartz, above n 1 at 768 and following.

[44] *Katz* v. *Oak Industries, Inc.*, 508 A 2d 873 at 879 (Del. Ch. 1986).

[45] See, e.g., Blair and Stout, above n 7.

[46] See, e.g., Freeman, above n 14.

[47] See, e.g., Blair and Stout, above n 7 at 258–65; L.A. Stout, "Bad and Not-So-Bad Arguments for Shareholder Primacy" (2002) 75 *Southern California Law Review* 1189; I. Anabtawi and L.A. Stout, "Fiduciary Duties for Activist Shareholders" (2008) 60 *Stanford Law Review* 1255.

[48] Blair and Stout, above n 7 at 269; Stout, above n 47 at 1192–5; Modern Corporation Project, "Statement on Company Law," available at https://themoderncorporation.wordpress.com/company-law-memo

shareholder wealth should be the sole corporate objective is that "[i]f directors were allowed to deviate from shareholder wealth maximization, they would inevitably turn to indeterminate balancing standards, which provide no accountability."[49] Harvard law Professor Mark Roe has suggested that "a stakeholder rule of managerial accountability could leave managers so much discretion that managers could easily pursue their own agenda, one that might maximize neither shareholder, employee, consumer, nor national wealth, but only their own."[50] Influential economist Michael Jensen similarly claims that "telling the manager to maximize current profits, market share, future growth profits, and anything else one pleases will leave the manager with no way to make a reasoned decision. In effect it leaves the manager with no objective."[51] Jensen concludes that we must "define a true (single dimensional) score for measuring performance for the organization."[52]

13.9 Systems Thinking and the Question of Corporate Purpose

It is important to recognize that systems thinking alone does not answer the fundamental question of what a particular system's function or purpose should be. Indeed, systems thinking teaches that the answer depends on many things, including (in the case of a designed system) the intentions of the system's creator. But systems thinking does shed light on the perennial debate over corporate purpose by demonstrating that the conventional justification for shareholder primacy that most commentators rely upon today – the justification that long-term shareholder value provides the single metric that is essential to ensure managerial accountability – is erroneous, for at least two reasons.

The first reason is that systems thinking shows that a single metric is not, in fact, essential to ensure managerial accountability. There are alternative methods for objectively assessing corporate performance and rewarding managers accordingly. For example, suppose that rather than asking corporate directors and executives to maximize accounting profits, we ask them instead to meet several different performance thresholds or

[49] S.M. Bainbridge, "A Duty to Shareholder Value," *New York Times* (Room for Debate), 16 April 2015.

[50] M.J. Roe, "The Shareholder Wealth Maximization Norm and Industrial Organizations" (2001) 149 *University of Pennsylvania Law Review* 2063 at 2065.

[51] M.C. Jensen, "Value Maximization, Stakeholder Theory, and the Corporate Objective Function" (2002) 12 *Business Ethics Quarterly* 235 at 238.

[52] *Ibid.* at 235.

"subgoals": to earn at least a certain level of profits, while keeping employee turnover beneath some rate, while meeting or exceeding standards for revenue growth. Even if the managers retain complete discretion over how to operate the company once these subgoals have been met, this is hardly "no accountability." Managers can be rewarded or punished according to whether they meet all the requisite subgoals. (And if they meet the subgoals, the company survives and thrives, generating products for consumers, salaries for employees, tax revenues for governments, and decent returns for investors – a pretty happy state of affairs.) We can even go further, and seek to "optimize within constraints" by using operational analysis to assess managerial performance in a more fine-grained fashion and identify possible incremental improvements in system function, perhaps measured according to some weighted-average multiobjective function.[53]

Systems thinking thus contradicts the claim that shareholder primacy is essential for managerial accountability. It is perfectly possible to task corporate managers with tending to the health of several different corporate subsystems, and the interests of many possible constituents, without releasing them to run amok.

But systems thinking offers a second important insight into the question of corporate purpose as well, an insight fatal to the traditional shareholder primacy view that corporate directors and executives should maximize "long run" shareholder value. In brief, systems thinking reminds us that *we simply do not know what will happen in the long run, or even how long the long run will last.* This makes the concept of long-term shareholder value fundamentally subjective, unobservable, and unquantifiable. As a performance measure, long-run shareholder value *offers no accountability at all.*[54] By forcing us to deal with messy complexities of corporate personality and perpetual life, systems thinking offers not just a viable alternative method for assessing manager performance, but a superior one.

13.10 Conclusion

The legal technology known as the corporate entity is an extraordinary – and extraordinarily important – invention. As legal persons with potentially perpetual lives, corporations can aggregate enormous resources and devote them to enterprises that span time periods much longer than

[53] Hitchens, above n 33 at 50; US Department of Commerce, above n 40.

[54] D. Radcliffe, "The Incoherence of Jensen's Value Maximization 'Scorecard'" (2015) (draft on file with author).

those allotted mortal human beings. This gives corporate entities a unique capacity to pursue large-scale, long-term projects: creating universities, cathedrals, and museums; exploring and developing new lands; building infrastructure and brand names; developing and commercializing new technologies. Such long-term projects historically have made, and in the future can continue to make, vital contributions to intergenerational equity and efficiency.

At the same time, the corporate entity's sempiternal nature raises exceedingly thorny problems of assessing corporate performance. In light of those problems, systems thinking may offer a more sensible method of assessing performance than the currently popular approach of treating metrics like accounting profits or TSR as outputs that should be maximized. System analysis recognizes that such backward-looking, relatively short-term metrics are not ends in themselves but, at best, sources of information about the health of certain of the corporation's essential subsystems. They are not, and should not be treated as, the ultimate corporate objective.

Epilogue

A Look to the Future

BARNALI CHOUDHURY AND MARTIN PETRIN

While the contributors to this book have provided new ways in which the modern company can be better understood, in the end, globally there remains little consensus as to what the company is and what its purpose should be. Numerous initiatives are taking place – both at national and international levels – that seem to promote the idea that a company is more than an avenue for generating profits and that aim to carve out the role of the company in society.[1] Similarly, scholarly views supporting these notions seem to far outweigh the espousal of converse views.[2] Of course, profit making remains an important objective for companies, which are, after all, primarily economic beings. Nevertheless, given the problems an exclusive focus on the profit making function of companies has given rise to, it is curious why a profit-driven – and accordingly, shareholder-centric – view of companies remains a dominant ideology.

One reason for this may be that a company as solely a vehicle for profit maximization reflects a long-standing, and thus deeply entrenched, ideological perspective. As one commentator has observed, a shareholder-centric view of the firm is "much beloved by law and economics scholars, financial economists, and dogmatic conservatives generally."[3] However, even beyond these individuals, a sole profit motive for the existence of companies reflects "conventional wisdom."[4] It is the message given out in

[1] See, e.g., the UN Guiding Principles on Business and Human Rights, the Conflict Mineral Rule in the United States, and the Modern Slavery Act in the United Kingdom.

[2] For recent examples, see L. Stout, *The Shareholder Value Myth: How Putting Shareholders First Harms Investors, Corporations, and the Public* (San Francisco: Berrett-Koehler Publishers, 2012); B. Sjafell and B.J. Richardson (eds.), *Company Law and Sustainability: Legal Barriers and Opportunities* (Cambridge University Press, 2015).

[3] C.C. Nicholls, "Governance, Mergers and Acquisitions, and Global Capital Markets," in J. Sarra (ed.), *Corporate Governance in Global Capital Markets* (Vancouver: UBC Press, 2003), 90.

[4] S. Denning, "The Origin of 'The World's Dumbest Idea': Milton Friedman," *Forbes*, June 26, 2013, available at www.forbes.com/sites/stevedenning/2013/06/26/the-origin-of-the-worlds-dumbest-idea-milton-friedman/#265e6a6e214c

business schools, the ethos followed by many corporate managers – as the Starbucks example described in the introduction reinforces – and the one often reflected in company or securities laws.[5]

A second reason may be because there is a lacuna in the law that fails to define corporate purpose. A logical solution to this gap would be, of course, to provide a definition. But providing a definition brings its own risks. Section 172 of the UK Companies Act was designed to bring clarity to the role of corporate managers, mandating that directors promote the success of the company for the benefit of its members while having regard to a number of other, broadly defined, stakeholder interests. In doing so, section 172 appears to clarify the beneficiaries of the company. It also stands in sharp contrast to corporate law in the United States, which does not contain a similar provision, and which has left the corporate purpose ambiguous.[6] Still, attempting to define the corporate purpose under UK company law has not substantially clarified it and caused confusion as to its precise effects and application. In part, this is because the wording of section 172 appears to prioritize the interests of shareholders over stakeholders – particularly if there is a conflict between the two interests. Moreover, since other aspects of the Companies Act were not altered, section 172 remains enforceable only by shareholders, not other stakeholders. Thus, if the idea was to use the wording of section 172 to suggest that the corporate purpose was something other than shareholder wealth maximization, it is unclear whether this clarification has progressed our understanding of the corporate purpose.

More likely, the persistence of the shareholder wealth maximization narrative survives because of path dependency. As Bebchuk and Roe have observed, corporate law can create path dependency in two ways.[7] The first is structure driven, in that an economy's ownership structures are

[5] For a good description of the origins of shareholder wealth maximization thinking, see L.A. Stout, "The Problem of Corporate Purpose" (2012) 48 *Issues in Governance Studies*, available at www.brookings.edu/wp-content/uploads/2016/06/Stout_Corporate-Issues.pdf; Darrell West, "The Purpose of the Corporation in Business and Law School Curricula" (2011) *Governance Studies at Brookings*, available at www.brookings.edu/wp-content/uploads/2016/06/0719_corporation_west.pdf

[6] See, e.g., C.M. Bruner, "The Enduring Ambivalence of Corporate Law" (2008), 59 *Alabama Law Review* 1385; B. Choudhury, "Serving Two Masters: Incorporating Social Responsibility into the Corporate Paradigm," (2009) 11 *University of Pennsylvania Journal of Business Law* 631.

[7] L.A. Bebchuk and M.J. Roe, "A Theory of Path Dependence in Corporate Ownership and Governance" (1999) 52 *Stanford Law Review* 127.

determined by its initial pattern of corporate ownership structures.[8] This may be a result of, among other factors, sunk adaptive costs both by the firm and other entities and institutions as well as endowment effects.[9]

The second source of path dependency is rules driven.[10] As Bebchuk and Roe explain, corporate rules depend on and reflect the economy's initial ownership and governance structures. While again they note that this source of path dependency arises from sunk adaptive costs and the maintenance of the status quo,[11] the authors further observe that rules-driven path dependency may also arise because of the influence of interest groups. Corporate rules, Bebchuk and Roe conclude, may be affected by the relative power of interest groups.[12] However, since the existing corporate ownership structures affect the resources and resulting political influence of certain interest groups, these groups will always be able to shape later corporate rules. Roe even refers to the political environment in which a firm operates as an "elephant," a giant force that can "deeply affect" its "shape, structure and governance."[13]

Thus, shareholder wealth maximization appears to have become an entrenched norm, in part, because of sunk adaptive costs and political will. In addition, by perpetrating the status quo as well as by its continued dominance, shareholder wealth maximization endures as the default driver of the corporate purpose.

Yet whether it is ideology, gaps in the law, or path dependency propelling the maintenance of shareholder wealth maximization, the good news is that none of these factors are static. In particular, ideology and political will – which underlie all three factors – are amenable to change. Thus, despite the predominance of the shareholder wealth maximization norm today, the role and purpose of the company is unlikely to be reflective of that norm as time passes. Even Henry Hansmann, the co-author of *The End*

[8] *Ibid.* at 139.

[9] Bebchuk and Roe list the factors of structure-driven path dependency as sunk adaptive costs (the costs of adaptations by the firm), complementarities (the costs of adaptations by other entities and institutions), network externalities (i.e. the dominant structure in the economy), endowment effects (i.e. control structures), or multiple optima (i.e. the maintenance of the status quo). *Ibid.* at 139–42.

[10] *Ibid.* at 153.

[11] *Ibid.* at 155–6.

[12] *Ibid.* at 157.

[13] M.J. Roe, "Political Determinants of Corporate Governance: Political Context, Corporate Impact" (2003) *Harvard Discussion Paper No. 451*, at v.

of History for Corporate Law[14] – which concluded that shareholder wealth maximization was the ideal standard for the company – has recognized that the standard may involve "too steep a tradeoff between material prosperity and social order."[15] As he notes, society's recognition of this trade-off may dispute the legitimacy of the shareholder wealth maximization model in the future, "however much it may be in ascendance now."[16]

Indeed, as the prevalent ideology and political opinions slowly shift and the trade-offs that shareholder wealth maximization demands further emerge, it seems inevitable that the role and purpose of the company will also similarly evolve. As the winds of change begin to blow and increase their bluster, the hope is that contributions like this book will propel change even further.

[14] H. Hansmann and R. Kraakman, "The End of History for Corporate Law," (2001) 89 *Georgetown Law Journal* 439.

[15] H. Hansmann, "How Close Is the End of History?" (2006) 31 *Journal of Corporation Law* 745 at 747.

[16] *Ibid.*

INDEX